Contemporary Readings In
Sport Psychology

Contemporary Readings In Sport Psychology

Edited by

WILLIAM P. MORGAN, Ed.D., F.A.C.S.M.
Associate Professor of Physical Education
Human Performance Laboratory
University of Missouri

CHARLES C THOMAS · PUBLISHER
Springfield • Illinois • U.S.A.

Published and Distributed Throughout the World by

CHARLES C THOMAS · PUBLISHER

Bannerstone House

301-327 East Lawrence Avenue, Springfield, Illinois, U.S.A.

Natchez Plantation House

735 North Atlantic Boulevard, Fort Lauderdale, Florida, U.S.A.

With THOMAS BOOKS *careful attention is given to all details of manufacturing and design. It is the Publisher's desire to present books that are satisfactory as to their physical qualities and artistic possibilities and appropriate for their particular use.* THOMAS BOOKS *will be true to those laws of quality that assure a good name and good will.*

Printed in the United States of America

H-2

CONTRIBUTORS

John C. Bachman, Ed.D.
Professor of Physical Education and Kinesiology
Macalester College

Graham B. Blaine, Jr., M.D.
Chief of Psychiatry
Harvard University Health Services

B. Robert Carlson, Ph.D.
Assistant Professor of Physical Education and Recreation
University of Kansas

Lida R. Carmen, M.S.
Clinical Assistant in Psychiatry
Harvard University Health Services

Albert V. Carron, Ed.D.
Assistant Professor of Physical Education
University of Saskatchewan

Charles C. Cowell, Ph.D.
late, Professor of Physical Education
Purdue University

Bryant J. Cratty, Ed.D.
Professor of Physical Education and Director of the
Perceptual-Motor Learning Laboratory
University of California, Los Angeles

Frances Z. Cumbee, Ph.D.
Associate Professor of Physical Education
University of Wisconsin

Robert W. Dixon, Ph.D.
Professor of Educational Psychology
University of Michigan

Robert L. Foster, B.A.
Instructor of Physical Education
Vanden High School, California

Hiram L. Gordon, Ph.D.
Research Psychologist
Fort Logan Mental Health Center
Denver, Colorado

Dale L. Hanson, Ph.D.
Professor and Chairman
Department of Physical Education
Macalester College

Robert G. Harlow, Ph.D.
University of Minnesota
Private Practice
Minneapolis, Minnesota

Franklin M. Henry, Ph.D.
Professor of Physical Education
University of California, Berkeley

William W. Heusner, Ph.D.
Professor of Physical Education
Human Energy Research Laboratory
Michigan State University

Burris F. Husman, Ed.D.
Professor of Physical Education
University of Maryland

Daniel C. Hutton, Ph.D.
Formerly, Assistant Professor of Psychology
University of Maryland

A. H. Ismail, H.S.D.
Professor of Physical Education
and Director of Research
Purdue University

Warren R. Johnson, Ed.D.
Professor of Health Education and Physical Education and
Director, Children's Physical Developmental Clinic,
University of Maryland.
Visiting Lecturer, The Washington School of Psychiatry

Gerald S. Kenyon, Ph.D.
Professor of Physical Education
University of Wisconsin

Clyde G. Knapp, Ph.D.
Professor of Secondary Education
University of Illinois

Robert M. Kozelka, Ph.D.
Associate Professor of Mathematics
Williams College

Walter Kroll, P.E.D.
Professor of Physical Education
University of Massachusetts

Ward Lambert
Graduate Assistant, Department of Physical Education,
College of Physical Education, Recreation and Health
University of Maryland

Murney Lazier, M.A.
Evanston Township High School
Evanston, Illinois

Ronald A. Lee, M.S.
Graduate Assistant in Physical Education
University of Oklahoma

Robert M. Malina, Ph.D.
Assistant Professor of Anthropology
University of Texas at Austin

Ernest D. Michael, Jr., Ph.D.
Professor of Ergonomics and Physical Education
University of California, Santa Barbara

William P. Morgan, Ed.D.
Associate Professor of Physical Education
University of Missouri, Columbia

William E. Morris, Ph.D.
Division of Research Grants
National Institutes of Health

Richard C. Nelson, Ph.D.
Associate Professor of Physical Education
College of Health and Physical Education
Pennsylvania State University

Bruce C. Ogilvie, Ph.D.
Professor of Psychology
San Jose State College

Sheri L. Peterson, M.Ed.
Formerly, University of Oklahoma

William R. Pierson, Ph.D.
Chief Physiologist
Human Engineering Department
Lockheed-California Company

Philip J. Rasch, Ph.D.
Chief, Physiology Division
Naval Medical Fields Research Laboratory
Camp Lejeune, North Carolina

Margaret Robb, Ph.D.
Associate Professor of Physical Education
State University of New York
College at Cortland

John M. Roberts, Ph.D.
Professor of Anthropology
Cornell University

David Rosenberg, Ph.D.
Assistant Chief Psychologist
Veterans Administration Hospital
Marion, Indiana

E. Dean Ryan, Ed.D.
Professor of Physical Education
University of California, Davis

John N. Sage, Ed.D.
Assistant Professor of Physical Education
University of California, Riverside

Robert N. Singer, Ph.D.
Associate Professor of Physical Education
Michigan State University

Leon E. Smith, Ed.D.
Professor of Physical Education
University of Iowa

Arthur H Steinhaus, Ph.D., M.P.E.
Visiting Professor
Department of Health, Physical Education and Recreation
Michigan State University

Brian Sutton-Smith, Ph.D.
Professor of Psychology
Principal, Developmental Psychology
Teachers College, Columbia University

William W. Trousdale, Ph.D.
late, Assistant Professor of Psychology
University of Oklahoma

Jerome C. Weber, Ph.D.
Associate Professor of Physical Education
University of Oklahoma

W. I. Welker, Ph.D.
Professor of Neurophysiology
Laboratory of Neurophysiology
University of Wisconsin Medical Center

Harriet G. Williams, Ph.D.
Associate Professor of Education
University of Toledo

Jack H. Wilmore, Ph.D.
Assistant Professor of Physical Education
University of California, Berkeley

Joseph L. Zerman, M.D.
Cambridge, Massachusetts
Formerly, Assistant Psychiatrist
Harvard University Health Services

PREFACE

INDIVIDUALS from various disciplines have been interested in the psychological bases of muscular activity for many years, but the field of sport psychology has lacked any sort of formal orientation until quite recently. Organization of the International Society of Sport Psychology in 1965 and a North American Society in 1966, however, suggests that this specialized area of inquiry is becoming somewhat formalized. The highly successful Second International Congress of Sport Psychology, which was held in Washington, D.C., in 1968, further evidences this field's rapid growth.

Because of the embryonic nature of sport psychology, it is difficult to predict just what course the growth of this field will ultimately take. Indeed, perusal of the program of the Second International Congress suggests that workers in this area are presently concerned with many different specialized facets of psychology. Therefore, it seems appropriate to regard sport psychology as being multidimensional. For this reason, selections from comparative and physiological psychology, engineering psychology, learning theory, measurement, mental health, motor learning, motivation, perception, personality dynamics, psychophysiology, and social psychology appear in this volume. In addition, a section entitled *Cogent Commentaries* has been included to permit the inclusion of certain heuristic articles that tend to cut across the many categories.

I have taught an introductory course in sport psychology for several years, and each semester it becomes increasingly difficult to acquaint the beginning student with representative literature. Since sport psychology articles appear in a wide variety of journals, I found it necessary to assemble copies of significant articles and place them on library reserve. This approach seemed to be at least partially satisfactory in the beginning, but as more students became interested in this area of inquiry the approach became woefully inadequate. Furthermore, the sport psychology literature seems to have at least doubled in the past few years. This dilemma provided the primary impetus for the

[xi]

compilation of *Contemporary Readings in Sport Psychology*. A number of excellent readings books in both physical education and psychology already exist, and the intent of the present volume is not to replace any of these valuable sources, but rather, to serve as an adjunctive reading for those individuals concerned with human performance in the broad context, and to meet the specific needs of the beginning student in sport psychology. The volume should also be of value to courses concerned with the foundations of physical activity.

It is hoped that the book will also prove to be of interest as general reading for individuals from various disciplines. Most of the articles have been written by physical educators, but it will be noted that certain of the contributors are anthropologists, neurophysiologists, physiologists, clinical psychologists, and social psychologists.

The selection of articles was based on a number of criteria. Since it is hoped first of all that the present work will serve as a *springboard* for the beginning student, articles were consequently selected from the *whole* of sport psychology. For this reason many excellent articles had to be omitted less the work resemble, for example, readings in motor learning, personality theory, or motivation. Secondly, an attempt was made to select articles that represented on-going research efforts. Third, articles were selected that possessed a demonstrated or, in my opinion, heuristic potential. Fourth, I have relied heavily upon feedback from my students regarding articles which they have found to be of particular value. Articles that met all of these criteria became automatic selections; there was little difficulty in deciding to use these *classics*. In most instances, however, I relied upon the opinion of colleagues, far too numerous to cite, regarding specific entries.

I shall welcome comments from readers regarding the addition of articles that they feel would be appropriate in subsequent editions. I should also welcome comments from professors and students pertaining to those articles that they feel have been of special help to them in their work.

W.P.M.

ACKNOWLEDGMENTS

I WISH TO EXPRESS my appreciation to the various authors and publishers for their contributions to this volume. This production would not have been possible without their generous cooperation. Thanks are due Mr. Payne Thomas for his advice and encouragement throughout the preparation of this book. I wish to acklowledge my teachers, B. H. M., P. B. J., W. R. J., and W. F. U., for reasons far too numerous to mention. Special thanks are due my wife, Grace, for proofing the entire manuscript and serving as a constant source of encouragement.

CONTENTS

PART ONE

COMPARATIVE AND PHYSIOLOGICAL PSYCHOLOGY

PART TWO

ENGINEERING PSYCHOLOGY

PART THREE

LEARNING THEORY

[xv]

PART NINE

PERSONALITY DYNAMICS

PART TEN

PSYCHOPHYSIOLOGY

Contemporary Readings In
Sport Psychology

PART ONE

COMPARATIVE AND PHYSIOLOGICAL PSYCHOLOGY

Chapter 1

EFFECTS OF DIFFERING PREPUBERTY EXERCISE PROGRAMS ON THE EMOTIONALITY OF MALE ALBINO RATS*

JEROME C. WEBER AND RONALD A. LEE

INTRODUCTION

THIS STUDY was done to determine if differing types of prepuberty exercise programs had any effects on the emotionality exhibited by male albino rats at puberty. The term *emotionality* is defined as the state of being emotional, a state which consists of a group of organic and expressive reactions, and which denotes a generally upset or excited condition in the organism. The term *emotionality* is used as a convenient title which describes a complex of factors. Emotionality is generally thought of as a trait, since organisms will differ in the extent to which they display those reactions covered by this term.

REVIEW OF LITERATURE

The emotionality of animals has long been observed and a large number of methods to measure emotionality have been proposed.[5, 6, 10, 12, 14]

Weininger,[13] Greenman and Duhring,[4] Ader,[1] Hunt and Otis,[7] and Denenberg and others[3] have reported that animals which are handled early in life exhibit less emotionality than animals which have not been handled. The literature supports the hypothesis that the amount of emotionality exhibited by a given organism is, at least to some degree, subject to environmental influences.

* J. C. Weber and R. A. Lee: Effects of differing prepuberty exercise programs on the emotionality of male albino rats. *Res Quart Amer Ass Health Phys Educ*, *39*:748-751, 1968. Reproduced here with the permission of the authors and the American Association for Health, Physical Education, and Recreation. This study was supported by grants from the University of Oklahoma Faculty Research Committee and Alumni Development Fund.

[5]

No studies were found which investigated the effects of exercise as an independent variable which affected the dependent variable of emotionality.

Michael[8] concluded that activity probably results in a more efficient reaction to stress situations because of a heightened sensitivity in the enlarged adrenals due to activity. Bartlett[2] found that adaptation to exercise appeared to protect the organism against the emotional stress produced by restraint. Renold[9] found that when eosinophil count was used as an index of adrenal cortical function, the coxswain and the coach of a racing crew showed responses comparable to those of the oarsmen.

Selye[11] suggested that bodily stress reactions were generally independent of the specific stress agent and that adaptation to one type of stressor may be valuable in aiding the organism to deal with other types of stresses. If this general adaptation process carries over from situation to situation, it seems reasonable to hypothesize that animals subjected to the stresses of forced exercise would exhibit less emotionality in response to the stress of an open-field testing situation.

METHODS

Forty-eight male albino rats of the Sprague-Dawley strain, born on the same day but not litter mates, were randomly assigned to one of the following groups:

Sedentary. Those animals which were restricted to 10 by 8 by 7 inches animal cages and received no exercise other than that which was available in their confined cage area.

Voluntary exercise. Those animals which were housed in similar living cages but which were also allowed access to a freely revolving exercise wheel which was five inches wide and fourteen inches in diameter. These animals were free to exercise at their own volition.

Forced exercise. Those animals which were kept under the same conditions as the animals in the voluntary exercise group and which, in addition, were forced to swim for thirty minutes each day with an overload of 2 percent of their body weight added in the form of lead weights.

All groups were fed Wayne Lab Blox *ad libitum* and were allowed constant access to water. Other relevant variables such as room temperature, humidity, amount of daily handling, and position in the cage racks were not controlled but were the same for all groups. The experimental period was the thirty-five days from the animals' thirty-first day of life to the animals' sixty-fifth day of life.

On the sixty-sixth day of life the animals were tested in random order. An animal was placed in the center square of a standard open field consisting of forty-nine squares each measuring 7½ by 7½ inches. The squares were numbered consecutively. The experimenter recorded the animal's activity on a scale reproduction of the open field by placing a check in every square in which the animal placed all four feet. The animal remained in the open field for five minutes. The experimenter was unaware of the group to which the animal he was observing belonged. The field was cleaned after each trial to be sure that no scent remained which a subsequent animal would follow.

Two measures of emotionality were recorded: (1) the total number of squares traversed by an animal and (2) the total number of squares traversed by an animal toward the center. A one-way fixed-effects model of the analysis of variance was used to analyze the total number of squares traversed (parametric data). The Kruskal-Wallis one-way analysis of variance was used to analyze the total number of squares traversed towards the center of the open field (nonparametric data). The .05 level was selected for significance for all statistical tests.

RESULTS

The analysis of variance detected significant differences between groups for total number of squares traversed. The group means were as follows: sedentary = 57.38 squares, voluntary = 72.56, forced exercise = 93.37 squares. The Tukey test indicated that the mean of the forced exercise group was significantly greater than the means of the voluntary exercise group and the sedentary group. There were no significant differences between the voluntary exercise and sedentary groups. The results of the analysis of variance are presented in Table 1-I.

The Kruskal-Wallis one-way analysis of variance detected significant differences between groups for the total number of squares

TABLE 1-I

ANALYSIS OF VARIANCE OF TOTAL NUMBER OF SQUARES
TRAVERSED

Source	Sums of Squares	Degrees of Freedom	Mean Squares	F	F.95 (2,45)
Between	50,116.64	2	25,058.32	26.86	3.20
Within	41,969.13	45	932.64		
Total	92,085.77	47			

traversed toward the center. The group means were as follows: sedentary = .357 squares, voluntary exercise = .625 squares, forced exercise = 5.312 squares. The Mann-Whitney U test indicated that the mean of the forced exercise group was significantly greater than the means of the voluntary exercise group and the sedentary group. There were no significant differences between the voluntary exercise and sedentary groups. The results of the Kruskal-Wallis nonparametric analysis of variance of total number of squares traversed toward the center were (2 df) H = 9.67 and H .95(2) = 5.99.

CONCLUSIONS

The results of the present study indicate that the type of prepuberty exercise program to which a male albino rat is subjected is a significant variable in determining the amount of emotionality the animal exhibits in an open-field testing situation at puberty.

It is hypothesized that the forced exercise during the experimental period constituted a stress to which the animals in the forced exercise group became adapted. Further, this adaptation carried over so that these animals were better able to deal with a new and different type of stress situation, namely, the open field.

These results support the theory that adaptation to one stress by means of the general adaptation syndrome is valuable to the organism in dealing with the same or other stressors at a later date.

While the present results cannot be used to directly imply that a similar carry-over of the adaptation process occurs in man, examination of the relationship, if any, between reaction and adaptation to physical and mental stress in man seems a promising avenue of inquiry for the physical educator.

REFERENCES

1. ADER, R.: The effects of early experience on emotionality. *Amer Psych, 12*: 410-16, 1957.
2. BARTLETT, R. G., Jr.: Stress adaptation and inhibition of restraint induced (emotional) hypothermia. *J Appl Physiol, 8*:661-63, 1956.
3. DENENBERG, V. H., and others: Effects of infantile shock upon emotionality at weaning. *J Comp Physiol Psych, 55*:703-10, 1962.
4. GREENMAN, M. I., and DUHRING, F. L.: *Breeding and Care of the Albino Rat for Research Purposes.* Philadelphia, Wistar Institute of Anatomy and Biology, 1931.
5. HALL, C. S.: Emotional behavior in the rat. I. Defecation and urination as measures of individual differences in emotionality. *J Comp Physiol Psych, 18*:385-403, 1934.
6. HALL, C. S.: Drive and emotionality. Factors associated with adjustment in the rat. *J Comp Physiol Psych, 17*:89-108, 1934.
7. HUNT, H. F., and OTIS, L. S.: Restricted experience and timidity in the rat. *Amer Psych 10*:432, 1955.
8. MICHAEL, E. D.: Stress adaptation through exercise. *Res Quart Amer Ass Health Phys Educ, 28*:50-54, 1957.
9. RENOLD, A. E.; QUIGLEY, T. B. and THORN, G. W.: Reaction of the adrenal cortex to physical and emotional stress in college oarsmen. *New Eng J Med, 244*:754-77, 1951.
10. SADVONI, K., and KOLTZOVA, M. P.: Genetic analysis of temperament in rats. *J Exper Zool 45*:301-18, 1925.
11. SELYE, H.: *The Stress of Life.* New York: McGraw, 1956.
12. UTSURIKAWA, N.: Temperament differences between out- and inbred strains of the albino rat. *J Animal Behav, 7*:111-29, 1917.
13. WEININGER, O.: The effects of early experience on behavior and growth characteristics. *J Comp Physiol Psychol, 49*:1-9, 1956.
14. YERKES, R.M.: The heredity of savageness and wildness in rats. *J Animal Behav, 3*:286-96, 1913.

Chapter 2

SOME DETERMINANTS OF PLAY AND EXPLORATION IN CHIMPANZEES*

W. I. WELKER

INTRODUCTION

IN RECENT YEARS, an increasing number of experiments have appeared which have attempted to study the behavior of animals when not motivated by the so-called primary drives. These studies have shown that certain characteristics of the external environment in themselves will elicit behavior. Such behavior has usually been called exploration (or curiosity) and, sometimes, play.

The study reported below was designed to test four specific hypotheses, suggested by the literature, concerning stimulus determinants of play and exploration. These hypotheses are as follows: (1) A relatively new, novel, or different stimulus situation will elicit more exploratory and play behavior than a relatively old, familiar, or unchanged one; (2) with repeated presentation, responsiveness to a novel situation decreases, not only within any one session, but from one session to another; (3) a stimulus object which, when manipulated, causes a change in the situation, will elicit more exploration and play than one which does not cause a change when manipulated, and (4) the animal will preferentially explore and play with those stimulus objects which have greater stimulation value, that is, it will prefer (within limits) larger, brighter, and more heterogeneous objects.

* W. I. Welker: Some determinants of play and exploration in chimpanzees. *J Comp Physiol Psychol, 49*:84-89, 1956. Copyright (1956) by the American Psychological Association, and reproduced here with permission of the author and the American Psychological Association. This chapter is a portion of a dissertation submitted in partial fulfillment of the requirements for the Ph.D. degree at the University of Chicago.

METHOD

Subjects

Six chimpanzees were the *Ss* of this study. The three in the younger group (Chow, Kathy, Lad) were between three and four years of age, and the three in the older group (Dehn, Hank, Dag) were between seven and eight. All the animals were in good health throughout the experimental period.

Apparatus

Fifteen stimulus situations were designed (Fig.2-1). Two situations (No. 1 and 11) consisted only of the presentation board, measuring 23½ inches by 40 inches and not pictured in Figure 2-1. Two (No. 10 and 15) were placed inside the animal's cage, and the other eleven consisted of different sets of stimulus objects which were bolted to the presentation board. All these sets of objects, except those in Situation 7, consisted of pairs of objects. The two objects of each pair were similar in all except one or two main stimulus conditions. Figure 2-1 shows the objects used in each situation, the number of the

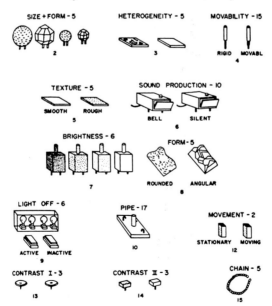

FIGURE 2-1. Stimulus objects.

situation (printed below the object sets), the stimulus variable involved in the situation and the number of sessions for which it was presented (printed above the object set), and, where not obvious, the characteristics which distinguished each object from the other of a pair (printed beneath the object set). Duplicate pairs of objects were prepared in Situations 3, 4, 5, 6, and 8. In Situations 13 and 14 one object of each pair was painted the same color as the presentation board on which it was mounted, and the other object was of a contrasting color. The contrasting and blending colors in Situation 14 were the reverse of those in Situation 13.

Procedure

Each situation was presented to each animal in a series of six-minute sessions. Each situation was repeatedly presented until responsiveness to the objects (group average) began to approach an asymptote of satiation. When responsiveness to one situation reached the criterion of satiation, a new situation was introduced. This new situation was likewise run for several sessions and in this manner a total of fifteen situations was presented. The several sessions of Situations 7 and 8 were presented alternately. The sessions of all other situations were presented consecutively. All six animals were run in close succession for a particular session each day, and the order of testing the animals was randomized from day to day. No attempt was made to schedule equal intervals between successive sessions. In most instances, only one session was presented each day, but sometimes two sessions were presented. In one case, as many as five sessions were given on one day (Situation 5). In addition, inclement weather and other exigencies necessitated some variation in the time of day at which the tests were given. However, varying the time of testing did not have significant effects on the results.

Since the animals were in their outside cages during testing, some external distractions were inevitable. Many of these external factors were clearly contiguous with the animal's distraction from the experimental situations. Among these, the animal in the adjacent cage was a major factor. However, most of the external stimuli were sporadic and of short duration, and often were not disturbing to the animals. Temperature and humidity readings were taken daily; they bore no consistent relationships to the results.

The presentation board, with or without attached objects, was placed before the cage of the chimpanzee while E sat nearby and recorded the behavior of the animal in shorthand symbols for the six-minute session. Manipulations (M) and head-orientations (O) directed toward the stimulus objects were recorded. The objects were so spaced on the presentation board that discrete manipulations of each object could be observed. With the aid of a watch with a sweep secondhand and a time-ruled data sheet, each five-second period during which the animal oriented toward, or manipulated, one or another of the stimulus objects was recorded.

A manipulation was recorded if the animal made contact with an object (i.e. mouthing, biting, smelling, scratching, slapping, rubbing, grasping) during a five-second period. If S continued to touch the object, all five-second periods of maintained contact were recorded. If manipulation occurred to two objects during the same five-second period, both were recorded.

An orientation was recorded if the animal looked at the stimulus objects during a five-second period without manipulating them. The exact focus of attention could not be determined with certainty. However, it could be determined whether or not the animal was looking at the situation in general.

A measure of total responsiveness (ΣR) during a single minute or session was obtained by summing the number of five-second periods during which an animal responded (sum of M and O) to the experimental situation.

The reliability of the written recording technique was checked in two ways: by electrical counters (in Situation 6) and by movie records. The electric counter and written records showed close correspondence in direction and amount of change in average ΣR from session to session. The written record was found to overestimate the time spent in manipulating (from 7 to 17%), and to underestimate the time spent in orienting (from 4 to 14%) and in not reacting (from 1 to 8%) when compared with the movie record. These discrepancies are explicable in view of the fact that the written unit was a five-second period, whereas the movie unit was 1/16 second (the time interval between successive exposures), thus affording greater accuracy. The direction of overestimation or underestimation was the same for all animals in each response category.

RESULTS

The statistical significance of all the results reported below was tested by the Sign Test. [1] The two-tailed test was used in every case.

Approach to Novelty

If the total responsiveness (ΣR) in the session during which a new set of objects was first introduced is compared with ΣR to familiar objects in the preceding session, a significant increase in reactivity to new situations by all animals is found. This result is significant at the .01 level for each animal. Merely changing the color of the presentation board from gray to red (Situation 11) was sufficient to elicit increased duration of response in all animals.

Satiation

A response decrement or satiation effect was found with repeated presentation of each situation throughout several successive sessions and is depicted in Figure 2-2, which shows the average number of

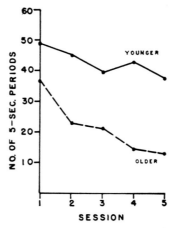

FIGURE 2-2. Session-by-session response trend (two age groups).

five-second periods the two age groups spent reacting to the experimental stimuli. The data are plotted for the first five consecutive sessions of twelve situations. In this analysis, a comparison was made of the responsiveness of each animal on the first and fifth sessions of all twelve situations. The Sign Test was applied to the several pairs of scores for each animal. Four animals showed significant session-to-session satiation (.05 level or better). The two animals that did not show such satiation were in the younger age group.

Minute-by-minute satiation, determined by comparing ΣR on the first and sixth minutes within each of 112 sessions, was significant for each animal beyond the .01 level. Figure 2-3 presents the combined session and minute trends in ΣR for twelve situations which

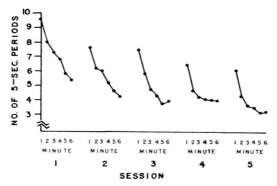

FIGURE 2-3. Intrasession and intersession response trends.

were presented to the animals for at least five sessions. This figure shows that there was an average increase in responsiveness during the first minute of each session over the last minute of the preceding session. This increase was significant at the .01 level for Chow, Dehn,

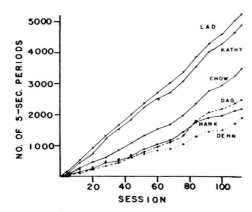

FIGURE 2-4. Cumulative ΣR curves over 112 sessions.

Hank, and Dag, but not for Kathy or Lad, who also did not exhibit significant session-by-session satiation.

Although decrease in ΣR occurs toward any particular situation over time, there is an overall linearity of the cumulative response curves of each animal (Fig. 2-4).

Object Preferences

It was found that the animals preferred certain objects to others. The object preferences were determined by comparing the ΣR of the two objects of a pair during successive minutes. Out of seventy-two possible preferences, twenty-three occurred which were significant at the .05 level or better (Table 2-I). Of these, seventeen were in the predicted direction (see *d* in Introduction). The remaining six preferences were significant in the direction opposed to that which was predicted (italic values in Table 2-I); four animals preferred the spheres in Situation 2; in Situation 8, one preferred the rounded objects, and in Situation 13, one animal preferred the noncontrasting object.

TABLE 2-I

PROBABILITIES OF DIFFERENCES IN SITUATIONS
DESIGNED TO TEST FOR PREFERENCES

	Animal					
Situation	*Chow*	*Kathy*	*Lad*	*Dehn*	*Hank*	*Dag*
2, Size	.01	.01	>.25	.05	.01	.05
2, Form	<.75	*.99*	<.75	*.95*	*.99*	*.95*
3, Heterogeneity	.05	.25	>.25	>.25	>.25	>.25
4, Movability	.01	.01	.01	>.25	.01	.25
5, Texture	<.75	.50	<.75	.10	>.25	<.75
6, Sound	<.75	.01	>.25	.10	<.75	>.25
7, Brightness	<.75	.01	>.25	>.25	.05	>.25
8, Form	<.75	*.99*	.10	<.75	>.25	<.75
9, Light off	>.25	.05	.25	<.75	>.25	>.25
12, Movement	.05	.05	<.75	*	*	.05
13, Contrast I	.10	*.95*	<.75	<.75	<.75	>.25
14, Contrast II	>.25	*	<.75	>.25	*	>.25

* Insufficient number of observations.

A more detailed analysis of the data indicates how responses to the objects of a pair were distributed over time. The records from the situations in which preferences occurred show that although all objects were touched, responsiveness to the objects often alternated.

However, the animals touched the preferred objects more frequently and for longer periods of time. Thus, the data from the ten sessions of Situation 4 were analyzed for length and number of contacts made to both the preferred and nonpreferred objects. Sixty pairs of observations were available for both these measures (ten sessions from each of the six animals). Application of the Sign Test revealed that the length of contacts was greater on the average to the preferred objects (.01 level), but the number of contacts with the preferred objects was not significantly greater ($p = .10$).

If it can be assumed that ΣR to one situation is independent of ΣR to any other situation, objects that were placed inside the cage (Situations 10 and 15) were preferred by the total group to all those that were placed outside the cage. In this analysis, the comparisons were made between different situations, rather than within situations as were the above preference analyses. Pairs of scores were formed comparing Situations 10 and 15 with each of the other situations. The Sign Test was applied, and it was found that the animals were more responsive to Situation 10 than to any other situation (.05 level). They were more responsive to Situation 15 than to any other situation (.05 level) except Situation 4 (.25 level).

Variability

The records were analyzed for variability (or moment-to-moment changes) in behavior to stimulus objects. Three characteristics of the behavior were selected as indicating such variability: (1) contacts, or the number of times an animal touched an object for one or more five-second periods after it had been touching either some other experimental object, or some nonexperimental stimulus, (2) shifts, or the frequency of shifts of response from one object to another, and (3) the frequency of withdrawals from the experimental situation. The relative frequencies of these measures tell us how variable the animal has been in a given situation during a given period of time.

It was found that the frequency of contacts, shifts, and withdrawals was positively associated with the frequency of ΣR. Thus, the animals that were most responsive to the objects also exhibited a greater frequency of behavior changes in relation to the objects than did those animals that were least responsive. In this analysis there were six situations (Situations 2, 7, 9, 12, 13, and 14) from which it was possible to ascertain whether or not a particular object of a pair had been touched, and if so, in what order. A total of twenty-four sessions had been presented to each animal involving these six situations. The animals were ranked according to their total responsiveness in each of these sessions. Then the corresponding measures of behavior change (contacts, shifts, withdrawals) were assembled for each animal. These data for all sessions were then summed and averaged for each animal. The differences in frequency of contacts, shifts, and withdrawals between the highest-responding and lowest-responding individuals are significant for each measure at the .01 level. In the above analysis the ΣR of one animal was contrasted with that of another. However, each animal could also be considered individually by comparing its sessions of highest responding with those of lowest responding. Again the same relationships were found. Although it is theoretically possible for a low-responding animal to be more variable than a high-responding animal, such was never the case.

Age Differences

The three younger animals were significantly more responsive to all situations throughout the 112 sessions than were the three older animals (.01 level; see Fig. 2-2 and 2-4). There were no significant age-group differences in ΣR during the first minute when new situations were presented, but a significant age difference was apparent by the sixth minute. This faster satiation rate for the older animals is apparent in both the minute and session trends.

Situations 10 and 15 were presented to test whether or not the age differential might be due to the greater difficulty of the larger (older) animals in reaching their arms through the two-inch mesh wire of the cage. In both these situations, the objects were placed inside the cage. The difference between the age groups was maintained despite this change, however. The Sign Test was applied to fifteen pairs of scores (per age group) obtained from each of these two situations. These scores consisted of the ΣR of each animal during the last five sessions of Situation 10 and of all five sessions of Situation 15.

The age differences for these two situations were significant at the .01 and .05 levels, respectively.

DISCUSSION

In accordance with traditional usage, the behavior under investigation here has been termed play and exploration. Such behavior consists of variable responses to novel objects. The influence of novelty of stimulus in eliciting such behavior is indicated by (1) an increase in responsiveness upon appearance of a new set of objects, (2) an increase of responsiveness to the same set of objects after an intersession interval, and (3) a decrease of interest in the objects with repeated exposure. That the older, more experienced, animals were less attracted to the new objects further attests the significance of the novelty factor. The phenomenon here called satiation is seen to be relatively long lasting (persisting from day to day and becoming cumulatively effective), and probably represents a sort of learning.

Stimulus preferences were also found to be important in the activity pattern which occurred. Such preferences were predominantly to the more movable, larger, brighter, more heterogeneous, and changing (auditory, visual) stimulus configurations. Although such preferences may be special cases of preference for novelty (i.e. spatial or temporal changes), preferences for qualitative stimulus characteristics also occurred (e.g. preference for curvilinear objects). That preferences were not more consistently shown by all the animals may be understood when one considers the importance of novelty. The effectiveness of novelty may have overshadowed the effects of the differential stimulus conditions.

Variability of behavior was an outstanding characteristic of the play and exploration observed. The animals never continued to respond to only one object or aspect of the experimental situation which confronted them. They responded first to one object, then to another, and to various aspects of a single object as well. Such behavior changes may be understood in terms of the three concepts discussed above. Attraction to novelty, and satiation of interest with familiarity were salient characteristics of the session-by-session and minute-by-minute behavior changes. Although the data do not lend themselves to such an analysis, it is possible that moment-to-moment behavior changes show these same characteristics. Thus, an animal touching a wooden block would satiate swiftly and become attracted to other blocks that were, at that moment, more novel. Response to the second block would satiate quickly and shift subsequently to another stimulus relatively more novel than the first. In the sequence of such actions the animal would linger longer with certain preferred stimuli, or return to them more frequently than it would to other, less preferred stimuli. Although such an interpretation seems to this author to best fit the data on variability, further experimentation is necessary to test the validity of these concepts.

SUMMARY

Six young chimpanzees (3 to 8 years old) were exposed successively to fifteen different stimulus situations during a total of 112 six-minute sessions. The introduction of novel or different stimulus objects elicited increased responsiveness. With repeated exposure to these objects, a decrease in total responsiveness occurred for all animals within sessions and for all but the more highly responsive animals from session to session. For a given set of objects there was an increase in responsiveness from the last minute of one session to the first minute of the subsequent session. Certain object preferences were exhibited by all animals. The three younger animals were more responsive than the three older animals. All animals were more variable (in terms of frequency of contacts, shifts, and withdrawals) when they were more highly responsive (in terms of total time of contact). Motivation to play and explore was maintained as long as new objects were periodically introduced. Specific characteristics of the stimulus situations were thus shown to be determinants of play and exploration, and the behavior was shown to be patterned over time in certain specifiic ways.

REFERENCES

1. Dixon, W. J., and Massey, F. J., Jr.: *Introduction to statistical analysis.* New York: McGraw, 1951.
2. Welker, W. I.: Play and exploration in chimpanzees. Unpublished doctor's dissertation, University of Chicago, Dept. of Photographic Reproduction, Thesis N. 2387, 1954.

PART TWO
ENGINEERING PSYCHOLOGY

Chapter 3

EFFECTS OF VARIED INFORMATION FEEDBACK PRACTICE CONDITIONS ON THROWING SPEED AND ACCURACY*

ROBERT M. MALINA

INTRODUCTION

STUDIES OF MOTOR learning have unequivocally stressed the importance of providing the learner with as specific and as immediate knowledge of his performance as possible.[2, 3, 5] However, much of the research on this aspect of skill learning has been limited to simple, discrete motor responses. Since gross motor skills have been noticeably omitted from such analyses one may raise questions concerning the influence which feedback mechanisms may have on the development of proficiency in gross motor tasks. The present study, therefore, was designed (1) to analyze performance patterns in speed and accuracy of overarm throwing behavior during repeated practice sessions involving different conditions of information feedback—the external, quantifiable information of the speed and/or accuracy of performance made available to the subject after each throw and (2) to determine the effect of the different practice conditions on subsequent performance in throwing for speed and accuracy.

Studies of the role of information feedback in the speed and accuracy of throwing behavior are lacking. Nevertheless, a variety of studies has shown that such feedback in the form of knowledge of results is a significant factor in the development of proficiency in tasks requiring a high degree of accuracy. Providing feedback improved

* Robert M. Malina: Effects of varied information feedback practice conditions on throwing speed and accuracy. *Res Quart Amer Ass Health Phys Educ, 40*:134-145, 1969. Reproduced here with the permission of the author and the American Association for Health, Physical Education, and Recreation. Data for this study were from a research project conducted to fulfill requirements for the Ph.D. degree at the University of Wisconsin, under the supervision of G. Lawrence Rarick, 1963.

accuracy in tracking,[11, 12, 20] aiming,[23] lever displacing,[6, 7] control-stick manipulation,[1] and inscribing lines.[4]   On the other hand restricting or delaying feedback had the effect of impeding the acquisition of accuracy in ball tossing,[14, 16] two-hand positioning,[8] lever displacing,[6, 7] control-stick manipulation,[1] and inscribing lines.[4]   Research is lacking on the effect of such information feedback on the speed and accuracy of throwing. Implications, however, are apparent. Smith and Smith,[19] for example, showed that visual direction alone was not an adequate basis for accurate ball tossing performance, which suggests that factors other than visual cues are essential to accurate throwing. Furthermore, throwing is a ballistic skill;[10] since it is difficult to modify a ballistic movement during its execution, information feedback would be used to amend the response in the succeeding performance. It is dependent, of course, on the performer's ability to identify the information value of the feedback and then incorporate this information into the subsequent trial.

PROCEDURES

Fifty-five high school freshman males, fourteen to sixteen years of age, were the subjects of the study. They were randomly divided into five groups of eleven each on the basis of the practice conditions specifically defined for each group:

Group I: controls; no practice

Group II: speed information feedback only

Group III: accuracy information feedback only

Group IV: speed-accuracy information feedback

Group V: no information feedback

In addition to initial and final tests, Groups II through V received twelve practice sessions under the information feedback conditions defined for each group. The sessions were scheduled on alternate days, three days a week, over a 4-week period. The performance task and directive were the same for all subjects in the test and practice sessions—twenty overarm throws at a distance of thirty feet, striving for a maximum speed and maximum accuracy; that is, with equal emphasis on both variables in question. Each subject performed individually for test and practice sessions.

The apparatus used to measure the speed and accuracy of throwing performance and to systematically report this information to the subject has been described in detail in separate reports.[17, 18] Essentially it consisted of a target and a photoelectric-vibration system, so arranged that as the light source to the photocells was interrupted at ball release, relays controlling the electric timer and target lamps were activated. As a result the timer was started, the target lamps were shut off, and the target area was completely darkened. As the ball contacted the target the vibration system was activated and stopped the timer. The target lamps were restored manually. It should be noted that the target lamp arrangement was such that it could be excluded from the photoelectric circuit for those conditions permitting accuracy information.

Information of accuracy performance was provided in the form of direct vision of ball-target contact, and was withheld by restricting the subject's vision of the target area at the ball release. Speed information feedback was provided verbally as the time of flight. It was reported to the subject in relation to his fastest time from previous test or practice sessions. The rationale underlying this procedure was to insure an equal emphasis on both speed and accuracy during all sessions. In the case of accuracy, the bull's eye was the guide. A throw that missed the bull's eye did not represent maximum accuracy. In the case of speed there was no such guide. By reminding the subject of his fastest speed a speed guide analogous to the bull's eye was provided. Speed feedback was withheld simply by not reporting the elapsed time to the subject.

The accuracy and speed of each throw were recorded as the point of ball-target contact and as the time of flight respectively. Accuracy was scored in three dimensions: concentric circle, and horizontal and vertical deviations. The time of each throw was converted to velocity in feet per second. The details of the scoring and conversion procedures as well as reliabilities have been presented in previous reports.

RESULTS

Mean performances for all groups are presented in Figures 3-1 through 3-3. It was apparent that the groups which received speed information feedback, Groups II and IV, showed gradual improvement in throwing speed over the practice program (Figure 3-1). On

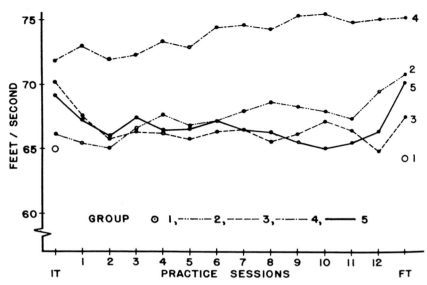

FIGURE 3-1. Mean group performances in throwing velocity.

the other hand Groups III and V, which practiced without speed feedback, demonstrated a reduced throwing speed. After an initial decrease in speed, both groups showed a moderately stable but reduced level of speed throughout the program.

On the concentric circle basis (Fig. 3-2), the accuracy information feedback groups, Groups III and IV, showed a relatively stable level of accuracy during the initial practice sessions, followed by a gradual improvement. The accuracy-restricted groups, II and V, showed a sharp deterioration in concentric circle accuracy early in practice, followed by a fluctuating level through the central portion of the program. As practice continued Group II showed a steady recovery while Group V continued at variable accuracy levels.

The changes in concentric circle accuracy were closely paralleled by changes in the vertical and horizontal deviation accuracy measures (Fig. 3-3). Group IV's deviation accuracy in the vertical plane remained relatively stable, showing improvement in the later practice sessions. On the other hand the group's horizontal deviation accuracy showed fluctuations similar to those evident in concentric circle accuracy. Group III's deviation accuracy in the vertical plane showed a steady improvement over the first six sessions, and as such, closely

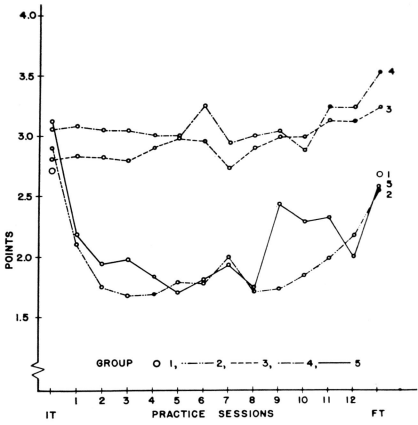

Figure 3-2. Mean group performances in concentric circle accuracy.

matched the group's concentric circle performance. The deviation in the horizontal plane, however, remained relatively stable early in practice, showing a slight improvement. During the later sessions deviation accuracy in both horizontal and vertical planes showed gradual improvement.

Groups II and V, the accuracy-restricted feedback groups, demonstrated different deviation accuracy trends. Both decreased steadily in vertical deviation accuracy during the early practice sessions. Later in practice, performance in this dimension was relatively stable for Group II and variable for Group V. In the horizontal plane, both groups showed reduced but variable deviation accuracy.

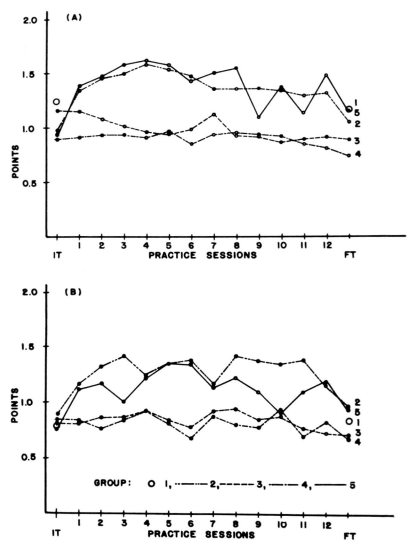

FIGURE 3-3. Mean group performances in deviation accuracy: (A) vertical. (B) horizontal.

The final test session (FT in the figures) actually represented a restoration of feedback for Groups II, III, and V in accuracy, speed, and speed and accuracy respectively. The groups responded to the restored feedback by increased levels of performance in the respective variables relative to the last practice session.

To ascertain treatment effects of the practice program upon subsequent performance, the final test means were tested for homogeneity by analysis of covariance procedures.[15] Since all F values were significant (Table 3-I), the difference between each individual pair of

TABLE 3-I

ANALYSES OF COVARIANCE OF FINAL MEANS ADJUSTED
FOR INITIAL DIFFERENCES

Variable	Sources of Variation	Adjusted Sum of Squares	df	Adjusted Mean Square	F
Velocity	Tr.[a]	387.86	4	96.96	4.84[d]
	E[b]	981.96	49	20.04	
	T[c]	1369.82	53		
Concentric Circle Acc.	Tr.	9.111	4	2.278	11.31[d]
	E	9.866	49	.201	
	T	18.977	53		
Horizontal Deviation Acc.	Tr.	.913	4	.288	4.98[d]
	E	2.242	49	.046	
	T	3.155	53		
Vertical Deviation Acc.	Tr.	1.196	4	.299	4.68[d]
	E	3.125	49	.064	
	T	4.321	53		

[a] Treatment
[b] Error
[c] Total
[d] Significant beyond .01 level

adjusted final means for each variable was tested by the Kramer extension of the Duncan Multiple Range Test.[13]*

The final speed performance of Group IV, the speed-accuracy feedback group, was not significantly greater than that of Group II, the speed information group. Groups II and IV, however, were significantly superior in throwing speed to Groups I and III, the control and accuracy feedback groups respectively. On the other hand, the

* The Kramer analyses have been deleted in the present reproduction, but these are available in the original article.

TABLE 3-II
CORRELATION COEFFICIENTS AMONG GROUP AND WITHIN GROUPS[a]

Correlation	df	Time	Velocity	Concentric circle acc.	Horizontal dev. acc.	Vertical dev. acc.
Among groups	3	.744	.673	.096	—.300	.374
Within groups	53	.909[c]	.905[c]	.644[c]	.510[c]	.539[c]
Within group I	9	.948[c]	.958[c]	.893[a]	.609[a]	.844[b]
Within group II	9	.878[c]	.878[c]	.402	.599	.041
Within group III	9	.923[c]	.851[c]	.691[a]	.751[b]	.406
Within group IV	9	.902[c]	.885[c]	.770[b]	.653[a]	.577
Within group V	9	.933[c]	.943[c]	.785[b]	.262	.548

[a] P = .05
[b] P = .01
[c] P = .001

differences in speed between Groups II and IV and Group V were not of statistical significance. The differences between Groups I, III, and V likewise failed to show significance.

The concentric circle accuracy and horizontal and vertical deviation accuracy performances of Group IV were not significantly different or greater than the accuracy performances of Group III. Groups III and IV, however, were significantly superior to Groups I, II, and V in concentric circle accuracy, but significantly superior only to Groups II and V in vertical and horizontal deviation accuracy. Group V was significantly inferior to Group I in concentric circle accuracy, while there was no difference in concentric circle accuracy between Groups I and II. In the deviation accuracy measures, the differences between Groups I, II, and V were not statistically significant.

Correlations among and within groups on the initial and final measures are shown in Table 3-II. The correlations among the means for the groups on the time and velocity measures indicated a tendency toward group stability on the initial and final tests. The high significant correlations within all groups suggested a decided tendency for the subjects who were fast on the initial test to be fast on the final test. This stability was more apparent in the high correlation within each specific group, thus suggesting similar treatment effects for subjects within their respective groups.

Correlations among the means of the groups on the three accuracy measures were low and not significant, indicating differential treatment effects. The correlations within all groups combined were moderately high and significant. However, there was a wide range of variation among the coefficients within each specific group.

DISCUSSION

Accuracy appeared to be more affected by withholding accuracy information than speed was affected by withholding speed information feedback. On the other hand, both speed and accuracy, as measured in the various dimensions employed, improved under practice conditions in which the respective type of information feedback was provided. Improvement in accuracy, however, was more variable than improvement in speed. For example, it was not until the second half of the practice program that groups receiving accuracy information feedback showed definite indications of improvement, suggesting perhaps that practice programs attempting to improve throwing accuracy should be continued for a longer duration.

The findings of the present study agree in principle with the results reported by Fulton[9] and Solley [21, 22] in studies of speed and accuracy in lunging skills. Under practice conditions emphasizing speed, accuracy, or speed and accuracy, greater proficiency was evident in the emphasized factor(s), while proficiency in the unemphasized factor(s) was reduced and more variable. Although the directive throughout the present study was to strive for maximum accuracy and maximum speed, the speed information feedback group improved in speed and regressed in accuracy, while the exact opposite was true for the accuracy information feedback group. The subjects apparently directed their attention towards the factor for which information feedback was readily available with the neglect of the factor for which it was withheld. On the other hand, the speed-accuracy information group improved in both variables during the practice program, suggesting that, when the premium is on both factors and information feedback is provided for both, the subjects directed their attention to both speed and accuracy. The degree to which the subject is able to utilize the information value of the feedback is, of course, dependent upon his ability to effectively combine the speed and accuracy information in subsequent trials. The performance curves of Group IV, the speed-accuracy information group, suggest that the subjects experienced difficulty in combining speed and accuracy effectively early in practice when speed improved and accuracy was relatively stable. As practice continued the subjects learned to effectively incorporate both factors into the throw, showing an improvement in accuracy with a moderately stable speed. This interpretation appears in agreement with Ammons' [2] discussion of the specificity of knowledge of performance:

> The point of optimum specificity of knowledge of performance is related to some extent to the stage of learning. At the start of learning a new task, the subject can use little information. As learning proceeds, he is able to use more and more. Learning is, in fact, dependent upon the subject's acquisition of techniques for utilizing a greater range of information.

The accuracy performance curves of Groups II and V suggested that the subjects were adapting to the lack of accuracy information feedback during the later practice sessions. It was more evident in Group II, which received speed information feedback only. This suggested, therefore, that vision of the bull's eye prior to and during the throwing act to ball release was sufficient to guide the subjects in accuracy performance. By doing so, the subjects may have disregarded their subjective impressions of accuracy or inaccuracy of the preceding throw. Further exploration of this area is necessary for it is entirely possible that the subjects might eventually have surpassed their initial accuracy levels had the practice program been continued.

Improvement or reduction in performance on the final test was specific to the type and completeness of information feedback provided or withheld during the practice program. There was, however, one significant exception. Group V, which practiced without information feedback, showed no appreciable change in throwing speed on the final relative to the initial test. This apparent discrepancy merits speculation. The subjects perhaps could not effectively combine the speed and accuracy information made available to them during the final test since they had just completed a practice program during which neither speed nor accuracy information feedback was provided. Since the contributory components of throwing speed are rather gross, the adjustments essential for improved speed were perhaps easier to make than the finer adjustments necessary to improve accuracy. Hence the subjects improved in speed at the expense of accuracy.

An apparent logical inconsistency was also evident in the Kramer analysis of the velocity scores. Groups II and IV were significantly different from Groups I and III, but none of the four was significantly different from Group V. This logical paradox was perhaps a function of inferential procedures; that is, the chances of random differences between Groups II and IV and Groups I and III were less than the chances of random variation between Groups II and IV and Group V. Care must be taken in interpreting these findings. The effects of practice were not as pronounced in the case of Group

V. The need for further exploration of this area is definitely indicated.

REFERENCES

1. ABBEY, DAVID S., and COWAN, PHILIP A.: Incomplete visual feedback and performance on the Toronto Complex Coordinator. *Percept Motor Skills, 11*:43-45, 1960.

2. AMMONS, R. B.: Effects of knowledge of performance: A survey and tentative theoretical formulation. *J Gen Psychol, 54*:279-99, 1956.

3. ANNETT, JOHN: *The role of knowledge of results in learning: A survey.* U. S. Naval Training Development Center. TR No. 342-3, 1961.

4. BAKER, C. H., and YOUNG, PHYLLIS: Feedback during training and retention of motor skills. *Canad J Psychol, 14*:257-64, 1960.

5. BILODEAU, EDWARD A., and BILODEAU, INA McD.: Motor skills learning. *Ann Rev Psychol, 12*:243-80, 1961.

6. BILODEAU, EDWARD A.; BILODEAU, INA McD., and SCHUMSKY, DONALD A.: Some effects of introducing and withdrawing knowledge of results early and late in practice. *J Exp Psychol 58*:142-44, 1959.

7. BILODEAU, INA McD.: Accuracy of a simple positioning response with variation in the number of trials by which knowledge of results is delayed. *Amer J Psychol 69*:434-37, 1956.

8. ELWELL, J. L., and GRINDLEY, G. C.: The effect of knowledge of results on learning and performance. I. Coordinated movements of the two hands. *Brit J Psychol, 29*:39-54, 1938.

9. FULTON, RUTH E.: Speed and accuracy in learning movements. *Arch Psychol, 41* (300):1-53, 1945.

10. HUBBARD, ALFRED W.: Homokinetics: muscular function in human movement. In Warren R. Johnson (Ed.): *Science and Medicine of Exercise and Sports.* New York, Harper and Brothers, 1960.

11. HUNT, DARWIN P.: The effect of precision of informational feedback on human tracking performance. *Hum Factors, 3*:77-85, 1961.

12. ———. Effects of nonlinear and discrete transformation of feedback information on human tracking performance. *J exp psychol, 67*:486-94, 1964.

13. KRAMER, C. Y.: Extension of multiple range tests to group correlated adjusted means. *Biometrics, 13*:13-18, 1957.

14. LAVERY, J. J. The effect of one-trial delay in knowledge of results on the acquisition and retention of a tossing skill. *Amer J Psychol, 77*:437-43, 1964.

15. LINDQUIST, E. F. *Design and Analysis of Experiments in Psychology and Education.* Boston, Houghton, 1953.

16. LORGE, I., and THORNDIKE, E. L.: The influence of delay in the aftereffect of a connection. *J Exp Psychol, 18*:186-94, 1935.

17. MALINA, ROBERT M.: Reliability of different methods of scoring throwing accuracy. *Res Quart Amer Ass Health Phys Educ, 39*:149-60, 1968.

18. ———, and RARICK, G. LAWRENCE: A device for assessing the role of information feedback in the speed and accuracy of throwing performance. *Res Quart Amer Ass Health Phys Educ, 39*:220-23, 1968.

19. SMITH, PATRICIA C., and SMITH, OLIN W.: Ball throwing responses to photographically portrayed targets. *J Exp Psychol, 62*:223-33, 1961.

20. SMODE, ALFRED F.: Learning and performance in a tracking task under two levels of achievement information feedback. *J Exp Psychol, 56*:297-304, 1958.

21. SOLLEY, WILLIAM H.: Speed, accuracy, or speed and accuracy as an initial directive in motor learning. *Motor Skills Res Exch, 3*:76-77, 1951.

22. ———.: The effects of verbal instruction of speed and accuracy upon the learning of a motor skill. *Res Quart Amer Ass Health Phys Educ, 23*: 531-540, 1958.

23. STOCKBRIDGE, H. C. W., and CHAMBERS, B.: Aiming, transfer of training, and knowledge of results. *J Appl Psychol, 42*:148-53, 1958.

Chapter 4

FEEDBACK AND SKILL LEARNING*

Margaret Robb

INTRODUCTION

T<small>HE</small> <small>IMPORTANCE</small> of feedback in learning is well recognized. According to Bilodeau and Bilodeau[1] feedback is one of the strongest and most important variables controlling performance and learning. Wiener[3] and psychologists working in the human performance area have stated that feedback provides the information which makes possible the comparison between output and a reference or standard. In other words, feedback can be thought of as error information.

Feedback can be further distinguished by the arrival time of information about a performance. If, for example, a summary score is given to a subject after a defined performance has been completed, it is labeled *terminal feedback*. If the information is ongoing or is provided for moment-to-moment regulation of behavior, it is referred to as *concurrent feedback*. In some studies feedback has been defined by classifying the mode used in obtaining information. That is, sense organs which are stimulated from outside the body and provide knowledge of events happening outside the body are known as *external feedback modes*. *Internal feedback modes* refer to those receptors which register or provide information regarding the action

* Margaret Robb. Feedback and skill learning. *Res Quart Amer Ass Health Phys Educ,* 39:175-184, 1968. Reproduced here with the permission of the author and the American Association for Health, Physical Education, and Recreation. This research was conducted in partial fulfillment of the requirements for the degree Doctor of Philosophy at the University of Michigan, Katherine Ley, Chairman, and was supported by the National Aeronautics and Space Administration, Office of Advanced Research and Technology under contract No. NASr-(06) with the Department of Psychology, Human Performance Center and the Department of Aerospace Engineering, Information and Control Engineer Program, University of Michigan.

of the body itself. Kinesthetic sense, or the more recently used term, proprioceptive sense, is one type of internal feedback.

PURPOSE

The major purpose of this study was to investigate the course of learning a specified arm-movement pattern under conditions which varied as to the type of frequency of feedback information. A secondary purpose was to determine the subject's ability to perform the same pattern in the absence of explicit visual feedback. A movement was planned which resembled a sport movement. Many sport movements have an address or set position, some type of preparation (e.g. backswing), an acceleration or downswing, a follow through or deceleration, and a return to a starting position. The equipment allowed for a one-dimensional arm-movement and the above-mentioned characteristics were incorporated into the design of the pattern. A tracking task* was employed to determine if information could be gained about methods of training which might enhance learning. The subjects in this study were specifically trained with some type of feedback followed by testing under conditions in which part of the feedback was absent. It was hypothesized that the different modes of feedback used during training would have significantly different effects on the performance of the subjects as demonstrated in the performance of the task without explicit visual feedback.

METHOD

Subjects

Forty undergraduate students, twenty men and twenty women, served as subjects. They were secured from a pool of right-handed students who had applied to the Department of Psychology, University of Michigan, to serve as paid subjects. Their ages ranged from eighteen to twenty-three years. Males and females were randomly

---

* A pursuit tracking task was used in this study. A pursuit tracking task is one in which a subject is presented with a display containing a target and a cursor. The target is caused to move by an input signal, and the subject's task is to move the control device which in turn moves the cursor and superimposes the cursor over the target.

assigned to five different groups so that each group consisted of four men and four women.

Apparatus

The subject sat in a soundproof compartment in front of a display and a control approximately fifty centimeters from the oscilloscope. Therefore, one centimeter of target displacement corresponded to $1.41°$ of visual angle. The arm-movement pattern to be learned was displayed to subjects as a target moving in the desired pattern on a five-inch Fairchild oscilloscope (see Fig. 4-1). The subject grasped the handle of the control device and moved the control, which in turn moved a cursor on the display. By moving the control properly the cursor could be superimposed over the target. The subject wore Willson sound barrier earphones which allowed the experimenter to communicate with him.

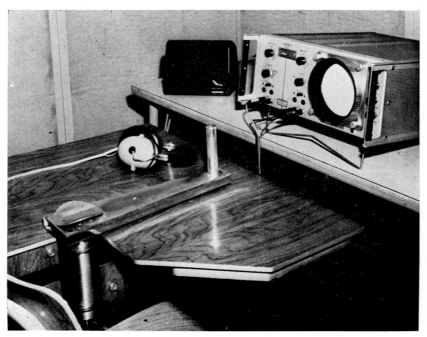

FIGURE 4-1. Display and control equipment used by subjects. A—oscilloscope, B—earphones, C—control.

FIGURE 4-2. Experimenter's equipment. A—analog computer, B—X-Y plotter, C—brush pen recorder.

The experimenter's equipment consisted of an analog computer, associated electronic components, a Veriplotter model X-Y plotter, and an eight-channel brush pen recorder (see Fig. 4-2).

Data Collected

Two types of data were collected. The mean error score, termed Integrated Absolute Error (IAE), was recorded for each trial. This score was calculated automatically by the analog computer and was proportional to the average difference between input and output without regard for sign accumulated during each trial. The lower the error score the more closely the output resembled the input. In order to provide some groups with another type of terminal feedback, selected trials were recorded on the X-Y plotter to give graphic knowledge of results. The X-Y plotter graphed the subject's output as the pattern was performed. After a trial was completed the input pattern was superimposed over the output pattern. These graphs were also analyzed to determine position and timing errors during training and testing.

Procedure

Five groups of eight subjects each were trained to perform the movement pattern. Each group trained under a different condition. The five conditions of training were labeled *blanked, vision, vision-blanked, passive-active,* and *slow-standard*. The specific feedback conditions emphasized during training for each group were as follows:

(1) *Blanked.* The subjects in group 1 watched the target and cursor disappear from view after 0.5 second. During this blanked-out period, the subjects relied on cues provided by the manipulation of the control device and memory of the pattern to perform the movement. This group received two types of terminal feedback. The IAE scores were reported to each subject after each practice trial. Immediately following trials 10, 20, and 30, the subject left the booth and was shown the graphic records generated by the X-Y plotter. After viewing these records the subject returned to the booth and performed ten more trials. By viewing the graphs the subject could see his point-for-point errors during performance of the previous trial.

During the sixth session, the criterion test for the blanked group was just another session like all their training sessions. The training condition for this group was the same condition used by all other groups of subjects as the criterion test.

(2) *Vision.* Subjects in the second group watched the target, and moved the control device in an attempt to superimpose the cursor over the target, i.e. they performed a pursuit tracking task. Concurrent feedback was obtained from visual viewing of the position of the target and cursor during each trial and from internal cues through manipulation of the control stick. These subjects also received the same two forms of terminal feedback as did the subjects in the blanked group (IAE and graph readings).

(3) *Vision-blanked.* Subjects in this group were trained under a combination of the conditions specified for the subjects in groups 1 and 2 by alternating the two conditions in blocks of ten trials. Sub-

jects performed the first block of ten trials, and later the third block of ten trials, under conditions specified for the vision group. The second and fourth blocks of ten trials were practiced under the conditions specified for the blanked group.

(4) *Passive-active.* Subjects in the fourth group combined passive participation with active performance. At the beginning of the first and third blocks of ten trials, the subjects were instructed to remove the hand from the control device and merely watch the target traverse the screen in the desired pattern. During the second and fourth blocks of ten trials the subjects performed a pursuit tracking task with vision. This procedure of alternating blocks of watching the target and performing the movement was carried out during each of the five practice sessions.

(5) *Slow-standard.* The condition utilized for the subjects in this group consisted of practicing the pattern under two different speeds in alternating blocks of ten trials. During the first and third blocks of ten trials, the subjects practiced the pattern while the target traversed the screen at a speed such that the total movement took 8.6 seconds to complete. During the second and fourth blocks the standard speed of 3.46 seconds was utilized. (All the other groups utilized the standard speed time.) Subjects in the slow-standard group were reminded at the beginning of each practice session that the criterion test to be performed after several days of practice would be at the faster of the two speeds.

The subjects in all the groups were run individually for five practice sessions. Each practice session consisted of forty trials and lasted approximately thirty minutes. At the beginning of the first session, the subjects received a brief orientation to the equipment. All the subjects, except those in the group that were never to see the target on the scope (the blanked group) were informed that after several days of practice they would be asked to move the control device to perform the movement pattern in the absence of visual information.

RESULTS

The main dependent variable was integrated absolute error. It was used as a measure of each subject's improvement with practice in his ability to minimize the difference between desired input and

actual output averaged over the time of a trial. It also provided
the primary measure for comparing performance under different
feedback conditions.

The subjects in each of five groups showed considerable learning
during the five training sessions. The data obtained during training
and testing are illustrated in Figure 4-3. Each point represents the
mean IAE scores for a group of eight subjects in blocks of ten trials.
During the training session the subjects in the vision group displayed
the lowest error scores, and the subjects in the slow-standard group
had the lowest error scores during the slow speed practice. None
of the other methods (vision-blanked, passive-active, or blanked) resulted in error scores as low as those methods where concurrent visual
feedback was always provided.

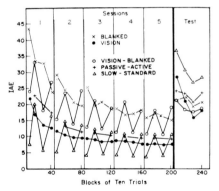

FIGURE 4-3. Mean error scores of blocks of 10 trials for subjects in blanked,
vision, vision-blanked, passive-active, and slow-standard groups during training
and testing.

During the sixth session the criterion test was administered. A
test of homogeneity of variance failed to reject the hypothesis that
the variance obtained during the criterion test was from the same
population. Therefore, a two-way analysis of variance of groups by
blocks of ten trials was performed to determine if the difference among
the mean error scores of the five groups was significant. The summary of the analysis of variance can be seen in Table 4-I.

The Newman-Keuls method[4] was used to test the difference between the means of the five groups. The results of this test showed

TABLE 4-I

ANALYSIS OF VARIANCE FOR IAE SCORES OF ALL SUBJECTS
OBTAINED DURING THE CRITERION TEST

Source of Variance	SS	df	MS	F	
Between subjects	9727.35	39			
A (Groups)	2757.06	4	689.26	3.46[a]	.05
Subject within Groups	6970.29	35	199.15		
Within subjects	13214.54	120			
B (trials)	1135.60	3	378.53	3.66[b]	.05
AB	1226.04	12	102.17		
B x subjects within groups	10852.90	105	103.36		

[a] $F .95(4,35) = 2.65$
[b] $F .95(3,105) = 2.71$

that the mean error score for the subjects in the slow-standard groups during the criterion test was significantly different from the mean error scores of the other four groups. The other groups (vision, blanked, vision-blanked, and passive-active) did not differ significantly from each other.

Four graphic records from the X-Y plotter were selected for each subject per session to study the specific kinds of errors the subjects made while performing the movement pattern. The three peaks on each of the four graphic records were scored. A peak occurred whenever there was a change of direction from right to left, or left to right in the movement pattern. The method of scoring the graphs was patterned after a technique suggested by Poulton.[2]

The results of the graph analysis regarding position errors can be seen in Figure 4-4. A position error occurred when the subject moved the control device to the wrong place at the right time, i.e. the subject may have gone too far or not far enough to the right or left and hence he either overshot or undershot the desired amplitude. As can be seen in Figure 4-4, during the first five sessions the subjects who used some form of visual information (vision, slow-standard, and passive-active) performed the pattern better than subjects who did not have access to visual error information. During the criterion test, subjects in the slow-standard group performed more poorly with regard to the position errors. This difference was not significant. These findings suggest that the subjects in the slow-standard group, although performing at a higher error score, were able to learn the

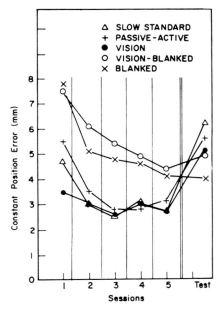

FIGURE 4-4. Constant position errors taken from graphic records.

amplitude pattern about as well as subjects who trained under the other conditions.

An examination of the timing errors during the criterion test indicated that subjects in the slow-standard group had higher timing errors than the subjects in the other four groups (see Fig. 4-5).

A one-way analysis of variance was performed to determine if the difference in the timing errors which occurred during the performance of the criterion test were significant. The results of the analysis of variance are shown in Table 4-II. A *t*-test between means revealed that the error scores for the subjects in the slow-standard group differed significantly from the error scores of the other groups. This result in-

TABLE 4-II

ANALYSIS OF VARIANCE FOR CONSTANT TIMING ERROR SCORES
DURING THE CRITERION TEST

Source of Variance	SS	df	MS	F
Groups	71.00	4	17.75	2.71[a]
Error	230.00	35	6.58	

[a] $F .95(4,35) = 2.65$

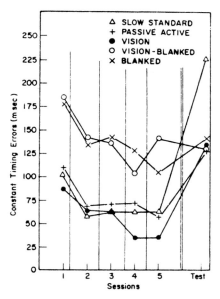

FIGURE 4-5. Constant timing errors taken from graphic errors.

dicated that the subjects in the slow-standard group were not able to learn the timing requirements of the task as well as the subjects in the other groups.

DISCUSSION

Subjects in the vision group received the optimum amount of feedback information during training. They received both forms of concurrent feedback (visual and proprioceptive) and both forms of terminal feedback (graphic knowledge of results and IAE). During training their error scores reflected the use of this information. The blanked group received concurrent proprioceptive feedback and terminal feedback supplied by the experimenter (graphs and IAE). Their error scores were higher and more erratic than those of the vision group during training. The task appeared to be more difficult because less feedback information was received. When the vision group transferred to the blanked condition during the criterion test their error scores immediately were higher, and the effect of taking away visual error information was noticeable. However, these subjects adjusted to this condition after ten trials, and showed a drop in error scores which was equal to that of the blanked group after ten trials.

The subjects in the slow-standard group received the same type of feedback as did the subjects in the vision group. However, the pattern was slowed down for alternate blocks of ten trials. Their error scores on the slow speed trials were lower than any of the other four groups during training, which indicated that during slow practice, their output was more nearly like the input pattern than any other group. If it is assumed that one must perform the exact response in order to learn the *feel* of the pattern, then these subjects certainly had more opportunity than the subjects in the other groups. When these subjects transferred to the blanked condition and feedback was reduced to only that which was available from internal cues and memory, they had significantly higher error scores than the subjects in the other groups. Although there was an improvement in error scores during the criterion test, this improvement was not great enough to effect the significant difference. Further analysis of the data revealed that these subjects had learned the amplitude pattern as well as the other subjects, but not the timing requirements.

Emphasizing concurrent visual feedback during a block of trials followed by a block of trials in which only concurrent proprioceptive feedback was available did not aid in faster or better learning of the arm-movement pattern. This result was somewhat unexpected. The investigator had assumed that under this condition (vision-blanked) the subjects would have had an early opportunity for the practice of a condition equivalent to the criterion test. It was assumed that this practice would aid subjects during the criterion test. The data showed that these subjects did no better than the blanked group during training and testing. Either subjects were more confused than helped by the alternation of conditions during practice, or the early use of this type of feedback during training was not helpful for later performance.

The passive-active group received knowledge of the input pattern during the *watching* trials. If one agrees with Wiener[4] that feedback is error information, then these subjects were not actually receiving feedback during the watching trials. Instead they were receiving information as to the objective of the task, or learning the exact pattern of the input signal. Subjects, during their active trials, performed at a higher error rate than the vision group. These data appear to agree with Bilodeau and Bilodeau[1] that feedback is one of the more important variables for learning a task. However, when subjects in this group performed the criterion test, they were able to perform it as well as the other groups. Apparently the limited practice on the active-visual condition was sufficient to prepare these subjects to perform the criterion test.

CONCLUSIONS

Although practice was very important in learning the arm-movement pattern, the key to effective learning was practice plus feedback information. Concurrent visual feedback was the most important variable for learning the movement pattern.

One conclusion appears valid concerning both terminal and concurrent feedback. A measure of performance obtained during the continuous execution of the skill may be more valuable to the learner than a measure of terminal performance.

The use of slow practice, especially alternating slow and standard speed practice, was questioned as a method of learning a pattern in which timing is important.

The results of the criterion test showed that there was some indication that after a basic pattern was established through practice with some type of visual information, subjects were able to rely on internal cues sufficiently well enough to judge output and regulate performance.

REFERENCES

1. BILODEAU, E. A. and BILODEAU, I. McD.: Motor skills in learning. In Paul Farnsworth (Ed.): *Annual Review of Psychology*. Palo Alto, Annual Reviews, 1961.
2. POULTON, E. C.: On simple methods of scoring tracking errors. *Psychol Bull, 59*:30-328, 1962.
3. WIENER, N. W.: *Cybernetics*. Cambridge, M.I.T., 1965.
4. WINER, B. J.: *Statistical Principles in Experimental Design*. New York: McGraw, 1962.

PART THREE
LEARNING THEORY

Chapter 5

A THREE-LEVEL THEORY OF PERCEPTUAL-MOTOR BEHAVIOR*

Bryant J. Cratty

The student of human behavior arrives at valid inferences by observing people and through the careful collection and analysis of
meaningful data. When conflicts arise between behavior as observed
and behavior as measured, they may be resolved either by a re-
examination of the rationale upon which investigations have been
based, by a reassessment of evaluative procedures, and/or through
the development of theoretical models which attempt to synthesize
the data of observations and of measurement.

In the study of perceptual-motor behaviors a primary conflict
arises between the common observation that some individuals seem
to evidence proficiency in a number of skills, and the frequent experimental finding that "skill is specific." Proponents of the generality
of perceptual-motor skill continue to utilize such terms as coordination, agility, and balance as though they were unitary factors applicable to a variety of situations. These individuals persist in the
invention of various movement exercises which are purported to transfer to a variety of specific situations.

The strict experimentalist on the other hand seems to suggest that
the specificity of perceptual-motor attributes is so marked that the
only way in which an athletic team may defeat another is to actually
confront them on a given day and at a given place. They suggest
that no amount of preparation can really duplicate the exact circumstances that will be encountered on the day of a confrontation between two teams. Furthermore, it is usually stated that transfer be-

* B. J. Cratty. A three-level theory of perceptual-motor behavior. *Quest* (Monograph VI), May, 1966, pp. 3-10. Reproduced here with permission of the author
and the *Quest* Board.

tween skills occurs with such infrequency that practicing for transfer would seem a waste of time.

The argument concerning the specificity or generality of human attributes has had a relatively long history in the experimental literature. Spearman,[24] in 1904, was one of the early advocates of the generality of human intelligence. His initial study, in 1904, utilized the then new tool of factor analysis. In subsequent years Guilford,[15] Thurstone,[27] and others interested in human cognition have suggested that intellectual behavior is highly specific, and may be fractionalized into several components.

Experimentalists interested in perceptual-motor functioning have added further evidence to both sides of the arguments concerning the specificity versus generality of human skill. Henry[17] and his students, for example, argue for the specificity of movement speed, strength, and reaction time. They have found that even endurance is specific to the movement; and that therefore to suggest that a general state of cardiovascular readiness to perform is inaccurate. Rather, one must consider endurance at doing *what* to be scientifically accurate.[1]

Edwin Fleishman[11] and his colleagues have factored manual ability into five components; strength has been divided into four parts, while balance has been fractured into four balances.

Is there then a hypothetical construct, a meaningul and scientifically accurate model which is compatible both with the experimental findings and common observations of human skill? Is there a lucid explanation which accurately portrays the situation as it actually is with regard to the performance and learning of perceptual-motor tasks? Several have constructed such a model to explain intellectual performance. Spearman,[25] for example, speaks both of a *g* (general) and an *s* factor in intelligence. Thurstone[29] and Kelley[19] have also maintained that mental operations are governed by both a common primary factor as well as by specific factors. Burt,[3] Eysenck,[10] and Vernon[30] share the opinion that intellectual attainment is molded by a general or universal factor at the top of a hierarchy of second-level group factors. Vernon postulates second-order visual educational factors and practical-mechanical factors underlie human thinking. At the base of Vernon's pyramidal construct are placed specific unique factors influencing a trait or test.[30] Burt[3] further divides these kinds of specific factors into *accidental factors* (those largely due to chance), and factors specific to the situation.

In a previous effort to resolve this general proplem as related to perceptual-motor functioning, this writer proposed a theory which suggested that constructs at two levels mold performance; those specific to the task and general ones such as the ability to analyze an activity, freedom from excess tension, and the like.[6] The statement which follows represents a refinement of this model. A framework is proposed which is composed of factors at three levels. It is believed that this refined statement does not conflict with the available experimental evidence, but on the contrary is rather a comprehensive consideration of the results from a variety of types of studies, investigations which support the supposition that general kinds of behavioral tendencies support and mold perceptual-motor performance and learning, and research which indicates that skilled output is highly specific.

This theory assumes that factors at three levels influence final performance and learning output. At the base level (we are inverting Vernon's Pyramid) are General Behavioral Supports, including aspiration level, arousal, ability to analyze a task, and perhaps various perceptual abilities. Attributes at this level, it is believed, can be demonstrated to influence a variety of kinds of human behaviors, including verbalization, cognition, and tasks which might be classified as intellectual as well as perceptual-motor abilities. These qualities at the base of our pyramid are relatively fixed, but in turn are influenced and modified by an individual's self-assessments of performance attained.

At the second level are various perceptual-motor factors spawned by the factorial studies. Ability Traits such as static strength, extent flexibility, and the like are placed here. These intermediate traits are influential of perceptual-motor performance and are usually not demonstrated as supportive of cognition or verbal behavior.

At the apex of the triangle are placed factors specific to the task and situation. Such factors as the unique energy demands of the task, the immediate values impinging upon the motivational state of the performer, the perceptual components specific to the task, the unique kinds of past experiences in the task, practice conditions, the social characteristics of the situation in which the task is performed, as well as the task's specific movement patterns (i.e. *force* requirements and *velocities*) may be found here.

This three-level theory may thus be diagrammed as follows in Figure 5-1.

Experimental evidence supporting the existence and importance of general factors named may be found at several sources. The work of Frank, for example, supports the importance of a general level of aspiration operative to support performance.[14] More recent evidence

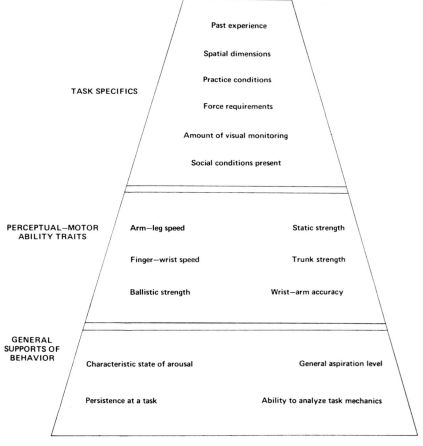

FIGURE 5-1. A three-factor theory of perceptual-motor behavior.

collected at the University of California at Davis, by Ryan,[23] also supports the supposition that an individual's feelings about his performance potential and strivings may influence performance and learning in a diversity of tasks. These latter investigations found that overachievers possessing only moderate intellectual endowments who were securing high grades within a university setting also reached superior levels of achievement on a test of perceptual-motor ability.

The recent review of the literature on arousal and activation by Duffy[9] supports the contention that individuals not only are activated to meet specific demands placed upon them in a given situation, but also habitually function at a predictable level of arousal throughout the day. Duffy cites innumerable investigations which support the content that a general level of arousal unique to each individual influences the manner in which a variety of perceptual-motor activities are performed.[9] Additional evidence from Magoun[21] and his co-workers interested in the reticular activating system supports the importance of general activation level in the formation of behavior.

Studies by this writer and his students also support the inference that a general spatial factor, independent of the musculature involved in a task, influences the ability to perform skills.[5, 7, 8] These studies indicate that musculature and spatial dimensions of the task are controlled by separate neural mechanisms and that a general spatial factor may be operative in a variety of perceptual-motor activities involving accurate movement.

The factorial work of Fleishman[12] and his co-workers indicates that the ability to analyze the mechanics and spatial dimensions of tasks influences learning and performance, particularly during the initial stages of skill acquisition. An investigation by Kreiger[20] indicates that figure-ground perception may be influential of the ability to intercept balls in a variety of situations; while the investigation by Benson[2] indicates that accurate perception of residual muscular tension contributes to relaxed and efficient performance in swimming.

Several investigations also indicate that with sustained practice in groups of skills, higher intercorrelations will result. These kinds of findings indicate that many of the investigations which purport to investigate transfer specifics and intercorrelations of performance levels may produce confounding results due to the fact that they may be actually sampling performances on several different points on curves based upon learning schedules which were initiated long before the adult subjects found themselves in the experimental situation. Hebb,[16] for example, suggests that transfer of skill in adult subjects has already occurred prior to the experimental examination of transfer.

There is an indication that skill specificity may hinge upon the use of vision when performing motor acts. Transfer seems more likely in tasks when vision is eliminated than when vision accompanies complex coordinations. The neurological evidence relating to the vast amount of the brain devoted to visual functioning, as well as the complexity of the visual cortex, supports the contention that visual-motor performance may be highly specific; while movements performed in the absence of vision may be more highly related. Cells in the fovea of the eye are represented in the brain at a 1 to 1 ratio, while muscle receptors are probably afforded no such liberal representation in the cortex.

Evidence that skilled output is also governed by factors specific to the task and to the situation is also abundant. Strong's[26] investigation, for example, clearly points to the influence of specific motivating conditions related to the social context upon measures of fitness. The innumerable studies by Henry[17, 18] and his students also attesting to the specificity of motor output have been mentioned. Namikas[22] and others have also found that extreme specificity is evidenced when the performances of highly similar tasks are contrasted. Some recent factor analyses may be criticized in so far as the initial matrices obtained containing low correlations were further subjected to factor analyses in an attempt to isolate factors which in truth may not have been present. The recent investigation by Alderman[1] points to the high specificity of apparently similar endurance tasks.

Declarations, therefore, that perceptual-motor skill either is specific or general, become indefensible. The shape of the typical motor learning curve attests to the influence of past experience during the *discovery phase* of learning. The learner during the initial stages of learning an action initially seems to organize the required response pattern by reference to similar activities within his repertoire of past experience.

On the other hand, for the coach or physical education teacher to ignore the specifics of skill acquisition is also fraught with peril. Particular problems will be generally encountered when attempting to elicit a new response pattern with a situation containing stimuli similar to those in a previous situation.

The effective teacher should thus be sensitive to these three levels of influence upon perceptual-motor performance and particular attention should be directed toward their mutual influence. The lower levels constitute the basic orientation and alertness of the performer, but in turn are influenced by his constant assessment of the performance output at the apex of the construct. Ability Traits within the middle of the model are influential not only of the particular task under consideration but to varying degrees of other and similar perceptual-motor activities. Ability Traits in turn are changed if the individual continues to practice activities which enhance these attributes, or begins to avoid activities which result in a diminution of certain movement capacities.

Developmentally the varying importance of the three levels of factors probably change. For example, during infancy and early childhood the influence of Ability Traits and General Supports from the lower two levels are perhaps more influential of performance. During later childhood, adolescence, and adulthood, more importance might be attached to the specific influences at the apex of the pyramid.

The previous statements may seem to assume that the writer considers the intellectual and perceptual-motor functioning of man as separate behaviors. Essentially it is believed that while human behavior may not be fragmented when subjected to philosophical speculations, scientific inquiry demands that at times we consider behavior in the plural. There seems to be kinds of behavior which, when observed, would likely be classified as either verbal, perceptual, motor, cognitive, etc.

The conceptual framework presented, it is believed, represents only transitory truth. However, at the same time it would seem to begin to explain factors which cause human movements as they really exist. Consideration of these levels of factors, it is believed, may aid in the teaching-learning process, particularly as the instructor gains first an awareness of their relative influence upon the task at hand, and then becomes able to discriminate between those which are modifiable in a short period of time versus factors which are relatively fixed.

Several of the previous assumptions need further verification in the form of scholarly research. For example, the generality versus specificity of human skill as a function of the amount of visual monitoring necessary is in need of further investigation. The generality versus the specificity of aspiration level also needs further clarification. Particular emphasis should be placed upon the extent to which various perceptual qualities underlie several kinds of perceptual-motor skill. Such factors as perceptual anticipation, figure-ground perception and similar attributes need further clarification with particular emphasis placed upon determining whether they contribute to a group of skills or only to specific skills. To state that *skill is specific* is not very helpful, as most of the teaching-learning processes cannot duplicate the multitude of conditions which later might be encountered by the learner. Thus, it is believed the search for basic, general factors which mold a number of kinds of perceptual-motor performances should be continued with vigor. Failure to consider the basic perceptual-motor capacities, and the reasons for superior and inferior functioning in movement tasks constitutes a serious omission from a scholarly discourse on the total human personality.

REFERENCES

1. ALDERMAN, RICHARD B.: Specificity of individual differences in arm movement fatigue within two levels of work load. *Res Quart Amer Ass Health Phys Educ, 36*:227-232, 1965.
2. BENSON, DAVID: "Effects of Concomitant Learning in Relaxation and Swimming on Swimming Improvement." Unpublished Study, University of California, Los Angeles, 1958.
3. BURT, C.: *The Factors of the Mind.* London, University of London Press, 1956.
4. BUXTON, E. E., and L. G. HUMPHREYS: The effect of practice upon intercorrelations of motor skills. *Science, 81*:441-442, 1935.
5. COHEN, PAUL. "Performance Times in Large Maze Tasks." Master's Thesis, University of California, Los Angeles, 1963.
6. CRATTY, BRYANT J.: *Movement Behavior and Motor Learning.* Philadelphia, Lea & Febiger, 1964.
7. CRATTY, BRYANT J. The influence of small-pattern practice upon large pattern learning. *Res Quart Amer Ass Health Phys Educ, 33*:523-535, 1962.
8. CRATTY, BRYANT J.: A comparison of the learning of a fine motor skill to

learning a similar gross motor task, based upon kinesthetic cues. *Res Quart Amer Ass Health Phys Educ, 33*:212-221, 1962.

9. DUFFY, ELIZABETH: *Activation and Behavior.* New York, Wiley, 1962.

10. EYSENCK, H. J.: *The Structure of Human Personality.* London, Methune, 1953.

11. FLEISHMAN, EDWIN A., and GAYLOR D. ELLISON: A factor analysis of fine manipulative tests. *J Appl Psychol, 46*:96-105, 1962.

12. FLEISHMAN, EDWIN A., and WALTER E. HEMPEL, JR.: Changes in factor structure of a complex psychomotor test as a function of practice. *Psychometrika, 19*:239-252, 1954.

13. FLEISHMAN, E. A., and W. E. HEMPEL, JR.: The relation between abilities and improvement with practice in visual discrimination reaction task. *J Exper Psychol, 49*:301-312, 1955.

14. FRANK, J. D.: Recent studies of the level of aspiration. *Psychol Bull, 38*: 218-226, 1941.

15. GUILFORD, J. P.: The structure of intellect. *Psychol Bull, 53*:267-293, 1956.

16. HEBB, D. O.: *The Organization of Behavior.* New York, Wiley, 1949.

17. HENRY, FRANKLIN: Increased response latency for complicated movements and a 'memory drum' theory of neuromotor reaction. *Res Quart Amer Ass Health Phys Educ, 31*:448-457, 1960.

18. HENRY, FRANKLIN and WHITLEY, J. D.: Relationships between individual differences in strength, speed, and mass in an arm movement. *Res Quart, Amer Ass Health Phys Educ, 31*:24-33, 1960.

19. KELLEY, T. L.: *Crossroads in the Mind of Man.* Stanford, 1928.

20. KREIGER, JANE C. "The Influence of Figural-Ground Perception on Spatial Adjustment in Tennis." M.A. Thesis, U. of Calif., Los Angeles, 1962.

21. MAGOUN, H. W.: *The Waking Brain.* Springfield, Thomas, 1958.

22. NAMIKAS, GEDIMINAS, and ARCHER, E. JAMES: Motor skill transfer as a function of inter-task interval and pre-transfer task difficulty. *J Exper Psychol, 59*:109-112, 1960.

23. RYAN, DEAN E.: Relative academic achievement and stabilometer performance. *Res Quart Amer Ass Health Phys Educ, 34*:185-190, 1963.

24. SPEARMAN, C.: General intelligence objectivity measured and determined. *Amer J Psychol, 15*:201-293, 1904.

25. SPEARMAN, C.: *The Abilities of Man: Their Nature and Measurement.* London, Macmillan, 1927.

26. STRONG, CLINTON H.: Motivation related to performance of physical fitness test. *Res Quart Amer Ass Health Phys Educ, 34*:497-507, 1963.

27. THURSTONE, L. L.: The vectors of the mind. *Psychol Rev, 41*:1-32, 1934.

28. THURSTONE, L. L.: *Primary Mental Abilities.* Chicago, U. of Chicago, 1938.

29. THURSTONE, L. L.: *Some Primary Abilities in Visual Thinking.* Chicago, University of Chicago, Psychometric Laboratory Report, 1950, p. 59.

30. VERNON, P. E. *The Structure of Human Abilities.* London, Methune, 1953.

Chapter 6

INCREASED RESPONSE LATENCY FOR COMPLICATED MOVEMENTS AND A "MEMORY DRUM" THEORY OF NEUROMOTOR REACTION*

Franklin M. Henry**

INTRODUCTION

THE TIME REQUIRED for a muscle to begin to respond to direct stimulation is about .015 second. A simple reflex response such as the eye wink is made in .04 second, while the reflex to a blow on the patellar tendon requires about .08 second. The simplest voluntary response to a stimulus (simple RT) requires .15 second under the most favorable circumstances; .20 to .25 second may be considered more typical. When complications such as discrimination between several stimuli and/or choice between several possible movements are introduced (disjunctive RT), the required time increases and may be as long as .50 second. It should be noted that RT "is not the time occupied in the execution of a response; rather, it is the time required to get the overt response started." [11]

THEORETICAL CONSIDERATIONS

Early experimental psychologists considered RT to be a measure of the cumulated time required for a series of mental processes, including stimulus perception and the willing of the movement. This concept was gradually discarded during the period 1873-93 in favor

* F. M. Henry and D. E. Rogers: Increased response latency for complicated movements and a *memory drum* theory of neuromotor reaction. *Res Quart Amer Ass Health Phys Educ, 31*:448-458, 1960. Reproduced here with the permission of the authors and the American Association for Health, Physical Education, and Recreation. This investigation was supported by a grant from the Faculty Research Fund of the University of California.
** With the technical assistance of Donald E. Rogers.

of the idea that the stimulus simply triggered off a prepared reflex, the voluntary mental phase of the process being limited to the preparation, i.e. the development of a state of readiness to make a specific planned movement. This is essentially the same as the modern view. A reaction cannot be broken up into a series of successive mental and motor acts. The response is a total reaction in which perception of the stimulus runs concurrently with the motor response, with much of the perceptive process and all the overt movement occurring after the reaction i.e. following the true RT, which is defined as the latent period between the stimulus and the first beginning of physical movement. Woodworth has traced the historical development of these ideas in considerable detail.[10]

While the traditional prepared reflex theory of RT may be accepted in its general aspects, the present writer proposes considerable modification designed to recognize current knowledge of the neuromotor system and its control by the cephalic nervous centers. There is no reflex in the modern physiological use of the term, since a reflex must be nonwillful and not voluntary. There is probably not more than a minimal involvement of the cerebral cortex in the RT response, because the neuromotor coordination centers and pathways are chiefly cerebellar or subcortical without cortical termination.[9] Perhaps in consequence of the neuroanatomy, neouromotor perception is extremely poor, although neuromotor coordination or kinesthetic adjustment (with the absence of perceptual awareness) is exceptionally well developed in humans.[4]

Performance of acts of skill (even though relatively simple) may be assumed to involve neuromotor memory. This may be operationally defined as improved neuromotor coordination and more effective response, the improvement being the result of experience and practice, possibly accumulated over a period of many years. An implication of the neuroanatomy of the system as outlined above is that such memory must be different from ideational or perceptual memory, since conscious imagery is indefinite and largely excluded.

Nevertheless, a rich store of unconscious motor memory is available for the performance of acts of neuromotor skill. Added to this are innate neuromotor coordinations that are important in motor acts. The tapping of the store may be thought of broadly as a memory storage drum phenomena, to use the analogy of the electronic computer. The neural pattern for a specific and well-coordinated motor act is controlled by a stored program that is used to direct the neuro-motor details of its performance. In the absence of an available stored program, an unlearned complicated task is carried out under conscious control, in an awkward, step-by-step, poorly coordinated manner.*

Voluntary consideration of a particular movement that has already been learned, and is to be accomplished at maximum speed, occurs during the classical foreperiod (an interval of readiness while the subject is attentively waiting for the reaction-causing stimulus). Such consideration may involve visual imagery of the specific intended movement, but it is chiefly the development of a strong intent to start that movement in immediate response to the stimulus. It is not concerned (and indeed cannot be) with the actual formation of the already learned or structured specific program that will guide the released outburst of neural impulses through the proper centers, sub-centers, and nerve channels so that it will produce the intended movement. The crucial willful act in the simple reaction is the release of the outburst of neural impulses that will result in the movement. Normally this act is voluntary and intentional rather than reflex, although in special circumstances it may become almost reflex. The term release is used advisedly; impulses are already present in the cephalic nervous system in the form of brain waves and afferent neural discharges from various sources and are directed and channeled rather than created. This is another point of distinction between a voluntary reaction and a simple automatic stimulus-response reflex.

The above concepts can lead to a number of testable predictions in the area of motor coordination. Keeping in mind that the programing of the movement can constitute only a part of the total latency (because synaptic conduction in and of itself requires time) it might, for example, be expected that a minor program change

---

* Subsequent to the preparation of this article the writer has become aware of an interesting observation by J. E. Birren: "When skills are acquired the component movements appear discrete and are then gradually combined into a continuous pattern. Furthermore, as a skill deteriorates (because of aging) it may again assume the quality of separate movements." (*Psychological Aspects of Aging,* Washington, American Psychological Association, 1956, p. 100).

for a simple movement would be easy to accomplish, whereas a long or rather complicated program should be difficult to change after it starts organizing the channels. Various implications of the theory will be examined in subsequent articles.

PROBLEM INVESTIGATED

One of these implications, which will be investigated in the present study, is the theoretical requirement that there should be a longer reaction latency for a complicated movement than for a simpler movement. This is because a more comprehensive program, i.e. a larger amount of stored information, will be needed, and thus the neural impulses will require more time for coordination and direction into the eventual motor neurons and muscles.

The voluntary decision to make a movement when the stimulus occurs is thought to cause a state of readiness to respond to (and be triggered by) the stimulus. During this foreperiod, there is some amount of preliminary neuromotor response. It is known that some premovement tension may develop in the muscles that are to make the overt response, but such tension is sometimes absent and sometimes of an inappropriate nature.[10] Action potentials, however, reveal fairly consistent foreperiod excitation of both the reacting and noninvolved muscles. It is argued here that this may indicate alertness rather than implicit or partial reaction.[11] Whether this interpretation is correct or not, it seems obvious that when the movement is complicated and requires considerable skill, it is not possible for the tension during the foreperiod to be related to more than the very first phase of the overt movement. Moreover, a complicated movement necessarily involves several muscle groups and several specific areas of neuromotor coordination centers; more extensive use of learned and stored neuromotor patterns are surely required to initiate the overt motor action in this case. Thus it may be hypothesized that with richer and more complicated patterns involved, a longer latent time for the more complicated circulation of neural impulses through the coordination centers is inevitable. The situation is probably analogous to (but not identical with) the events, whatever they are, that cause greater response latency when there is a choice of movement in the reaction.[10]

The hypothesis can be tested experimentally by observing the simple

RT required for the initiation of movements that vary from simple to complex. Note that there can be a simple RT for a complex movement. If the situation for a particular response involves no discrimination as between two or more stimuli, and no choice (at the time of reaction) between which of two or more movements is to be made, the RT is simple, regardless of the complexity of the movement itself.

REVIEW OF LITERATURE

While there has apparently been no investigation which approached the problem from the point of view stated above, there have been, over the years, a few researches that are pertinent. The first was a study by Freeman in 1907, which reported that in drawing geometric figures such as a straight line, a circle, and a pentagon, the RT became longer as the figure increased in complexity.[3] In explanation, it was contended that the cause was antagonistic muscular tensions originating from anticipation of the necessary movement reversals. Unfortunately, the data were only secured on four individuals, so although the results are statistically inconclusive, they are in the anticipated direction.

On the other hand, Fitts[2] stated in 1951 that "the latent time is independent of the rate, extent or direction of the specific movement required by the stimulus," basing his interpretation on the 1949 experiment of Brown and Slater-Hammel,[1] although he cites some other references that are less directly related. It may be noted that the experiment in question involved only the variation of the length or direction of a simple movement; complexity was not studied.

Several reports from our laboratory have included data on the RT for movements that differ in complexity. Unfortunately, with respect to the present issue, the experimental designs were oriented to the problems that were being investigated; no attempt was made to control or balance out the practice effect. The most recent of these was by Mendryk,[7] who used two movements that differed considerably in length and slightly in complexity. In subjects of three age groups (N = 50 in each), the RT's were .002, .004 and .009 second faster for the longer and more complex movement. However, each subject had been given fifty trials with the short movement and thirty practice trials with the longer movement before the tabled values for the latter were recorded, so there may have been a considerable practice effect acting to decrease the RT and thus occlude the complexity effect.

Mendryk has made available to the writer his data for the last twenty trials with the short movement and the first twenty trials with the subsequent longer and more complex movement, which makes possible a comparison involving less of the practice effect. In his twelve-year-old group the RT for the longer movement is .004 second slower than for the short movement ($t = 1.2$), in the twenty-two-year-old group it is .009 second slower ($t = 3.8$), and in the forty-eight-year-old group it is .006 second slower ($t = 2.2$). Thus while the effect is small, and not completely controlled as to practice, it is in the anticipated direction and is statistically significant for the two adult groups.

METHODOLOGY

Apparatus and Movements

A reaction key was mounted at the forward end of the flat foundation board of the instrument. This was a sensitive key; the weight of the subject's finger was sufficient to keep it closed. At the back end of the board an upright supported a red warning light at eye level. A silent control switch was operated by the experimenter out of sight of the subject. When it was turned to its first position, the warning light came on. After a lapse of one to four seconds (in chance order), the switch was turned to the second position, which sounded the stimulus gong and simultaneously started the RT chronoscope. When being tested with Movement A, the subject simply lifted his finger a few millimeters, which permitted the reaction key to open and stopped the chronoscope.

Movement B was more complicated. A tennis ball hung by a string which placed it about fifteen centimeters above the reaction key and thirty centimeters further back, away from the subject. In response to the stimulus signal, he reached forward to grasp the ball. When the ball was touched, the upper support end of the string pulled out of a switch clip, thus freeing the ball to permit a follow-through.

A second chronoscope, which also connected to the reaction key, recorded movement time (MT). It stopped when the string pulled out of the switch clip.

Movement C was somewhat more complicated; it included a series of movements and reversals. A second tennis ball (C), also supported by a string and clip, was hung thirty centimeters to the right of ball B. In response to the stimulus, the subject moved his hand from the key, reaching forward and upward to strike ball C with the back of the hand, then reversed direction to go forward and downward, touching a dummy push button on the baseboard to the left of the reaction key, and finally reversed again to go upward and forward, striking down ball B. This two-ball apparatus was illustrated in an earlier publication from this laboratory,[5] which listed references to detailed descriptions of the device. It should be mentioned that the circuits included provisions for using an auditory stimulus (an electric gong), and this was used in the present study.

Experimental Design

There were two experiments. In the first, designated Experiment I, there was continuous rotation of conditions, trial-by-trial, with Movement A required for the first trial, B for the second, C for the third, A for the fourth, and so on. Before each trial, the subject was reminded as to which movement was to be made; moreover, he could see from the way the apparatus was set up that there were no balls, or one, or two, to be hit. Fifteen practice trials were given, followed by thirty trials (10 for each movement) which were used for the statistical analysis. While this design offered the advantage of very exact balancing out of possible practice and fatigue effects, there was a remote possibility that even though the instructions were carefully given, and the nature of the required movement for a particular trial was obvious, some cases may have occurred in which there might have been some element of choice of movement.

Experiment II involved one practice trial with Movement A, followed by ten trials with that movement. After a brief rest, a practice trial was given on B, followed by ten trials with that movement. After another rest, one practice trial was given on C, followed by ten trials with that movement. A third of the subjects followed the A-B-C sequence, another third the sequence B-C-A, and the final third the sequence C-A-B. Each person had thirty trials (10 on each movement) in addition to the practice before each series of ten. All subjects used in Experiment II were well practiced in the movements, since they had gone through Experiment I approximately one week earlier.

Subjects

Group 1 consisted of thirty undergraduate college men. Group 2 was composed of thirty undergraduate college women. In each group approximately half were physical education majors. These groups were tested only under the conditions of Experiment I. Group 3 consisted of twenty young men ranging in age from nineteen to thirty-five years (average 24), and included college students, high school teachers, and others. Group 4 was made up of twenty eighth-grade boys, age eleven or twelve, and Group 5 was composed of twenty fourth-grade boys age eight or nine. Not one of these 120 individuals was (or could be) selected in any way, either intentionally or unintentionally, with respect to the possibility that he would do better with one of the movements than with another one. In other words, the samples are completely unbiased with respect to the variable under consideration, which is the RT for Movement A compared with B or C.

RESULTS AND DISCUSSION

Reaction Time vs Complexity

The data of Table 6-I show that all groups react more slowly as the movement becomes more complex. The reaction preceding Movement B is about 20 percent slower, on the average, than the RT for A, and the reaction preceding Movement C is about 7 percent slower than the RT for B. Even though the groups are relatively small, the differences between the RT's are without question statistically significant in each, as may be seen by the *t*-ratios in Table 6-I. Moreover, the differences are approximately as large and significant under the conditions of Experiment II as under the conditions of Experiment I.

Since the findings are positive in each of five groups of subjects

TABLE 6-I

MEAN REACTION TIMES OF THE VARIOUS GROUPS

Group	Movement A		Movement B		B-A	Movement C		C-B
	M (sec.)	σ	M (sec.)	σ	tᵃ	M (sec.)	σ	tᵃ
1(I) Men	.163	.018	.195	.026	8.6	.204	.031	2.9
2(I) Women	.174	.027	.205	.026	8.3	.219	.034	3.8
3(I) Age 24	.158	.025	.197	.034	9.4	.213	.034	5.3
4(I) Age 12	.178	.023	.214	.035	8.1	.226	.033	3.4
5(I) Age 8	.238	.038	.275	.042	8.4	.295	.026	4.9
3(II) Age 24	.144	.019	.186	.031	10.1	.199	.032	3.4
4(II) Age 12	.159	.015	.201	.031	7.5	.214	.033	3.8
5(II) Age 8	.214	.031	.253	.024	7.0	.270	.039	4.0

[a] A t-ratio of 1.70 is significant at the 5 percent level for Groups 1 and 2 (N = 30), while 1.73 is required for Groups 3, 4, and 5 (N = 20). The statistical hypothesis is single-tailed, since the direction of the differences is predicted by the experimental, i.e., alternative, hypothesis. It will be noted that all of the t-ratios are significant and quite large; the smallest is 2.9.

that differ in age and sex, and are positive under both of the experimental conditions, the evidence seems adequate to claim that the hypothesis of slower RT for movements of increased complexity, based on the memory drum theory of reaction latency, has been confirmed. It should be emphasized that the simple movement was very simple indeed. Furthermore, the amount of movement required to actuate the reaction key was only a fraction of a millimeter; in other words, the RT did not involve movement in the ordinary meaning of the word. (Some experiments that have purported to measure RT have actually included considerable amounts of movement.) The additional serial elements and reversals of direction in Movement C, as compared with B, caused only about a third as much change in RT as did the type and amount of complexity difference of B as compared with A.

The determination of the crucial elements of the complexity effect, and of just how much of a change in complexity is required to produce a noticeable change in RT, will require further investigation. It seems reasonable to expect that increased movement complexity occurring early in a movement will have a much greater influence on RT than if the complexity appears late in a movement that was simple in its early phases. Whether increased demand for accuracy and precision of movement, and increased involvement of feedback, will slow RT as implicitly predicted by the theory, are among the important questions that remain to be answered.

SECONDARY PROBLEMS INVESTIGATED

Age and Sex Differences in Reaction Time

It will be noticed that RT is slower in the younger age groups (Table 6-I), although no statistical evaluation of the differences has been made because the influence of age on RT is already well established.[11] This is not true in the case of MT. Data on that problem have only become available recently;[7, 8] the current results will be given in the next section of the report.

In the present set of experiments, the RT's of men and women subjects do not differ significantly. The *t*-ratios for the differences are 1.7 for A, 1.5 for B, and 1.7 for C; these are within the expectations of random sampling variability. As might have been hoped, the two samples of adult males have very similar RT's, the differences within each movement condition being nonsignificant ($t = 0.8$, 0.3, and 0.9). It may be seen in Table 6-I that RT's are faster for all ages in Experiment II as compared with Experiment I; this is of no consequence because these subjects necessarily had practice in the reactions and movements before doing Experiment II (since they had already done Experiment I), and would be expected to profit by that experience. The amount of practice was of course equal for all three movements.

Age and Sex Differences in Movement Time

The mean movement times are given in Table 6-II. In Movement B the eight-year-old boys are 52 percent slower than the twelve year olds in Experiment I, and 27 percent slower in Experiment II. In the case of Movement C, the figures are 54 and 33 percent. All these differences are significant. However, the differences between the twelve-year-old boys and the fifty adult males are not significant; the *t*-ratios are 0.9 for B and 1.1 for C and hence fail to overthrow the null hypothesis. The two samples of adult males do not differ significantly one from the other, either for Movement B ($t = 1.9$) or

Movement C ($t = 1.6$). It will be recalled that Movement A was not timed, because it was simply a finger withdrawal.

The college women are 40 percent slower than the college males in Movement B and 14 percent slower in Movement C. These differences are clearly significant, as evidenced by large *t*-ratios (Table 6-II).

TABLE 6-II

MEAN MOVEMENT TIMES OF THE VARIOUS GROUPS

Group		Movement B			Movement C		
		M (sec.)	σ	t (groups)	M (sec.)	σ	t (groups)
1(I)	Men	.093	.024		.481	.079	
2(I)	Women	.130	.027	5.6(#2-#1)[a]	.552	.094	3.1(#2-1#)[a]
3(I)	Age 24	.078	.029		.437	.103	
4(I)	Age 12	.097	.023	2.1(#4-#3)[a]	.493	.108	1.6(#4-#3)
5(I)	Age 8	.147	.043	4.5(#5-#4)[a]	.762	.131	6.9(#5-#4)[a]
3(II)	Age 24	.081	.013		.391	.161	
4(II)	Age 12	.091	.021	1.8(#4-#3)	.438	.208	0.9(#4-#3)
5(II)	Age 8	.117	.026	10.3(#5-#4)[a]	.582	.103	2.7(#5-#4)[a]

[a] A t-ratio of 2.0 is significant at the 5 percent level.

Intercorrelations

The correlation between RT and MT varies considerably among the five groups of subjects, which is not unexpected because the number of cases in any one group is rather small for this type of analysis. The relationship has been examined for Experiment I only. For Movement B, the values range from $-.323$ to $+.212$, with the average (using the z transformation) at $r = .064$. In the case of Movement C, the values range from $-.088$ to $+.420$, with the average at $r = .180$. There seems to be no particular tendency for the amount of correlation to vary systematically with age or sex. These results are in agreement with the findings of others, which have recently been reviewed.[6, 7] The problem here is not really whether the correlation is or is not statistically significant, since it might or might not be found significant in one particular study. Rather, the concern is whether the real correlation is low (tending to be close to zero), or substantial, i.e. moderate, or relatively high. Evidence is accumulating that it is a very low order relationship, having little or no predictive value.

The correlation of MT itself as between the B and C types of movement is somewhat higher. It is true that for age groups eight and twelve the values are very low, namely, .084 and −.002. However, in the adults the figures are .562 for the women, .489 for the college males, and .427 for the group of twenty men. When the five groups are averaged (using the z transformation), $r = .329$. While the correlation may be considered significantly different from zero for each group of adults, their average value (.493) certainly does not indicate a high degree of relationship.

The odd-even MT reliability coefficients (S-B corrected) for the three groups of adults are .982, .919, and .796 for Movement B and .988, .966, and .684 for Movement C. Using these values to correct the correlations between the two movements is r^2, which is .326, .269, and .335 in the above three relationships after the influence of error variance (unreliability) has been removed.

Now the amount of common variance of individual differences as between the two movements in r^2, which is .326, .269, and .335 in the above three groups of adults. (These values may be multiplied by 100 to convert them to percent.) It follows that the amount of individual difference variance that is not common to the two movements, and is not error variance, is given by the squared coefficient of alienation k^2, which is defined as $1 - r^2$. It is obvious that k^2 is to be identified as the specificity of individual abilities in the two movements, while r^2 is the generality of individual abilities. The values of k^2 for the three groups are .674, .731, and .665, and may be converted to percents by multiplying by 100. The relatively large values for k^2 justifies the statement that ability to make a fast arm-hand movement of the type used is quantitatively determined to a greater extent (69%) by abilities that are specific to one or the other of the two movements, and to a lesser extent (31%) by a general speed ability that is involved in both movements. This analysis has, moreover, presented the most favorable case for generality, since it has been limited to the three groups of adult subjects; the correlation between movements approximated zero in the younger groups. The results with adults agree with those of a recent study that utilized other types of arm movements, finding 74 percent specificity and 26 percent general arm speed ability.[7]

SUMMARY AND CONCLUSIONS

Following a consideration of prevailing concepts of reaction time and modern knowledge of the operation of the neuromotor nervous system, a theory has been developed which places heavy reliance on nonperceptive use of motor memory in voluntary acts involving motor coordination. Innate and particularly learned neuromotor coordination patterns are conceived of as stored, becoming accessible for use in controlling the act by a memory drum mechanism that requires increasing time for its operation as the motor act becomes more complex.

To test the hypothesis that the simple reaction time becomes lengthened with increased movement complexity, data were secured on 120 individuals, including both sexes and (in the case of males) three age groups. Sixty of the subjects were tested with two experimental procedures in order to improve the adequacy of the control conditions. Three types of movement varying in complexity were used: both reaction time and movement time were measured.

The data were also examined with respect to several problems secondary to the main study. These included the influence of age and sex on net movement time, and the amount of generality and specificity of individual differences in speed of arm movement ability.

Results of the statistical analysis of the data seem to justify the following conclusions:

(1) Under controlled conditions, simple reaction time becomes longer when the type of movement which follows the reaction is varied from very simple to relatively complex. Further increase in complexity produces additional slowing, but to a lessened degree.

(2) College women have less arm-speed ability than college men.

(3) Eight-year-old boys have less arm-speed ability than twelve-year-old boys. (While the data suggest that twelve-year olds are slower than young adults, the statistical results are inconclusive.)

(4) Individual differences in speed of arm-movement ability are predominately specific to the type of movement that is made; there is only a relatively small amount of general ability to move the arm rapidly.

REFERENCES

1. BROWN, J. S., AND SLATER-HAMMEL, A. T.: Discrete movements in the horizontal plane as a function of their direction and extent. *J Exper Psychol, 38*:84-95, 1949.
2. FITTS, P. M.: Engineering psychology and equipment design. In Stevens, S. S. (Ed.): *Handbook of Experimental Psychology.* New York, Wiley, 1951.
3. FREEMAN, F. N.: Preliminary experiments on writing reactions. *Psychol Monogr, 8*(34):301-33; 1907.
4. HENRY, F. M.: Dynamic kinesthetic perception and adjustment. *Res Quart Amer Ass Health Phys Educ, 24*:176-87, May, 1953.
5. HOWELL, M. L.: Influence of emotional tension on speed of reaction and movement. *Res Quart Amer Ass Health Phys Educ, 24*:22-32; March 1953.
6. LOTTER, W. S.: Interrelationships among reaction times and speeds of movement in different limbs. *Res Quart Amer Ass Health Phys Educ, 31*:147-55; May 1960.
7. MENDRYK, S.: Reaction time, movement time, and task specificity relationships at ages 12, 22, and 48 years. *Res Quart Amer Ass Health Phys Educ, 31*:156-62; May 1960.
8. PIERSON, W. R.: The relationship of movement time and reaction time from childhood to senility. *Res Quart Amer Ass Health Phys Educ, 30*: 227-31; May 1959.
9. WENGER, M. A.; JONES, F. N., AND JONES, M. H.: *Physiological Psychology.* New York, H. Holt, 1956.
10. WOODWORTH, R. S.: *Experimental Psychology.* New York, H. Holt, 1938.
11. WOODWORTH, R. S., AND SCHLOSBERG, HAROLD: *Experimental Psychology,* rev. ed. New York, H. Holt, 1954.

PART FOUR
MEASUREMENT

Chapter 7

A METHOD FOR EVALUATING THE SIGNIFICANCE OF DIFFERENCES OBSERVED IN A CASE STUDY*

William W. Heusner

INTRODUCTION

IN RECENT YEARS, the single-subject case study has become increasingly popular as a research tool in physical education. Frequently, the scope of the data desired, a limited availability of subjects having particular qualities, and economy of test administration dictate at least a pilot investigation using the single-subject case study technique. Several examples[1, 2, 5, 6, 8] of this type of research are listed in the references. Such studies present inherent difficulties, however, if one wishes to evaluate the significance of the differences observed between test scores obtained before and after the introduction of an experimental factor, EF.

In a limited number of these investigations, two sets of data may be obtained for each variable by testing the subject several times in a relatively constant state both before and after the EF. Within each of these sets of data, the test scores may then be considered to be cases with the mean of the test scores representing an approximation to the subjects's *true score* for the test item at that time. Under these circumstances, the standard *t*-test may be used to evaluate the significance of the observed differences between means.

Unfortunately, in most studies this retesting procedure is unacceptable. In some instances, the process of retesting introduces a training or a learning factor. At other times, especially when data

* William W. Heusner: A method for evaluating the significance of differences observed in a case study. *Res Quart Amer Ass Health Phys Educ, 30*:363-366, 1959. Reproduced here with the permission of the author and the American Association for Health, Physical Education, and Recreation.

must be collected at the termination of exercise, a single measurement at a specified moment is all that is possible. Under conditions such as these where the number of cases, N, is limited to 1, the *t*-test becomes useless. That is, regardless of the size of the observed difference, the value of *t* disappears since the standard error of the difference between means is infinite.

COMPARISON WITH NORMAL DISTRIBUTION

In order to evaluate the significance of the differences observed when N = 1, it is necessary to compare the observed differences with the normal distribution of scores for the variable in question. The measure which is used most commonly to denote the dispersion of obtained scores around true scores is the standard error of estimate,[3, p. 404]

$$Se = \sigma x \sqrt{1 - r_{12}}$$

where: σx is the standard deviation of raw scores, and r_{12} is the coefficient of reliability based upon test-retest stability.

This statistic frequently is called the *standard error of measurement* or the *standard error of an obtained score*. However, SE is not quite a suitable measure for evaluating the significance of the difference between two single test scores. That is, when two observed values are being compared, each represents an estimate of a true score. The difference between an observed score and the corresponding true score is an error of measurement. Therefore, two errors of measurement are involved.

Gulliksen[4] describes an applicable statistic which is based upon theory similar to that used in the derivation of SE, which he calls the *standard error of a difference for the case in which the two standard deviations are alike*, S_d. This statistic was presented earlier by Kelley,[7] who called it the *standard deviation of differences between scores on two similar forms*.

DERIVATION OF S_d

Before applying S_d to the case study technique, one should understand the basic concepts underlying its derivation. In summary, S_d is obtained as follows:

The difference between two raw scores, X_1 and X_2, of an individual on two parallel tests, t_1 and t_2, may be denoted by d. That is

$$d = X_1 - X_2.$$

Next, the individual's true score on any test, t_j, can be denoted by T_j. If the parallel test, t_1 and t_2, are a test and a retest, and there is no reason to believe that the individual has changed with respect to the attribute measured by the test in the interval between the test and the retest, then

$$T_1 = T_2 = T.$$

T represents the individual's true score on the attribute measured by t_1 and t_2. Now, the deviation score x_j is defined as the deviation of an observed score X_j from a true score T_j, or as

$$x_j = X_j - T_j.$$

Consequently, the difference between two raw scores in the case of a test and a retest is

$$\begin{aligned} d &= X_1 - X_2 \\ &= (x_1 + T) - (x_2 + T) \\ &= x_1 - x_2. \end{aligned}$$

If the same test-retest has been given to a sample group of N persons, drawn at random from the same population as the individual subject, the differences between the N pairs of scores will fluctuate randomly by chance. If, then, a population of all such differences is defined, one can compute the variance of the differences between these N pairs of observed scores as

$$\frac{\Sigma d^2}{N} = \frac{\Sigma(x_1 - x_2)^2}{N}.$$

Substituting SD^2 for the left-hand member and expanding the right-hand member of the previous equation yields

$$Sd^2 = \frac{\Sigma x_1{}^2}{N} + \frac{\Sigma x_2{}^2}{N} - \frac{2\Sigma x_1 x_2}{N}.$$

However, since

$$\sigma x^2 = \frac{\Sigma x^2}{N}$$

(See p. 95-96 and p. 157 in Ref. 3.)

$$r_{xy} = \frac{\Sigma xy}{N\sigma x\sigma y}$$

then,

$$S_d{}^2 = \sigma x_1{}^2 + \sigma x_2{}^2 - 2rx_1x_2\ \sigma x_1\sigma x_2.$$

For ease of notation, let

$$r_{12} = rx_1x_2.$$

Now, assuming that the standard deviations of the test and retest are equal, and thus may each be denoted by σx,

$$S_d{}^2 = 2\sigma x^2 - 2\sigma x^2 r_{12}$$
$$= 2\sigma x^2(1 - r_{12}).$$

Taking the square root of both sides of this equation gives

$$S_d = \sigma x \sqrt{2(1 - r_{12})}$$
$$S_d = \sigma x \sqrt{1 - r_{12}} \sqrt{2}$$
$$= Se \sqrt{2.}$$

APPLICATION OF S_d

It is now apparent that in a case study one may test the significance of a given difference, d_k, in the usual manner by the use of a critical ratio which has the standard error, S_d, as the denominator and d_k as the numerator. That is, an observed difference in an individual may now be compared with the standard error of the population of such differences to determine whether or not the size of the observed difference is greater than one would expect it to be if only random variations were operating. When S_d has been computed on a large N, normal curve tables may be used. For small samples, Student's Tables provide the exact random sampling distribution.

It should be noted that several basic assumptions underlie the use of S_d. In the first place, the variable must be normally distributed. Secondly, the standard error of measurement and the true mean of the group tested must remain constant during the interval of the test-retest period. Finally, one must assume that the subject being tested is a member of the same population as the group on whom S_d was computed.

RELIABILITY UNDETERMINED

At times, especially in pilot investigations, one may wish to use a test item, the reliability of which has not been adequately demonstrated. The researcher employing the case study technique may find it quite inconvenient, if not impossible, to test and retest a large sample group. Consequently, in such instances only one set of test scores will be available, and a coefficient of correlation, r_{12}, indicating reliability cannot be computed. Yet, without r_{12} there is no direct method of obtaining S_d. Nevertheless, this does not prohibit entirely the use of the technique presented in this paper. S_d can be estimated maximally from other data.

Guilford[3, p. 478] defines the index of reliability, r_{01}, as the correlation between true scores and obtained scores on a given test item. Therefore, r_{01}^2 is an index of determination denoting the proportion of the variance in the test scores which is determined by the variance in the true scores. The same information is given by r_{12}. Therefore,

$$r_{01} = \sqrt{r_{12}}.$$

Guilford[3, p. 479] also states, "Nothing can correlate with obtained scores higher than their correlation with corresponding true scores." That is, the maximum limit of the correlation of a test with anything else is r_{01}. Consequently, the coefficient of reliability for any test item, X, must be at least as great as the square of the correlation of that item with some other variable, Y. The use of the largest available r_{xy}^2 as a minimal estimate of r_{12} in the computation of S_d would be justified then so long as the investigator realizes that an overestimation of S_d results, thus increasing the severity of the test for significant differences. That is, a type II error of accepting the null hypothesis when it is false is more likely to be made.[3, p. 210] Although in some instances statistical significance may be overlooked, this procedure strengthens the claim of significance for those cases in which it has been demonstrated mathematically.

CONCLUSIONS

Contrary to prevalent belief that data collected in a single-subject case study cannot be adequately treated statistically, the use of S_d as the denominator of a critical ratio enables one to evaluate the significance of observed differences in the standard manner. Where reliability has not been determined, it may be estimated minimally from the largest available correlation with some other variable.

REFERENCES

1. CAMPNEY, H. K.: "The Effects of a Combined Program of Physical Activity on the Physical Fitness of an Adult Male." Master's thesis. Urbana, U. of Illinois, 1953.
2. CURETON, T. K.: Physical fitness improvement of a middle-aged man, with brief reviews of related studies. *Res Quart Amer Ass Health Phys Educ,* 23:149-60; May 1952.
3. GUILFORD, J. P.: *Fundamental Statistics in Psychology and Education.* New York, McGraw, 1950.
4. GULLIKSEN, H.: *Theory of Mental Tests.* New York, Wiley, 1950, p. 40.
5. HEUSNER, W. W.: Progressive Changes in the Physical Fitness of an Adult Male During a Season of Training for Competitive Swimming. Doctor's thesis. Urbana, U. of Illinois, 1955.
6. HORNOF, Z., AND KREMER, M.: Biologický Podklad Vytralostníich Vykonu Světového Rekardmana Zátopka. *Sokol* 72:167-203, 1952.
7. KELLEY, T. L.: *Interpretation of Educational Measurements.* New York, World Book Co., 1927. p. 180-81.
8. WALTERS, C. E., AND PARTRIDGE, M. J.: Electromyographic study of the differential action of the abdominal muscles during exercise. *Amer J Phys Med,* 36:259-68; October 1957.

Chapter 8

SIX SCALES FOR ASSESSING ATTITUDE TOWARD PHYSICAL ACTIVITY*

Gerald S. Kenyon

INTRODUCTION

. . . all of us are forced to behave cleverly or stupidly according as our attitude and inner resistances ordain.—Sigmund Freud

An UNDERSTANDING of the social and psychological significance of sport and physical activity necessitates paying careful attention to concepts and constructs employed by workers in the several behavioral disciplines. Among the more promising social psychological units of analysis is that of attitude. Although attitude dynamics are not fully understood, sufficient progress has been made to warrant their serious investigation in the realm of physical activity. An adequate characterization and assessment of attitudes in this domain would open the door to numerous studies, the findings from which would contribute to a greater understanding of social reality, and thus aid in the development of a sociopsychological theory of sport. The purpose of this paper is to report one approach to the measurement of attitude toward physical activity.[†]

* Gerald S. Kenyon: Six scales for assessing attitude toward physical activity. *Res Quart Amer Ass Health Phys Educ, 39*:566-574, 1968. Reproduced here with the permission of the author and the American Association for Health, Physical Education, and Recreation. Supported by National Institute of Mental Health grants MH 08214-01 and MH 11038-01, and the University of Wisconsin grant 63-851. Appreciation is expressed to John W. Loy, Jr., for assistance with various phases of the project.

† An appendix to this article containing ATPA scales, form D, has been deposited as Document number 9983 with the ADI Auxiliary Publications Project, Photoduplication Service, Library of Congress, Washington, D. C. 20540. A copy may be secured by citing the document number and remitting $1.25 for photoprints or $1.25 for 35mm microfilm. Advance payment is required. Make checks or money orders payable to: Chief, Photoduplication Service, Library of Congress.

ATTITUDE: A PROBLEM OF DEFINITION AND MEASUREMENT

Attempts to determine social attitudes have been plagued by two closely related problems—definition and measurement. Considerable theoretical and empirical work has been done, however, in an effort to overcome problems presented by each.

Defining Attitude

Although often used with different connotations, the term attitude has been a part of psychological literature for at least a century.[2] Herbert Spencer made reference to attitudes and their relations to beliefs as early as 1862. Not much later, German experimental psychologists were describing a variety of mental and motor sets— *Aufgabe,* or preparedness—influencing thought and action.[11] In 1918, attitude was given new status as a social psychological variable with the publication of the five-volume work by Thomas and Znaniecki, *The Polish Peasant in Europe and America.*[16] These writers went so far as to define social psychology as the *scientific study of attitudes.*

Despite a relatively long history, consensus about the definition of attitude has been slow in coming. After surveying the use of the term over the years, Allport[2] concluded that, "Attitude cannotates a neuropsychic state of readiness for mental and physical activity." Thurstone[17] defined attitude as ". . . the intensity of positive or negative affect for or against a psychological object." More recently, attitude has been defined as ". . . a consistency among responses to a specified set of stimuli, or social objects;"[6] as a projection onto the evaluative dimension of semantic space:[13] as ". . . the predisposition of the individual to evaluate some symbol or object or aspect of his world in a favorable or unfavorable manner;"[8] as "An enduring system of positive or negative evaluations, emotional feelings, and pro or con action tendencies with respect to a social object"[10] (thus suggesting cognitive, affective, and action tendency components of attitude); and as "an acquired behavioral disposition."[4] In an attempt to reflect contemporary writing on the subject, attitude, for this paper, is held to be *a latent or nonobservable, complex, but re-*

latively stable behavioral disposition reflecting both direction and intensity of feeling toward a particular object, whether it be concrete or abstract.

Measuring Attitude

However latent attitudes may be, their measurement depends upon some overt behavior, that is, a response elicited by some stimulus. Although all techniques rely upon observing responses to specific stimuli, the form of the latter varies widely, from the use of direct questioning or direct observation, to the use of attitude scales. In view of the several weaknesses of direct questioning,[5] most recent work has employed as stimuli verbal attitude statements in one form or another. By collecting several statements about the psychological object in question, a scale can be formed which measures the degree of affect, usually with satisfactory reliability.

Serious attempts to *scale* attitudes began almost forty years ago. Cognizant of developments in psychophysics, particularly by Fechner and Weber, Thurstone [18, 19] began experimenting with similar techniques in areas where there was no corresponding physical manifestation of the phenomenon. His work not only led to the development of attitude scales with a form of interval measurement, but also set the stage for psychological scaling in general—a field which now boasts a sizable literature. Today, attitude scales are developed most often by (1) specifying the domain of the psychological object in question, and defining its universe of content, (2) selecting or developing stimuli (usually verbal) to represent the domain, and (3) formulating scales, using either judgment or response methods[20] with an appropriate sample.

The reliability of attitude scales usually has been determined psychometrically using either internal consistency measures or equivalent forms. Validity, however, is another problem. Since attitude, as a latent variable, cannot be observed directly, face or intrinsic validity is relied upon rather heavily, i.e. by showing items to be logically representative of the attitude universe in question. Another approach is the use of reference groups, whose attitudes are inferred from the actions of their members.

Assessing Attitude Toward Physical Activity and Sport

Over the years a number of studies have appeared in the research literature addressed to the subject of attitudes toward physical activity. Although a variety of techniques has been employed, in general they have suffered from a number of shortcomings. First, sufficient attention has not been paid to the characterization of *physical activity* in its broadest sense; efforts to date have usually limited the inquiry to a somewhat restricted domain such as *physical education, team game competition,* or *sports.* Second, instruments seldom were based upon a thorough application of appropriate test construction procedures so long a part of the measurement literature, such as item analysis and psychological scaling techniques. When such methods were used, too often data were acquired from relatively small samples. Third, where scaling procedures were employed, such as in the development of instruments by Wear,[21] Richardson,[14] Adams,[1] and Mason and Ventre,[12] there has been a failure to account for the possible, and indeed likely, multidimensionality of the domain in question. This paper describes efforts to overcome such problems; that is, an attempt was made to construct within the context of a model characterizing physical activity (the *psychological object*), relatively independent univocal scales for determining attitudes toward physical activity.

PROCEDURE

A procedural schematic showing the steps taken in developing both the conceptual model and the attitude scales is shown in Figure 8-1.

The Model or Frame of Reference

The rationale underlying the model used for characterizing physical activity has been presented in a companion paper.[9] In brief, it was assumed that *physical activity* can be reduced to more specific, or meaningful components (i.e. a set of all physical activities can be reduced to logical subsets) and that a meaningful basis for such a procedure was the *perceived instrumentality* of each class of physical activity. The results of this work provided a definition of the psy-

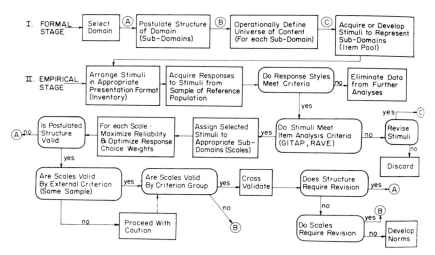

FIGURE 8-1. Procedural schematic showing model formulation and scale development.

chological object toward which attitudes are held. The six dimensions (or subdomains) of the model are as follows: physical activity perceived as (1) a social experience, (2) health and fitness, (3) the pursuit of vertigo, (4) an aesthetic experience, (5) catharsis, and (6) an ascetic experience.

Developing the Scales

For each of the six subdomains of the hypothesized model, a universe of content was identified and defined. Seven alternative, Likert-type attitude statements (the stimuli) thought to be representative of each dimension were evaluated by judges, revised, and incorporated into two separate but similar inventories, one for college men and one for college women. This paper presents the results using a second revision of the inventories—Form C (CM-men, CW-women). Many of the items in Form C had already been shown to have considerable merit as a result of their previous use in earlier forms (A and B). The inventories were administered to samples with N's between 200 and 360 for each sex.* Response styles were checked using four re-

_____

* Data were obtained from lower division undergraduates enrolled in the River Falls and Oshkosh divisions of the State University of Wisconsin.

TABLE 8-I

ILLUSTRATION OF ITEM ANALYSIS STATISTICS PROVIDING CRITERIA FOR ITEM SELECTION AND INVENTORY EVALUAIION

I. STIMULUS

Item 83 (Form CM). "I would enjoy engaging in those games and sports that require a defiance of danger."

II. RESPONSE STATISTICS (N = 353)

A. For hypothesized subdomain (physical activity as the pursuit of vertigo)

Choice	A priori weights	Optimized weights	p^a	r_{bis}	X_{50}^b	Beta^c
VSA	7	5	.02	.57	3.75	0.69
SA	6	5	.08	.55	2.54	0.67
A	5	5	.32	.53	0.85	0.64
U	4	4	.09	.04	-	-
D	3	4	.33	—.28	—1.56	—0.29
SD	2	3	.11	—.55	—2.23	—0.65
VSD	1	1	.05	—.96	—1.70	—3.41

B. For nonhypothesized subdomain (physical activity as an aesthetic experience)^d

Choice	A priori weights	Optimized weights	P	r_{bis}	X_{50}	Beta^c
	U					
VSA	N		.02	—.27	—7.81	—0.28
SA	W		.08	.15	9.52	0.15
A	E		.32	.00	—270.48	0.00
	I					
U			.09	—.10	-	-
	G					
D	H		.33	.03	13.31	0.03
SD	T		.11	—.14	—9.05	—0.14
VSD	E		.05	.20	8.23	0.20
	D					

^{a} Proportion of subjects responding to each response choice.
^{b} Position on the criterion scale corresponding to the median of the item characteristic curve (z-score units).
^{c} The reciprocal of the standard deviation of the item characteristic curve (indicating degree of discrimination).
^{d} Statistics clearly reveal that item does not function for this subdomain.

peated items.[†] Reliability coefficients based upon Hoyt's procedure,[7] response frequencies, and item discrimination statistics were computed for each of six scales. The reliability of each scale was maximized by rescaling the *a priori* weights of the best items using a reciprocal averages procedure.[3] Selection of the best items (and thus yielding Form D) was based upon the distribution of response choice fre-

---

[†] If responses to repeated items on a given inventory varied by two or more scale positions on more than two of the items, data from that inventory were excluded. For each group this criterion was met by all but ten or fewer subjects.

quencies, three-item discrimination statistics, and the range and distribution of rescaled weights. Statistics used as decision criteria are illustrated in Table 8-I. In addition, factor loadings generated by factor analyses of Forms A and B, were used to aid in the selection of promising items for Form C.

Since attitude, as a behavioral disposition,[4] is nonobservable, validity cannot be determined directly. However, an attempt was made to infer the validity of each scale by using preferred type of activity—through direct or vicarious participation—as a criterion. Thus, it was postulated that subjects expressing a strong preference for a particular type of activity (determined through the use of separate questions) would possess a positive attitude toward that activity. For each activity type strong and weak preference groups were compared by testing for the significance of the difference between means on the appropriate scale. To test the stability of Forms CM and CW, a procedure somewhat akin to double cross-validation[15] was used based upon data acquired from subjects at different but comparable institutions. The construct validity for the conceptual model upon which the scales are based has been reported elsewhere.[9]

RESULTS

Reliability

Hoyt reliabilities for the six scales of Forms CM and CW are shown in Table 8-II, based upon a rescaling of both original and *best* items. For both men and women maximized Hoyt r's were lowest for the *social experience* scale (.72 and .72 respectively), and highest for the *pursuit of vertigo* scale (.89 and .86 respectively).*

Validity

Scale scores differentiated between strong and weak preference groups in the predicted direction for all scales† except *catharsis*

---

* Use of a slightly modified version of Form D (best items from Form C) with English secondary school pupils yielded reliabilities slightly higher than those reported here.

† Although of no general significance, the writer has noted with interest that an active sport parachutist scored 68 out of a maximum 70 (*a priori* weights) on the *vertigo* scale.

TABLE 8-II

HOYT RELIABILITIES FOR EACH OF SIX SCALES FOR ASSESSING
ATTITUDE TOWARD PHYSICAL ACTIVITY: BASED
ON SAMPLES OF 353 MEN AND 215 WOMEN

Scale	Original items (form C)		Best items (form D)	
	n_I[a]	Hoyt r	n_I	Hoyt r
1. Social experience				
men	14	.70-.72[b]	10	.70-.72
women	14	.70-.74	8	.68-.72
2. Health and fitness				
men	14	.74-.77	10	.79
women	14	.79-.82	11	.83
3. Pursuit of vertigo				
men	14	.88-.89	10	.88-.89
women	14	.83-.84	9	.86
4. Aesthetic experience				
men	14	.80-.82	10	.82
women	14	.83-.85	9	.87
5. Catharsis				
men	14	.69-.78	9	.77
women	14	.72-.80	9	.79
6. Ascetic experience				
men	14	.82-.82	10	.81
women	14	.74-.79	8	.74-.78

[a] Number of items used to represent each scale.
[b] The first coefficient is based upon *a priori* weights, the second based upon weights rescaled to optimize reliability. Where rescaling did not increase *r*, only the original coefficient is given, i.e., based upon the *a priori* weights one through seven.

(Table 8-III). A thorough reanalysis of the data has failed to provide a satisfactory explanation for the latter finding. However, a restudy of the pattern matrix together with the intercorrelations among factors provided a clue. First, the factor that was identified as representing *catharsis* contained some loadings ($> .30$) that were representative of other domains: particularly *health and fitness,* social experience, and ascetic experience. Such contamination was reflected also in the magnitude of the correlations between factors identified as representing these dimensions (up to .52). Clearly, the validity of the *catharsis* scale has not been established. Items and statistics are reported, however, in the event the reader should be interested in exploring this domain further.

Statistics generated through *cross-validation* are given in Tables 8-IV and 8-V. Upon examination of means, standard deviations, and reliability coefficients, considerable stability is apparent when the two samples are compared.

TABLE 8-III

SCALE VALIDATION USING PREFERENCE FOR A GENERALIZED ACTIVITY TYPE AS CRITERION

Preference criterion[a]	Scale	Sex	Preference group[b]	N	X	s	t	p
1. "Physical activity for social purposes"	Social experience	Men	Strong	86	43.3	3.7	9.03	<.001
			Weak	115	41.6	4.3		
		Women	Strong	111	34.8	2.8	3.85	<.001
			Weak	36	32.6	3.6		
2. "Physical activity for health and fitness"	Health and fitness	Men	Strong	143	42.9	4.1	3.59	<.001
			Weak	55	38.6	3.8		
		Women	Strong	78	47.9	4.2	6.51	<.001
			Weak	48	42.6	4.7		
3. "Physical activity for thrills and excitement"	Pursuit of vertigo	Men	Strong	142	44.8	6.6	10.51	<.001
			Weak	81	36.4	3.8		
		Women	Strong	47	41.3	3.3	9.89	<.001
			Weak	98	34.9	3.8		
4. "Physical activity for aesthetic experience"	Aesthetic experience	Men	Strong	10	40.3	4.8	2.34	<.02
			Weak	297	38.2	3.7		
		Women	Strong	35	40.0	5.8	7.98	<.001
			Weak	92	33.4	3.4		
5. "Physical activity for recreation and relaxation"	Catharsis	Men	Strong	184	37.1	3.1	−10.82[c]	<.001
			Weak	54	42.5	3.8		
		Women	Strong	128	35.8	4.6	−3.02[c]	<.01
			Weak	20	39.1	4.6		
6. "Physical activity to meet a physical challenge"	Ascetic experience	Men	Strong	135	43.7	4.0	13.22	<.001
			Weak	104	36.8	4.1		
		Women	Strong	27	35.9	4.8	7.02	<.001
			Weak	129	30.8	3.1		

[a] Each criterion was defined to reflect the intended characteristics of the activity type.
[b] To be assigned to the "strong preference" group, subjects ranked the activity type in question either first or second out of the six possibilities. The "weak preference" group ranked the same activity either fifth or sixth.
[c] A careful analysis of the data has failed to provide an explanation for these findings. Further study of this dimension is clearly needed.

TABLE 8-IV

SCALE STABILITY AS REFLECTED IN MEANS, STANDARD
DEVIATIONS, AND HOYT RELIABILITIES: FORM DM
(N = 353 AND 310, RIVER FALLS AND OSHKOSH RESPECTIVELY)

Scale			Weighting System		
	$n_I{}^a$	RF with RF^b	OSK with OSK	RF with OSK	OSK with RF
1. Social	10				
X̄		42.5	39.6	39.5	42.4
s		4.1	3.5	3.2	3.7
r		.72	.71	.63	.61
2. H and F	10				
X̄		41.3	40.4	40.3	41.3
s		4.1	4.0	4.0	3.9
r		.79	.75	.74	.71
3. Vertigo	10				
X̄		40.7	42.1	42.3	40.4
s		6.2	4.6	5.2	5.0
r		.89	.82	.85	.79
4. Aesthetic	10				
X̄		38.6	39.3	39.3	38.7
s		3.9	4.2	3.7	4.3
r		.82	.83	.79	.82
5. Catharsis	9				
X̄		37.5	38.1	38.2	37.3
s		4.0	3.8	3.9	3.6
r		.77	.69	.71	.66
6: Ascetic	10				
X̄		40.3	41.9	41.0	41.2
s		5.0	4.6	4.8	4.6
r		.81	.78	.79	.74

[a] Number of items.
[b] Statistics generated by Wisconsin State University, River Falls data using River Falls rescaled weights.

SUMMARY

An attempt was made to develop attitude scales representing each of the dimensions of a multidimensional model for characterizing physical activity. With the exception of *physical activity as catharsis,* a moderately reliable and valid scale consisting of a relatively small number of items was developed for each subdomain. The use of these scales, however, should be restricted to research purposes. Instructions, items, and their scale designations are given in an appendix.*

REFERENCES

1. ADAMS, R. S.: Two scales for measuring attitude toward physical education. *Res Quart Amer Ass Health Phys Educ, 34*:91-94, 1963.

* Available from ADI, Auxiliary Publications Project, Photoduplication Service, Library of Congress, Washington D.C. 20540.

TABLE 8-V

SCALE STABILITY AS REFLECTED IN MEANS, STANDARD
DEVIATIONS, AND HOYT RELIABILITIES: FORM DW (N = 215 AND
306, RIVER FALLS AND OSHKOSH RESPECTIVELY)

Scale	$n_I{}^a$	Weighting System			
		RF with RF	*OSK with OSK*	*RF with OSK*	*OSK with RF*
1. Social	8				
$\overline{X}$		34.0	32.0	32.2	33.7
s		3.0	3.0	2.5	2.8
r		.72	.69	.59	.61
2. H and F	11				
$\overline{X}$		45.4	44.3	44.3	45.3
s		4.9	4.0	4.5	3.9
r		.83	.75	.78	.66
3. Vertigo	9				
$\overline{X}$		37.4	36.6	36.8	37.1
s		4.4	5.3	4.8	4.7
r		.86	.87	.84	.84
4. Aesthetic	9				
$\overline{X}$		35.1	35.8	35.7	35.2
s		4.2	3.6	3.9	3.6
r		.87	.82	.82	.75
5. Catharsis	9				
$\overline{X}$		36.7	35.1	35.7	36.5
s		4.1	4.5	4.5	3.8
r		.79	.79	.78	.73
6. Ascetic	8				
$\overline{X}$		31.5	31.3	31.5	31.2
s		4.1	3.6	3.9	3.6
r		.78	.70	.74	.66

2. ALLPORT, G. W.: Attitudes. In Murchison, C. (Ed.): *A Handbook of Social Psychology*. Worcester, Clarke University Press, 1935.

3. BAKER, F. B.: Univac scientific computer program for scaling of psychological inventories by the method of reciprocal averages. *Behav Sci, 5*: 268-69, 1960.

4. CAMPBELL, D. T.: Social attitudes and other acquired behavioral dispositions. In Koch S. (Ed.): *Psychology: A Study of a Science*. Vol. 6. New York, McGraw, 1963.

5. EDWARDS, A. L.: *Techniques of Attitude Scale Construction*. New York, Appleton, 1957.

6. GREEN, B. F.: Attitude measurement. In Lindzey, G. (Ed.): *Handbook of Social Psychology*. Vol. 1. Reading, Addison-Wesley, 1954.

7. HOYT, C.: Test reliability estimated by analysis of variance. *Psychometrika* 6:153-60, 1941.

8. KATZ, D.: The functional approach to the study of attitudes. *Public Opin Quart, 24*:163-204, 1960.

9. KENYON, G. S.: A conceptual model for characterizing physical activity. *Res Quart Amer Ass Health Phys Educ, 39*:96-105, 1968.

10. KRECH, D.; CRUTCHFIELD, R. S.; AND BALLACHEY, E. L.: *Individual in Society.* New York, McGraw, 1962.
11. LANG, L.: Neue Experimente Über den Vorgang der Einfachen Reaction auf Sinneseindrucke. *Phil Stud, 4*:479-510, 1888, cited by Allport, *op cit.*
12. MASON, M. G., AND VENTRE, A. G. L.: Attitude to athletics in second and fourth year boys in secondary schools. *Res papers phys educ, 1*:42-50, 1965.
13. OSGOOD, C. C.; SUCI, G. J.; AND TANNENBAUM, P. H.: *The Measurement of Meaning.* Urbana, U of Illinois, 1957.
14. RICHARDSON, C. E.: Thurstone scale for measuring attitudes of college students toward physical fitness and exercise. *Res Quart Amer Assoc Health Phys Educ, 31*:628-43, 1960.
15. Symposium: The need and means of cross-validation. *Educ Psychol Meas, 11*:5-28, 1951.
16. THOMAS, W. I. AND ZNANIECKI, F.: *The Polish Peasant in Europe and America.* Boston, Badger, 1918.
17. THURSTONE, L. L.: Comment. *Amer J Sociol, 52*:39-50, 1946.
18. ————.: Attitudes can be measured. *Amer J Sociol, 33*:529-54, 1928.
19. ————.: A law of comparative judgment. *Psychol rev, 34*:273-86, 1927.
20. TORGERSON, W. S.: *Theory and Methods of Scaling.* New York, Wiley, 1958.
21. WEAR, C. L.: Construction of equivalent forms of an attitude scale. *Res Quart Amer Assoc Health Phys Educ, 26*:113-19, 1955.

Chapter 9

RELIABILITY THEORY AND RESEARCH DECISION IN SELECTION OF A CRITERION SCORE*

Walter Kroll

INTRODUCTION

When several trials on a particular test are available the question of which trial or trials to use as a criterion measure arises. McCraw[18] considered this problem briefly in his study comparing various methods of scoring motor learning tests and he recommended that the maximum or best performance be selected. In 1950, Henry[8] presented empirical evidence that the discarding of discrepant data, even on the basis of fixed tolerance limits, lowered rather than raised the precision of prediction in a timing situation. Yet in 1959, Henry[7] selected the maximum grip strength from several available trials as the criterion measure in an excellent paper considering reliability problems. In effect, Henry, in 1959, discarded all but the maximum score while, in 1950, he warned against discarding discrepant data.

Recently, Whitley and Smith[19] challenged the *accepted and common practice* of using a subject's best score as a criterion measure when several trials were available on a strength measure. These authors offered evidence for using the mean of all available trials as the criterion measure by showing that the mean of all strength trials correlated higher with a speed criterion than other combinations of trial strength scores. Subsequently, Berger and Sweney[2] questioned this position contending the use of mean

* Walter Kroll: Reliability theory and research decision in selection of a criterion score. *Res Quart Amer Ass Health Phys Educ, 38*:412-419, 1967. Reproduced here with the permission of the author and the American Association for Health, Physical Education, and Recreation.

[95]

strength as a criterion measure over best trial "has no sound or logical basis." *

The necessity of selecting a criterion score when several trials are available represents a frequently called-for research decision. There is, fortunately, a sound and logical basis for making such research decisions, although it involves careful consideration of reliability analysis and theory. It is understandable that confusion exists in such matters since much of the theoretical basis for reliability analysis is steeped in psychological test nomenclature. Although principles of reliability analysis appear in almost every textbook in statistics, application of theory to everyday research situations seems to remain a problem.

PURPOSE

The purpose of this paper is to briefly review pertinent principles of reliability analysis and to present a theoretically defensible procedure for the selection of a criterion score when several trials are available. In order to recommend such a procedure it will be necessary to first consider some selected rudiments of reliability theory. It would be impossible and undesirable, of course, to attempt a comprehensive review. The interested reader is referred to suitable texts for fuller treatments of reliability analysis.[5, 6, 9, 10, 15, 20]

RUDIMENTS OF RELIABILITY THEORY

Variance Components

Any observed score is composed of two major components, a true score and an error score. Under appropriate conditions, the true score can be estimated and the error portion subdivided into a number of different variance components. Suppose, for example, that we are interested in assessing isometric strength of the wrist flexors in college males. Because we are concerned with test-retest reliability, we give five trials spaced a minute apart on one occasion and repeat the measurement schedule two weeks later. We wish to secure a criterion measure representing strength for our subjects and in estimating reliability of such a criterion measure as well.

---

*(See also Henry, Franklin M. *Best* versus *average* individual scores. *Res Quart Amer Assoc Health Phys Educ, 38*:317-20, 1967, for additional comment on this subject.)

If we let i = individuals, j = trials, and k = test days, the observed strength score X_{ijk} is in theory equal to

$$X_{ijk} = X + e_i + e_j + e_k + e_{ij} + e_{ik} + e_{jk} + e_{ijk}$$

That is, the criterion measure X_{ijk} is composed of a hypothetical true score (X), three sources of error due to subjects (e_i), trials (e_j), days (e_k), and the interactions of these three random error components $(e_{ij}, e_{ik}, e_{jk}, e_{ijk})$.

In order to define the X_{ijk} score we are interested in using as our criterion measure, we must consider the influences error variances have upon the observed score. We want an unbiased, reliable, criterion score and to achieve this we must apply the principles of reliability analysis. Reliability analysis necessitates a set of assumptions basic to the development of any reliability estimates. These assumptions are essential to a meaningful interpretation of any reliability estimate we may eventually derive and wish to evaluate. To calculate any correlation coefficient to be used as an estimate of reliability, we must assume that an observed score is comprised of a true score and an error score. We must assume the measures are of the same thing and that the error components are random and uncorrelated with themselves and the true score. In other words, the error components occur at random, independently of each other and the true score. The magnitude of error components will remain relatively constant regardless of the magnitude of the true score. We must also assume that the mean of these random and uncorrelated error scores is zero.

These assumptions, it must be emphasized, are inherent in any reliability estimate because reliability is defined as the ratio of true variance (σ^2 true) over total observed variance (σ^2 obs.). The observed variance is, of course, composed of σ^2 true plus σ^2 error, and we may write:

$$\text{reliability} = \frac{\sigma^2 \text{ true}}{\sigma^2 \text{ true} + \sigma^2 \text{ error}} = 1 - \frac{\sigma^2 \text{ error}}{\sigma^2 \text{ observed}}$$

Clearly then, a test is "unreliable in proportion as it has error variance." [16]

Applied to our example of wrist flexor strength, the total observed variance can be defined as equal to:

$$\sigma^2 \text{ observed} = \sigma^2_i + \sigma^2_j + \sigma^2_k + \sigma^2_{ij} + \sigma^2_{ik} + \sigma^2_{jk} + \sigma^2_{ijk} + \sigma^2 \text{ true.}$$

Since the basic definition of reliability involves the ratio of true variance over true variance plus error variance, it is clear that a number of reliability estimates are possible depending upon our ability to estimate the various error components and make decisions in defining certain variance sources as part of the true variance or as an error variance. To derive estimates of the components of variance associated with observed scores it is necessary to abandon the traditional use of a product-moment correlation since it cannot differentiate from the several sources of variance with which we are normally concerned. We can secure estimates of the several variance components by use of an appropriate analysis of variance model.[6, 15]

The advantages of an analysis of variance approach to reliability analysis are considerable. Reliability analysis through analysis of variance is achieved through intraclass correlation. Readers may consult any of a number of texts [6, 10, 15, 20] or *Research Quarterly* articles [3, 4, 13] for explanations of the intraclass correlation approach to reliability estimation. In particular, the relationships between interclass and intraclass correlation merit special attention.

Although intraclass and interclass correlation techniques are related, they are not identical.[6, 13] The product-moment r has the major disadvantage of being unable to distinguish among several sources of error variance which may be present in an observed score. It is thus hazardous to attempt a complete analysis of variance components via product-moment correlation by manipulation of the data into various combinations producing two sets of scores for correlation computation.

In an excellent study assessing several variance components in muscle strength and vertical jump tests,[7] estimates of appropriate variance components were apparently made in this fashion; i.e., computing a product-moment r for a test-retest situation and then estimating other variance components. Unless the full, appropriate analysis of variance model is employed which correctly defines variance components and associated degrees of freedom, an investigator may derive incorrect estimates. For example, this study analyzed a total variance ($\sigma^2 x$) for male grip strength of 26.507 into variance components representing between days ($\sigma^2 a - b/2 = 6.553$), measurement error ($\sigma^2 e = 0.984$), intraindividual ($\sigma^2 j = 5.569$), and interindividual ($\sigma^2 t = 19.954$). These separate variance components added up to 33.060 while the total variance being analyzed was only 26.507. This was true for all four sets of data analyzed.

Kinds of Reliability Estimates

First of all, there is no such thing as *the* reliability of a test. Most investigators are familiar with the traditional types of reliability estimates called internal consistency, equivalence, and stability.[5] The meaning of these three types will not be reviewed here other than to note that each specifies a certain group of decisions concerning the definition of true variance and error variance. Reliability estimates have usually been secured by product-moment correlation, r, necessitating the manipulation of data into two sets of scores. When data have been forced into such sets and r computed, the nature of the ratio of true variance over true variance plus error variance has been prescribed.

Consider our example of wrist flexor strength data. If we execute a test-retest product-moment correlation by using the mean of each subject's five trials on each occasion, we are defining the reliability ratio as one composed of σ^2 true over σ^2 true plus an σ^2 error where the error variance is due to variations within individuals between days. Such a ratio ignores error variance due to trial-to-trial variation on each of the test occasions. In the case of an internal consistency method via split halves, the resulting reliability estimate ignores day-to-day fluctuations and defines variation from trial-to-trial as error variance.

This means that logical considerations enter into any decision making about appropriate definition and allocation of variance components to true or error variance when several sources of variation are present. The basic problem thus becomes one of defining (and estimating) true variance and error variances. The several kinds of reliability estimates will produce several kinds of correlation coefficients since each method has a different set of rules for defining true and error variances.

Interpretation of a Correlation Coefficient as an Estimate of Reliability

Mistakenly, investigators have often considered the highest correlation coefficient *r* as the most desirable. This is not always true for several reasons. Since *r* is affected by the variability of the data from which it is computed, it is always necessary to consider the range of talent effect. Indeed, the most significant factor in determining *r* for a set of data is the range of ability in the sample.[16] This holds true because of effects upon the ratio which defines reliability. If the amount of variance between individuals increases while the error variances remain relatively constant, the obtained *r* is inflated. If the variance between individuals is decreased, the range of talent is decreased and the obtained *r* is expected to be decreased. Since basic assumptions stipulate that error variances are random and uncorrelated, error variances have no relationship to the true variance and are expected to remain relatively constant. It is clear, then, that if the error variance (σ^2 error) remains relatively constant, major effects upon *r* can be produced by increases or decreases in the observed variance because reliability is equal to

$$1 - \frac{\sigma^2 \text{ error}}{\sigma^2 \text{ observed}}$$

To interpret an estimate of reliability it is necessary to have not only the computed *r* but the standard deviation of the sample from which it was secured. With such information it is possible to estimate a standard error of measurement (σ meas.) by the formula:

$$\sigma \text{ meas.} = \sigma \text{ sample } \sqrt{1 - r}$$

The σ measurement is presumed to be independent of the range of talent in the group for which it was determined,[17] giving an indication of the absolute accuracy of measurement.

Thus it can be seen that an *r* of .90 with an observed standard deviation of 100 may not be preferable to an *r* of .50 with an observed standard deviation of 10. Since the range of talent determines the σ observed, the effects of reported *r*'s can be considerable. Indeed, a standard formula is available for estimating the *r* of a test when used in a population with a different standard deviation.[5]

It must be noted throughout that reliability theory prescribes effects that tend to be produced. In any set of particular data, some relationships prescribed by reliability theory may be masked or even reversed due to other relationships in reliability theory. Such effects were excellently demonstrated in an empirical study of measurement errors by Johnson.[12]

APPLICATION AND RECOMMENDED PROCEDURE

Since basic assumptions stipulate that an observed score is composed of two major components, true and error, and that error components are random and uncorrelated with themselves and the true score, the proper procedure for deciding which score or scores to select as a criterion measure when several trials are available is straightforward. If the error variances (σ^2 error$_1$ . . σ^2 error$_j$) are random and uncorrelated, then the proper procedure is to use the mean of all available trials. If this assumption can be shown to be untenable, then the investigator is faced with several and mostly unpleasant alternatives.

When several trials are available, the assumption of random, uncorrelated error variance due to trials can be tested quite simply by an analysis of variance design for repeated measures. In effect, we merely test the hypothesis that there are no differences between trials. Jackson[11] calls this a test for *trial effect* or *practice effect* while Alexander[1] calls it a *trend effect*. If the between trials F is nonsignificant it is then obvious that trial means do not fluctuate in any pattern; i.e. it is reasonable to assume there is no systematic error variance associated with observed trial scores. The assumption of error variance due to trials being random and uncorrelated would be considered tenable and the investigator would justifiably use the mean of all available trials as the criterion score.

Consider now that there was no significant trial-to-trial variance but the investigator still chose the highest trial score as the criterion measure. In effect, he would be ignoring the assumption of random, uncorrelated error variance associated with trials. His operating assumption, that is, the assumption he is unconsciously advocating, is that trial error variances are all negative and can best be overcome by choosing the trial score with the lowest negative error (the highest observed score). If he selected the lowest trial score, his operating assumption would be that all error variances are positive. Thus, choosing the lowest score makes as much sense as choosing the highest depending upon the logic of the reliability situation. It is clear, however, that when no systematic trial error variance is present, use of a criterion measure other than the mean of all trials is incorrect. This holds true regardless of what r's are obtained by various selection procedures (high, low, mean) and *sized up* for appropriateness.

In the note by Whitley and Smith,[19] their data showed no significant F for four strength trials given. These data clearly met the requirement of random, uncorrelated error variance due to trials and the authors were justified in using the mean of all trials as the criterion measure. Their data also showed that the mean of all trials correlated higher with a speed criterion measure than the *best score*, the *next best* score, or a three-trial average which omitted the lowest score. The results obtained reflect very well the operation of reliability theory concerning the assumption of trial error variance.

The study by Berger and Sweney[2] cannot, however, be properly evaluated in a similar manner. In this study, hypothetical data were used to compute test-retest r's by different methods of criterion score selection when several trials were available (high-high, high-mean, and mean-mean). The report presented only computed r's but not the necessary data with which to consider a range effect. The r effects demonstrated in this paper may have been due simply to range effects since the three sample groups considered were constructed to produce marked differences in group variability while keeping each subject's set of scores within a range of thirty. As might be expected, reported r's increased from low variability to high variability groups. Since the error variance due to trials was kept relatively constant by restricting the trial range within each subject to thirty or less while the variance between subjects in each group was increased, the effects upon the reliability ratio of σ^2 true$/\sigma^2$ true $+$ σ^2 error would lead to the trend of r's reported simply because of a range effect. Any procedure which produces an increased σ^2 observed will tend to produce higher r's assuming the error variance remains relatively constant. An evaluation of the differences between methods of criterion score selection within each of the three variability groups studied cannot be made for the simple reason that the observed variance of the new distribution of criterion scores (i.e. high-high, high-mean, mean-mean) was not reported.

Consider now the case in which the treatment by subjects design indicates a significant F between trials constituting evidence for a systematic error variance due to trials. In strength measures, for example, repeated trials may produce a significant monotonic decrease in observed strength over trials. This means that the error variance due to trials does not meet the assumption of being random and uncorrelated. Here the selection of the highest trial score might be defensible. Even more appropriate, however, would be to seek a measurement schedule which was free of a systematic error variance due to trials. Conversely, if the trial scores systematically decrease, say, in a learning experiment where rapid progress is made in the elimination of errors during the first few trials, selection of the lowest score (McCraw's maximum performance) would be defensible. Here again, however, there is a more appropriate practice.

As Liba[14] has shown, systematic trial-to-trial variance affects reliability estimates by the tendency to lower them. Liba concluded that if the presence of systematic trial variance was shown, the analysis of variance intraclass correlation model was not appropriate. This is not necessarily true since an estimate of reliability can still be made. In fact, it is possible to assess the magnitude of the trend effect and compute a reliability estimate with the trend effect subtracted out from the total variance.[1, 6]

The practice of allowing for a trend effect would seem inappropriate for most applications in physical education research. In situations where systematic trial-error variance or trend effects occur, an investigator should, if at all possible, search for a measurement schedule which results in criterion estimates free of systematic measurement error variance. If this is impossible, the choice of a high, low, or even mean score may represent the only alternative available to the investigator. Selection of a logical criterion score in this unpleasant and very infrequent situation is defensible, however, only if the theoretical assumptions of reliability analysis are kept in mind.

For most situations the investigator should search for a measurement schedule free of systematic error variance. This involves not only freedom from systematic error variance due to trials but on observed scores from day to day in a test-retest situation as well. This is nothing more than a search for a stable baseline with which to compare possible treatment effects. Until evidence is demonstrated for such a stable baseline any possible treatment effects demonstrated are suspect since they may be seriously confounded with errors in criterion measure assessment.

Thus, there is quite clearly a sound and logical basis for *choosing* a criterion measure when several trials are available. It is to be hoped that application of this sound and logical basis may encourage an investigator to reexamine his entire method of criterion measure assessment, or even to abandon it and search for a reliable method. Surely, however, it is time to stop making less than sophisticated pronouncements about research decisions which should be made on the basis of underlying theory and not overlying desires reflected in *sizing up* the data for correspondence to some imagined desirable result.

REFERENCES

1. Alexander, Howard W.: The estimation of reliability when several trials are available. *Psychometrika, 12*:79-99, 1947.
2. Berger, Richard A., and Sweney, Arthur B.: Variance and correlation coefficients. *Res Quart Amer Ass Health Phys Educ, 36*:368-70, 1965.
3. Brozek, Josef, and Alexander, Howard: Components of variation and the consistency of repeated measurements. *Res Quart Amer Ass Health Phys Educ, 18*:152-66, 1947.
4. Feldt, Leonard S., and McKee, Mary Ellen: Estimation of the reliability of skill tests. *Res Quart Amer Ass Health Phys Educ, 29*:279-93, 1958.
5. Guilford, J. P.: *Psychometric Methods.* New York, McGraw, 1954.
6. Haggard, Ernest A.: *Intraclass correlation and the analysis of variance.* New York, Dryden Press, 1958.
7. Henry, Franklin: Influence of measurement error and intra-individual variation on the reliability of muscle strength and vertical jump tests. *Res Quart Amer Ass Health Phys Educ, 30*:155-59, 1959.
8. Henry, Franklin: The loss of precision from discarding discrepant data. *Res Quart Amer Ass Health Phys Educ, 21*:145-52, 1950.
9. Jackson, R. W. B.: *Studies on the reliability of tests.* Bull. No. 12, Dept. of Educ. Research, U. of Toronto, 1940.
10. Jackson, R. W. B.: *Application of the analysis of variance and covariance method to educational problems.* Bull. No. 11, Dept. of Educ. Research, U. of Toronto, 1940.

11. JACKSON, R. W. B.: Reliability of mental tests. *Brit J Psychol, 29*:267-87, 1939.

12. JOHNSON, HELMER G.: An empirical study of the influence of errors of measurement upon correlation. *Amer J Psychol, 57*:521-36, 1944.

13. KROLL, WALTER: A note on the coefficient of intraclass correlation as an estimate of reliability. *Res Quart Amer Ass Health Phys Educ, 33*:313-16, 1962.

14. LIBA, MARIE: A trend test as a preliminary to reliability estimation. *Res Quart Amer Ass Health Phys Educ, 33*:245-48, 1962.

15. LINDQUIST, E. F.: *Design and Analysis of Experiments in Psychology and Education.* Boston, Houghton, 1956.

16. LINDQUIST, E. F., (Ed.): *Educational Measurement.* Washington, D. C.: American Council on Education, 1951.

17. LINDQUIST, E. F.: *A first course in statistics.* Cambridge, Riverside Press, 1942.

18. McCRAW, L. W.: Comparative analysis of methods of scoring tests of motor learning. *Res Quart Amer Ass Health Phys Educ, 26*:440-53, 1955.

19. WHITLEY, J. D., AND SMITH, L. E.: Larger correlations obtained by using average rather than *best* strength scores. *Res Quart Amer Ass Health Phys Educ, 34*:248-49, 1963.

20. WINER, B. J.: *Statistical Principles in Experimental Design.* New York, McGraw, 1962.

Chapter 10

EFFECT OF KNOWLEDGE OF RESULTS ON ISOMETRIC STRENGTH SCORES*

WILLIAM R. PIERSON AND PHILIP J. RASCH

INTRODUCTION

IT IS COMMONLY supposed in strength testing that a subject's knowledge of his performance favorably influences the results, and strength tests are frequently administered in such a way that the subject is unaware of his scores, at least until the testing has been completed. Arps[1,2] noted that his three subjects increased isotonic endurance from 5 to 35 percent when they had knowledge of their performance, but most methods of strength testing are isometric, or very nearly so, and there is little justification in the literature for *blind* testing of isometric strength. The purpose of the present study was to investigate the effects of knowledge of performance on isometric strength test scores. A secondary consideration was to determine the effect of the day of week on such scores.

METHOD

Subjects were fifteen paid volunteer upper class students of the California College of Medicine. They were tested for isometric strength by means of an apparatus which consisted of a short bar connected by airplane cable and adjustable link chain to a Baldwin-Lima SR-4 load cell, which activated a Triplett model 626 dial indicator placed in full view of the subject. The subject was positioned in front of the bar, erect, and holding it in both hands. By means of the adjustable link chain, the forearms of the subject were positioned at 90° to the pendant humeri. This position was chosen be-

* William R. Pierson and Philip J. Rasch: Effect of knowledge of results on isometric strength scores. *Res Quart Amer Ass Health Phys Educ, 35*:313-315, 1964. Reproduced here with the permission of the authors and the American Association for Health, Physical Education, and Recreation.

cause the isometric strength curves of Williams and Stutzman[3] indicate that at 90° the elbow flexors exert maximum torque. The subject was instructed to make an isometric contraction with the arms only. While one investigator read the dial, the other observed the subject for obvious synergistic action and/or change in body position. Each subject exerted a maximal pull against the bar twice a day, once with the dial visible to him and once with it hidden, five days a week, for two weeks. A rest of not less than 5 minutes was taken between each of the daily trials. The experimental design was that of a split-plot Latin square, in which the effects of day of week and priority of administration were balanced. In the statistical analysis, a probability of .01 or less was used to indicate significance.

RESULTS

The mean strength score with no knowledge of results was 97.9 pounds (SD = 17.0) as compared to 100.8 pounds (SD = 15.6) with knowledge. The correlation between the two test scores was significant ($r = 0.98$) and the t-test for related samples indicated that the difference in mean scores was not due to chance (t = 3.38). The analysis of variance for day of week resulted in nonsignificant scores for both the tests with knowledge and without knowledge of results (F = 0.28 and 0.26 respectively).

CONCLUSIONS

The results of the present study indicate that, for the population represented by the sample tested, isometric strength scores are greater when the subject has knowledge of his performance than when he does not. They also indicate that the day of week is not an important variable in isometric strength scores.

REFERENCES

1. ARPS, G. F.: A preliminary report on "Work with knowledge versus work without knowledge of results." *Psychol Rev, 24*:449-55, 1917 (cited in Woodworth, R. S., and Schlosberg, H. *Experimental Psychology.* Henry Holt and Company, 1954).
2. ARPS, G. F.: Work without knowledge of results versus work with knowledge of results. *Psychol Monogr,* No. 125, 1920.
3. WILLIAMS, M. E., AND STUTZMAN, L.: Strength variation through the range of motion. *Phys Ther Rev, 39*:145-52, 1959.

PART FIVE
MENTAL HEALTH

Chapter 11

USE OF THE HARVARD PSYCHIATRIC SERVICE BY ATHLETES AND NON-ATHLETES*

Lida R. Carmen, Joseph L. Zerman, and Graham B. Blaine, Jr.

INTRODUCTION

THE IMPRESSION at the Harvard University Health Services that fewer athletes than nonathletes used the Psychiatric Service prompted the study on which this paper reports.

Statistical comparison of the use of the Psychiatric Service by athletes and nonathletes during a five-year period showed that athletes had, in fact, used the service less. (The term *athlete* designates any undergraduate who has participated in extramural sports as a member of a team and who has been awarded a varsity letter or a freshmen numeral.) Over this period, 7.0 percent of the athlete population had come to the Psychiatric Service as patients, compared with 8.5 percent of the nonathlete population.

This finding evoked a number of questions and speculations: Does less frequent use of the Psychiatric Service by athletes mean that they have fewer problems than nonathletes? Do athletes have the same number of problems as nonathletes, but use ways other than psychiatric help to deal with them? Are athletes more reluctant to ask for help when they have problems? What kinds of problems trouble them, and how do these problems compare with those of nonathletes?

PROCEDURE

The study consists of two parts: (1) a large survey that covered

* L. R. Carmen, J. L. Zerman, and G. B. Blaine, Jr.: Use of the Harvard psychiatric service by athletes and non-athletes. *Mental Hygiene, 52*:134-137, 1968. Reproduced here with the permission of the authors and The National Association for Mental Health, Inc.

[111]

the five academic years 1957-1962 and included all athletes who were seen in the Psychiatric Service of the Harvard University Health Services, a total of 106 students; (2) a smaller study, carried on in the final year of the survey, that focused on the twenty-six athletes who applied to the Psychiatric Service in the academic year 1961-1962 and a control group drawn randomly from the nonathlete applicants of that year. The sports represented included football, baseball, basketball, wrestling, swimming, Rugby, hockey, lacrosse, fencing, golf, skiing, riflery, sailing, crew, track, squash, tennis, and soccer.

Information for both studies was obtained from the clinical records, and included the following: (1) source of referral of the student; (2) the student's scholastic year at the time he came to the Psychiatric Service; (3) the nature of the problems presented and the symptoms associated with these problems; (4) the number of clinic visits; (5) whether college attendance was interrupted; (6) whether the student graduated. Comparative survey statistics for nonathletes were obtained from the annual reports of the University Health Services.

The *presenting problem* as referred to in this study was the predominant reason for the student's search for help from the Psychiatric Service, i.e. the problem that was reported initially in the record, the precipitating problem or chief complaint. Any others mentioned subsequently were regarded as attendant problems, whether or not they were directly related to, or associatd with, the presenting problem.

Reasons for seeking help were classified according to the major areas of the student's life that were affected. They included study, family-marriage, social interactions, and sexual relationships. Other categories were career plans, specific physical symptoms or complaints, speech difficulties, information seeking, administrative problems, and disciplinary problems. Symptoms of depression and anxiety were noted when associated with the various groupings.

FINDINGS

Sources of referral were found to be the following: the athlete himself (41%); an authority representing the college, such as a dean, tutor, proctor, or teacher (31%); physicians in other clinics of the

University Health Services (15%); or a variety of other people such as friends, relatives, ministers, and other counselors (13%).

Of the 106 athletes who applied, twenty-two did so as freshmen, forty-four as sophomores, twenty-one as juniors, and nineteen as seniors.

The commonest presenting problems among athletes were found to be study (41%), social difficulties (12%), sexual preoccupations (11%), and career worries (7%). The presenting problems of the remaining 29 percent were divided among family troubles, information seeking, administrative routines, physical complaints, and disciplinary measures. About 25 percent complained of anxiety and depression.

The commonest complaint in the category of *secondary problems* was social difficulty (40%). Family problems were cited by 37 percent. Study problems were third (29%), followed by career (22%) and sexual problems (12%). The seniors had the fewest social concerns both in presenting and secondary problems, but were more uncertain about careers. Although only a few freshmen and sophomores complained about sexual problems, there was a sharp rise in such complaints among the juniors; as secondary problems, they rose to 68 percent among the seniors.

Physical complaints were largely secondary worries and were confined almost wholly to the sophomore class. About 50 percent of the athletes complained of three major problems; another 36 percent presented two problems; only 14 percent had a single complaint.

Eight athletes were hospitalized in mental hospitals, one in his freshman year, four in the sophomore year, two as juniors, and one in his senior year. The hospitalized athletes included three swimmers, two football players, one tennis player, one fencer, and one rifleman.

The sports most heavily represented were football,[14] swimming,[14] crew,[13] basketball,[9] and fencing.[9] Track, wrestling, and soccer contributed five members each. There was a sprinkling of skiers and baseball, hockey, squash, and lacrosse players. Only 19 percent reported that their sports activity was affected by their problems.

The group sustained a 41 percent dropout rate. Specifically, this meant that forty-six students dropped out at least once before graduation. Of this number, nineteen dropped out twice; one student dropped out three times. Seventy-nine percent graduated, 8 percent are still enrolled, and thirteen students have not returned. The hospitalized group graduated four; two are currently enrolled; and two others have not returned after an absence of three years each.

About 66 percent of the athletes came for a maximum of five interviews. Fourteen percent had six to ten sessions; 20 percent came for more than ten interviews. Few athletes (13%) reapplied for help in the academic years following their initial care.

Nonathletes reapplied almost three times as frequently as athletes, i.e. about 36 percent returned for further treatment in subsequent years. Referrals of athletes by school authorities were 10 percent greater than those of nonathletes. These findings seem to support the hypothesis that athletes were more reluctant applicants and needed to be sent to the clinic by others. Also, they complained less frequently about medical troubles, for their referrals from the medical clinics were 14 percent fewer than those of nonathletes.

The athlete group, in comparison with the figures for nonathletes, seemed to contain a high percentage of sophomores. In the five years, athlete sophomores averaged about 41 percent of the total athlete group seeking psychiatric help as compared with 29 percent of sophomores in the nonathlete group. In the three other classes, athletes represented a smaller proportion than nonathletes, ranging from 2 percent less in the freshman class to 6 percent less in the senior class. Four of the students who became psychotic were sophomores compared with one freshman, two juniors, and one senior. The evidence seems to warrant the conclusion that some disappointments in competition in sports and achieving awards impelled more sophomore athletes to apply for psychiatric help than sophomore nonathletes. Their problems apparently came to the attention of others first, for as many were referred by school authorities as referred themselves.

The small study confirmed that athletes were *self-referred* less often than nonathletes. It showed the athlete group as having more three-problem applicants (42%) than the nonathletes (11%). Only 23 percent of the athletes presented a single problem, whereas 42 percent of the nonathletes did so.

Difficulty with study was the chief presenting problem for both groups, but was somewhat higher for athletes. In other major areas, such as sex, career choice, and family conflicts, athletes showed a higher number of concerns. Only in the social area were athletes significantly less troubled (30% athletes compared with 46% non-athletes).

In spite of their array of problems, the athletes appeared to be no more depressed than the nonathletes. Once in treatment, they followed through as well as nonathletes. Though they seemed to find the scholastic road somewhat more difficult, ultimately they graduated at almost the same rate as nonathletes.

DISCUSSION

The small study seems to verify the facts and figures of the larger survey. It gives some emphasis to the picture of athletes as persons beset not by fewer, but possibly by more, problems than nonathletes, a speculation offered in a study by Davie.[1]

The athletes' better social adjustment would seem to validate other studies of athletic achievement. One, by Benson and Summerskill,[2] found that successful athletes clearly felt that their esteem on the campus was greater because of their athletic achievement. In this study, athletes expressed themselves as deeply satisfied with their social interactions and team spirit. Another study[3] presented the view that there was an interacting relationship between athletic achievement and adjustment; a third[4] held, similarly, that participation in interpersonal and intramural athletics played an important part in making a student well liked by his peers.

The fact that most athletes in the large survey were able to carry on sports activities despite multiple personal problems seems to indicate that sports may have other meanings and functions. They appear to serve as a defense against depression and/or anxiety and as a denial of weakness. The records of athletes frequently contain comments describing the meaning of sports to them. To one crewman, his sport seemed to mean dispelling a depression—"I get a big lift in the spring from rowing in crew workout after feeling low." To a runner, his activity meant keeping down fat and feminine tendencies. A football player talked about the "pleasure of knocking people down," presumably as an outlet for aggressive feelings.

For many athletes, physical activity, rather than talking things out, appears to offer a means of expressing feelings and aggressions.[5] Perhaps this substitution of action for words contributes to the seeming reluctance of athletes to come to a service that requires that they articulate their feelings.

An addendum to the use of sports for defensive purposes is the choice of sports by different personalities. One study [6] has suggested that athletes who participate only in individual sports score significantly higher in the *depression* variable of the MMPI than those who participate only in team sports. Such a theory could account for the number of depressed swimmers in our large survey—ten of the fourteen swimmers in this survey were depressed.

SUMMARY AND CONCLUSIONS

A survey of 106 athletes known over a five-year period to the Psychiatric Service revealed that they used the facilities of the service less frequently than nonathletes. The largest single problem area of the athletes was difficulty with studies. Sophomore athletes came in greater proportion than sophomore nonathletes, which suggests the hypothesis that increased competition for varsity awards was an added stress. Football players, swimmers, and crewmen contributed the largest number of those seeking help.

A smaller study of twenty-six athletes, using twenty-six nonathletes as a control, showed that the athletes who came for treatment tended to have a greater number of problems than did the nonathletes. These problems were spread over a broad range and were significantly fewer than those of nonathletes only in the area of socialization. This study supported the finding that athletes came somewhat less frequently on their own initiative. The increased pressure on sophomore athletes was apparent also in the smaller study. Denial of a wish for help and determination not to give in to *weakness* were often given as reasons for reluctance to apply for treatment.

REFERENCES

1. Davie, J. S.: Who Uses a College Mental Hygiene Clinic? In Wedge, B. M. (Ed.): *Psychosocial Problems of College Men.* New Haven, Yale, 1958, p. 148.
2. Benson, T. B., and Summerskill, J.: *Res Quart Amer Ass Health Phys Educ,* 26:9, 1955.

3. BUDDOLF, L. G.: *Res Quart Amer Ass Health Phys Educ, 25*:1, 1954.

4. McGRAW, L. W.: *Res Quart Amer Ass Health Phys Educ, 24*:70, 1953.

5. JOHNSON, W. R., AND HUTTON, D. C.: *Res Quart Amer Ass Health Phys Educ, 26*:49, 1955.

6. BOOTH, E. G., JR.: *Res Quart Amer Ass Health Phys Educ, 29*:127, 1958.

Chapter 12

LEISURE ACTIVITIES OF SCHIZOPHRENIC PATIENTS AFTER RETURN TO THE COMMUNITY*

Hiram L. Gordon, David Rosenberg, and William E. Morris

INTRODUCTION

There has been little systematic study of the leisure activities of psychiatric patients in the community. Robertson [1] surveyed the chief types of recreation of 953 patients before admission to an English mental hospital. Harrington and Cross,[2] also in England, studied the activities of 187 psychiatric patients prior to the onset of their acute symptoms. Neither study found a significant relationship between the leisure activities of these patients and their subsequent psychiatric diagnoses or responses to treatment.

The present investigation is concerned with the leisure activities of a group of adult male schizophrenic patients after release from three psychiatric hospitals. An attempt was made to find out how their activities in the community compared with those of *normal* adult males in type and amount of activity. The study was also designed to determine the relationship between number and type of leisure activities, including intensity of participation, and the psychiatric condition and work status of the patients after nine months in the community.

Harrington and Cross[2] have pointed out that many psychiatrists assume that the mental health of a person depends on a proper balance between work and leisure and that "a failure to use leisure time sensibly is often a precursor and an accompaniment of mental illness." Leisure

* H. L. Gordon, D. Rosenberg, and W. E. Morris. Leisure activities of schizophrenic patients after return to the community. *Mental Hygiene, 50*:452-459, 1966. Reproduced here with the permission of the authors and the National Association for Mental Health, Inc.

activity is particularly important for released schizophrenic patients because they usually have large amounts of free time.

Many schizophrenics, particularly those from Veterans Administration Hospitals, do little work after returning to the community. In a study of a large number of adult male schizophrenic Veterans, the Veterans Administration Program Evaluation Staff [3] found that, after nine months in the community, "70 percent of the total time during which the overall sample was available (for work), it was not employed; 23 percent of the time was spent in full-time nonsheltered employment." Fifty-three percent of the sample had not done even three days' work in any one week during the nine months of the follow-up study. About half of the subjects had made no definite effort to find a job. Such factors as the somewhat advanced average age of the sample, the prejudice of some employers against hiring former psychiatric patients, and the receipt of a pension or other compensation contributed to the high rate of unemployment. However, the main reasons for not working were found to be the poor emotional and mental integration of these ex-patients.

METHOD

The subjects in the present study were 172 adult male schizophrenics who had been released from three Veterans Administration Psychiatric Hospitals in widely separated areas of the country— Colorado, Indiana, and North Carolina. The subjects ranged in age from eighteen to fifty-five, with an average age of thirty-eight. Their educational achievement ranged from one to sixteen years, with a mean education of ten years. Most of the subjects were from the upper-lower or middle-lower social and economic class. None had any major physical disability that would prevent him from participating in ordinary recreation or work.

These ex-patients were also subjects in a broader study, made by the Program Evaluation Staff at twelve hospitals, of work in the community after hospitalization. Each subject's condition was rated by a psychiatric social worker nine months after he had left the hospital.* Each ex-patient was rated as to his participation in each

* The authors wish to thank the following social workers for doing the community ratings: Clarence Groth, Veterans Administration Hospital, Fort Lyon,

of twenty activities on a scale ranging from 0 (no participation) to 4 (frequent, interested participation). Two measures of participation were thus computed for each subject: the number of the twenty activities in which he had participated, even if to a limited degree, and the intensity (personal involvement) of his participation in these activities. This was accomplished by summing for each ex-patient his participation score in each of the activities. The resulting total gave an estimate of the *intensity* of the subject's leisure activities. (We have called this measurement a *weighted participation score;* it is a more meaningful, yet more subjective, measurement than the first one.) In addition, the sum of the rating of all subjects for a specific activity gave a measure of the popularity and availability of that activity.

The social worker found out how much time each subject had spent working during the first nine months after leaving the hospital. He also evaluated the subject's degree of mental illness (hereafter termed *mental status*) on a six-point scale ranging from 1 (not at all ill) to 6 (extremely ill). This information was used to evaluate his community adjustment. The first criterion of adjustment was whether the ex-patient did any work for pay during nine months in the community. The second criterion, mental status, was perhaps the more relevant of the two, but may have been somewhat *contaminated.* The social worker may not have been able to keep his knowledge of the subject's leisure activities from influencing his judgment of his current mental status. Perhaps the interviewer, like the psychiatrists referred to earlier,[2] tended to consider how a person spent his leisure time as one element in rating the degree of mental disorder.

The interviewer also obtained information as to whether the ex-patient performed an activity alone, with a significant *other* (usually wife or mother), with other members of the family, or with persons other than family members.

RESULTS

The most frequent leisure activity of these patients in the com-

Colo.; Charles F. Hansen and Ernest V. Webber, Veterans Administration Hospital, Marion, Ind.; and Leo B. Larabee, Veterans Administration Hospital, Salisbury, N. C.

munity was watching television and listening to the radio. This was true of 97 percent of the subjects, for 72 percent of whom this activity was frequent. Other common leisure activities, in order of frequency were reading newspapers, going for drives, visiting friends and relatives, reading material other than newspapers, attending church, working in the garden or yard, and engaging in hobbies. Not one of our subjects took any part in dramatics; very few attended a lecture or play, took a correspondence course, or played a musical instrument.

Therapists planning recreation for schizophrenic patients need to know which sports and hobbies the patients preferred in the hospital and which of these activities were continued in the community. Before leaving the institution, our subjects named their favorite recreational activities in the hospital. The most favored activities were watching television, playing pool, reading, watching movies, swimming, taking walks, softball and baseball, volleyball, playing cards, dancing, bowling, listening to music, and attending parties. These choices expressed an interest in far more sports and social activities than the same patients showed in the community. Patients expressing a liking for passive activities in the hospital, such as watching television or reading, almost always continued these activities after leaving the hospital. On the other hand, patients expressing a liking for sports and entertainment involving interaction with other people seldom continued these in the community. For example, forty-three patients chose playing pool as the preferred leisure activity in the hospital, but only five of these men played pool in the community. Nineteen chose swimming, eighteen, softball and baseball, sixteen, volleyball, and ten, attending parties; but none of the patients making these choices actually engaged in these activities after returning to the community.

Bowling and playing pool were the sports most frequently enjoyed by our subjects once they were in the community. Of the 172 subjects, fifteen participated in each of these. No more than three ex-patients participated in any other sport.

If one excludes watching television and reading, most of the subjects had no hobbies. Only a very small number of these ex-patients participated in energetic hobbies, even though such activities were counted if there had been only minimal or token participation.

The three most frequently listed hobbies were watching athletic contests (eight subjects), doing handicrafts of various kinds (eight subjects), and listening to music (seven subjects). Of these three hobbies, watching athletic contests and listening to music are usually quite passive, and only doing handicrafts could be considered active or creative.

It was possible for subjects to participate in an activity, but infrequently and with little interest. We devised an intensity score based on both a subject's frequency of participation and interest shown. The intensity scores for television showed that 167 of 172 subjects watched television in the community, and usually with considerable interest. Few subjects participated in hobbies, but those that did also showed considerable interest in them. Most of the subjects read newspapers and were taken on automobile rides; a moderate interest was shown in these activities. The subjects attending church, as well as the few taking part in sports, showed moderate interest in these activities. The subjects usually showed a low interest in participating in the other activities surveyed.

The patients who were more active in recreational activities while in the hospital showed a significant tendency toward greater participation in leisure activities during their nine months in the community than did the less active patients.

In seeming contradiction to earlier findings [4, 5, 6] on *normal* populations, the average age of our subjects was not significantly related to the number of different leisure activities they participated in or to the amount of their participation. The number of activities and the amount of participation of the married, separated, or divorced subjects were not significantly different from those of the subjects who had never married.

We had thought that participation in certain types of activity in the community might predict working behavior and mental status at nine months. This was found *not* to be the case for the three following groups: (1) ex-patients participating in sports, hunting, or fishing; (2) those who attended club meetings or went to parties or dances; (3) those who participated in hobbies or home study courses, attended lectures or the theatre, or went to movies. Seemingly, participation in no one type of activity was predictive of superior mental status or of work.

Mental status of a subject after nine months in the community was significantly related to the number of leisure activities in which he participated, his weighted participation score, and whether he took part in leisure activities with people other than members of his family. More favorable mental status was associated with more activities, higher participation scores, and some activity with a person outside the family. Whether a patient worked in the community or not was related only to his amount of participation in the twenty leisure activities studied; high participation scores were associated with a greater likelihood of compensated work.

DISCUSSION

It is difficult to compare findings on recreational participation from different studies. The ages, incomes, and social classes of the samples used are different; the activities measured vary and are categorized in unique ways; the specification of the amount of participation is either vaguely defined or different from other studies, and the time period studied varies considerably.

Since 1950 there have been at least three extensive surveys of recreational participation of *normal* American adults. The 1962 survey of the Outdoor Recreation Resources Review Commission (ORRRC) [6] sampled 2,750 adults. It studied participants among heads of households and their spouses in ten listed recreational activities plus any other leisure activities spontaneously mentioned. This seems to be the most extensive study reported concerning recreation; but, for comparative purposes, it has a disadvantage in that it is oriented primarily to outdoor recreation. The Opinion Research Corporation (ORC) [5] study of 1954, based on a national *probability sample* of 5,021 people age fifteen and over, attempted to find what proportion of people engaged *yesterday* in various leisure activities. The J. A. Ward study of 1954 [7] was based on the mean amount of time between 6 a.m. and 11 p.m. devoted to certain listed activities (not all of which were recreational) by a sample of about 1,600 people. Obviously, one must exercise considerable caution in comparing the present data with those from any of the above three surveys, particularly the last two mentioned.

Some idea of the relative amount of participation in nine important leisure activities can be obtained by comparing *frequent participation* of our subjects with *regular participation* shown for adult males in the ORRRC report. The ratios participating for the latter group are higher for each of the activities. Nearly as high a proportion of our subjects reported participating in use of television and radio, reading, going for pleasure drives, and attending church and clubs as were shown for the normal male group. However, markedly lower ratios of our subjects reported participation in sports, working in garden or yard, hobbies, visiting friends and relatives, and attending lectures and plays. For example, 55 percent of normal adult males took part in sports regularly, but only 12 percent of our ex-patients reported such participation. Sixty-three percent of the ORRRC sample visited friends and relatives regularly whereas only 23 percent of our sample reported such visits. It may then be concluded that the subjects in this sample participated much less frequently in recreational activities than does the average American male.

The inactivity of the ex-patient population can be further shown by what they did not do in the month studied. For example, of the 172 ex-patients, 97 percent *never* attended a lecture or went to the theatre, 92 percent *never* went to a library, 87 percent *never* went fishing or hunting, 84 percent didn't attend or even belong to a club, 81 percent took no part in sports, 79 percent had no hobby, 68 percent never went to movies, 60 percent didn't write letters, 60 percent didn't use the telephone, 54 percent didn't go to church, and 11 percent did no reading of any kind. Ex-patients participated in a mean of only 6.6 activities of the twenty investigated.

The authors do not maintain that the diagnosis of schizophrenia and the hospital stay of this sample are the only reasons for the subjects' low participation in leisure activities. It has been shown[5, 6, 8] that leisure activities of most kinds tend to be less among men of small income, limited education, or advanced age. The men in the present sample, as a group, were below average in both social class and income, and would attend few lectures and plays whether or not they were schizophrenic. However, difference in social class or income could scarcely account for the large difference between this sample and a normal group in such activities as working in the garden or yard and visiting friends and relatives. Other studies[5, 6] have suggested that the amount of participation in these activities has little relation to the social class or income of the participants.

The most frequent community activities of our subjects were all rather passive ones, requiring a minimum of physical or mental activity. These were not the types of activity in which one could set goals of output or performance and thus feel a sense of failure or guilt from lack of attainment. Certainly watching television, listening to the radio, reading, and visiting friends and relatives are passive and noncompetitive activities. Others of the nine most frequent activities of our sample might be considered somewhat active in a normal population, but apparently they were not for these ex-patients. For example, going for a drive was considered passive because 82 percent took drives with other people who, according to the reports of the social workers, usually did the driving. Going to church was passive because only 18 percent of the church-goers ever attended alone and few, if any, ever took any responsibility in the church. Seemingly they were taken to church by their families or foster home sponsors. There was no activity definitely requiring extensive physical activity, concentrated effort, or real initiative among the most frequent activities.

Use of television and radio was by far the most frequent leisure activity of these subjects. Earlier studies have also found that watching television was the most frequent leisure activity among the general population[5, 6] and for British psychiatric patients before entering treatment.[2] Clearly most of our subjects watched television often, either from choice or because other members of the family were utilizing the most convenient living spaces for that purpose.

Whether a subject's intensity score was above or below the average for the entire group of subjects was not related to whether he worked or to his mental status after nine months in the community. Only the total amount of recreational activity of a subject in the community was significantly related to whether he did any work. In an earlier study by the present investigators,[9] the amount of recreational activity in the hospital by individual patients was not associated with the amount of time subsequently spent in the community, mental status after nine months, or whether the patient worked. Variables at departure from the hospital that did differentiate patients who worked from those that did not were an optimum amount of energy displayed in speech, gait, and posture, a more favorable mental status, a reported preference for outdoor sports, and a dislike for table games.[9, 10]

Our survey supports the findings of Harrington and Cross[2] that there are considerable differences between what patients *say* they want to do and what they actually do. The National Recreation Association [11] found the same mechanism operative in the general population. Eight of the ten most frequently chosen leisure activities were passive or sedentary, whereas all but one of the activities most aspired to were active pursuits. Anderson [12] tells us that when people are asked what they do with their leisure time they apparently give answers aimed to fit the social expectations of their listeners.

Why is it that many patients express a preference for sports and social activities and then, in the community, do not participate in this type of activity? Possible explanations are the following:

(1) These subjects, as a group, display a lack of energy, because of which they would be more content to remain passively in their homes. Hodgen and Reimer,[13] McFarland and Huddelson,[14] Rice, Rosenberg, and Radzyminski,[15] and Rosenberg and Rice[16] have all shown that schizophrenic patients have a lower level of physical fitness than normal subjects. A considerable number of the present sample did not seem to be physically able to take part successfully in active sports. Often they did not recognize this fact because of disordered thought processes.

(2) The patients with better mental status have some doubts about their adequacy and physical ability. Expressing preferences for such activities as hunting and fishing, baseball, and bowling not only serves to reassure the patients but, hopefully, enhances their images. Just saying that they are interested in active sports and social activities may make the patients feel more adequate.

(3) The ex-patients, partly through lack of judgment and partly through lack of recent community experience, did not fully appreciate the difficulties in participating in sports and social events. As Anderson[12] points out, most of these activities call for "planning, getting dressed, going to places and arriving on time; getting organized." Also, our subjects had little consideration of the cost of such activities. When they stated that they were interested in playing golf, they did not consider the cost of furnishing their own equipment or the fact that there was limited availability of golf courses in the neighborhood where they would be residing.

In the ORRRC study,[6] 60 percent of the people interviewed expressed a desire to engage in more outdoor activities. When asked what prevented them, 52 percent answered "lack of time." Most people crave more free time. On the other hand, Harrington and Cross[2] pointed out that many psychiatric patients did not regard their free time as a precious commodity that could be used for pleasure or advantage. These investigators remarked that "it was often difficult to see how so much time could apparently be filled with so little." Our interviewers often expressed the same thought. Most of our subjects had little realization that the use they made of their leisure time might be related to the success of their adjustment. Most men and women work to obtain free time, and carefully plan how to spend it. For many of our subjects, their large amount of free time was something to be endured with boredom and resignation.

Anderson[12] has also pointed out that many people think that leisure time must be earned; it can be enjoyed only if a person "has earned it by the sweat of his brow." Many schizophrenic patients returning to the community have a history of not working or making constructive social contributions in the previous few years. In our culture they may feel guilty about this, and such guilt possibly could inhibit them from participating in, or enjoying, leisure activities as much as normal men of their age. Certainly our interviewers had the impression that the ex-patients of this study secured little enjoyment from their leisure activities.

Most former schizophrenic patients need to participate in recreational activities in the community to help them keep physically fit and to prevent deterioration of their intellectual and social abilities. This study has indicated that male schizophrenics who return to the community, if left to their own devices, do not participate in active recreation to the extent that they should. This may well be true for other patient groups also. Former mental patients need to avail themselves of community recreational facilities. Participation in community recreational programs would probably need to be prescribed for the departing patient by his hospital physician and a referral made to the recreation director in the ex-patient's home community. The program itself would need to be somewhat directive, with the therapist arranging participation in specified recreational activities until the ex-patient had established a habit of self-engagement. In the present study the activities that patients said they most enjoyed in the hospital were often ones that were prescribed and controlled to a considerable extent by the therapists.

SUMMARY

The purpose of this study was to gather information about the recreational activities of psychotic patients after they have returned to the community. The subjects were 172 adult male schizophrenic patients leaving three Veterans Administration Hospitals. Each subject was interviewed and evaluated at the time he left the hospital and again after nine months in the community.

This group of ex-patients definitely had fewer recreational activities than did *normal* male adults. Their main recreational activities in the community were passive and involved little physical effort or creativity. Watching television was by far the most common activity. Other frequent activities were reading, listening to radio and music, going for drives, visiting relatives and friends, and attending church or club meetings. There was little participation in sports or hobbies.

The two criteria of community adjustment were (1) whether the ex-patient did any compensated work and (2) his mental status after nine months. Only the total amount of community recreational participation of an ex-patient was related to whether he did any work. Favorable mental status was significantly related to the number of recreational activities, amount of recreational participation, and engaging in recreation with people other than the patient's immediate family.

Patients who indicated a preference for sports while in the hospital seldom participated in them after returning to the community. On the other hand, patients who indicated that they preferred passive activities, such as watching television and reading, almost always participated in these after returning to the community.

These ex-patients frequently did not regard their leisure time as an asset to be enjoyed or used for self-improvement. Many schizophrenic patients leaving the hospital definitely need recreational guidance from community workers until they have formed a habit of participation in recreation of their own accord.

REFERENCES

1. ROBERTSON, J. P. S.: *J Clin Psychol, 13*:56, 1967.
2. HARRINGTON, J. A., AND CROSS, K. W.: *Ment Hyg, 46*:580 (October), 1962.
3. GUREL, L.: Personal Communication, 1964.
4. CHALFEN, L.: *J Genet Psychol, 88*:261, 1956.
5. Opinion Research Corporation: The Public Appraises Movies: A Survey for the Motion Picture Association of America, Inc. Princeton, N. J., Opinion Research Corporation, 1957.
6. Outdoor Recreation Resources Review Commission: Participation in Outdoor Recreation: Factors Affecting Demand among American Adults (Report #20). Washington, D. C., Government Printing Office, 1962.
7. Ward, J. A., Inc.: A Nationwide Study of Living Habits: A National Survey Conducted for the Mutual Broadcasting System in 1954. Quoted in De Grazia, S.: Of Time, Work and Leisure. New York, Twentieth Century Fund, 1962.
8. WHITE, R. C.: *Amer J Sociol, 61*:145, 1951.
9. MORRIS, W. E.; GORDON, H. L.; AND ROSENBERG, D.: *Ment Hyg, 49*:172 (April), 1965.
10. MORRIS, W. E., AND JENSEN, M. B.: *Ment Hyg, 45*:77 (January), 1961.
11. National Recreation Association: The Leisure Hours of 5000 People. New York, National Recreation Association, 1934.
12. ANDERSON, N.: Work and Leisure. Glencoe, Free Press, 1961.
13. HODGEN, R. E., AND REIMER, D.: *J Assoc Phys Ment Rehab, 14*:38, 1960.
14. McFARLAND, R. A., AND HUDDELSON, J. H.: *Amer J Psychiat, 93*:567, 1936.
15. RICE, D. C.; ROSENBERG, D.; AND RADZYMINSKI, S. F.: *J Assoc Phys Ment Rehab, 15*:143, 1961.
16. ROSENBERG, D., AND RICE, D. C.: *J Assoc Phys Ment Rehab, 18*:73, 1964.

Chapter 13

SELECTED PHYSIOLOGICAL AND PSYCHOMOTOR CORRELATES OF DEPRESSION IN PSYCHIATRIC PATIENTS*

William P. Morgan

INTRODUCTION

IT HAS BEEN emphasized by a number of investigators [5, 9, 10] that the psychokinetic aspects of psychiatric disorders require that a kineto-therapeutic approach be employed as an adjunct to the psychothera-peutic process. It is thought that a therapeutic approach through motor activities should result in psychological changes. The literature contains a number of investigations which show that motor dysfunction is closely related to the degree of psychopathology. [2, 4, 7, 8, 11, 12, 13, 15, 16] These findings must be treated cautiously, however, because of the uncontrolled factors in most of these studies. For example, researchers in this area have failed to define rigidly the independent variable; that is the nosological contaminants associated with psychiatric diag-nosis were not controlled. Another shortcoming has been the failure to control for the contaminating effects of pharmacologic therapy.

Surveys have indicated that approximately 50 percent of all medical and surgical patients suffer from illnesses that are primarily emotional in nature. [14] More than half of these disturbances are depressive dis-orders. In view of the fact that both physiological and psychomotor disturbances represent the primary symptoms of depression it may be argued intuitively that a causal relationship exists. On the other

* W. P. Morgan. Selected physiological and psychomotor correlates of depres-sion in psychiatric patients. *Res Quart Amer Ass Health Phys Educ, 39*:1037-1043, 1968. Reproduced here with the permission of the author and the American Association for Health, Physical Education, and Recreation. This study was sub-mitted in partial fulfillment of the requirements for the Ed.D. degree at the Uni-versity of Toledo under Wynn F. Updyke. This study was supported in part by a fellowship from the Vocational Rehabilitation Administration.

hand, the physiological and psychomotor disturbances that are reported by the depressed patient may, in fact, not exist. Hence it is necessary that normative data be made available on depressed and nondepressed psychiatric patients in order to prescribe exercise therapies.

PROBLEM

The primary problem of the present investigation was to compare selected physiological and psychomotor variables of depressed and nondepressed psychiatric patients. A secondary problem was a comparison of the fractionated depression (D) scale of the Minnesota Multiphasic Personality Inventory (MMPI) and Zung's Self-Rating Depression Scale (SDS). A further subsidiary problem related to the role of alcoholism in depression as it contributed to selected physiological and psychomotor variables.

PROCEDURES

During the spring of 1966 an exploratory investigation was conducted at the Toledo State Hospital in which (1) the practicality and reliability of a tentative test battery was evaluated, (2) those porions of the battery which did not prove to be appropriate were deleted or modified, and (3) the relationship of selected physiological and psychomotor characteristics to depression was examined.

The main study was conducted during the summer of 1966. Male patients (N = 69) between the ages of twenty and fifty years served as subjects. The mean age was thirty-six, and the standard deviation was 9.61. Patients having a physical disability (i.e. tuberculosis, diabetes, cardiovascular impairment), organic brain disorder, or a history of psychosurgery were not included in this study. Of the patients tested, only two were unable to complete all tests. In both instances these patients began to hallucinate actively during the administration of the various tests.

The entire testing program was handled as a routine admission procedure. All tests were performed within forty-eight hours after admission and prior to the administration of medication, thus eliminating those patients who required immediate drug therapy or who were on medication at the time of admission. All tests were administered between 9:00 and 11:00 a.m. in an examination room on the central admission ward. The temperature in the examining room over the three month period ranged from 73° F to 78° F.

The *independent* variable investigated in this study was depression which was measured by means of both the D scale of the MMPI* [6] and the Self-Rating Depression Scale (SDS).[19] The SDS served as the criterion measure, and the MMPI D Scale was employed to confirm the validity of the SDS as reported by Zung.[20] The MMPI D Scale was administered first and was usually completed in approximately fifteen to twenty minutes. The SDS was administered following the MMPI D Scale, and it was usually completed in about five minutes.

Once the depression scales were completed the subject was tested on the following *dependent* variables: (1) Hoffmann sign; (2) Babinski sign; (3) percent body fat; (4) reaction time; (5) strength of grip; and (6) muscular endurance. In addition, a blood sample was drawn by a lab technician during the same morning but prior to the administration of the tests comprising the dependent and independent variables. Hemoglobin and hematocrit determinations were performed on this sample, these representing the seventh and eighth dependent variables. It should be emphasized that the experimenter performed all tests in a blind setting; that is, he was not aware of the subject's depression rating until after administration of the physiological and psychomotor tests.

When the previously cited testing had been completed each patient was interviewed regarding his use of alcohol and was classified as an alcoholic or as a nonalcoholic. The criterion used to classify the patient as an alcoholic or nonalcoholic was the clinical diagnosis provided by the patient's psychiatrist.

Testing Instruments

The test for the Hoffmann sign was performed, as reported by Chusid and McDonald,[3] by flicking the distal phalanx of the index

---

* Since there is evidence to indicate that item responses obtained to selected items isolated from the context of a personality inventory may not be comparable to those obtained within the context, the results of this research should not be considered applicable to the standardized complete form of the inventory. The Psychological Corporation must be contacted for permission to fractionate the MMPI scales, and the above statement must be included in any reports.

finger. A clawing movement of the finger or adduction of the thumb was regarded as a positive sign.

The test for the Babinski sign was performed by stroking the plantar surface of the foot with the superior surface of the experimenter's flexed thumb. Extension of the large toe with fanning of the small toes upon stimulation of the plantar surface of the foot was regarded as a positive sign.

Percent of body fat was estimated from selected skinfolds which were measured with a Lange skinfold caliper. All measurements were performed on the left side of the body. The technique reported by Sills[18] was employed in this study.

Reaction time was measured with involvement of both small and large muscle groups, respectively. Following a description of the test each subject was given a practice trial followed by two timed trials for both large and small muscle reaction times. The lowest time of the two trials was regarded as the representative score. Time was recorded to the nearest 1/100 second with a Dekan timing device.[1] A paired auditory-visual stimulus (light-buzzer) was presented. The length of time required by the subject to press his thumb against a button, the shaft of which was held in his right hand, was considered as small muscle reaction time (SMRT). The subject then assumed a standing position on a rubber mat with the knees slightly flexed. The stimulus was presented and the subject jumped from the mat (abduction of the legs), which in turn broke the circuit. This measurement was regarded as large muscle reaction time (LMRT).

Strength of grip was measured in pounds with a Narragansett hand dynamometer. The subject was given two trials with each hand. The higher performance for each hand was regarded as the representative score.

The muscular endurance test was performed with the dominant hand on a finger ergometer. The subject assumed a sitting position with the ulnar aspect of his forearm resting on the ergometer pad and the upper arm at a 90° angle with the vertical; that is, the upper arm was parallel to the surface of the table. The ergometer rested on an adjustable table which could be manipulated to the desired height within a few seconds. Each complete pull of the trigger represented approximately .290 foot pounds of work. The trigger was pulled at a

rate of sixty times per minute in rhythm with a metronome which provided both a visual and auditory stimulus. The endurance score was
the length of time the subject could perform the test. Time was
measured to the nearest tenth of a second and rounded off to the
nearest whole second for purposes of recording.

Blood samples were drawn from antecubital veins by a laboratory
technician. The hemoglobin and hematocrit assays were performed
in the pathology laboratory at the Toledo State Hospital. The hemoglobin count was measured in grams per 100 cc by the Cyanmethemo-
globin method, and hematocrit was measured as percentage of red
cells by the micromethod.[17]

ANALYSIS OF DATA

On the basis of their SDS depression scores the sixty-nine subjects
were classified into one of the following groups: (1) depressed
group (N = 25); (2) neutral group (N = 22); and (3) nondepressed group (N = 22). Observation of the data indicated that the
three groups did not differ with respect to incidence of Hoffmann
or Babinski signs; hence these data were not analyzed statistically.
Group differences on the remaining dependent variables were compared by means of a one-way ANOVA. The significance of the differences between means was tested with the Duncan's New Multiple
Range Test (Table 13-I).

The sixty-nine subjects were also classified as either alcoholic (N =
46) or nonalcoholic (N = 23). Observation of the data indicated

TABLE 13-I

F TESTS FOR THE VARIABLES OF THE DEPRESSION GROUPS (N = 69)

Varviables	*Depressed group* (N = 25) Mean	SD	*Neutral group* (N = 22) Mean	SD	*Nondepressed group* (N = 22) Mean	SD	F^a
Age	37.32	10.17	32.64	9.71	37.73	8.33	2.00
Body fat	11.92	5.28	11.64	4.35	11.77	4.26	.02
LMRT	0.43	0.14	0.36	0.10	0.39	0.09	2.36
SMRT	0.28	0.14	0.23	0.14	0.20	0.04	2.66
Grip (R)	109.96	30.74	110.00	16.85	113.36	23.15	.40
Grip (L)	97.64	26.35	102.45	12.23	105.45	20.05	.86
Endurance	99.72	75.49	119.77	85.68	172.27	135.54	3.15
Hemoglobin	14.86	1.11	15.07	1.31	15.44	1.10	1.45
Hematocrit	43.48	3.32	44.09	3.58	44.77	3.49	.82

[a] An F value of 3.13 is required for significance with 2 and 68 degrees of freedom.

TABLE 13-II

INDEPENDENT *t* TESTS FOR THE ALCOHOLIC (N = 46) AND
NONALCOHOLIC (N = 23) GROUPS

Variables	$Mean_{NA}$	$Mean_A$	Diff.	t
Age	33.34	37.26	3.92	1.61
MMPI D	48.21	50.52	2.31	.91
SDS	48.17	48.43	.26	.08
Body fat	12.26	11.54	.72	.61
Reaction time (L.M.)	.43	.37	.06	2.04[a]
Reaction time (S.M.)	.26	.23	.03	1.01
Grip (R)	113.34	108.28	5.06	.81
Grip (L)	103.08	100.95	2.13	.40
Endurance	130.13	128.80	1.33	.05
Hemoglobin	15.06	15.14	.08	.25
Hematocrit	44.21	44.02	.19	.22

[a] Significant at the .05 level.

that the two groups did not differ with respect to incidence of neuro-
logic signs; therefore, these data were not analyzed statistically. The
significance of the differences between means was tested by the *t*-test
for independent means (Table 13-II).

All variables except the Hoffmann and Babinski signs (nominal
data) were intercorrelated for the total group (N = 69) using the
Pearson *r*. The correlation matrix is shown in Table 13-III.

RESULTS

The only dependent variable on which the three depression groups
differed was finger ergometer endurance. The mean scores were 99.72
seconds for the depressed group, 119.77 seconds for the neutral group,
and 172.27 seconds for the nondepressed group. This *F* ratio was
significant at the .05 level and when multiple comparisons were made
with the Duncan's New Multiple Range Test, it was found that the
depressed group had less finger endurance than the nondepressed
group. These two groups did not differ from the neutral group (Table
13-I).

In addition to the depression classification the subjects were also
categorized as alcoholic (N = 46) or nonalcoholic (N = 23) for
the purposes of a separate analysis. The significance of differences
between means for all variables were tested with an independent *t*-test.
The only variable on which the two groups differed was large muscle

TABLE 13-III

CORRELATION MATRIX FOR ALL SUBJECTS (N = 69)

	1	2	3	4	5	6	7	8	9	10
1. Age										
2. MMPI	.16									
3. SDS	.01	.72[a]								
4. Body fat	.15	.16	.01							
5. LMRT	.33[a]	.38[a]	.14	.28[a]						
6. SMRT	.27[a]	.37[a]	.30[a]	.11	.63[a]					
7. Grip (R)	-.05	-.29[a]	-.17	.16	-.17	-.34[a]				
8. Grip (L)	-.01	-.21	-.13	.28[a]	-.11	-.22	.78[a]			
9. Endurance	-.28[a]	-.20	-.27[a]	.01	-.16	-.13	.12	.18		
10. Hemoglobin	-.11	-.09	-.24[a]	.04	-.00	.09	.16	.26[a]	.22	
11. Hematocrit	-.16	-.07	-.21	.07	.04	.04	.20	.22	.24[a]	.96[a]

[a] r = .24 required for significance at the .05 level.

reaction time. The mean scores were .37 second for the alcoholic group and .43 second for the nonalcoholic group; a significant difference which favored the alcoholic group.

The data for all of the subjects were intercorrelated for all variables. The correlation between Zung's Self-Rating Depression Scale and the MMPI D Scale was .72. Additional significant correlations were observed when all variables were intercorrelated for the sixty-nine subjects but these were not sufficiently high to be of practical significance.

DISCUSSION

It was hypothesized that the population means of the three depressive groups were equal. With the exception of finger ergometer endurance this hypothesis was not rejected for all of the dependent variables; it was rejected for the endurance variable, however. Previous research indicating that motor dysfunction was closely related to the degree of psychopathology was generally not substantiated by this investigation. Since the finger ergometer test was capable of discriminating between depressed and nondepressed patients it was tentatively suggested that this particular test was more of a psychological than a physical measure; that is, it probably tapped a psychological factor such as drive. It was concluded that the patient's verbalization of physiological and psychomotor retardation appeared to mirror his affective state rather than his physical competence.

Zung reported a correlation of .70 between the SDS and the D Scale of the MMPI when the complete MMPI was administered. It was hypothesized in the present study that the correlation in the population between Zung's SDS and the MMPI D Scale was zero. The correlation between these two tests was .72 which resulted in a rejection of the hypothesis. Since the correlation between the MMPI D Scale and the SDS ranges from .70 to .72, and since the SDS can be completed in several minutes as opposed to a half-hour to two hours for the MMPI, employment of the SDS rather than the MMPI seems justifiable if the tester is interested in a quantitative assessment of the common clinical view of depression.

The patients were also classified as being either alcoholic or non-alcoholic. It was hypothesized that the population means of these two groups were equal. With the exception of large muscle reaction time (LMRT) this hypothesis was not rejected. This hypothesis was not accepted for LMRT because the alcoholic group was significantly faster than the nonalcoholic group. It is possible that the alcoholic patient was characterized by an elevated "preparedness to react."

REFERENCES

1. Anonymous: *Dekan Timing Device Manual.* Glen Ellyn, Dekan Timing Devices Company, 1966.
2. BAMFORD, DANA, AND SWAN, DONALD W.: A Study to ascertain the effects of thorazine on chronically regressed schizophrenic patients receiving adapted physical education. *J assoc phys ment rehabil, 12*:23-24, 1958.
3. CHUSID, JOSEPH G., AND MCDONALD, JOSEPH J.: *Correlative neuroanatomy and functional neurology.* Los Altos, Lange Medical Publications, 1960.
4. CURETON, THOMAS K., JR.: Improvement of psychological states by means of exercise-fitness programs. *J assoc phys ment rehabil, 17*:14-25, 1963.
5. GREENWOOD, E. D.: Corrective therapy as it relates to the neuropsychiatric patient. *J assoc phys ment rehabil, 4*:26-30, 1950.
6. HATHAWAY, S. R., AND MCKINLEY, J. C.: Scale 2 (Depression). In Welsh, G. S. and Dahlstrom, W. G. (Eds.): *Basic Readings on the MMPI in Psychology and Medicine.* Minneapolis, U of Minnesota, 1956.
7. HODGDON, ROBERT E., AND REIMER, DELILAH: Some muscular strength and endurance scores of psychiatric patients. *J assoc phys ment rehabil, 14*: 38-44, 1960.
8. ————.: Exercise and pulse rate response in psychiatric patients. *J assoc phys ment rehabil, 16*:41-46, 1962.
9. KNUDSON, A. B. C., AND DAVIS, JOHN E.: Medically prescribed exercises for neuropsychiatric patients. *JAMA, 140*:1090-95, 1949.
10. LAYMAN, EMMA M.: *Mental Health Through Physical Education and Recreation.* Minneapolis, Burgess Publishing Co., 1955.
11. ————.: Physical activity as a psychiatric adjunct. In Johnson, Warren R. (Ed.): *Science and Medicine of Exercise and Sports.* New York, Harper, 1960.
12. LINTON, J. M.; HAMELINK, M. H.; AND HOSKINS, R. G.: Cardiovascular system in schizophrenia studied by the Schneider method. *Arch neurol psychiat, 32*:712-22, 1934.
13. MCFARLAND, R. A., AND HUDDELSON, J. H.: Neurocirculatory reactions in the psychoneuroses studied by the Schneider method. *Amer j psychiat, 93*:956-57, 1936.
14. POE, RICHARD O., and Others: Depression: study of 100 cases in a general hospital. *JAMA, 195*:345-50, 1966.
15. RICE, DENNIS C.; ROSENBERG, DAVID; AND RADZYMINSKI, S. F.: Physical fitness of the mentally ill; the effect of hospitalization. *J assoc phys ment rehabil, 15*:143-44, 1961.

16. ROSENBERG, DAVID, AND RICE, DENNIS C.: Physical fitness and psychiatric diagnosis. *J assoc phys ment rehabil, 18*:73-74, 1964.

17. SEIVERD, C. E.: *Hematology for medical technologists.* Philadelphia, Lea and Febiger, 1964.

18. SILLS, FRANK D.: Anthropometry in relation to physical performance. In Johnson, Warren R. (Ed.), *Science and Medicine of Exercise and Sports.* New York, Harper, 1960.

19. ZUNG, WILLIAM W. K.: Self-rating depression scale. *Arch gen psychiat, 12*: 63-70, 1965.

20. ————.: Self-rating depression scale in an outpatient clinic. *Arch gen psychiat, 13*:508-15, 1965.

PART SIX
MOTIVATION

Chapter 14

MOTOR PERFORMANCE UNDER STRESS*

Albert V. Carron

INTRODUCTION

In recent years anxiety (or level of emotionality) as measured by the Taylor manifest anxiety scale[17, 18] has frequently been considered to be one of the factors contributing to the total effective drive level of the organism. In the Hullian-Spence[5, 14] framework, habit strength (sHr) and drive (D) jointly determine response strength (sEr). Thus, whether performance will be facilitated or deterred by high drive will depend upon the relative strengths of the competing response tendencies. In regard to simple tasks, i.e. those tasks with only a small number of habits or competing response tendencies, the implication is clear—the performance level of the high-anxious subjects should be superior to that of the low-anxious subjects by virtue of their higher drive, which theoretically will combine with the simple correct habit. This has been confirmed by Montague,[10] Spence, Farber, and McFann,[15] Spence, Taylor, and Ketchel,[16] Taylor[19] and Taylor and Chapman.[20]

On the other hand, in complex tasks, i.e., those tasks containing a large number of habits or competing response tendencies, it may be expected that the performance of high-anxious subjects will be inferior to that of low-anxious subjects.

While the results of Axelrod, Cowen, and Heilizer[1] and Spence, Taylor, and Ketchel [16] failed to verify this latter prediction, it was confirmed by the findings of Farber and Spence,[4] Korchin and Levine,[6] Lucas,[9] Montague,[10] Ramond,[11] Spence, Farber, and Mc-

* A. V. Carron. Motor performance under stress. *Res Quart Amer Ass Health Phys Educ, 39*:463-469, 1968. Reproduced here with the permission of the author and the American Association for Health, Physical Education, and Recreation. The author is indebted to W. R. Morford for his advice and encouragement.

Fann,[15] and Taylor and Spence.[21] Unfortunately, only two of the above studies were concerned with tasks of a *motor nature* and consequently, the implications of drive theory for large muscle motor tasks are not clear. In what appear to be the only studies concerned with this problem, Ryan [12, 13] observed that although a shock stressor impaired performance in a difficult task when it was introduced early in the learning process,[13] it had no effect on performance when it was introduced late.[12]

PURPOSE

The present study is concerned with the effect of an electric shock stressor upon the performance of high-anxious and low-anxious subjects practicing on a difficult motor task.* The shock stressor was introduced early in practice when the strength of the correct habit would be expected to be approximately the same as that of the incorrect competing response tendencies, and late in practice when the strength of the correct habit should be stronger than that of the competing incorrect tendencies. Thus it was hypothesized that the early stress would have a detrimental effect upon the performance of the high-anxious subjects and would either not effect or would improve the performance of the low-anxious subjects. It was further hypothesized that the late stress would have a facilitative effect upon both groups, but this improvement would be most marked in the high-anxious subjects.

METHOD

Subjects

The 120 subjects (60 high-anxious and 60 low-anxious) were selected from the University of Alberta freshman male population (1,272 students) on the basis of their extreme scores on the Taylor manifest anxiety scale. (A score of 7 or below was designated low-anxious and a score of 21 or above was designated high-anxious.)

---

* While it is virtually impossible to evaluate the number and strength of competing response tendencies present in any motor task, the stabilometer used in the present study satisfied the requirements of the operational definition of difficult since the subjects continued to demonstrate mean performance improvements up to the seventieth (or last) practice trial.

When they arrived to be tested, the subjects were assigned in a fixed order to one of the following three conditions:

(1). *Control.* The twenty high-anxious and twenty low-anxious subjects practiced for two days (35 trials per day) on the stabilometer. They were never exposed to the experimental stress.

(2). *Stress-early.* On trials 4, 5, and 6, the twenty high-anxious and twenty low-anxious subjects were given the electric shock stressor.

(3). *Stress-late.* On trials 65, 66, and 67, the twenty high-anxious and twenty low-anxious subjects were given the electric shock stressor.

Apparatus

The task consisted of balancing on a stabilometer. The range of motion of the platform was $\pm\ 20°$ from the horizontal. Motion of the board over this arc was measured in electrical *movement units* with 1° of movement scored as one movement unit. All subjects were given seventy twenty-second trials over a two-day period (35 trials per day). The rest interval between trials was twenty to thirty seconds.

A model 250 constant current electronic stimulator was used to administer the shock stressor. The stimulus was applied through finger electrodes fastened to the right index finger.

Experimental Design

On the first day, the control and stress-late subjects were given thirty-five twenty-second trials. The stress-early subjects were given three practice trials and then, before trial 4, it was explained that they would receive either 0, 1, 2, or 3 electric shocks per trial for three trials. It was emphasized that these shocks were unavoidable and were in no way related to performance. Although the subjects were given the option of dropping out of the experiment at this point only three chose to do so. After trial 6, the electrodes were removed and the stress-early subjects then practiced under control conditions.

On the second day, the stress-early and control subjects were given thirty-five twenty-second trials under normal (control) conditions. The stress-late subjects were given twenty-nine trials and then, prior to trial 65, the shock stressor was introduced. After the stress period of three trials, the stress-late subjects were given the remaining three trials under control conditions.

RESULTS

Stress-Early

The results obtained when a variance analysis was used for the data from the prestress, stress, and poststress periods (an average of three trials was used to represent each period) are presented in Table 14-I. Although there were no differences in the performance levels of the six groups in the prestress period, in the stress period there were differences between the high-anxious and low-anxious subjects ($F = 6.55$, $p < .05$) as well as between the two stress-early experimental groups and the other four groups ($F = 4.26$, $p < .05$). However, when the ordered means from this latter variance analysis were subjected to the Duncan multiple range test, only the high-anxious stress-early group was inferior in performance level to the other groups.

TABLE 14-I

EARLY STRESS: VARIANCE ANALYSIS OF THE PERFORMANCE
LEVEL SCORES FOR THE PRESTRESS PERIOD, STRESS PERIOD,
AND POSTSTRESS PERIOD

Source of Variance	df	Prestress Period MS	F^a	Stress Period MS	F^a	Poststress Period MS	F^a
Anxiety level	1	9893.50	1.45	35845.62	4.89	21176.29	3.39
Experimental condition	2	983.61	0.15	23339.57	3.18	10964.81	1.71
AL x EC	2	11652.70	1.71	1418.49	0.19	5961.01	0.93
Error	114	6802.00		7335.49		6418.85	

[a] For df 1,114; 2, 114; F must exceed 3.92 and 3.07 respectively for significance at the .05 level.

In the immediate poststress period (trials 7 to 9) there were no differences in the performance levels of the six groups. That is, once the shock stressor was removed, the differences between the two stress-early groups and the other four groups seem to have been erased.

Another way of analyzing the effect of the shock stress upon performance involves studying the amount of change from period to period, i.e. from the prestress to the stress, and from the stress to the poststress. This resulting score is designated the delta, or difference score.

The results from an analysis of variance of the delta scores for the changes from the prestress to the stress period are presented in Table 14-II. The significant experimental conditions effect ($F = 5.004$, $p < .05$) indicates that the improvement of the stress-early groups during the stress period was less than that shown by the other four groups. When these results were subjected to a Duncan multiple range test, the amount of improvement of the high-anxious stress-early group was found to be significantly inferior to that of all other groups (except low-anxious stress-early, with this difference just failing to reach significance) while the low-anxious stress-early group did not differ from any other group in amount of improvement during the stress-early period.

TABLE 14-II

EARLY STRESS: VARIANCE ANALYSIS OF THE CHANGES IN PERFORMANCE (AS EXPRESSED BY A DELTA SCORE) FROM THE PRESTRESS PERIOD TO THE STRESS PERIOD AND FROM THE STRESS PERIOD TO THE POSTSTRESS PERIOD

Source of Variance	df	Prestress to Stress MS	F[a]	Stress to Poststress MS	F[a]
Anxiety level	1	6386.04	2.37	1806.52	1.30
Experimental condition	2	13569.45	5.04	2753.49	1.98
AL x EC	2	4692.72	1.74	1931.98	1.40
Error	114	2690.14		1388.49	

[a] For df 1,114; 2,114; F must exceed 3.92 and 3.07 respectively for significance at the .05 level.

The high-anxious stress-early and low-anxious stress-early groups did not differ from the other four groups in amount of improvement from the stress period to the poststress period (Table 14-II). It would seem, therefore, that while the shock stressor had a depressant effect upon the amount of improvement shown by the high-anxious group during the stress period, this effect did not persist once the electric shock threat was removed.

Stress-Late

As the analysis of variance reported in Table 14-III indicates, there were significant differences between the performance levels of the high-anxious and low-anxious subjects in the prestress, stress, and poststress periods but there was no *experimental condition* effect during these periods. However, studying the performance level alone is not adequate since both the high-anxious stress-late and the low-anxious stress-late did show a marked decrement in performance level during the stress period. This is not reflected by the variance analysis of performance levels because the low-anxious stress-late group was superior to all other groups prior to the introduction of the shock stressor. Thus, the performance decrement during the stress period resulted in their achieving approximately the same performance level as the other groups.

TABLE 14-III

LATE STRESS: VARIANCE ANALYSIS OF THE PERFORMANCE LEVEL SCORES FOR THE PRESTRESS PERIOD, STRESS PERIOD, AND POSTSTRESS PERIOD

Source of Variance	df	Prestress Period		Stress Period		Poststress Period	
		MS	F^a	MS	F^a	MS	F^a
Anxiety level	1	12038.03	7.23	11507.17	6.02	9194.50	5.72
Experimental condition	2	7.49	0.00	3036.01	1.59	780.30	0.49
AL x EC	2	154.26	0.09	1749.95	0.92	1244.14	0.77
Error	114	1665.87		1912.15		1608.37	

[a] For df 1,114; 2,114; F must exceed 3.92 and 3.07 respectively for significance at the .05 level.

The more meaningful analysis of the changes in performance resulting from the electric shock stressor was provided by the delta-score technique (see Table 14-IV). The two stress-late groups exhibited a change in performance from the prestress to the stress period that was significantly ($F = 9.45$, $p < .01$) inferior to that of the other four groups while the low-anxious stress-late group differed from the two stress-early groups only.

TABLE 14-IV

LATE STRESS: VARIANCE ANALYSIS OF THE CHANGES IN PERFORMANCE (AS EXPRESSED BY A DELTA SCORE) FROM THE PRESTRESS PERIOD TO THE STRESS PERIOD AND FROM THE STRESS PERIOD TO THE POSTSTRESS PERIOD

Source of Variance	df	Prestress to Stress		Stress to poststress	
		MS	F^a	MS	F^a
Anxiety level	1	1.99	0.00	85.34	0.22
Experimental condition	2	3287.77	9.45	6617.86	17.01
AL x EC	2	140.57	0.40	67.09	0.17
Error	114	347.97		389.07	

[a] For df 1,114; 2, 114; F must exceed 3.92 and 3.07 respectively for significance at the .05 level.

In the poststress period, the two stress-late groups showed a significant improvement in performance ($F = 17.01$, $p < .01$). A Duncan analysis indicated that both the high-anxious stress-late and the low-anxious stress-late groups improved significantly more ($p < .05$) than any of the other groups for this period.

DISCUSSION

According to Ryan,[12] two important factors which help to determine the effect that stress will have upon performance are the difficulty of the task and the proficiency of the individual when the stress is introduced. In the Hullian framework where the difficulty of the task is related to the number and strengths of the competing response tendencies present, it may be expected that when stress is introduced early in a difficult task, it will have a detrimental effect upon performance, while stress introduced late may be expected to be beneficial to performance. However, the anxiety level factor (with the underlying assumption that manifest anxiety scale scores reflect emotional responsiveness, which in turn reflects drive level) complicates this picture. The available literature in which stress was used on manifest anxiety scale subjects[2, 7, 8, 19] indicated that both levels of anxiety were affected in the same direction and to the same degree by stress. In the single exception, Deese, Lazarus, and Keenan[4] found that while the differences between high-anxious and low-anxious subjects increased under shock stress, this was due primarily to the disruptive effect of the shock on the low-anxious subjects.

In the present study, the results for the stress-late period were in the opposite direction expected—the stress was detrimental to performance.

In the stress-early period, the results closely approach theoretical expectations: namely, the stress was detrimental to the performance of the high-anxious subjects while the low-anxious subjects were essentially unaffected.

Some possible explanations for this failure to meet theoretical expectations for the stress-late period are as follows: First, sufficient practice might not have been given before the stressor was introduced. Thus, although the habit strength of the correct response tendency was probably stronger relative to the strengths of the incorrect response tendencies, the latter might not have been sufficiently reduced in the response hierarchy with regard to their excitatory potential (E) to ensure that they would not appear. The increase in drive level (by virtue of the shock stressor) would then have been sufficient to bring the incorrect tendencies over the minimum threshold level (L) necessary to make their probability of occurrence possible.

The second possibility which arises relates to the nature of the stressor. Since the shock was unavoidably introduced, the subject could do nothing to prevent its administration. It was nondirective and unrelated to performance, and consequently, rather than contribute to drive level, the shock may have been distractive and a detriment to the effective drive level. Thus, it is possible that had the subject been informed that he could avoid the electric shock by showing an improvement in performance, a facilitative effect might have resulted. The weakness of this explanation is its inability to explain the differences between the high-anxious and low-anxious subjects in magnitude of reaction to the early stress.

CONCLUSIONS

Within the limitations of the present study, the following conclusions appear justified:

(1) Stress, introduced early, had a differential effect upon the improvements in performance of the high-anxious and low-anxious subjects. The low-anxious stress-early group was not affected by stress, but the performance improvement of the high-anxious stress-early group was significantly inferior to that of all other groups during the stress period.

(2) During the stress-early period, the level of performance of the low-anxious stress-early group did not differ from any other group, while the level of performance of the high-anxious stress-early group was significantly inferior to that of the low-anxious control and stress-late groups.

(3) Stress, introduced late, resulted in a significant decrement in amount of performance improvement for both high-anxious and low-anxious subjects. Upon removal of the shock stressor, both the high-anxious and low-anxious subjects significantly improved in performance, thereby achieving their prestress levels of performance.

REFERENCES

1. Axelrod, H. S.; Cowen, E. L.; and Heilizer, F.: The correlates of manifest anxiety in stylus maze learning. *J exp psychol, 51*:131-38, 1956.
2. Davidson, W. Z.; Andrews, T. G.; and Ross, S.: Effects of stress and anxiety on continuous high speed color naming. *J exp psychol, 52*:13-17, 1956.
3. Deese, J.; Lazarus, R. S.; and Keenan, J.: Anxiety, anxiety reduction, and stress in learning. *J exp psychol, 46*:55-60, 1953.
4. Farber, I. E., and Spence, D. W.: Complex learning and conditioning as a function of anxiety. *J exp psychol, 45*:120-25, 1953.
5. Hull, C. L.: *Principles of Behavior.* New York, D. Appleton-Century, 1943.
6. Korchin, S. J., and Levine, S.: Anxiety and verbal learning. *J abnorm soc psychol, 54-55*:234-40, 1957.
7. Lazarus, R.; Deese, J.; and Hamilton, R.: Anxiety and stress in learning: The role of intraserial duplication. *J exp psychol, 47*:101-14, 1954.
8. Lee, L. C.: The effects of anxiety level and shock on a paired-associates verbal task. *J Exp Psychol, 61*:213-17, 1961.
9. Lucas, J. D.: The interactive effects of anxiety, failure and intraserial duplication. *Amer J Psychol, 65*:59-66, 1952.
10. Montague, E. K.: The role of anxiety in serial rote learning. *J Exp Psychol, 45*:91-96, 1953.
11. Ramond, C. K.: Anxiety and task as determiners of verbal performance. *J Exp Psychol, 46*:120-24, 1953.
12. Ryan, D. E.: Motor performance under stress as a function of the amount of practice. *Percept Motor Skills, 13*:103-106, 1961.
13. Ryan, D. E.: Effects of stress on motor performance and learning. *Res Quart Amer Ass Health Phys Educ, 33*:111-19, 1962.
14. Spence, K. W.: Theoretical interpretations of learning. In Stevens, S. S. (Ed.), *Handbook of Experimental Psychology.* New York, Wiley, 1951.
15. Spence, K. W.; Farber, I. E.; and McFann, H. H.: The relation of anxiety (drive) level to performance in competitional and noncompetitional paired-associates learning. *J Exp Psychol, 52*:296-305, 1956.
16. Spence, K. W.; Taylor, J.; and Ketchel, R.: Anxiety (drive) level and degree of competition in paired-associates learning. *J Exp Psychol, 52*:306-10, 1956.
17. Taylor, J. A.: A personality scale of manifest anxiety. *J Abnorm Soc Psychol, 48*:285-90, 1953.
18. Taylor, J. A.: Drive theory and manifest anxiety. *Psych Bull, 53*:303-20, 1956.
19. Taylor, J. A.: The effects of anxiety level and psychological stress on verbal learning. *J Abnorm Soc Psychol, 55-56*:55-60, 1963.

20. TAYLOR, J. A., and CHAPMAN, J. P.: Paired-associates learning as related to anxiety. *Amer J Psychol, 68*:671, 1955.
21. TAYLOR, J. A., and SPENCE, K. W.: The relation of anxiety level to performance in serial learning. *J Exp Psychol, 45*:61-64, 1952.

Chapter 15

EFFECT OF DIFFERENTIAL MOTIVE-INCENTIVE CONDITIONS ON PHYSICAL PERFORMANCE*

E. Dean Ryan

INTRODUCTION

THE FACT has been well established that certain motive-incentive conditions have a marked influence on learning and performance of verbal material.[2, 5] While attempts to manipulate the level of motivation in performers of physical skills through special incentives have been common, research as to the effects of those incentives has been limited. Further, those studies that do exist are contradictory to the extent that some show improvement under motive-incentive conditions and others show no effect.

REVIEW OF LITERATURE

Ulrich and Burke[7] tested a group of eighteen subjects on a bicycle ergometer under two varieties of motivational stress. All subjects received three trials. On the first trial, subjects were told to pedal for one minute, doing as well as possible. Scores were reported at thirty and forty-five seconds. On the second and third trials subjects were again asked to do as well as possible, equaling or improving on the first trial. They were instructed that a bell would ring periodically if their performance improved, but if their performance was below the previous standard a buzzer would ring. Unknown to subjects, it was determined prior to testing whether the buzzer or bell would ring during the trials, regardless of performance. All groups heard the bell

---

* E. D. Ryan. Effect of differential motive-incentive conditions on physical performance. *Res Quart Amer Ass Health Phys Educ, 32*: 1961, 83-87. Reproduced here with the permission of the author and the American Association for Health, Physical Education, and Recreation.

[153]

on one trial and the buzzer on the other. Results indicated no difference in total work output between the two motivating conditions, although both of these conditions were significantly better than the initial trial.

Fleishman,[1] after giving 400 subjects preliminary training on a rudder control test (maneuvering a type of Link trainer in response to visual signals), divided the subjects into two groups, giving one a variety of motive-incentive instructions and the other no instructions or encouragement after the preliminary test. The performance of the motivated group was significantly better than that of the control group. When the groups were divided into best and poorest performers on the basis of test scores, there was no significant difference between the performers of the poorest half of the control group and the poorest half of the experimental group. The best performers in the motivation group, however, had significantly better test scores than the best performers in the control group.

Noble,[6] using 400 subjects, gave a preliminary practice period on a two-handed coordination test (tracking). At varying periods of practice, experimental groups were informed of their average score and were told that they must improve if they were to pass. The author concluded that the incentive-motive conditions did not affect performance.

Johnson[3] had fifty-nine junior high school boys, with instructions to do as well as possible, pedal a bicycle ergometer against a fixed resistance of five pounds. The subjects were given eight thirty-second trials, with a thirty-second rest between each trial. Each subject had two tests, one with continuous verbal encouragement, the other with no encouragement. There was no significant difference between performance under the two conditions.

PROBLEM INVESTIGATED

A review of the literature reveals little as to the effect of various types of incentives on physical performance. Therefore the purpose of this experiment was to determine the relative effect of four different motive-incentive conditions on a simple task that required neither endurance nor skill. In addition the effect of the motive-incentive conditions at varying levels of performance was investigated. The specific task studied was grip strength as measured by a hand dyna-mometer.

METHODOLOGY

Eighty male university students participated in the experiment. All were volunteers, obtained from voluntary physical education classes. No particular systematic method of selection was used. All subjects, using only the right hand, were given a preliminary test of grip strength, consisting of three trials with a hand dynamometer. They were told that this was a test to determine their grip strength. Special emphasis was placed on the fact that maximum effort was essential. Results were not shown to the performers.

A second test was administered seven days later and the subjects were told that this test would determine, among other things, the reliability of grip strength. The same general procedures used in the first test were followed with one exception. On the second test each subject received one of four different motive-incentive conditions. Group 1, the control group, was given the same instructions as on the first test, being told to squeeze as hard as possible and to make a maximum effort on each trial. Group 2, the verbal group, was told to try to improve on their first score (they had no knowledge of initial scores), and as they performed were verbally encouraged to improve with such statements as "harder, harder, much harder." Group 3, the knowledge of results group, knew their initial scores, were allowed to watch the dynamometer scoring dial, and were told to make every effort to improve on the initial score. Group 4, the shock group, had an electrode attached to the left wrist, were informed of initial scores, and were told that failure to improve on each trial would result in receipt of a severe electric shock.

APPARATUS

To provide the electric shock a transformer increased the 120-volt supply to 350 volts and insulated the power line and its ground for safety reasons. Sufficient resistance was placed in the circuit to limit the electrode current to 4.4 milliamps per square centimeter of contact area. The electrodes were nine by eleven millimeters in size, separated by seven and one-half millimeters distance from edge to edge, mounted in a small plastic strip and held on the wrist by an elastic strap.*

A Lafayette hand dynamometer was used to measure grip strength. Although the dial of the dynamometer was marked in kilograms, it was necessary to multiply obtained scores by 0.88 and add 15.5 to obtain true kilograms. In this study, however, all scores reported were taken directly from the dial without conversion.

RESULTS AND DISCUSSION

In designing the experiment the author reasoned that differences in performance between subjects on the initial test might be attributed to varying levels of motivation, with higher levels of motivation resulting in superior scores. If this hypothesis were true, added incentive would be expected to produce greater gains in the lower scoring subjects.

Therefore, this experiment was designed to provide a test to determine whether or not the four types of incentives had the same relative effect at all levels of strength, and at the same time provide a test of the null hypothesis that there were no differences between the four types of motive-incentive conditions.

Subjects were arranged on the basis of their initial strength test, from strongest to weakest, and were divided into four levels of strength, with the strongest twenty assigned to the superior group, the next twenty to the good group, the third twenty to the fair group, and the weakest twenty to the poor group. Within each of the four levels the subjects were randomly assigned to one of the four motive-incentive groups, twenty per group. Thus all groups were matched with reference to the initial strength score.

The results of a simple variance analysis on initial strength measures, shown in Table 15-I, indicate no differences between the four groups ($F = 0.02$) prior to the application of the motive-incentive conditions. The reliability of the test-retest on the initial strength measures was .88.

Mean scores for the four motive-incentive conditions are shown in Table 15-II. While three of the four groups appear to be equal,

* See description of apparatus used by F. M. Henry in the article "Increase in Speed of Movement by Motivation and by Transfer of Motivated Improvement" which appeared in the May, 1951 *Res Quart Amer Ass Health Phys Educ.*

TABLE 15-I

ANALYSIS OF VARIANCE FOR INITIAL STRENGTH SCORES

Source of Variance	SS	DF	MS	F
Between	42.28	3	14.09	0.02
Within	89,337.96	96	930.60	
Total	89,380.24	99		

TABLE 15-II

MEAN SCORES FOR THE FOUR MOTIVE-INCENTIVE GROUPS[a]

(Groups X Levels)

	Knowledge	Verbal	Control	Shock
Superior	184.0	179.4	188.8	191.4
Good	154.8	153.4	145.2	163.8
Fair	130.8	151.6	143.8	157.0
Poor	129.0	134.8	130.4	146.6

[a] Scores are the sum of three trials on the dynamometer.

TABLE 15-III

ANALYSIS OF VARIANCE FOR MOTIVE-INCENTIVE GROUPS

Source of Variance	SS	DF	MS	F
Groups	2,621.9	3	873.9	2.34[a]
Levels	28,632.4	3	9,544.1	———
(Cells)	(32,824.0)	(15)		———
Groups X Levels	1,569.7	9	174.4	0.47[b]
Within	23,872.8	64	373.0	———
Total	56,696.8	79		

[a] F = 2.75 for significance at the 5 percent level.
[b] F = 2.02 for significance at the 5 percent level.

scores for the shock group are considerably higher. Results of the analysis of variance, shown in Table 15-III, however, indicate that the differences between groups are not significant ($F = 2.34$, with $F = 2.75$ required for significance at the 5% level.)

When strength scores are broken into groups by levels (Table 15-II) the mean scores for the superior group are quite similar. At the lower three levels both the shock group and the verbal group appear to have higher mean scores than the control group. These observed differences are not significant, however, with $F = 0.46$ for the interaction of groups by levels. (For significance at the 5% level, F had to equal 2.02.)

On the basis of studies done in other areas an assumption could be made that threat of electric shock, verbal encouragement, and knowledge of results would improve performance. The results of this experiment indicate, however, that on a simple task that requires neither endurance nor skill, there appears to be no difference in performance under the various motive-incentive conditions.

The apparent contradiction of Fleischman's study[1] can be explained. His primary objective was to design an experiment to obtain improvement. He selected a task that seemed most susceptible to the experimental treatment and loaded the experimental instructions. In the discussion of results, Fleischman states that while the differences were statistically significant, they were not large and should be interpreted with caution. Further he did not compare different types of motive-incentive conditions but utilized several motive-incentive conditions simultaneously in the experimental group. Ulrich and Burke found no differences in performance between the two types of motivational stress, which is in agreement with the present study.

The explanation for differences between performance on a physical task of this nature and performance on verbal material may be due to the nature of the physical test itself. Subjects in physical performance tests appear to be highly motivated, expressing a keen interest in their performance and the performance of others. It seems probable that the nature of simple tests of physical performance provides sufficient incentive to elicit maximal performance without additional motivation.

SUMMARY AND CONCLUSIONS

It was the purpose of this experiment to determine the effects of four types of motive-incentive conditions on grip strength. Eighty male subjects were divided into four subgroups, all groups being matched on the basis of a preliminary grip test. Group 1 was simply told to do as well as possible on the retest, group 2 was verbally exhorted to improve, group 3 was given the results of the previous test and was allowed to watch the dynamometer dial on the retest, and group 4 was threatened with electric shock for failure to improve.

There were no differences in performance between the four motive-incentive conditions, and no differences in performance between groups at the various performance levels. These results have practical implications for measurement programs in physical education. In the past, very little attention has been directed to the control of motivation when testing strength. This study suggests that as long as an effort is made to have subjects understand the importance of giving a maximum effort, no additional incentive is necessary. Further, additional incentive, if given, should not bias results.

REFERENCES

1. FLEISCHMAN, E. A.: A relationship between incentive motivation and ability level in psychomotor performance. *J Exp Psychol, 56*:78-81; July 1958.
2. HOVELAND, C. L.: Human learning and retention. *Handbook of Experimental Psychology.* Stevens, S. S. (Ed.), New York: Wiley, 1951.
3. JOHNSON, BIRGER: Influence of puberal development on responses to motivated exercise. *Res Quart Amer Ass Health Phys Educ, 27*:182-93; May 1956.
4. LINDQUIST, E. F.: *Design and Analysis of Experiments in Psychology and Education.* San Francisco, Houghton Mifflin Co., 1953.
5. McGEOCH, S. A., and IRION, A. Z.: *The Psychology of Human Learning.* New York, Longmans, Green and Co., 1952.
6. NOBLE, C. E.: An attempt to manipulate incentive-motivation in a continuous tracking task. *Percept Motor Skills, 5*:65-69, June 1955.
7. ULRICH, CELESTE, and BURKE, ROGER K.: Effect of motivational stress upon physical performance. *Res Quart Amer Ass Health Phys Educ, 28*:403-12; December 1957.

Chapter 16

INFLUENCE OF MOTIVATION ON PHYSICAL WORK CAPACITY AND PERFORMANCE*

JACK H. WILMORE

INTRODUCTION

IT HAS BEEN KNOWN for a number of years that the so-called maximum strength and endurance of an individual can be altered simply by changing the physical or psychological environment in which that individual performs. A number of unique examples have been cited in the popular as well as the scientific literature, where individuals placed quite by chance in situations of extreme stress have performed superhuman feats of strength. Likewise, carefully controlled scientific investigations have suggested that either or both strength and endurance capacities can be exceeded when their subjects were subjected to drugs,[1, 10, 12] hypnosis[10, 11, 16] or various forms of motivation.[9, 10]

In the majority of the above cases, it was hypothesized that the psychological barriers which normally establish limits to one's ultimate capacity are broken down, thus allowing the individual to surpass that level previously designated as his physical capacity. Although this hypothesis appears tenable, very little is known about the subsequent alterations in the various physiological parameters which accompany and possibly facilitate these increases in performance to supramaximal [†] levels. It has yet to be determined whether these increased performances, in specific reference to endurance activities, result from an

* J. H. Wilmore. Influence of motivation on physical work capacity and performance. *J Appl Physiol, 24*: 1968, 459-463. Reproduced here with the permission of the author and The American Physiological Society. This study was supported in part by a University of California faculty research grant.

† The term supramaximal performance is defined as a performance, illicited within either or both an altered physical or psychological environment, which exceeds limits or levels previously defined as maximal.

increased tolerance to withstand the greater degree of anaerobic metabolism, i.e. increasing lactate levels, or whether there is a further increase in the provision of blood and thus oxygen to the active tissues, i.e. an increasing oxygen intake above the assumed maximal value.

If supramaximal endurance performances are solely attributable to the ability to exceed psychological barriers or limitations, i.e. an increased tolerance to anaerobic metabolism, then it is hypothesized that there would be no significant concomitant alterations in the maximal oxygen intake as defined during normal maximal performances. Thus, the purpose of this study was to test the above hypothesis by determining $\dot{V}_{O_2 max}$ and the related cardiorespiratory responses to maximal exercise, under conditions requiring both maximal and supramaximal performances.

EXPERIMENTAL DESIGN

The initial sample consisted of thirty normal and healthy male volunteers who were all undergraduate students at the University of California, Berkeley. Eight of these subjects failed to complete all phases of the experiment and were thus omitted from the statistical analyses of the resulting data. The physical characteristics of the twenty-two subjects are presented in Table 16-I.

TABLE 16-I
PHYSICAL CHARACTERISTICS OF SUBJECTS

	Mean	Standard Deviation	Range
Age, years	22.3	3.54	18.2-30.5
Height, cm	178.34	6.76	163.9-194.6
Weight, kg	77.25	10.19	61.63-98.51
Lean body weight,* kg	69.70	9.19	53.54-95.46
Percent body fat*	9.32	7.13	0.00-24.86

* These values were obtained by the densitometric technique[6] using the formula developed by Rathbun and Pace.[14]
* This is the result of a specific gravity value in excess of 1.100.

Each subject performed three work-capacity tests on a bicycle ergometer under two identical control conditions (C_1 and C_2) and under one experimental condition (E). These tests were separated from one another by no less than one week and no more than three weeks. The experimental condition (E) required an environment conducive to a supramaximal performance. It was felt that this could best be accomplished through motivation by placing the subject in a competitive situation. To obtain this situation, all of the subjects participating in this study were paired according to the amount of work they performed (kilopond-meters) in C_1. Thus, under condition E, two subjects matched by their initial (C_1) work outputs, performed their work-capacity tests simultaneously (Fig. 16-1), each attempting to outperform the other. In addition to this competition between individuals, each subject was informed of the duration of his initial performance and was told to observe a timer (used only in test E), in an attempt to exceed his previous effort. It was felt that either one or both of these competitive situations would insure the desired results of an increased or supramaximal performance, although it is conceded that competition can negatively influence performance in certain individuals.

The procedures were the same for all three tests except for the

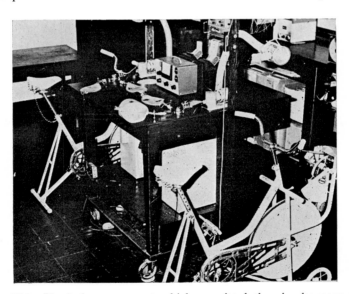

FIGURE 16-1. Physical arrangement which permitted the simultaneous testing of endurance capacity of two paired subjects under condition E. It should be noted that the subjects were placed side by side, each having an independent but identical system for monitoring and collecting expired air and each having an unhindered view of the timer which indicated the duration of the test.

experimentally induced motivation under condition E. Each subject was first tested under condition C_1, since the primary purpose of this test condition was to obtain the initial work outputs used for matching the paired subjects under condition E. The major hypothesis of this study was to be tested by comparing only condition C_2 with condition E. Thus, to theoretically balance out the influence of any extraneous factors on this comparison which might result from all subjects performing under these two conditions in the same order, i.e. training or learning effect, the influence of E on C_2, the subjects were divided into two subgroups. The first subgroup (n = 12) performed the three tests in the sequence, C_1-E-C_2, and the second subgroup (n = 10) performed in the sequence C_1-C_2-E.

All work-capacity tests were performed on friction-type, mechanically braked bicycle ergometers. A pedaling rate of sixty rpm was established for the entire test and the subjects were able to maintain this rate throughout all but the last few minutes of the exercise. The actual rate per minute and the total number of revolutions for each test were recorded by a microswitch and a battery-operated counter, thereby enabling an accurate calculation of the amount of work performed (kilopond meters) during the test. The friction load was set at a level of 12 kpm (720 kpm of work per minute) for the first five minutes of the exercise, and then immediately increased and maintained at a level of twenty-seven kpm (1620 kpm of work per minute) for the remainder of the test. Each test was terminated when the subject was no longer able to turn the pedals. The total riding time during the heavy work load (27 kpm), in addition to the total work output during the heavy work load, were used as the criteria for endurance capacity.

Heart rates were interpreted from both electrocardiograms and a Parks Electronics Laboratory heart rate monitor, model 503, during a five-minute preexercise resting period and at one-minute intervals during the exercise. The subjects' expired air was passed through a Collins triple J mouthpiece into a Parkinson-Cowan low-resistance, high-velocity gas meter. Aliquots of this expired air, representing one-minute samples, were collected during the preexercise rest period, during the first and fifth minute of the submaximal exercise (12-kpm work load), and continuously during the maximal exercise (27-kpm work load). These aliquots were analyzed immediately by means of a Beckman, model E2, oxygen analyzer and a Godart Pulmo-Analysor (CO_2). These two analyzers were calibrated at the beginning and end of each test with commercially prepared gas cylinders whose contents approximated the percentage range of respiratory gas mixtures. The cylinders were periodically reanalyzed by means of a Scholander microgas analyzer.

In those tests where the subjects rode in pairs, a complete duplicate set of equipment was provided in order not to place either of the subjects at a disadvantage. Thus, such factors as the type of bicycle, type of mouthpiece, airway resistance, aliquot-sampling system, etc., were identical for each subject for each of his three tests (see Fig. 16-1).

In addition to the above measurements, each subject underwent a densitometric determination of lean body weight and percent body fat [6] using the formula of Rathbun and Pace.[14] Although these determinations were peripheral to the problem under investigation, it was felt that they would be of general interest not only in further describing the characteristics of the subjects, but also as a reference for oxygen-intake values.

RESULTS

The means and standard deviations for the total work output (kilopond meters) and duration of maximal effort (riding time) are presented in Table 16-II. While the mean work output and riding time were significantly greater under condition E than under either condition C_1 (19 and 38%, respectively) or condition C_2 (10 and 21%, respectively), there was also a difference noted in the mean riding time between condition C_1 and C_2 which just attained significance at the 0.05 level. Therefore, the data were organized and analyzed not only by the condition of testing, i.e. C_1 and C_2 and E, but also by the order of testing, i.e. *day 1, day 2,* and *day 3,* in order to further evaluate the extent of the suggested training or learning effect (Table 16-II).

A significant training or learning effect is indicated in Table 16-II between the first and second day of testing. Thus, the mean maximal physiological responses to the work capacity test were likewise analyzed

TABLE 16-II

MEAN WORK OUTPUTS AND RIDING TIMES FOR HEAVY (27 KPM) WORK LOAD WITH DATA GROUPED BY ORDER AND CONDITION OF TESTING

	Work Output, kpm	Riding Time, sec
Condition of testing		
C_1	8,760±3,187	332±160
E	11,136±4,199	457±233
C_2	9,798±3,484	379±180
t ratios		
C_1-E	5.35*	4.56*
C_1-C_2	1.93	2.28*
E-C_2	3.31*	3.25*
Order of testing		
Day 1	8,760±3,187	332±160
Day 2	10,246±3,271	404±169
Day 3	10,688±4,415	432±246
t ratios		
Day 1-day 2	2.99*	3.46*
Day 1-day 3	3.67*	3.41*
Day 2-day 3	0.90	0.97

Values are means ± standard deviations.
* A ratio of 2.045 was needed for significance at the 0.05 level (two-tailed test, df = 21).

according to both the condition and order of testing (Table 16-III). It is obvious that the increased performance resulting from condition E was not accompanied by any statistically significant alterations in the maximal physiological responses. Similarly, the observed training or learning effect did not result from, nor did it alter, these maximal physiological responses. Of the small differences noted for each variable between each of the three conditions or orders of testing, only the maximal heart rate exhibited significant differences between any two tests.

To further define the variability of any one parameter under the three separate test conditions and between *days 1 through 3*, a matrix of zero-order intravariable correlations was computed. The coefficients for both work output and riding time ranged between $r = 0.85$ and $r = 0.95$, for $Vo_{2 \, max}$ they ranged between $r = 0.82$ and $r = 0.92$, for maximum heart rate they ranged between $r = 0.79$ and $r = 0.89$, and for ventilation they ranged between $r = 0.48$ and $r = 0.71$. These coefficients were all significant at the 0.05 level.

The continuous monitoring of the physiological responses at one-minute intervals during each test was of little value in relation to

TABLE 16-III

MEAN MAXIMAL PHYSIOLOGICAL RESPONSES TO WORK-CAPACITY TEST WITH DATA
GROUPED BY ORDER AND CONDITION OF TESTING

	Ventilation BTPS, liters/min	Oxygen Intake STPD			Heart Rate, beats/min	Oxygen Pulse, ml/beat
		ml/min	ml/kg per min	ml/LBW per min		
Condition of testing						
C_1	145.8±20.2	3756±542	48.8±5.1	54.0±4.9	189.6±11.5	20.71±2.86
E	149.6±22.4	3813±447	49.5±3.9	54.9±4.4	187.2±10.5	21.18±2.95
C_2	151.8±19.6	3820±442	49.7±5.0	55.0±4.2	187.2±9.4	22.29±2.38
t ratios						
C_1-E	0.80	1.16	1.29	1.43	2.18*	1.219
C_1-C_2	1.83	0.95	1.02	1.09	1.55	1.376
E-C_2	0.59	0.14	0.15	0.11	0.00	0.279
Order of testing						
Day 1	145.8±20.2	3756±542	48.8±5.1	54.0±4.9	189.6±11.5	20.71±2.86
Day 2	152.7±23.4	3792±438	49.3±4.2	54.6±4.6	187.1±9.7	21.24±2.51
Day 3	148.8±18.1	3840±449	50.0±4.7	55.3±3.9	187.3±10.3	21.23±2.84
t ratios						
Day 1-day 2	1.77	0.57	0.59	0.78	2.16*	1.202
Day 1-day 3	0.71	1.58	1.80	1.82	1.52	1.293
Day 2-day 3	1.07	0.02	1.07	0.66	0.15	0.055

Values represent means ± standard deviations.
* A ratio of 2.045 was needed for significance to the 0.05 level (two-tailed test, df = 21).

assessing variations in submaximal values resulting from the above experimental conditions. This was due to the fact that the subjects did not all perform for the same length of time nor produce the same amount of work. However, these successive values were of importance in evaluating each individual's oxygen intake curve for each of the three tests. Either a plateau or a decline was noted in these curves following the attainment of $\dot{V}_{O_2\,max}$ in all but three of the subjects, and the latter was probably a result of their inability to continue the heavy work load beyond three minutes.

DISCUSSION

The intercorrelations between the three tests for each variable measured in this study are within the ranges reported in previous investigations even though the present correlations were not truly representative of test-retest conditions.[5, 13, 19-21] While these test-retest correlations are of considerable interest and give added insight into any one particular study, they should be interpreted with caution as they are highly dependent on both the size of the sample and the degree of interindividual variability. One would expect a high coefficient when the n is small and the interindividual variability is high, and a lower coefficent when these two conditions are reversed. This might partially explain the wide range of test-retest correlations for maximal oxygen intake ($r = 0.70$ to 0.99) previously reported in the literature.[5, 19]

The mean maximal physiological values obtained in this study were comparable to those obtained by other investigators for males of approximately the same ages and levels of physical conditioning (Table 16-IV). This fact, in addition to the high intercorrelations between the three tests conditions for each variable and the attainment of either a plateau or a slight decline in the majority of the individual oxygen intake curves during the last few minutes of the maximal exercise, indicate that maximal physiological values were indeed obtained in this study.

The significant training or learning effect found for work output and riding time between *day 1* and *day 2* was not unexpected.[5, 8] Since the mean differences for the same performance variables between *day 2* and *day 3* were extremely small (3% difference) and

TABLE 16-IV

COMPARISON OF MEAN MAXIMAL PHYSIOLOGICAL VALUES WITH PREVIOUS INVESTIGATIONS

Investigator	Age Group, yr	Condition	N	Heart Rate, beats/min	Ventilation BTPS, liters/min	Oxygen Intake STPD		
						ml/min	ml/kg per min	ml/LBW per min
Robinson (1938)	20-29	N	11	189.0	118.2	3530	48.7	
Taylor (1944)	19-33	N	31	198.1	104.1	3480		
Åstrand (1952)	20-33	P	42	194.0	111.3	4110	58.6	
Slonim et al. (1957)	18-25	T	50	188.0	147.0	4050	55.4	
Buskirk and Taylor (1957)	18-29	N	39			3440	44.6	53.1
		A	15			3950	52.8	57.5
		R	5			4320	65.8	71.2
Mitchell et al. (1958)	20-29	N	36		94.9	3370	44.7	
DeVries and Klafs (1965)	20-26	P	16			3870	50.5	
Glassford et al. (1965)	17-33	N	24			3758	50.0	
Wilmore* (1967)	18-30	N	22	188.0	149.1	3796	49.3	54.6

N = normal, A = athletes, T = trained, R = runners, P = physical education majors.
* Values represent the average of the three tests.

not significant, it would seem evident that this effect is essentially dissipated after a second work-capacity test. Even though this training, practice, or learning effect was present, it is assumed that it had no significant influence on the major theses of this study, as the sample was balanced according to their order of testing and the comparisons of importance involved the second and third days of testing (conditions E and C_2) between which no significant training or learning effect was found.

A statistically significant increase in endurance capacity (work output and riding time) above either of the two control conditions resulted from the experimental condition where the subject was motivated by a competitive situation. This increase was expected in light of previous investigations which have used various means to gain increases in endurance capacity above maximal levels. Roush[16] found that hanging-by-hands endurance times were significantly greater in the hypnotic state when compared with the waking state. Likewise, Johnson and Kramer[11] found that a supine press of a forty-seven-pound barbell to exhaustion improved in the hypnotic state. Lehmann, Straub, and Szakáll[12] found up to a threefold increase in the performance to exhaustion on a bicycle ergometer when the subjects were adminstered Pervitin (1-phenyl-2-methylaminopropane), without significant concomitant circulatory adjustments or metabolic changes. Their maximal values, however, were considerably lower than any of those reported by the investigators cited in Table 16-IV. Similar results have been reported for strength tests.[10, 16]

The fact that the maximal physiological responses to the work capacity tests in the present study were essentially the same under all three conditions indicates that the increased performance (work output and riding time) brought about by motivation did not occur as a result of alterations in the maximal levels of the measured variables. Thus, it is concluded that the maximal values for these physiological variables are essentially fixed or absolute for any one individual on any specific testing apparatus, i.e. bicycle ergometer and are independent of any additional work performed beyond that needed to obtain these maximal values.

Although blood lactate levels and oxygen debts were not measured, it would appear that this reserve in work output above a predetermined capacity is made possible through an increased anaerobic metabolism coupled with an increased tolerance to the associated pain. This would essentially be in agreement with those investigators who have hypothesized that strength and endurance are limited by psychological inhibitions, and that supramaximal performances result from the breaking down of these psychological inhibitions or barriers.[1, 10, 12, 16]

REFERENCES

1. ALLES, G. A., AND FEIGEN, G. A.: The influence of benzedrine on work-decrement and patellar reflex. *Amer J Physiol, 136*:392-400, 1942.
2. ÅSTRAND, P.-O.: *Experimental Studies of Physical Working Capacity in Relation to Sex and Age.* Copenhagen, Munksgaard, 1952.
3. ÅSTRAND, P.-O.: Measurement of maximal aerobic capacity. *Can Med Assoc J, 96*:732-734, 1967.
4. ÅSTRAND, P.-O., AND SALTIN, B.: Oxygen uptake and muscular activity. *J Appl Physiol, 16*:977-981, 1961.
5. BUSKIRK, E., AND TAYLOR, H. L.: Maximal oxygen intake and its relation to body composition. *J Appl Physiol, 11*:72-78, 1957.
6. CONSOLAZIO, C. F.; JOHNSON, R. E.; AND PECORA, L. J.: *Physiological Measurements of Metabolic Functions in Man.* New York, McGraw, 1963, p. 288.
7. DeVRIES, H. A., AND KLAFS, C. E.: Prediction of maximal oxygen intake from submaximal tests. *J Sports Med, 5*:207-214, 1965.
8. GLASSFORD, R. G.; BAYCROFT, G. H. Y.; SEDGWICK, A. W.; AND MacNAB, R. B. J.: Comparison of maximal oxygen uptake values determined by predicted and actual methods. *J Appl Physiol, 20*:509-513, 1965.
9. HELLEBRANDT, F. A.; AND WATERLAND, J. C.: Indirect learning: the influence of unimanual exercise on related muscle groups of the same and the opposite side. *Amer J Phys Med, 41*:45-55, 1962.
10. IKAI, M., AND STEINHAUS, A. H.: Some factors modifying the expression of human strength. *J Appl Physiol, 16*:157-163, 1961.
11. JOHNSON, W. R., AND KRAMER, G. F.: Effects of stereotyped nonhypnotic, hypnotic, and post hypnotic suggestions upon strength, power, and endurance. *Res Quart Amer Ass Health Phys Educ, 32*:522-529, 1961.
12. LEHMANN, G.; STRAUB, H.; AND SZAKÁLL, A.: Pervitin als leistungsstei-gerndes mitter. *Arbeitsphysiol, 10*:680-691, 1939.
13. MITCHELL, J. H.; SPROULE, B. J.; AND CHAPMAN, C. B.: The physiological meaning of the maximal oxygen intake test. *J Clin Invest, 37*:538-547, 1958.
14. RATHBUN, E. N., AND PACE, N.: Studies on body composition. I. The determination of total body fat by means of the body specific gravity. *J Biol Chem, 158*:667-676, 1945.

15. ROBINSON, S.: Experimental studies of physical fitness in relation to age. *Arbeitsphysiol, 10*:251-323, 1938.

16. ROUSH, E. S.: Strength and endurance in the waking and hypnotic states. *J Appl Physiol, 3*:404-410, 1951.

17. ROWELL, L. B.: Commentary on measurement of maximal aerobic capacity. *Can Med Assoc J, 96*:735, 1967.

18. SLONIM, N. B.; GILLESPIE, D. G., AND HAROLD, W. H.: Peak oxygen uptake of healthy young men as determined by a treadmill method. *J Appl Physiol, 10*:401-404, 1957.

19. TAYLOR, C.: Some properties of maximal and submaximal exercise with reference to physiological variation and the measurement of exercise tolerance. *Amer J Physiol, 142*:200-212, 1944.

20. TAYLOR, H. L.; BUSKIRK, E., AND HENSCHEL, A.: Maximal oxygen intake as an objective measure of cardio-respiratory performance, *J Appl Physiol, 8*:73-80, 1955.

21. WILMORE, J. H., AND SIGERSETH, P. O.: Physical work capacity of young girls, 7-13 years of age. *J Appl Physiol, 22*:923-928, 1967.

22. WYNDHAM, C. H.; STRYDOM, N. B.; LEARY, W. P., AND WILLIAMS, C. G.: Studies of the maximum capacity of men for physical effort. I. A comparison of methods of assessing the maximum oxygen intake. *Arbeitsphysiol, 22*:285-295, 1966.

PART SEVEN
MOTOR LEARNING

Chapter 17

SPECIFICITY VS. GENERALITY IN LEARNING AND PERFORMING TWO LARGE MUSCLE MOTOR TASKS*

John C. Bachman

INTRODUCTION

THE ISSUE of generality vs specificity of individual differences in large muscle coordination or skill and in motor learning ability has recently aroused considerable interest. Factual data are establishing with increasing clarity that motor skills and large muscle psychomotor abilities are far more specific than has previously been realized. In a paper concerned with generality vs. specificity in the area of motor learning, Henry[3] points out that it is no longer possible to justify the concept of unitary abilities such as coordination and agility, since the evidence shows that these abilities are specific to the task or activity. It is not illogical to assume that individual ability in the learning of motor tasks may also be specific to the task.

PROBLEMS INVESTIGATED

The present study investigates task specificity vs. generality in the learning of two motor skills involving balance coordinations. In addition, with initial and final performance scores also available, an opportunity is present to investigate the specificity of motor performance as between tasks.

REVIEW OF RECENT LITERATURE

Scott[6] in 1955 summarized a large number of studies (many of

* J. C. Bachman. Specificity vs. generality in learning and performing two large muscle motor tasks. *Res Quart Amer Ass Health Phys Educ, 32*: 1961, 3-11. Reproduced here with the permission of the author and the American Association for Health, Physical Education, and Recreation.

[175]

them unpublished theses) in the area of balancing tests and other performances involving kinesthesia. Interest was centered on tests requiring no special apparatus, so that they could readily be used practically by teachers. Original data were also presented. Perhaps her most important conclusion was that "These tests in general show little interrelationship. This would lead one at present to assume considerable specificity of function." In a 1956 review of research on coordination and motor learning, Henry[2] found that the weight of evidence indicated that individual abilities in large muscle motor skills are highly specific to the particular motor task that is studied.

A more recent review[3] was concerned primarily with task specificity as compared with generality of motor learning ability. In this study there were citations of unpublished as well as published reports, and some original data were presented. In discussing the older views advocating the concept of general motor ability and educability, it was pointed out that when test batteries which incorporate a number of motor skill items are used, there is necessarily some appearance of general motor ability even though no common element is present among the items. A twenty-one-item correlation matrix published in 1957 by Cumbee, Meyer, and Peterson[1] has furnished evidence of the extreme specificity of motor coordination abilities and performances. Another 1957 study by Nelson[5] has found that transfer of motor learning is highly specific.

APPARATUS AND METHOD

Stabilometer

This instrument consisted of a horizontally pivoted board upon which the subject stood erect, with his feet fourteen inches apart and straddling the supporting axle. The center of rotation in the model used in this experiment was ten inches higher than the board upon which the subject stood, as shown in the photograph (Fig. 17-1). This model of the stabilometer was developed in connection with an experiment on kinesthetic factors in wrestling.[4] Presumably the low position of the board made the balancing test easier than in the ordinary stabilometer, particularly for short subjects.

Motion of the board was measured by a work adder. Any movement was transmitted by a 1.5 inch lever arm which was mounted

FIGURE 17-1. Stabilometer. A short cord drive lever is screwed into the protruding end of the main axle just above A. The cord passes downward and bends over a large pulley on the back of the work-adder dial B, terminating at a coil spring fastened to the frame just above C. A pawl at D engages the milled periphery of the work-adder dial, restricting its turning to a single direction so that movement of the platform is cumulated on the dial. Various A-frame rods brace the platform and the vertical posts that rise from the base to carry the main axle.

on the axle. A waxed string which was fastened to the lever arm passed over the groove of a pulley 3.63 inches in net diameter that was independently pivoted, the spring being held taut by a coil spring exerting 150 g. tension. The pulley carried a flat disc six inches in diameter and $\frac{1}{8}$ inch thick, with a milled or knurled edge. A pawl rested against this edge, permitting easy rotation in one direction, but preventing any movement in the opposite direction. (In the latter case, the string slipped in the pulley groove.) The disc carried a calibrated dial which was scaled in 100 arbitrary units. Each scale unit represented twelve degrees of back and forth platform tilting. Microswitches were fastened under each end of the tilting board and wired in series with an electric clock so that no time was registered during such periods as the subject had the board completely out of balance and against the baseboard and could thereby rest without movement. This provision insured that each thirty-second trial represented that much net time of actual balancing effort.

The subject stood on the pivoted platform in an erect position with his eyes open, straddling the pivot rod axle with one foot on either side of it. Each scoring period (trial) lasted thirty seconds of net exposure as registered by the clock. Between trials, the subject stepped off the board for thirty seconds. Ten trials were given rather than five as in previous experiments.[4]

Ladder Climb

This apparatus* was in reality two parallel ladders with one side in common, the total width being fourteen inches (see Fig. 17-2). The rungs (made of one inch dowling, five inches apart) were staggered in the two sections so that the distance from the bottom of the ladder to rung number sixteen (the top) was forty inches. A vertical extension was adjusted for each subject in such a manner that its top rung could just be grasped by his upward extended hand. Climbing

FIGURE 17-2. Ladder balance apparatus.

---

* This test was devised by the author.

was done near the middle of a five feet by ten feet mat to lessen fear of injury in case of a fall. Tennis shoes were worn by subjects to prevent, as much as possible, slipping off the ladder rungs. In the starting position, the ladder was held by the subject directly in front of him with the toes of both feet placed on the bottom crosspiece. It was required that climbing be done one step at a time.

A trial period lasted thirty seconds; there was a thirty-seconds rest period between trial periods. During each period the subject climbed as high as possible before toppling. He then stepped off and started reclimbing immediately. The highest rung upon which a foot was placed (with a deduction for any missed steps) was recorded as the score for that climb. The cumulated rung scores for each thirty-seconds period constituted the score for that trial period. It was emphasized that when balance was lost it was important to hold on to the ladder and start climbing again as soon as possible. An extra thirty-seconds rest was given after the fifth trial, since some subjects tended to fatigue during the experiment.

In both experiments, the subjects were kept informed as to the score after each trial. No prepractice contact of any kind with either the stabilometer or the ladder was permitted. If it had been, the initial scores would have been of questionable value.

Subjects

Three hundred and twenty subjects, 160 male and 160 females, were tested on both the stabilometer and the ladder climb. There were eight male and eight female subjects in each of twenty single-year groups, which ranged from six to twenty-six years.*

The subjects were student volunteers. They were unselected insofar as factors which might be expected to influence motor performance were concerned. They were obtained from Chico State College and from the public schools of Chico, California. College-age subjects were obtained from the student body as a whole, rather than just from the physical education classes.

---

* While the factual data will be presented in tables that differentiate the subjects with respect to sex and age, these variables are not of primary concern in the present study. A subsequent report will analyze in detail the role of sex and age in motor learning and performance.

RESULTS

Reliability of Individual Differences

The reliability coefficients shown in Table 17-I are the correlations between skill and initial trials 1 and 2, between final trials 9 and 10, and between the two learning scores (trial 1 minus trial 9, and trial 2 minus trial 10). It should be recognized that the estimated reliability of the individual differences is necessarily lower for learning than for initial or final scores, because a learning score is computed by subtracting the latter from the former, and any random error variances in the two measurements will be additive.

TABLE 17-I

RELIABILITY OF INDIVIDUAL DIFFERENCES[a]

Group	N	Stabilometer Learning	Initial	Final	Ladder Learning	Initial	Final
Age 6-11							
Male	48	.587	.860	.870	.578	.933	.944
Female	48	.804	.921	.965	.831	.935	.967
Age 12-18							
Male	56	.662	.830	.760	.803	.869	.734
Female	56	.724	.906	.931	.903	.856	.958
Age 19-26							
Male	56	.764	.876	.900	.746	.875	.879
Female	56	.595	.829	.896	.845	.870	.945
Age 6-26							
Male	160	.685	.902	.917	.791	.918	.935
Female	160	.745	.908	.943	.872	.904	.955
Mean[b]							
Male	160	.678	.857	.853	.720	.897	.878
Female	160	.719	.891	.937	.864	.893	.955

[a] All coefficients have been corrected to the full test values by the Spearman-Brown method.
[b] Average of the subgroup coefficients using the Z-transformation method.

Significance of Learning

Learning scores for both sexes show that a highly significant amount of improvement took place in performance of both tasks. In the stabilometer task the t-ratios for differences between initial and final trials or gain in performance (the learning scores) were $t = 30.4$ for trial 1 minus trial 9; and 24.0 for trial 2 minus trial 10 for all males. They were 30.1 for 1 minus 9, and 27.8 for 2 minus 10 for the females. The corresponding t-ratios for the ladder climb were 24.1, 16.9 for males, and 25.6 and 19.5 for the females. Even for the age group with the smallest learning score on the stabilometer (males age 7), the *t*-ratio was 3.76, which is significant at the 1 percent level.

Task Specificity

The cross correlations for learning and for performance for all three age groups and each sex are small even though fully corrected for attenuation. These correlations are shown in Table 17-II. Only the initial performance of males age nineteen to twenty-five shows a correlation significantly different from zero. This is probably just an aberrant correlation such as might be expected occasionally among eighteen correlations based on noncorrelated *true* relationships. The negative sign of this correlation shows that individuals who had good scores (low) on the stabilometer had poor scores (low) on the ladder climb task and vice versa. When this nineteen to twenty-five year age group is divided into subgroups, the younger one (19-21 years, N = 24) shows a correlation of —.409, and the older one (22-25 years, N = 32) shows a correlation of .269. Neither is statistically significant.

TABLE 17-II

CORRELATION BETWEEN STABILOMETER AND LADDER
BALANCING ABILITIES

Group	N	Learning[a]	Initial[a]	Final[a]
Age 6-11				
Male	48	—.165	—.168	—.110
Female	48	.064	—.034	.049
Age 12-18				
Male	56	.052	—.170	—.065
Female	56	.042	—.130	.039
Age 19-26				
Male	56	—.003	—.424[c]	—.152
Female	56	.140	—.052	.249
Mean[b]				
Male	160	—.039	—.260[c]	—.111
Female	160	.082	—.072	.113

[a] The algebraic signs have been reversed for the coefficients of the initial and final scores, since high skill is represented by a low stabilometer score or a high ladder balance score. All correlations are based on the average of two trials per subject. The coefficients have been fully corrected for attenuation in both variables, using the reliability coefficients reported in Table I.
[b] Average of the subgroup coefficients using the Z-transformation method.
[c] Significant at the 1 percent level.

TABLE 17-III

SPECIFICITY VS GENERALITY OF STABILOMETER AND LADDER BALANCING ABILITIES

Group	N	Learning		Initial Skill		Final Skill	
		Generality	*Specificity*	*Generality*	*Specificity*	*Generality*	*Specificity*
Age 6-11							
Male	48	2.71%	97.29%	2.83%	97.17%	1.20%	98.80%
Female	48	0.41%	99.59%	0.12%	99.88%	0.24%	99.76%
Age 12-18							
Male	56	0.27%	99.73%	2.88%	97.12%	0.42%	99.58%
Female	56	0.17%	99.83%	1.69%	98.31%	0.15%	99.85%
Age 19-26							
Male	56	0.01%	99.99%	18.00%	82.00%	2.32%	97.68%
Female	56	1.97%	98.03%	0.27%	99.73%	6.21%	93.79%

Since the error variance has been removed from the correlations by the correction for attenuation, the correlation r is a measure of generality of abilities, uncontaminated by the influence of imperfect reliability. The coefficient of alienation k is related to r by the well-known mathematical definition $r^2 + k^2 = 1$. Thus k can be considered to be a measure (in correlation units) of the amount of specificity of abilities. Multiplying each term in the formula by 100 makes it possible to table the percentages of individual differences that are general, i.e. common to both motor tasks, and specific, i.e. unique to only one of the tasks. This has been done for the six subgroups in Table 17-III.

DISCUSSION

The reliabilities of individual differences in performance, both initial and final, are relatively high in comparison with other co-ordination or kinesthesis tests.[6] It is difficult to find data in the literature on the reliability of learning, when learning is defined as the improvement in performance resulting from practice in large-muscle motor tasks. The values obtained in this study may be considered fairly good, even though one would like to see them larger. It is doubtful if there is any alternative method of handling the scores that would be much better. It is possible that more reliable individual differences in learning might be measurable by fitting individual learning curves to the data. While this would be extremely laborious by conventional methods, the use of modern electronic computers may bring this method within the scope of practicality. It would be desirable to add two more trials to the practice period, since this would permit a more accurate estimate of the final skill level. If this is done, however, there may possibly be difficulties with fatigue and loss of motivation near the end of the experiment.

When all of the reliability coefficients of Table 17-I (learning, as well as initial and final scores for each sex group) are averaged together for each task, it is found that the mean reliability for the entire group (age 6 to 26) is only 3 percent larger in each task than the mean reliability of the subgroups. This finding indicates that for these particular motor tasks, heterogeneity of age has not inflated the correlations.

Both tasks are convenient and practical for testing members of either sex and for use with a wide range of chronological ages. No particular difficulty has been encountered, so far, with previous experience or practice in the skills involved, although this is potentially a menace in any learning experiment. The bongo board, in particular, might create a problem in some localities.

Neither task can be considered to measure the sense of balance. The stabilometer performance requires a large amount of almost continuous physical activity. The board does not remain stable, even for the final trials. Most of the large muscle groups are extensively involved. The balancing seems to involve kinesthesis more than semicircular canal function. The improvement in performance is probably an improvement in muscular coordination; movements become precisely adjusted so that the board remains relatively stable. Extensive physical activity of the large-muscle type is also required for the ladder balancing task. Even the final trials involve considerable movement, since static positions are brief and rare. Success seems to be related to the development of complex, precise, and highly coordinated large-muscle movements dependent upon kinesthetic information. It would seem that both these tasks should be described as complex large-muscle coordinations.

The absence of correlation between individual differences in performance abilities for these two similar motor tasks, or between individual differences in learning abilities for the two tasks, will probably surprise some readers. Certainly the outcome seems to rule out the presence of general motor coordination ability in the ordinary usage of the term; it also rules out the presence of a motor learning ability. Instead, the abilities are task-specific, both for performance and for motor learning.

It would not be difficult to alter the experiment in such a manner that a pseudogeneral ability would appear. For example, suppose that instead of testing volunteer subjects individually with particular attention to maintaining insofar as possible, equal motivation for all, there had been compulsory participation by members of a school class. In this situation some individuals would be motivated to a high degree, some would simply go through the motions, and others would be intermediate. The consequence of this differential motivation would be a correlation between scores in the two tests, even though the true abilities were actually uncorrelated. Or suppose that we are testing two skills that have considerable correlation with age or maturity or growth. Unless the influence of these variables was carefully eliminated, a pseudogeneral ability would appear. In older subjects, a comparable situation would be obtained for tests in which body size or structure was correlated with performance. It follows directly from these considerations that the mere occurrence of positive intertask correlations, or for that matter the emergence of a general or group factor in a more complicated situation, does not overthrow the theory of task specificity unless statistically spurious elements in the experiment are eliminated.

SUMMARY AND CONCLUSIONS

Three hundred and twenty subjects were tested on two large-muscle motor tasks in order to investigate task specificity vs generality in the initial performance and the learning of two large-muscle motor skills. In one task, the subject stood on a pivoted board (stabilometer) and attempted to keep in balance with a minimum of movement. In the other, he repeatedly climbed a free-standing vertical ladder as far as possible before it toppled over. Both tasks were novel and initially unpracticed. Each involved almost continuous motor activity even after the full amount of practice. Ten trials were given on each. Statistically significant learning was observed in all age groups on both tasks; on the average it amounted to 59 percent improvement for the stabilometer and 44 percent improvement for the ladder climb.

Insofar as can be generalized from the two tasks investigated, motor learning is remarkably task-specific. No correlation was found that was significantly different from zero for any of the age groups. The greatest percent of communality of function was found in the six-year-old to eleven-year-old boys; even in this case there was less than 3 percent of generality in learning the two tasks.

The results show little more than zero correlation between performance of the two tasks, and therefore substantiate the theory of task specificity of motor abilities. In the one instance out of twelve where a significant correlation was found, it was low, and its sign showed a negative relation between skills in the two tasks. Certainly one would have to be very optimistic to consider this evidence of a relationship of any importance.

REFERENCES

1. Cumbee, Frances Z.; Meyer, Margaret; and Peterson, G.: Factorial analysis of motor coordination variables for third and fourth grade girls. *Res Quart Amer Ass Health Phys Educ, 28*:100-108, May 1957.
2. Henry, F. M.: Coordination and motor learning. *College Physical Education Association Proceedings*. Washington, D. C., the Association, 1956.
3. Henry, F. M.: Specificity vs. generality in learning motor skills. *College Physical Education Association Proceedings*. Washington, D. C., the Association, 1958.
4. Mumby, H. H.: Kinesthetic acuity and balance related to wrestling ability. *Res Quart Amer Ass Health Phys Educ, 24*:327-34, October 1953.
5. Nelson, D. O.: Studies of transfer of learning in gross motor skills. *Res Quart Amer Ass Health Phys Educ, 28*:364-73, December 1957.
6. Scott, M. Gladys: Measurement of kinesthesis. *Res Quart Amer Ass Health Phys Educ, 26*:324-41, October 1955.

Chapter 18

A FACTORIAL ANALYSIS OF MOTOR CO-ORDINATION*

FRANCES Z. CUMBEE

PART I
THE ANALYSIS OF MOTOR CO-ORDINATION VARIABLES
INTRODUCTION

Diagnosis and prognosis of individual differences in human behavior have been a matter of keen concern for psychologists and educators for years. In an effort to get a clear understanding of these human differences, certain words, indicative of concepts, have been employed. These concepts about human behavior are, in essence, abstractions. They have not been measured directly.

One is faced, however, with the actuality, that these *named* concepts about human behavior have different meanings for different people. The different meanings have led to widely scattered and diversified selection of tests to measure the traits or abilities believed to be involved. The tests used to measure motor coordination have covered such abilities as throwing a ball, balancing a rod, hopping on one foot, holding the balance on tip toes, and patting the head and rubbing the stomach. In the absence of an agreed-upon definition of motor coordination, these tests have been used and listed as measures of coordination. The mere name assigning of coordination to those tests, however, does not insure their validity.

* F. Z. Cumbee: A factorial analysis of motor co-ordination. *Res Quart Amer Ass Health Phys Educ,* 25:1954, 412-428. Reproduced here with the permission of the author and the American Association for Health, Physical Education, and Recreation. The author wishes to thank Professor Emeritus T. L. Torgerson for his advice and guidance throughout the author's graduate work; Professor Chester W. Harris of the School of Education, for his generous expert advice in the application of the factor analysis technique as well as for statistical advice in handling the data in Part II; also the Computing Service of the University of Wisconsin for running the correlation coefficients on the IBM machines.

[187]

Perhaps, in the interest of reaching some agreement, it might be wise to ascertain what these *coordination* tests really measure. Such a procedure is not concerned with first establishing a valid criterion for *coordination*. Rather, it is concerned with the location of what is really being measured by a selected but diversified group of tests which claim to measure the same complex concept. It is essentially the type study which Thurstone[27] did with tests which claimed to measure intelligence. If the presence of what is being measured can be demonstrated, then perhaps workers in the field can agree upon an operational definition of motor coordination. Criteria may then be established, and tests devised for diagnosis and prognosis of individual weaknesses in motor coordination.

THE PROBLEM

Background of the Problem

Factor analysis has been used to explore a wide variety of motor skills tests in an effort to determine the underlying factors in motor ability. One of the first studies in physical education employing the factor technique was the one by Jones[13] using the tetrad difference criterion in an effort to locate a general motor ability similar to the Spearman g[23] in intelligence. Jones concluded that the emphasis should be on *abilities* rather than *ability*.

A number of the studies since that time have been exploratory.[3, 4, 6, 14, 15, 16, 17, 18, 28] The workers were looking for rather large dimensions such as strength, speed, coordination, endurance, rhythm, and balance as factors in motor ability.

Out of some thirty-six factors located in these studies, thirteen factors center around some form of coordination. The items appearing on these thirteen factors indicate the following variables: throwing, kicking, catching, striking, ball handling, running, jumping, Johnson motor educability items, quick change of direction items, and a few composite scores.

While the exploratory studies so far have not given a clear defini- of motor coordination, other workers have tested certain hypotheses about coordination. For example, H. G. Seashore[20] reported a study in which he attempted to locate some factor common to fine and gross coordinations. His analysis, however, showed no factors which had items of both fine and gross coordination. An excellent logical analysis of elements in fine coordinations has been made by R. H. Seashore.[22] Later, R. H. Seashore, Dudek, Holtzman[21] proposed the hypothesis of a steadiness factor in fine coordination. Rather than locating one factor of steadiness, they located a factor which seemed to indicate static steadiness, and another factor which seemed to indicate steadiness when the subjects were moving. So, testing of these hypotheses about fine and gross coordination and about steadiness as a factor in fine coordination still leaves many questions.

Earlier workers in the field of motor ability offer some interesting clues. Oseretsky[7] made use of such items as rod balance, two-handed coordinations, speed of movement of the arms and hands, balance, hop and jump, and to a certain degree, rhythm. Garfiel[8] made use of two-handed trick-type coordinations such as rubbing the stomach and patting the head, some measure of rhythm, tapping for speed, a ball toss at a target, and an item which would involve balance to successfully perform.

Thus, it seems that a combination of some of these items used by earlier workers and some of the items appearing on *coordination* factors in more recent studies offer interesting possibilities for a definition of motor coordination. Earlier workers in the field have been concerned with balance, both the balancing of objects and body balance. Consideration has been given in earlier work to the *rhythm* with which a person performed activities. It is conceivable that a person's ability to time his movements plays a major role in being *well coordinated*. In addition, the ability to change directions rapidly has been used by earlier workers and by more recent workers. To perform sports skills in a *coordinated* fashion, this ability seems important also.

The Problem and the Hypotheses To Be Tested

The problem of what factors are present in variables which have been used in the past as measures of some phase of *coordination* will be investigated. Two hypotheses will be tested:

(1) There are definable factors in tests which claim to measure motor coordination.

(2) Tests used to measure motor coordination group themselves

around such factors as: the ability to balance objects and maintain body balance; the ability to time movements of the body; and the ability to move rapidly with the moving parts changing directions.

PROCEDURE

The data for the twenty-one variables* were collected for 200 college Freshmen women with 92 percent visual acuity, binocular efficiency, and depth perception at far-point as measured by the Keystone telebinocular. The tests were administered a second time from 80 to 130 students in order that test-retest reliabilities† could be determined. Scores of the twenty-one variables were used to calculate the Pearson product-moment correlations. These coefficients were calculated on punched-card equipment by the Computing Service of the University of Wisconsin. The 210 intercorrelations made up the entries in the original correlation matrix, Table 18-I.

The centroid and the multiple-group method of factoring were used to determine the underlying factors. Dissatisfaction with the rotations and with the appearance of the residual matrix‡ after the extraction of nine factors by the centroid method resulted in changing to the multiple-group method of factoring. Formulas and calculation procedures for the multiple-group method of factoring as well as the outline of a technique for rotating the initial oblique solution to the primary solutions as given by C. W. Harris and Schmid[10] were followed.

DISCUSSION OF DATA

Interpretations of Factors

Table 18-II, the Oblique Factor Matrix, will be used to discuss the eight factors extracted. Factor A clearly is a *balance* factor. In view of the loadings of the three balancing-objects items, it would appear that one may give to this factor the name of *balancing objects*. This appears to be the first time when items of the balancing-objects

---

* See list of variables in Table 18-II.

† Test-retest reliabilities are given in Table 18-II.

‡ See Table 18-IV for doublets remaining after the extraction of nine centroid factors.

TABLE 18-1

ORIGINAL CORRELATION MATRIX (r) AND RESIDUALS[1]

	1	2	3	4	5	6	7	8	9	10	11	12	13	14	15	16	17	18	19	20	21
1																					
2	594																				
3	473	670																			
4	278	356	334																		
5	212	298	249	362																	
6	088	-026	014	046	135																
7	088	110	049	-003	059	258															
8	-037	041	-068	183	003	106	164														
9	067	042	037	088	112	029	150	-044													
10	065	052	022	162	152	041	-035	-030	300												
11	175	149	132	182	293	129	120	092	147	129											
12	126	129	105	100	185	-014	-041	061	040	156	326										
13	180	177	196	186	149	159	044	-038	124	117	175	117									
14	277	254	242	219	151	153	097	-008	065	108	145	042	317								
15	344	369	349	364	304	107	146	106	-016	062	264	178	183	352							
16	394	385	382	365	227	073	000	008	138	050	243	123	204	474	530						
17	288	358	288	395	206	099	109	078	038	-022	251	164	244	352	464	504					
18	213	377	292	309	292	000	061	097	022	054	235	120	207	245	311	553	496				
19	091	163	146	441	289	000	052	110	071	098	156	-047	221	288	239	289	292	189			
20	185	175	139	302	281	026	031	-033	049	191	285	070	195	247	191	217	206	260	429		
21	274	137	203	269	189	006	-013	026	090	149	281	085	239	396	327	373	340	215	382	241	

[1]Residuals are underlined. Decimal points have been omitted.

type have been included in a factorial analysis in the field of physical education. However, the ability to balance a rod on the index finger has seemed important as a measure of coordination by such people as Oseretsky, even though such skills have not been included in a factor analysis. Moreover, this factor is correlated with Factor E which is loaded heavily with the sports skills.

Factor B may be given the name *tempo*. The three highest items on this factor are those which required the subject to do a prescribed exercise in any tempo she liked, then repeat this tempo four more times. Allowing a student to perform at a preferred tempo in activities is the type activity Rimoldi[19] used for the majority of the tests in his personal tempo experiment. Rhythm has been exceedingly hard to measure objectively. This attempt to measure one phase of it (tempo) objectively still needs refinement. The test-retest reliabilities of these items were lower than those of other variables in the analysis, as may be seen in Table 18-II. Consequently, too great a dependence upon these items on this factor is not justified. Reference to the communalities in the same table, however, indicates that the variance accounted for is under the reliability estimates.

Factor C seems to be *two-handed agility*. The two variables which are high on this variable are the type tests which earlier workers in the field, Garfiel[8] and Oseretsky[7] seemed to consider important in coordination. The Army Air Corps[1] also used some two-handed variables in assessing the level of coordination of pilots. In all these two-handed variables, there seems to be some need for the subject to grasp or understand the situation before the motor operation can be put into practice. It would be interesting to see if variables which involved asymmetric movement of arms and legs would appear on this factor.

Factor D may readily be called *speed of change of direction of arms and hands*. Items 11 and 12 were designed to see how rapidly a person could move his arms and hands while performing a task which did not call for minute accuracy. The appearance of the static balance item on this factor is interesting. The subjects were seated on the floor while taking tests 11 and 12. There were no specified directions for the way the subjects were to sit. A large portion of the students leaned on one arm for support while taking the tests. This is a type of static balance and possibly had something to do with the performance on tests 11 and 12.

TABLE 18-II

OBLIQUE FACTOR MATRIX—V[1]

	A	B	C	D	E	F	G	H	h^2_j	Rel. Est.
1. 30-sec. rod balance	498	056	037	042	079	—075	—020	—084	524	785
2. 30-sec. rod balance, replacement	729	011	—012	—040	—056	054	040	—100	794	817
3. 2 rod balance	513	—068	—025	—009	077	021	—008	012	508	857
4. Dynamic balance	201	004	141	—012	133	367	437	080	557	921
5. Static balance	193	070	—033	230	—049	324	006	044	342	665
6. Tempo-long-short	—046	460	023	033	072	—045	—005	—063	231	335
7. Tempo-arm exercise	081	519	070	—064	—016	—071	—041	095	310	626
8. Tempo-total body	—034	260	—045	158	—056	116	411	—061	271	357
9. Crosses and vertical lines	—002	068	488	—063	029	—076	008	054	321	773
10. Nose and ear	022	—085	452	063	—029	076	108	—054	345	787
11. Stick placing	—024	225	—015	451	054	085	000	016	403	903
12. Block tapping	024	—012	016	530	—054	—085	132	—018	381	807
13. Burpee	008	079	120	054	218	015	—005	068	174	716
14. Short potato race	—069	133	153	—089	519	—085	—026	—003	458	675
15. Soccer kicks	098	196	—038	168	339	013	166	017	465	833
16. Basketball throw	039	—028	156	015	524	—090	143	095	560	921
17. Ball Catching	—053	133	—009	022	508	—031	131	469	678	756
18. Ball striking	057	000	—028	026	288	098	022	410	437	772
19. Johnson 3	—050	012	009	088	239	536	239	—082	586	822
20. Johnson 4	046	—059	—068	151	071	416	—087	035	380	753
21. Jump and reach	—081	—066	117	122	370	079	106	—034	347	934
Number of variables between ± .10	16	14	14	14	12	16	12	19		

[1] Decimal points have been omitted.

All variables appearing on Factor E have correlated with the *co-ordination* factor or factors identified in other studies, with the exception of the Johnson 4 item. Thus, this study verifies the selection of these items as having something in common. Other writers have called this factor *sensorimotor coordination, gross body coordination,* or *true motor educability*. It should be recalled that previous factorial analysis of sports skills have identified strength and speed by tests which seemed to be simple enough to permit rather clear interpretation. However, after these factors were extracted from the matrix, some grouping of sport skills which did not have any test simple enough to permit clear identity appeared. To this factor the authors gave the name *coordination*. It seems sensible to conceive of *coordination* as some combination of abilities which may be measured by rather simple tests rather than by complicated sports skills. It is for this reason that the present writer is dubious about calling this factor *motor coordination,* as it has been identified in other studies.

One is prone to wonder if this factor is not more of a total body *quick change of direction* factor. Two of the variables appearing on this factor, the Burpee and the short potato race, are what physical educators have called *agility* measures. They involve a total body *quick change of direction*. The present writer is hesitant to call this a quick change of direction factor because of the low correlation of the Burpee test with this factor. The choice of the Burpee as a quick change of direction item is probably a poor choice. The use of more tests such as the side-step, zig-zag, and dodging run might give more evidence that the type of ability involved on this factor is a quick change of direction. The *gross body coordination and agility* factor in the Larson study[15] had four quick change of direction items.

Factor F may be called *body balance*. One seems reasonably safe in identifying this factor as body balance, since these tests seem to be simple tests in that they are aimed at balance rather than at some such thing as motor educability. The latter is a more complicated concept. Bass[2] suggested that the dynamic balance test is measuring something besides the type balance in her study since the communality was low. She suggested that it might be some type of motor educability. Carpenter[3] suggested that the Johnson 3 and Johnson 4 items were on a factor which probably indicated *true motor educability*. It would seem reasonable to believe that, if more Johnson items were analyzed in terms of more simple tests such as balance, tempo, and various type floor patterns, clearer identification of what has been called motor educability would be possible.

Factor G was extracted to facilitate rotation of Factor C, and to indicate some possible verifications that are needed. It will not be named in this study. After the extraction of the first six factors there were two doublets left in the residual matrix. One of the doublets included variables 4 and 8, dynamic balance and tempo (jump and arm pattern) respectively. It may be possible that this sort of factor is getting at an awareness of position in space and an awareness of time-force relationships. Such an ability may be uncorrelated or independent of one's ability to perform at high speed, or to play baseball, or to strike an object. Rather, it may be a perception factor of where the body is in space, the amount of force, and when the force is applied to keep the body in that position.

Factor H was extracted because it was the only doublet left in the residual matrix and it was thought its extraction would help clarify the other factors. It will not be named. The two variables appearing high on this factor are the two which involved a ball that was thrown from a robot for the subject to catch or to strike. This would involve making judgments of the speed of the moving ball and of the space it would cover, and then adjusting the body to that moving object in order to perform the skill successfully. This factor, as well as Factor G, then, appears to be something of a perception factor.

Intercorrelation of Factors

Since this is an oblique solution, the factors are correlated. The intercorrelation of factors may be seen in Table 18-III, the ϕ matrix. Inspection of the twenty-eight intercorrelations reveals that eleven are zero. This indicates that these factors are at right angles and hence, independent, of one another. Seven of the intercorrelations are near enough to zero to be thought of as independent of one another. Ten of the intercorrelations have large enough correlations to warrant consideration. Of these ten, seven are positively correlated, indicating an acute angle between the factors; three are negative, indicating an obtuse angle. It should be kept in mind that the correlations between these factors are subject to change should other samples of different age levels and different sexes be used. The reader may wish to examine Table 18-III for a review of these intercorrelations. Comment will be made here only on the largest correlations in the ϕ matrix.

TABLE 18-III—Ø
INTERCORRELATION OF FACTORS

Factor	A	B	C	D	E	F	G	H
A	1.000							
B	.057	1.000						
C	.114	.105	1.000					
D	.287	— .044	.383	1.000				
E	.569	.083	.083	.304	1.000			
F	.097	.176	.386	.193	.344	1.000		
G	— .030	— .045	— .422	— .216	— .141	— .266	1.000	
H	.079	— .022	.027	.251	— .130	.002	.141	1.000

The .569 correlation between Factor A (balancing objects) and Factor E seems logical since a number of sports skills in Factor E require adjustments in the use of hand and arm for successful performance. Factor A requires small quick adjustments with hand and arm to keep the rod balanced. These balancing-objects items have not been included in a factor analysis in physical education studies before. Evidence here, however, suggests that they be given serious consideration in the analysis of sports skills.

RESULTS AND CONCLUSIONS

Eight factors were obtained from this analysis, five of which were given names. Five of these factors seem to permit clear interpretation by rather simple tests. Therefore, the first hypothesis has to be accepted.

The factors underlying the twenty-one variables used in this study seem to permit the following names: *Balancing Objects, Tempo, Two-Handed Agility, Speed of Change of Direction of the Arms and Hands, Body Balance.* Therefore, the second hypothesis has to be accepted.

This study seems to permit the following conclusions:

(1) Variables used in the past to measure motor coordination, motor proficiency, or sports skills do group themselves around certain abilities.

(2) While variables do group around certain abilities, there is an indication in this study that further factors, which have not been considered in studies of this kind, are pertinent to motor coordination. Factors G and H in this study indicate such a conclusion.

(3) Factor E confirms the selection of *coordination* variables from several factorial studies as having something in common. The author, however, questions naming this factor motor *coordination*.

(4) Factor A (balancing objects) warrants consideration in the analysis of sports skills because of the .57 correlation of this factor with Factor E.

(5) The two motor educability items used in this analysis are best identified in terms of total body balance.

(6) The appearance of the block-placing-for-speed and the kick-for-distance items on the tempo factor indicates that these variables require some degree of the ability to time movements of the body. However, the tempo items used in this study were a narrow interpretation of timing movements. No *timing* in relation to outside objects was considered in the tempo tests. Moreover, the tempo items were not vary reliable and need further refinement.

(7) The intercorrelation of factors indicates no relationship between the two-handed agility factor and Factor E. None of the sports skills appeared on the former factor. This could be due to an absence of similar movement patterns in the sports skills and the novel, trick-type tests by which Factor C was identified. In addition, the novel tests in Factor C seem to require some degree of concentration or ability to grasp what is expected in order that they may be executed properly. The two Johnson items also seem similar in this respect. There is some indication of relationship between this Factor C (two-handed agility) and Factor F on which the two Johnson items appear.

(8) No final definition of motor coordination can be given in terms of abilities from this study. Further clarification of Factors G and H seems needed, as well as more clarification of Factor E, which is primarily composed of sports skills.

(9) The multiple-group method of factoring these motor coordination variables gave a more decisive reduction of the intercorrelation matrix than did the centroid method.

PART II

COMPARISON OF THE CENTROID AND THE
MULTIPLE-GROUP METHODS OF FACTORING

The last conclusion in Part I suggests a possible discrepancy in factors obtained when different methods of factoring are used. In an effort to determine the number of factors present in the inter-correlation matrix, the solution of this problem began by extracting three centroids. Test-retest reliability estimates were used as communality estimates so that only reliable variance would be extracted from the intercorrelation matrix. After the extraction of three centroids, vectors were extended [25] and plots made. Since the variables seemed to cluster fairly well on the plots, the centroid approach was continued.

The question of when to stop factoring in factor analysis is an important one. Essentially, one attempts to reduce the intercorrelation matrix to zero. Two criteria were applied to determine when the factoring should be stopped. Thurstone[27] reported an empirical rule developed by Tucker. This rule is based on the idea that only chance variance will remain in the residuals when the significant factors have been taken out. Such a criterion is of course appropriate when factors are extracted one at a time as in the centroid method. Coombs[5] has given another criterion which is based on the idea that the number of negative signs (after sign change) expected in the residual matrix is a function of the number of variables. From his graph, a table was made from which one could determine directly the total number of negative signs to expect from a certain number of tests when the factoring was adequate.

Application of Tucker's and Coombs' criteria for when to stop factoring produced the results shown in Table 18-IV.

As can be seen, there is no consistency between the criteria applied. The negative signs should increase after each factor in Coombs' criterion, and the ratio in Tucker's criterion should increase. This was not the case. Rather, there was a constant fluctuation both within each criterion and between the two criteria. For example, after two factors had been extracted, Coombs' criterion suggested enough factors

TABLE 18-IV
APPLICATION OF TUCKER'S AND COOMBS' CRITERIA

		Coombs	Tucker
Factors extracted	*Critical values*	*160±10*	*.952*
9			.964
8		160	.918
7		144	.971
6		170	.941
5		140	.945
4		148	.946
3		153	.980
2		171	.944

had been extracted, while the Tucker criterion suggested the factoring be continued. After six factors had been extracted, Coombs' criterion once more suggested that the factoring should be stopped, but the Tucker criterion suggested factoring should be continued. (The Tucker criterion had suggested the factoring was adequate after three factors had been extracted) Then, after seven factors had been extracted, the Coombs criterion suggested a continuation, while the Tucker criterion suggested the factoring was adequate.

Although the criteria did not answer with complete satisfaction the question of when to stop factoring by this centroid method, it was decided to try to rotate five of the obtained factors to see if there was some interpretation possible. C. W. Harris[9] has given a method of direct rotation. This is done by looking at the plots of extended vectors to determine the points at which the planes intersect. The direction numbers of these points are taken as the basis for the transformation matrix of direction cosines. After the direct rotation was made, several adjustments were made by radial and by single plane rotations to try to put the variables in a hyperplane which permitted interpretation.

As indicated in Part I, dissatisfaction with the rotations, and with the appearance of the residual matrix after the extraction of nine factors resulted in changing to the multiple-group method of factoring. This change was made to see if clearer identification and a cleaner reduction of the intercorrelation matrix was possible. As may be seen by the residual matrix, Table 18-V, several doublets were left in the residual matrix after the extraction of nine factors by this centroid method.

TABLE 18-V

CENTROID RESIDUALS AFTER EXTRACTION OF NINE FACTORS[1]

	1	2	3	4	5	6	7	8	9	10	11	12	13	14	15	16	17	18	19	20	21
1	-014																				
2	107	005																			
3	-070	000	-005																		
4	002	012	-052	-053																	
5	-040	053	-007	050	047																
6	-029	-046	013	019	-012	-010															
7	013	040	011	-041	062	-013	-055														
8	-080	-036	-023	016	-031	001	-002	-053													
9	-002	-013	-003	-003	-012	004	-022	022	111												
10	-049	029	-082	-002	028	036	-048	-049	028	-038											
11	029	-016	-003	-033	-132	-063	-037	-049	-003	-062	107										
12	-036	-054	042	064	-040	-063	074	-019	068	-063	-021	020									
13	023	-010	-045	014	-002	009	-040	-043	005	044	022	002	-104								
14	-024	048	-056	-049	005	-034	008	064	-036	019	-019	-017	-016	-006							
15	019	-003	-028	-020	008	021	-024	003	-088	-070	-025	-016	-071	-028	-019						
16	023	012	012	-046	054	-014	-014	-019	033	037	-018	-064	017	033	035	-008					
17	-010	-028	-023	022	-014	-003	027	012	-003	009	014	023	-004	-002	032	-016	-074				
18	-013	-022	-013	-013	015	-047	033	002	-001	025	-004	052	005	-024	-009	-027	-016	-022			
19	018	-027	044	067	047	-005	009	-006	-066	-096	-012	013	047	-005	-116	-036	-040	-042	042		
20	-024	-023	-045	038	-077	-004	018	-012	-056	-036	-083	-001	-073	014	008	179	-040	003	001	-025	
Σ	001	-001	001	000	001	001	000	001	-001	-001	000	001	-001	-001	-001	-001	001	-001	001	-001	000

[1]Decimal points have been omitted.

PURPOSE

It is the purpose of this section to compare the centroid and the multiple-group methods of factoring the same empirical data.

PROCEDURE

Since the calculated communalities using the multiple-group method were smaller than the reliability estimates used in the first solution by the centroid method, the intercorrelation matrix once again was factored by the centroid method, using the same communalities as were used in the multiple-group method. Only six centroids were extracted, since the multiple-group method gave six factors which were interpreted.*

One method of comparing the centroid solution with the multiple group solution is to make a least squares approximation of one solution to the other. This is a well-established statistical procedure and has recently been reviewed by C. W. Harris.[11] In this instance a least squares approximation to the F matrix was made from the V matrix since V was of greater rank than F. The idempotent matrix X was computed from V and F, $[X = (V^1V)^{-1} V^1 F]$. V was multiplied by X to give the matrix F_1, the least squares approximation to the centroid solution, $(VX = F_1)$. F_1 was subtracted from F to show differences in the two solutions.

DISCUSSION OF DATA

Table 18-VI records residuals after the extraction of six centroids, using the same communalities as was used in the multiple-group method. Table 18-VII is the F matrix of the centroid solution; Table 18-VIII the least squares approximation matrix, F_1; Table 18-IX contains the difference between the F and the F_1 matrices. A comparison of Table 18-VII and Table 18-VIII indicates that the two solutions are quite similar. Further, inspection of Table 18-IX indicates that for all practical purposes the two solutions are comparable since the majority of the entries are essentially zero.

---

* It was suggested in Part I that Factors G and H were extracted to aid in rotation, to remove the two remaining doublets from the residuals, and to possibly indicate further clarifications needed.

TABLE 18-VI

RESIDUALS AFTER EXTRACTION OF SIX CENTROIDS[1]

	1	2	3	4	5	6	7	8	9	10	11	12	13	14	15	16	17	18	19	20	21
1	024																				
2	002	-029																			
3	-027	060	-033																		
4	002	-034	020	028																	
5	021	025	-002	-004	012																
6	033	-019	026	023	-074	-020															
7	-012	008	-008	-068	026	033	014														
8	000	026	-041	046	081	-037	-021	015													
9	044	-018	003	-052	003	057	-073	-013	024												
10	018	-016	023	-037	-015	012	024	-054	041	047											
11	-025	020	002	050	012	004	-017	-028	-020	-058	011										
12	-037	011	-008	-017	-011	053	073	-060	-037	049	040	047									
13	020	-006	-028	007	-015	-061	016	036	-022	-023	-019	021	016								
14	009	-050	-010	027	005	-022	-029	-003	-069	-016	-038	016	055	071							
15	002	-038	-003	022	-046	-018	006	006	062	-031	-008	-027	047	000	026						
16	013	036	011	-019	-001	-013	053	-011	080	-009	017	012	-063	032	-069	014					
17	012	-019	021	-038	-036	-007	-017	026	064	-005	-028	-008	004	-041	024	-017	061				
18	029	-023	-018	004	037	-008	-060	-013	032	003	-043	-108	021	-006	049	-038	051	083			
19	-025	022	005	-039	-029	-013	053	007	-011	060	007	023	-035	000	-004	001	001	045	047		
20	-040	-002	016	052	014	-009	-034	060	-070	-022	052	-043	015	033	018	-022	-027	023	-061	066	
21	-063	044	-009	-004	-004	060	033	-023	-022	011	071	010	013	036	-021	-007	-022	-060	-051	-019	-006
	000	000	000	001	-001	000	000	-001	000	002	002	-001	-001	-000	-003	000	-001	000	000	000	-001

[1] Decimal points have been omitted.

TABLE 18-VII
CENTROID FACTOR MATRIX—F[1]

	1	2	3	4	5	6	hj^2
1	5398	—3199	3119	1376	—0688	0997	5246
2	6012	—3684	3731	2181	2229	—1792	7657
3	5160	—3523	2520	1897	0869	—0890	5053
4	6001	0785	—1878	2547	2069	—1473	5309
5	4897	1726	0799	1013	1991	0147	3261
6	1885	2109	0888	—2948	—2079	—1933	2554
7	1856	1412	1427	—2533	—0519	—3148	2407
8	1117	1825	—1103	—2058	1619	—3516	2501
9	2133	2748	2175	0509	—3335	1163	2957
10	2353	3114	1209	2117	—1813	2271	2962
11	4682	2391	0769	—1678	0975	2128	3652
12	2599	1189	1924	—1924	2379	3093	3080
13	3926	0244	—0127	—0155	—1491	0811	1839
14	5254	—1390	—1778	—0468	—3485	0466	4528
15	6194	—1842	—0426	—1584	0328	—0593	4491
16	6433	—3218	—1219	—0392	—0919	0619	5461
17	6340	—2457	—2477	—2480	0928	0446	5958
18	5170	—1501	—1190	—0849	2216	2118	4052
19	4809	1752	—4489	3092	0072	—0864	5666
20	4425	1845	—1584	2020	0447	1115	3105
21	4950	—0329	—2234	0331	—1482	1102	3312

[1] Decimal points have been omitted.

TABLE 18-VIII
LEAST SQUARES APPROXIMATION MATRIX—F_1[1]

	1	2	3	4	5	6	hj^2
1	539	—325	326	112	—028	—033	5168
2	613	—371	393	222	226	—129	7849
3	519	—367	233	201	092	—023	5077
4	571	051	—194	237	179	—205	4965
5	473	180	047	127	170	065	3076
6	181	173	049	—259	—175	—148	1847
7	199	168	183	—271	—109	—241	2447
8	098	177	—108	—176	204	—303	2170
9	214	277	195	063	—296	156	2765
10	243	321	131	212	—193	202	3022
11	467	245	090	—206	088	198	3756
12	279	106	204	—194	220	299	3061
13	390	011	—017	—024	—108	097	1742
14	515	—167	—161	—054	—365	034	4563
15	617	—175	—077	—143	018	—057	4413
16	644	—294	—137	—024	—142	065	5449
17	643	—243	—232	—267	145	063	6226
18	517	—154	—130	—064	200	121	3666
19	539	208	—425	271	110	—097	5974
20	413	165	—159	234	076	138	3027
21	477	—044	—201	060	—135	155	3157

[1] Decimal points have been omitted.

TABLE 18-IX

DIFFERENCES BETWEEN F AND F_1[1]

	1	2	3	4	5	6	h_j^2
1	001	—005	—014	026	041	133	0078
2	—012	—003	—020	—004	—003	050	—0192
3	—003	—015	019	—011	—005	066	—0024
4	029	028	—006	018	028	—058	0344
5	017	—007	033	—026	029	—050	0185
6	008	038	040	036	033	045	0707
7	—013	—027	—040	—018	—057	074	—0040
8	014	005	002	030	—042	049	0331
9	—001	—002	023	—012	038	—040	0192
10	—008	—010	—010	000	—012	025	—0060
11	001	—006	—013	—038	010	015	—0104
12	—019	013	—012	—002	018	010	0019
13	003	013	—004	—009	041	—016	0097
14	010	—028	017	—007	—016	012	—0035
15	002	009	—034	015	015	002	0078
16	—001	028	—015	015	—050	—003	0012
17	—009	003	016	—019	—052	—018	—0268
18	000	—004	—011	020	022	091	0386
19	—058	—033	024	038	—003	—011	0308
20	029	020	—011	—032	—031	—026	0078
21	018	—011	022	—027	013	—045	0155

[1] Decimal points have been omitted.

In all probability, the use of the reliability estimates so that only reliable data would be factored was a poor communality estimate for the first centroid solution. These reliability estimates are higher than the calculated communalities, as may be seen by comparison of the h^2j and the reliability estimates in Table 18-II, Part I.

SUMMARY AND CONCLUSIONS

This section of the paper has been devoted to comparing the centroid and the multiple-group methods of factoring. A least squares approximation of the F matrix from the V matrix was made. It was shown that, for all practical purposes, the two methods yield similar solutions when the same communalities are used in both solutions.

The author is inclined to think there is merit in the use of the multiple-group method of factoring, however. The centroid method is a laborious method which requires the reproduction of the matrix after the extraction of each factor, while the multiple-group method requires a reproduced matrix after the extraction of several factors. Residuals after the extraction of one factor at a time often leave one in doubt about remaining factors. The simultaneous extraction of several group factors leaves residuals which, in many instances, indicate rather clearly the remaining groups.

REFERENCES

1. ARMY AIR FORCES AVIATION PSYCHOLOGY PROGRAM: Research Report, No. 4. *Apparatus Tests.* (By Melton, Arthur E., Ed.). Washington, Government Printing Office, 1947.

2. BASS, RUTH I.: An analysis of the components of tests of semicircular canal function and of static and dynamic balance. *Res Quart Amer Ass Health Phys Educ, 10*:35-52, May 1939.

3. CARPENTER, AILEEN: Factors in motor educability, *Res Quart Amer Ass Health Phys Educ, 14*:366-371, Dec. 1943.

4. CARPENTER, AILEEN: The differential measurement of speed in primary school children. *Child Develop, 12*:1-7, March 1941.

5. COOMBS, C. H.: A criterion for significant common factor variance. *Psychometrika, 6*:264-272. 1941.

6. CURETON, T. K.: *Physical Fitness Appraisal and Guidance. Factor Analysis of Twenty-two Physical Fitness Tests.* St. Louis, C. V. Mosby and Co., 1947.

7. DOLL, EDGAR A.: *The Oseretsky Tests of Motor Proficiency.* Minneapolis, Educ Test Bureau, Educ Pub, 1946.

8. GARFIEL, EVELYN: The Measurement of Motor Ability, *Archives of Psychol, 9*:1-47, April 1923.

9. HARRIS, C. W.: Direct rotation to primary structure. *J Educa Psychol, 39*:449-468, Dec., 1948.

10. HARRIS, C. W., and JOHN SCHMIDT, JR.: Further application of the principles of direct rotation in factor analysis. *J Exper Educa, 18*:175-193, March 1950.

11. HARRIS, C. W.: The symmetrical idempotent matrix in factor analysis. *J Exper Educ, 19*:239-246, March 1951.

12. HOLZINGER, KARL J.: A simple method of factor analysis. *Psychometrika, 9*:257-262, Dec. 1944.

13. JONES, L. M.: *Factorial Ability in Fundamental Motor Skills.* New York, Bureau of Publication, Contributions to Education No. 665, Teachers College, Columbia University, 1935.

14. LARSON, L. A.: A Factor Analysis of Motor Ability Variables and Tests, with Tests for College Men, *Res Quart Amer Ass Health Phys Educ, 12*: 499-517, May 1941.

15. LARSON, L. A.: A Factor and Validity Analysis of Strength Variables with a Test Combination of Chinning, Dipping, and Vertical Jump. *Res Quart Amer Ass Health Phys Educ, 11*:82-96, Dec. 1940.

16. McCLOY, C. H.: The measurements of motor capacity and general motor ability, *Res Quart Amer Ass Health Phys Educ, 5*:46-61, March 1934.

17. Metheny, Eleanor: Studies of the Johnson test as a test of motor educability. *Res Quart Amer Ass Health Phys Educ, 9*:105-114, Dec. 1938.
18. Phillips, Marjorie: Study of a series of physical education tests by factor analysis. *Res Quart Amer Ass Health Phys Educ, 20*:60-71, March 1949.
19. Rimoldi, Horacio, J. A.: Personal tempo. *J Abnorm Soc Psychol, 46*:283-303, July 1951.
20. Seashore, Harold G.: Some relationships of fine and gross motor abilities. *Res Quart Amer Ass Health Phys Educ, 15*:259-274, Oct. 1942.
21. Seashore, Robert H.; Dudek, Frank J.; and Holtzman, Wayne: A factorial analysis of arm-hand precision tests. *J Appl Psychol, 33*:579-584, Dec. 1949.
22. Seashore, Robert H.; Dudek, Frank J., and Holtzman, Wayne: An experimental and theoretical analysis of fine motor skills. *Amer J Psychol, 53*:86-98, 1940.
23. Spearman, C.: *The Abilities of Man.* New York, Macmillan, 1927.
24. Thurstone, L. L.: A multiple-group method of factoring the correlation matrix. *Psychometrika, 10*:73-78, June 1945.
25. Thurstone, L. L.: *Multiple Factor Analysis.* Chicago, U of Chicago, 1947.
26. Thurstone, L. L.: Note about the multiple-group method. *Psychometrika, 14*:43-45, March 1949.
27. Thurstone, L. L.: *Primary Mental Abilities.* Psychometric monographs, no. 1, 1938.
28. Wendler, Arthur J.: A critical analysis of test elements used in physical education. *Res Quart Amer Ass Health Phys Educ, 9*:64-76, March 1938.

Chapter 19

LEARNING TO JUGGLE: III. A STUDY OF PERFORMANCE BY TWO DIFFERENT AGE GROUPS*

Clyde G. Knapp, Robert W. Dixon, and Murney Lazier

INTRODUCTION

IN A PREVIOUS study of juggling[3] it was found that a short work-rest practice situation (5 minutes per day) facilitated more rapid learning than a longer work-rest practice situation (15 minutes every other day). The subjects of that investigation were male seniors at the University of Illinois who were majoring or minoring in physical education. Since these subjects were highly selected and had the maturity and ability needed for performing complex sensory-motor skills, the findings should not be applied indiscriminately to other groups. The present investigation was designed to determine whether similar results might be obtained by using unselected relatively immature high school subjects in a similar learning condition.

Any attempt to predict relative levels of motor performance of unselected high school and college seniors specializing in physical education would almost certainly point to superiority of the college student. The statement "boys continue to improve in physical skills at least through the seventeenth year"[1, p. 331] is representative of what the literature says on this subject. Espenschade's study[2] shows almost continual improvement in athletic performance during the adolescent years. Out of curiosity, several colleagues of the writers were queried and without exception they predicted that the college students would learn to juggle more rapidly than the high school subjects.

---

* C. G. Knapp, W. R. Dixon, and M. Lazier: Learning to juggle: III. A study of performance by two different age groups. *Res Quart Amer Ass Health Phys Educ*, 29:1958, 32-36. Reproduced here with the permission of Professor Clyde G. Knapp and the American Association for Health, Physical Education, and Recreation.

PROCEDURE

In the present study, the subjects were boys enrolled in physical education classes at Evanston Township High School. Selection of subjects was at random. Practice preparations and instructions duplicated those in the previous study. The criterion for learning—100 consecutive catches—was the same. Several demonstrations of juggling were presented, mimeographed rules and suggestions were given to each subject, and discussion was permitted for the purpose of clarifying understanding of procedure. The rules and suggestions, identical with those given the college seniors, were:

A. Rules

1. Only the whole method is permissible.
   a. You may not practice the hand movements without using balls.
   b. You may not practice the toss and catch using less than three balls.
2. During a juggle at least one ball must be in the air at all times. If two balls touch a hand simultaneously the count must stop.
3. Time and distribution of practice session, as stipulated for your group, must be followed exactly.

B. Suggestions

1. Start with two balls in the dominant hand.
2. Toss and catch balls with rhythmical movements.
3. In tossing let the ball leave the hand approximately in front of the chin with the head facing forward.
4. Toss the ball to a height approximately equal to the top of your head.
5. Toss the ball so that it may be caught about six inches to the left, or right, of the sternum line at a height slightly above the belt.
6. Toss the ball to the inside of the ball about to be caught.
7. Watch the balls with a minimum of eye movement.
8. Concentrate on your task.
9. Relax.

In one way the present procedure differed from that of the experiment with college seniors. In the previous study, one group practiced five minutes daily and another group fifteen minutes every other day with no interruptions for weekends. In the present study, *daily* was five days a week in physical education classes and *every other day* was three days one week, two days the next, etc. Thus, *daily* was every class period and *every other day* was every other class period.

RESULTS

Table 19-I presents the average time required by the high school subjects to learn to juggle. Notice that the mean score for the five minute group is 83.53 minutes, while the average score for the other group was 148.80 minutes. The significance of the difference between the two means was computed by using the Student-Fisher *t*-test. A *t*-value of 4.59 was obtained, and this is significant at the 1 percent level of confidence.

TABLE 19-I
A COMPARISON OF MEAN TIMES REQUIRED FOR HIGH SCHOOL
STUDENTS TO LEARN TO JUGGLE BY TWO WORK-REST
PRACTICE METHODS

Group	N	Mean	Std. Dev.	Diff.	t	P
Five minutes daily	19	83.53	40.12			
Fifteen minutes on alternate days	25	148.80	49.49	65.27	4.59	.01

The five-minute daily group learned to juggle significantly faster than the group which practiced fifteen minutes on alternate days. In the college investigation, one minute invested by the five-minute group was worth 1.80 minutes spent by the fifteen-minute group. The ratio in the present investigation was one minute to 1.78 minutes.

Table 19-II presents the results of comparing the performances of the high school students with those of the college subjects. No significance was found between the differences in means of comparable groups. A *t*-value of 1.01 was found when the two five-minute groups were contrasted and a *t*-value of 1.39 when the two fifteen-minute groups were analyzed. Neither of these *t*-values achieves the 5 percent level of confidence.

Tables 19-I and 19-II include only subjects who achieved the criterion of 100 consecutive catches. Not shown in the tables is the fact that more high school than college students failed to meet the criterion. In the five-minute groups there were twelve high school subjects who spent at least 165 minutes in practice who never completed 100 consecutive catches, whereas every college student who started met the standard. In the fifteen-minute groups, there were twenty-one high school boys who practiced 200 minutes, or more, and still did not meet the criterion, while only four college students did not succeed.

TABLE 19-II

COMPARISON OF MINUTES REQUIRED BY HIGH SCHOOL
STUDENTS AND COLLEGE STUDENTS TO LEARN TO JUGGLE

Group	N	Mean	Std. Dev.	Diff.	t	P
5-minute high school	19	.83.53	40.12	13.67	1.01	.30
5-minute college	35	69.86	48.20			
15-minute high school	25	148.80	49.49	23.00	1.39	.10
15-minute college	31	125.80	68.60			

Among subjects who met the standard, college students furnished both the fastest and the slowest learners. In the five-minute groups, the range of the college subjects was from nineteen to 210 minutes, while the high school students ranged from forty to 178 minutes. In the fifteen-minutes groups, the college students ranged from forty to 278 minutes, while the high school subjects varied from forty-five to 235 minutes.

DISCUSSION OF RESULTS

The shorter work-test situation produced learning in less practice time for high school subjects, as it did for college students. Thus, the present experiment has obtained additional evidence to support the idea that a shorter work-rest situation reduces the time required to learn.

There was no statistical difference between the time required for the high school boys to learn to juggle and time required by the college students. How can this result be explained? The selective nature of the college subjects and the *mine run* nature of the high school boys makes explanation in terms of maturation only impossible. However, one possibility would be that the task of juggling places no particular premium on such a variable as strength. Examination of the data compiled by Espenschade shows that in one of the athletic performances—target throwing—the oldest boys did not do as well as the youngest boys. In target throwing, there did not seem to be a significant change in performance within the age groups studied. It is quite possible that juggling presents a similar situation. Juggling may place little premium on either strength or other maturational changes customarily occurring between high school freshman and college senior ages.

The increase in the number of subjects who did not meet the criterion deserves comment. Actually, most of these subjects did achieve some measure of success. It might have been reasonable to establish a lower standard for the younger group. If, for example, twenty-five catches had been the criterion all but three of the five-minute group and all but six of the fifteen-minute group would have been successful. Nevertheless reasons for greater rate of failure in the high school group exist though they are not known. One explanation might be offered in terms of maturity. Perhaps the high school students who failed simply were not physically mature enough for the task. Another explanation might be offered in terms of motivation. Perhaps the *mine run* high school boys had less desire to learn to juggle than did college physical education major or minor seniors.

No significant mental maturational differences were found among the high school students who failed and those who succeeded. Table 19-III shows the status of the successful and unsuccessful subjects in terms of mental maturity.

Another possibility is to explain the increase in failures by the selection which has taken place. Whatever it is that is causing more high school students to fail has kept these boys out of physical education as a major or minor field. High school boys who fail have low motor

TABLE 19-III

COMPARISON OF CHRONOLOGICAL AGE, MENTAL AGE, AND INTELLIGENCE QUOTIENTS OF SUCCESSFUL AND UNSUCCESSFUL JUGGLERS AMONG HIGH SCHOOL SUBJECTS

		Chron. Age		Mental Age		IQ	
Group	*N*	*Mean*	*Range*	*Mean*	*Range*	*Mean*	*Range*
Successful	44	14.3	13-16	189 ms.	148-246	111	77-157
Unsuccessful	33	14.4	14-17	187 ms.	142-286	109	79-159

ability and do not choose a career in physical education. This hypothesis could be tested by securing a sample of non-physical education college seniors and studying their response to the task.

SUMMARY AND CONCLUSIONS

The present study reports data which were collected as high school freshmen attempted to learn to juggle under two different practice-rest conditions. The subjects in one group practiced juggling three paddle tennis balls for five minutes daily until they were able to make 100 consecutive catches, while another group practiced the same skill for fifteen minutes every second day. The evidence obtained from the high school freshmen was then compared with the results secured from a previous study group involving college seniors in physical education.

The following conclusions are indicated:

(1) The five-minute daily practice sessions secured more rapid learning than did the fifteen-minute every second day sessions. This was true for both the high school freshmen and the college seniors;

(2) There was no statistically significant difference between the time required to learn to juggle by the high school freshmen who met the criterion of 100 consecutive catches and by the college seniors in physical education;

(3) There was a sharp increase in the number of failures in the more immature group. These *failures* could have been practically eliminated if a lower criterion of success in juggling (20 to 25 catches) had been established. No explanation has been found in the data available for the increased rate of failure among the high school students.

REFERENCES

1. BRECKENRIDGE, MARIAN E., and VINCENT, E. LEE: *Child Development.* Philadelphia, Saunders, 1949.
2. ESPENSCHADE, ANNA: *Motor Performance in Adolescence.* Society for Research in Child Development, National Research Council, Washington, D.C., 1940.
3. KNAPP, CLYDE G., and DIXON, W. ROBERT: Learning to juggle: I. A Study to determine the effect of two different distributions of practice on learning efficiency. *Res Quart Amer Ass Health Phys Educ, 21*:331-336, Oct. 1950.
4. KNAPP, CLYDE G.: Learning to juggle: II. A study of whole and part meth-methods. *Res Quart Amer Ass Health Phys Educ, 23*:398-401, Dec. 1952.

Chapter 20

INFLUENCE OF NEUROMOTOR PROGRAM ALTERATION ON THE SPEED OF A STANDARD ARM MOVEMENT*

Leon E. Smith

INTRODUCTION

Recent theory concerned with discrete simple limb movements made at maximum speed holds that the motor action results from the triggering of a previously learned and stored CNS neural program (motor memory). Upon release, this program organizes and directs the detailed operation of synapses in the neuromotor centers, resulting in an outflow of appropriate motor nerve impulses, thus causing a reproduction of the previously learned limb movement. There is reason to believe that after the action has been triggered, the carrying out of the program progresses to completion in a manner that is remarkably resistant to modification (Henry, 1960 a, b; Henry & Harrison, 1961).

From this concept, it appears likely that, if one could create two different neural or CNS *programs* A and B (both of which would result in a substantially identical movement), then individual differences in the effectiveness of A in producing the fastest possible movement would have little or no correlation with individual differences in the effectiveness of B. This hypothesis follows from the theoretical postulation that individual differences in the maximal speed of a limb movement ordinarily reside in the CNS program directing that movement rather than in the ultimate capacity of the muscular tissue to create force (Henry & Whitley, 1960). Evidence supporting the postulate includes observations that the correlation between muscular

* L. E. Smith: Influence of neuromotor program alteration on the speed of a standard arm movement. *Perceptual and Motor Skills,* 15:1962, 327-330. Reproduced here with the permission of the author and publisher.

[213]

strength capacity measured statically in the movement position and maximal speed of the limb (which must reflect the force actually exerted in movement) is very small, even though both variables show high reliability. The findings have shown close agreement, although strength has been measured by several techniques, and different limbs and directions of movement have been employed (Clarke, 1960; Clarke & Henry, 1961; Henry, 1960 a; Rasch, 1954; Smith, 1961 a,b).

METHOD

The movement was the forward horizontal arm swing of approximately 100°, recently described by Henry (1961). Under procedure A, *S* rested his hand on the first timing key and started at his own initiative. His instructions were to move the arm as fast as possible throughout the arc. Under Procedure B, he performed two serial acts. In the first (untimed) he began at his own initiative by pulling maximally on the handle of a dynamometer placed in the starting position. After approximately thirty seconds, when he thought he had developed maximal tension, he began the second act by pressing a switch held in his free hand. This operated an electric mechanism which detached the handle from the dynamometer. As a part of the same action and while continuing to hold the handle (which weighed only 28 gm), he moved it off of the first timing key and swung his arm through the horizontal arc as rapidly as possible. Thus the starting position and movement (a 105° lateral straight-arm adduction at maximal speed) were identical for both A and B movements. Nevertheless, the time patterns of the excitation of the muscles, and therefore the CNS or neural programs, were necessarily different because of the premovement stimulation of the driving muscles in B.

In order to make sure that the results were not specific to a particular phase of the movement, four timing stations were used. Pull-out strings which operated microswitches were placed on the arc of a horizontal circle that had a radius of sixty-five centimeters. The first microswitch (Station O) was released when *S* first moved his hand counterclockwise to start the movement. Timing station No. 1 was at an arc distance of 17.3 centimeters, No. 2 was at 60.5 centimeters, No. 3 at 103.6 centimeters, and No. 4 at 121 centimeters. The target, a loose-hanging towel, was at 136 centimeters. The string supports and microswitches were attached to two plywood arcs of about sixty centimeters inner radius, separated vertically fifty centimeters and supported from the floor in an adjustable fashion. The construction was similar to an apparatus described by Henry (1960 a).

For both A and B, *S* sat erect in a chair with his right shoulder at the center of the arc radius determined by his arm length, using his feet and the free arm to brace himself firmly. The right arm was clenched and the arm rigidly extended sideward, with the hand on the No. 0 microswitch. The counterclockwise arm swing was performed with the arm kept rigid, pivoting at the shoulder without body twist except at the very last part of the movement. Release of the No. 0 microswitch started four S-1 electric chronoscopes, each of them being stopped in turn as the arm swept through the strings at the timing stations. The angular movement for the average *S* was approximately 15° at No. 1, 53° at No. 2, 90° at No. 3, and 105° at No. 4.

Sixty male college students, age nineteen years ($S = 1.06$), were tested. Half were given five practice trials and twenty tests with A, followed by five practice trials and twenty tests with B. The other half were tested in the reverse order.

RESULTS AND DISCUSSION

The *within-program* consistency of individual differences in speed of movement, estimated by the split-half reliability coefficients, is quite high (see Table 20-I). These are product-moment correlations without the Spearman-Brown correction. In contrast, the *between-program* correlations are very low, and none of them differs significantly from zero. The *ts* for the differences between the two types of correlations range from 50 to 53. The between-program correlations for *net* time between stations are .11 for 1 and 2, .13 for 2 and 3, and .14 for 3 and 4. Consequently, the hypothesis being tested, namely, that individual differences in the effectiveness of Program A in producing fast movements would have little or no correlation with individual differences in the effectiveness of Program B, is confirmed. The experimental evidence supports Henry's *program* theory of discrete movements that formed the basis of the hypothesis.

Quite aside from the implications for that theory, the results clearly

TABLE 20-I

CORRELATION COEFFICIENTS (r)

Timing Station (cumulative)	Within Program A	B	Between programs A vs B
1	.932	.965	.033
2	.944	.978	.059
3	.951	.980	.199
4	.949	.980	.219

demonstrate the extreme specificity of movement abilities. The doctrine of motor specificity has recently received considerable attention (Bachman, 1961; Henry & Smith, 1961; Lotter, 1961; Smith, 1961 a). While some psychologists have long been aware that motor abilities tend to be uncorrelated, it is now becoming evident that such a tendency is far more extreme than had been realized.

TABLE 20-II

SPEED OF MOVEMENT (cm./sec.)

Program	Mean Speed per Interval 1	2	3	4	Change in Speed 0-1	1-2	2-3	3-4
A	303	690	876	785	303	387	186	—91
B	216	616	760	662	216	400	144	—99
Diff.	87	74	116	123	87	—13	42	8

While the hypothesis under test was concerned with individual differences, it is interesting that the average S exhibits different speed patterns in the two programs. This is shown by the data on change in speed between intervals (Table 20-II). The difference between A and B, computed at the first timing station, is *positive* and statistically significant ($t = 11.5$, $p < .01$). This means that the *change* in speed from zero (no movement) to the average speed for the first interval was greater with A. The next computation involves the net gain in average speed for the second timing interval compared with the speed over the first interval. In this case, the difference in change is also significant ($t = 10.2$, $p < .01$), but it is *negative*, since the greater change occurred in B. Thus, the pattern of change is different with the two procedures, and inferentially for the two programs. It should be noted that the changes in speed in the table are simple increments. They are not stated in units of acceleration, because of the relatively large and unequal distances between successive timing stations, and uncertainty as to the mathematical form of the acceleration curve.

SUMMARY AND CONCLUSIONS

The maximal speed of a lateral adductive arm movement was measured in sixty male college students. Two *programs* were used. With the first, the movement was an arm swing from a resting start; with the other the muscles were pre-tensed before the start, the movement being identical with the first in other respects and the starting positions identical. There were four timing stations, placed at 15, 53, 90, and 105°. Using both cumulative and net times at each station, the correlations between speeds with each program were small and nonsignificant, although the reliability coefficients for scores within each program were very high. It is concluded that the results support the doctrine of extreme specificity of individual differences in movement ability. They also support the current movement theory that ascribes individual differences in maximal speed to differences in the CNS or neural program that controls the detailed muscular actions.

REFERENCES

1. BACHMAN, J. C.: Specificity vs. generality in learning and performing two large muscle motor tasks. *Res Quart Amer Ass Health Phys Educ,* 1961, *32,* 3-11.
2. CLARKE, D. H.: Correlation between the strength/mass ratio and the speed of an arm movement. *Res Quart Amer Ass Health Phys Educ,* 1960 *31,* 570-574.
3. CLARKE, D. H., and HENRY, F. M.: Neuromotor specificity and increased speed from strength development. *Res Quart Amer Ass Health Phys Educ,* 1961, *32,* 315-325.
4. HENRY, F. M.: Factorial structure of speed and static strength in a lateral arm movement. *Res Quart Amer Ass Health Phys Educ,* 1960, *31,* 440-447. (a)
5. HENRY, F. M.: Increased response latency for complicated movements and a *memory drum* theory of neuromotor reaction. *Res Quart Amer Ass Health Phys Educ,* 1960, *31,* 448-458. (b)
6. HENRY, F. M.: Reaction time-movement time correlation. *Percept Mot Skills,* 1961, *12,* 63-66.
7. HENRY, F. M., and HARRISON, J. S.: Refractoriness of a fast movement. *Percept Mot Skills,* 1961, *13,* 351-354.
8. HENRY, F. M., and SMITH, L. E.: Simultaneous vs. separate bilateral muscular contractions in relation to neural overflow theory and neuromotor specificity. *Res Quart Amer Ass Health Phys Educ,* 1961, *32,* 42-46.
9. HENRY, F. M., and WHITLEY, J. D.: Relationships between individual differences in strength, speed and mass in an arm movement. *Res Quart Amer Health Phys Educ,* 1960, *31,* 24-33.

218   *Contemporary Readings In Sport Psychology*

10. Lotter, W. S.: Specificity or generality of speed of systematically related movements. *Res Quart Amer Ass Health Phys Educ,* 1961 *32,* 55-62.
11. Rasch, P. J.: Relationship of arm-strength, weight and length to speed of movement. *Res Quart Amer Ass Health Phys Educ,* 1954, *25,* 328-332.
12. Smith, L. E.: Individual differences in strength, reaction latency, mass and length of limbs, and their relation to maximal speed of movement. *Res Quart Amer Ass Health Phys Educ,* 1961, *32,* 208-220. (a).
13. Smith, L. E.: Relationship between explosive leg strength and performance in the vertical jump. *Res Quart Amer Ass Health Phys Educ,* 1961, *32,* 405-408. (b)

Chapter 21

LEARNING*

Harriet G. Williams

INTRODUCTION

Not until recently has much thought or attention been given
to the effects of physical activity upon the learning capacities of the
individual. However, with the current upsurge in interest in the child
with special learning disabilities, physical education and physical education activities have assumed an increasingly important role in programs designed to enhance the cognitive or intellectual development of
the retarded or slow learner.

The assumption behind the involvement of physical activity in such
programs is that it is principally through appropriate motor experiences that a "veridical organization of the perceptual world is
possible" [16] and that only when such perceptual organization is
achieved can the individual realize his full intellectual potential. Consequently, physical activity has come to be regarded by some as "an
essential tool, indeed a primary tool, in inducing optimal mental development." [1] With such important responsibilities as these being
thrust upon the shoulders of physical education and physical activity,
it seems important for us, as physical educators, to look back and to
evaluate as objectively as possible what is fact and what is fancy about
the contributions of physical activity to the intellectual, cognitive, and
perceptual development of the individual.

EXERCISE AND MENTAL ABILITIES

Two main sources of information are pertinent to the discussion of
the effects of exercise upon the mental abilities of the individual with

* H. G. Williams: Learning. *J Hlth Phys Ed & Rec, 38*:1968, 28-31. Reproduced here with the permission of the author and the American Association for
Health, Physical Education, and Recreation.

[219]

average intelligence. First, there are the data derived from various studies that have taken some measure of physical fitness or physical proficiency and have correlated it with an index of academic success or mental capacity. Second, there are the data obtained from studies designed to look more directly at the effects of physical activity upon the performance of certain mental tasks.

By and large, results from correlational studies[8, 24, 31, 32] have suggested that there may exist a rather low but positive relationship between physical fitness or motor proficiency and general academic achievement, particularly if such achievement is measured by some sort of grade point average index (*r's* range from +.009 to +.660). Such data have frequently been used as the basis for extolling the benefits of physical exercise, inferring that the exercise habits of the individual were directly responsible for the academic success achieved. This is, of course, not legitimate since a correlation coefficient, regardless of how high or low it is, gives no information about cause and effect. With correlational data, one can never be quite certain whether individuals who exhibit greater academic success do so because they are physically fit or whether individuals who are academically successful simply happen to exercise more frequently than other individuals.

In studies where IQ and activity levels of younger children have been correlated, results have indicated that IQ and other measures of intelligence are in no way related to the general activity level of the individual.[18] In other words, children of average or below average intelligence (but not retarded) were shown to be as physically active as children of above average or superior intelligence. Studies which have been designed to assess the effects of exercise on intellectual performance in a more direct way have also indicated that participation in regular physical activity, either for brief or prolonged periods of time, has little or no effect upon such mental capacities as verbal comprehension and symbolic reasoning.[6, 20] Thus, although programs of exercise may bring about certain demonstrable physiological changes in the individual, accompanying changes in mental capacity as a result of such exercise are not as readily documented. Still, certain animal studies have shown that depriving the young animal of the opportunity for active physical exploration of his environment during the early developmental years may result in lowered performance on "animal intelligence tests." [4, 25]

EXERCISE AND THE MENTALLY RETARDED

Recent research indicates that the mentally retarded individual may derive a number of important benefits from planned programs of physical activity. For example, mentally retarded individuals show significant improvements in physical abilities when given specialized training or instruction in systematized programs of physical education.[13, 15, 22, 29]

Dramatic gains in the intellectual efficiency of the mentally retarded as a result of participation in programs of physical activity have also been noted.[3, 15, 22] Oliver[22] reported, for example, that participation in a ten-week program of organized physical education and recreational activities resulted in significant increases in the IQ's of 25 percent of the individuals participating in the program. No similar improvements were noted in a control group not allowed to participate in such a program.

Although improvements in intellectual capacities of the mentally retarded are frequently reported, the exact contribution of physical activity to such achievement is not as clearcut as it may seem at first glance. To illustrate, in a recent study concerned with the effects of physical education activities on the intellectual development of mentally retarded boys, Corder[3] attempted to control for the so-called *Hawthorne* or *extra attention* effect, a factor which many studies have disregarded. To do this, the investigator singled out a group of boys who were to be excused from regular routines to perform special jobs but were not to participate in any organized form of physical activity. Results indicated that, in terms of IQ gains, the extra attention group was not significantly different from the experimental group who participated in the planned program of physical activity, but neither were they significantly different from the control group who simply followed the regular school routine. This, of course, raises the question of just how much of the IQ gain observed in the experimental group was due to physical activity and how much to other factors at work in the situation.

THE DOMAN-DELACATO SYSTEM

In recent years, there has been considerable interest in, discussion about, and controversy over the system proposed by Glen Doman and

Carl Delacato for training children who are or have been diagnosed as brain-damaged.[5, 17, 27] This system of treatment is based upon the assumption that every individual must pass through a definite sequence of steps in his or her sensorimotor-cognitive development. If any one of these stages of development is skipped over or passed through improperly, the *neurological organization* of that individual may be faulty and the individual may experience certain perceptual and/or cognitive difficulties which are reminiscent of brain damage. A part of the treatment proposed for such individuals is a series of manipulated or patterned movements (including creeping and crawling), which are purportedly designed to reproduce the normal activity of undeveloped parts of the brain.

Proponents of the Doman-Delacato system have frequently reported large and dramatic gains in the cognitive or intellectual functioning of individuals who have been trained in such a program of patterned activity. Frequent and just criticisms have been made of these studies, however, on the basis of their failure to apply even the simplest and most basic elements of experimental and/or statistical design. In many cases, for example, control groups have not been used, a procedure which makes the results derived from such studies completely uninterpretable.[17] This is not meant to imply that the system itself is unsound but rather that we need to work out in a clearcut and scientific manner, the kinds of behavioral changes which can and cannot be attributed to the use of such a system.

Results from a recent study[27] carefully designed to test the Doman-Delacato rationale with retarded readers, through the use of both control and placebo groups and a large sample of subjects, revealed no significant differences between control, placebo, and treatment groups in terms of observable changes in reading performance. The program of patterned activity had little or no effect upon the reading capacities of retarded readers involved in the program. Thus in the eyes of many scientists, clearcut proof of the efficacies or benefits of planned programs of patterned activity upon cognitive or intellectual development in the individual has yet to be established.

OTHER COGNITIVE SKILLS

A few studies have reported that certain related aspects of the mentally retarded individual's cognitive behavior may be positively influenced by programs involving training in gross bodily coordination.[14, 15, 30] Troth [30] suggests that as a result of training in both gross and fine motor coordination tasks, mentally retarded individuals show a definite increase in the length of attention span as well as an observable improvement in the ability to recognize certain geometric and perceptual forms. There is some reason to believe that when simple movements of the body are involved in learning tasks which involve right-left discriminations, children of average intelligence are able to master such concepts significantly more quickly than when no such movement is involved.[14] Evidence from animal studies also suggests that early visual and motor experiences may play an important role in the ease with which certain complex mazes are learned.[4, 25] Although such evidence as this does indeed suggest that physical activity may be important in the development of certain perceptual-cognitive behaviors, such data are far from substantial enough to warrant any wholesale conclusions about physical activity and perceptual-cognitive functioning.

FINE PSYCHOMOTOR SKILLS

There is some evidence to suggest that mild forms of exercise may have a significant and positive effect upon the learning and performance of certain fine hand-eye coordination skills in mildly or severely retarded individuals. Harrison[7] reported, for example, that a group of nonverbal retardates improved significantly in their ability to unbutton a row of buttons of different sizes after a four-week period of planned physical exercise. Similar findings have been reported by Painter,[23] who found that exposure to programs of physical activity had a profound and positive influence upon the young child's ability to perform such fine perceptual-motor skills as drawing figures and copying complex geometric forms. It would appear then that certain fine neuromuscular coordinations may be improved through regular exposure to some form of physical activity. Because few if any of these studies have as yet been replicated, we cannot accept as universal fact these *apparent* benefits of exercise upon fine neuromuscular coordination.

VISUO-PERCEPTUAL CAPACITIES

Since much of learning takes place through the visual sense, it seems important to discuss what effects, if any, exercise may have upon the visuoperceptual capacities of the individual. It is interesting to note that although visual perception is believed to play an important role in skilled motor performance not a great deal is actually known about how such activity affects the individual's visuoperceptual capacities.

Muscular activity has been shown to affect certain perceptual capacities of both humans and animals. Several animal studies have indicated that when the young animal is prevented from moving freely about in his environment, depth perception faculties may fail to develop properly and visually guided behaviors may be considerably slower in appearing than in the normally reared animal.[10, 11, 25, 26] In man, the perception of size as well as recognition of specific visual forms appears to be dependent upon some degree of coordination between visual and motor experiences.[2, 9]

Although the basis for such prescription is not clearly understood, doctors have occasionally prescribed certain motor activities, including gross motor coordination skills, balance stunts, and eye-hand coordination tasks, to promote the development of visual perception skills in children.[21] One investigator has reported that participation in specifically designed sensorimotor activity programs appears to enhance the development of certain visuospatial abilities in the young child.[23]

Highly skilled athletes have also been shown to possess certain visual capacities which are superior to those of the nonathlete or poorly skilled individual.[28, 33] Such evidence does not, however, indicate in any way whether the individual's involvement in physical activity produced these superior visual skills or whether it was due to the possession of such capacities that the individual became an outstanding athlete.

ADAPTATION TO VISUALLY DISTORTED ENVIRONMENTS

It is widely recognized that for adaptation to a visually rearranged environment to occur, the individual must be able to move freely in and about his environment.[9,10,11,12] In other words, to regain mastery of fine hand-eye coordination skills or to overcome errors in visual localization of targets or objects in spatially rearranged visual fields, some gross bodily movement must occur.

Work by Held[11] has indicated that even spatial relationships within the individual's *real* visual field can become distorted if the individual has previously been exposed to certain visual conditions and forced to move actively about. On the other hand, if an individual is simply exposed to such visual conditions without being forced to move about, such distortions in the *real* visual world do not occur. It would seem then that there may be a very subtle but important relationship between certain veridical perceptions and the movement experience of the individual. Exactly how such functions are related to the learning process has yet to be outlined.

RECOMMENDATIONS FOR FUTURE RESEARCH

There appears to be considerable positive opinion with regard to the stimulating effects of physical activity upon certain intellectual-cognitive performances of the individual. However, a careful look at the available literature reveals that there is little if any systematic research which quantifies, in a clear and precise way, the effects of exercise or programs of physical activity upon the perceptual-cognitive-intellectual functioning of either the normal or the mentally retarded individual. This indicates a definite need for the following:

(1) Studies specifically designed to outline both the acute and chronic effects of exercise upon specific cognitive or intellectual behaviors of the individual. *Specific* behavior is stressed because it may well be that certain cognitive functions can be enhanced by participation or involvement in physical activity while others remain completely or relatively unchanged by any amount, kind, or dosage of physical activity. We need to differentiate between such capacities.

(2) Research which can answer, in certain terms, the question of whether or not physical activity can and does effect desirable changes in the perceptual capacities of the individual. Since cognitive and perceptual functions appear to be so closely linked in the human organism, this may be the point at which we should begin to unravel the puzzle of the relationship between perception, cognition, and motor activity.

(3) Replication of the work of various investigators in this field. Careful attention must be paid to the inclusion and reporting of detail pertinent to such replication. Only when we have done this and have numbers of studies which all point in the same general direction can we truly say that physical activity can and does bring about

positive changes in the perceptual-cognitive-intellectual functioning of the individual.

REFERENCES

1. BENOIT, J. PAUL: Extending the mind through the body. *J hyth phys ed rec, 37*:28-30, April 1966.
2. COMALLI, P. E., JR.; WAPNER, SEYMOUR, and WERNER, H.: Effect of muscular involvement on size perception, *Perceptual-Motor Skills, 9 (2)*:116, 1959.
3. CORDER, W. O.: Effects of physical education on the intellectual, physical, and social development of educable mentally retarded boys. *Exceptional Children, 32*:357-64, 1966.
4. FORGUS, R. H.: Early visual and motor experience as determiners of complex maze-learning ability under rich and reduced stimulation. *J Comp Physiol Psychol, 48*:215-20, 1955.
5. FREEMAN, ROGER D.: Controversy over *patterning* as a treatment for brain damage in children. *J Amer Med Assn, 202 (5)*:83-86, 1967.
6. GUTIN, BERNARD: Effect of increase in physical fitness on mental ability following physical and mental stress. *Res Quart Amer Ass Health Phys Educ, 37*:211-20, 1966.
7. HARRISON, W., and others: Effect of music and exercise on the self-help skills of nonverbal retardates. *Amer J Ment Defic, 71*:279-82, 1966.
8. HART, MARCIA E., and SHAY, CLAYTON: Relationship between physical fitness and academic success. *Res Quart Amer Ass Health Phys Educ, 35*: 443, 1964.
9. HELD, RICHARD: Motor-sensory feedback and the geometry of visual space. *Science, 141*:722-23, 1963.
10. HELD, RICHARD, and BOSSOM, J.: Neonatal deprivation and adult rearrangement: Complementary techniques for analyzing plastic sensory-motor coordination. *J Comp Physiol Psychol, 54*:33-37, 1961.
11. HELD, RICHARD, and HEIN, A.: Movement-produced stimulation in the development of visually-guided behavior. *J Comp Physiol Psychol, 56*: 872-76, 1963.
12. HOEPNER, B. J. Comparison of motor ability, new motor skill learning, and adjustment to a rearranged visual field. *Res Quart Amer Ass Health Phys Educ, 38*:605-14, 1967.
13. HOWE, C.: A comparison of motor skills of mentally retarded and normal children. *Exceptional Child, 25*:352-54, 1959.
14. JEFFREY, W. E.: Variables in early discrimination learning: Motor responses in the training of left-right discrimination. *Child Develop 29*: 269-75, 1958.
15. KARIGER, ROBERT L.: Physical education therapy. *Child Study Center Bulletin* State U of NY *3*:35-41, 1966.

16. KEPHART, N. C.: Perceptual-motor aspects of learning disabilities. *Exceptional Child, 31*:201-206, 1964.

17. KERSHNER, JOHN R.: Doman-Delacato's theory of neurological organization applied with retarded children. *Exceptional Child 441*-50, 1968.

18. MACCOBY, E. E.; DOWLEY, E. M., and HAGEN, J. W.: Activity level and intellectual functioning in normal, preschool children. *Child Develop 36*:761-70, 1965.

19. MURSTEIN, B. I., and LEIPOLD, W. D.: Role of learning and motor abilities in the Wechsler Belleview digit symbol subtest. *Educational and Psychological Measurement, 21*:103-12, Spring 1961.

20. McADAM, ROBERT E., and WANG, YUAN KAI: Performance of a simple mental task following various treatments. *Res Quart Amer Ass Health Phys Educ, 38*:208-12, 1967.

21. McKEE, G. W.: The role of the optometrist in the development of perceptual and visuomotor skills in children. *Amer J Optomet* and *Arch Amer Acad Optomet, 44*:297-310, 1967.

22. OLIVER, J. N.: Effect of physical conditioning exercises and activities on the mental characteristics of educationally sub-normal boys, *British J Educ Psychol, 28*:155-65, 1958.

23. PAINTER, GENEVIEVE: Effect of a rhythmic and sensory-motor activity program on perceptual-motor-spatial abilities of kindergarten children. *Exceptional Child, 33*:113-16, 1966.

24. RARICK, G. L., and McKEE, ROBERT: Study of twenty third-grade children exhibiting extreme levels of achievement on tests of motor proficiency. *Res Quart Amer Ass Health Phys Educ, 20*:142, 1949.

25. REISEN, A. H.: Plasticity of behavior: Psychological aspects. Pp. 425-50 in H. F. Harlow and C. N. Woolsey (Eds.): *Biological and Biochemical Bases of Behavior,* Madison, U. of Wis, 1958.

26. REISEN, A. H., and AARONS, L.: Visual movement and intensity discrimination in cats after early deprivation of pattern vision. *J Comp Physiol Psychol, 52*:142-49, 1959.

27. ROBBINS, M. P.: Test of the Doman-Delacato rationale with retarded readers. *J Amer Med Assn, 202*:87-92, 1967.

28. SLUSHER, HOWARD: Perceptual differences of selected football players, dancers, and nonperformers to a given stimulus. *Res Quart Amer Ass Health Phys Educ, 37*:424-28, 1966.

29. STEIN, JULIAN U.: Potential of physical activity for the mentally retarded child. *J Hlth Phys Educ Rec, 37*:25-27, April 1966.

30. TROTH, WILLIAM B.: Procedures and generalizations for remediation in motor coordination and perceptual training for the mentally retarded. *Train Sch Bull, 64*:77-80, 1967.

31. WEBER, JOHN R.: Relationship of physical fitness to success in college and to personality. *Res Quart, Amer Ass Health Phys Educ, 24*:471, 1954.

32. WEDEMEYER, CHARLES A.:   Gifted achievers and monachievers.   *J Higher Educ, 24*:25, 1953.
33. WILLIAMS, HARRIET G.:   *Effects of systematic variation of velocity and direction of object flight and of age and skill classifications upon visuoperceptual judgments of moving objects in three-dimensional space.* Toledo, Department of Physical Education, U of Toledo, January 1968.

PART EIGHT
PERCEPTION

Chapter 22

SPIROKINESIS*

BRYANT J. CRATTY AND JOHN N. SAGE

INTRODUCTION

STUDIES IN zoology and psychology since the turn of the century
have documented the tendency of motile organisms to veer and
spiral when deprived of external reference points. However, objective
evidence pinpointing the characteristics of this phenomenon in humans seems lacking. The previous studies might be best classified
as descriptive rather than scientific. Also, experimenters seemed
thwarted in their attempts to explain the movement characteristics.
Lund,[3] for example, while suggesting that the spiraling tendency was
due to differences in leg length present in about 80 percent of his
subjects, presented little objective evidence exactly describing the
amount of veer evidenced by them. Schaffer,[5] in the classic study of
"Spiral Movement in Man," on the other hand, suggested that veering
was due to some kind of neurological imbalance. In any case, the
tendency to veer and to spiral in the absence of orienting cues seems to
be a recognized facet of human locomotion.

REVIEW OF THE LITERATURE

Schaffer, in a series of studies dating from 1920 to 1929 based
upon observations of crabs, anelid worms, and small jellyfish, together
with a number of different kinds of spermatoza, found that they all
swam in spirals. When summarizing these observations, Schaffer

* B. J. Cratty and J. N. Sage: Spirokinesis. *Res Quart Amer Ass Health Phys
Educ,* 37:1966, 480-490. Reproduced here with the permission of Professor
Bryant J. Cratty and the American Association for Health, Physical Education,
and Recreation. This investigation was under the sponsorship of USPHS Grant
No. NB 05577-02S1 under the direction of the National Institute for Neurological
Diseases and Blindness. Data processed at the Health Sciences Computing Fa-
cility, UCLA.

[231]

stated that "No forward moving organism has yet to be found that does not move in some form of spiral path when there are no orienting senses to guide it." In a series of experiments with humans dating from 1918 to 1928, and summarized in an article in 1928, Schaffer attempted to determine whether the spiraling tendency was related to handedness, leg length, drugs, mental illness, and/or the media through which an individual moved (i.e. in water or on land). The methods employed and the records obtained in this research represents one of the most fascinating studies of human movement in the literature.[5]

In his conclusion, Schaffer stated that the tendency was for humans to move in a spiral, similar to a clock spring, when deprived of external cues; and that this spiraling tendency was due to neurological reasons, rather than to such factors as length of leg, handedness, and sex.

Lund also presented experimental evidence attempting to relate veer to leg length.[3] D'Olivera found that pilots tended to veer when walking, in the same direction they habitually veered their planes when flying,[2] while Banerjee found that when children were blindfolded and asked to walk in a straight line toward a point, errors to the left were twice as common as errors to the right.[1] Rouse and Worchel utilized blind subjects to evaluate the veering tendency and found that there were marked consistencies in veering patterns correctable only when a sound cue of high frequency was present.[4]

There were marked deficiencies in the experimental protocols employed in the previous studies attempting to evaluate veer. Schaffer, for example, merely drew his general impression of the pathways taken by his subjects; Rouse and Worschel utilized only eighteen subjects, while Lund, Banerjee,[1] and D'Olivier,[2] evaluated their findings utilizing only the most superficial of statistical procedures (i.e. percentages), nor did they attempt to control auditory cues which could have contaminated their findings.

PURPOSE

The present investigation was conducted to observe whether or not humans, deprived of auditory and visual cues, do veer or spiral when asked to walk a straight pathway, and, if so, to accurately assess the nature and amount of this veering tendency. It attempted to objectively describe rather than to determine causality. Subproblems included assessment of the effects of sex and reported hand and leg dominance upon the direction and/or amount of spiral evidenced.

DEFINITION OF TERMS

Spirokinesis

This is a spiraling movement seen when motile organisms are deprived of external cues.

Veering Tendency

This is the tendency to deviate to the left or to the right from an established pathway.

Homotropic Pattern

Individuals who consistently spiral to the left or to the right are considered to produce a homotropic pattern.

Heterotropic Pattern

Individuals who are inconsistent in their direction of spiral, sometimes moving to the left, and then to the right, are considered to produce a heterotropic spiraling pattern.

PROCEDURES

Preparation of Measurement Area

A large level athletic field was surveyed and found to evidence 1° of declination. A grid was laid out on this field 110 yards wide and 120 yards long, in squares ten yards by ten yards. A starting point was designated on one side of the field at a point sixty yards from either end. Comparable grids were drawn on graph paper on a scale of ¾ inch to ten yards. The subjects were started so that they began initially to walk uphill 1°. The testing took place within a single day, from 9 AM until 3 PM.

Subjects

The subjects consisted of 105 volunteer college-age students, seventy-six males and thirty-one females, enrolled at the University of California at Los Angeles. They were informed that they were going to take part in our experiment which was a pilot study for an investigation of the blind, and which would take only a short period of time (5-7 min.).

Task Administration

Each subject was informed that rubber ear plugs would be placed in his ears, with cotton on top of the ear plugs, and that he would be blindfolded. In addition, he was informed that a large black hood would be placed over his head. Next he was told that he would be led for five steps in a straight line and then released. He would then be asked to continue in a straight line as established by the initial five steps. Questions were answered, and then the above procedures were carried out. Following the masking of auditory cues, the subjects reported that they could hear only the voices of the experimenters when they were close at hand and speaking loudly. The subject was then led to the starting point on the large field.

The subject was then guided from behind at the elbows for five steps by an experimenter; he was released, and the experimenter followed close behind with a clipboard containing a copy of the grid upon which they were walking. Both the experimenter and the subject straddled the initial starting line while making these five steps, and the experimenter was careful not to disorient the subject when releasing him, but to remove both hands at the same time from the subject's elbows.

A mark was placed on a line on the graph when the subject crossed the corresponding line on the field. The subject was stopped after he had rotated 360° or had left the gridded area. He was then returned by the experimenter, by the shortest possible route, to the initial starting point. After being afforded a three-minute rest, he was given a second trial under the same conditions. After the completion of the second trial, the experimenter removed the hood, blindfold, and ear plugs, and asked the subject to fill out a questionnaire, giving age, height, weight, hand dominance, and leg dominance.

In addition, the experimenter asked the subject after each trial to report the direction he felt he was veering (if he felt that he had done so). Other subjective reports were collected relative to "unpleasant feelings."

The subjects were tested individually, but it was impossible to shield the field testing area from the view of prospective subjects. In all, 105 subjects were tested.

Treatment of the data

Several kinds of measures of veer were experimented with; however, it was finally decided to plot the amount of angular rotation, to the nearest degree, evidenced after the subjects had walked 100, 200, 300, and 400 feet (if they walked that far on the grid). Initially, the first 100 feet were laid out on the line inscribed on the plotting grid, after affording the subject an initial fifty feet in which he was permitted to establish his subjective "straightness." In other words, after releasing him, the actual measurement of rotation was not made until after he had proceeded fifty feet. The rotational measurement was made through the use of a map measurer on the line of veer, marking 100, 200, and 300 feet of progress with a point. Lines were then drawn tangent to the points, and a comparison of angular difference between these lines computed, resulting in measures of angular rotation at 100, 200, 300, and 400 feet. In order to reproduce the average curves walked by the various groups, the x and y coordinates of the points of the pathways of each subject were measured at 100, 200, and 300 feet by the use of a cellulose overlay containing a grid corresponding to the chart used when the data were originally collected on the field.

These coordinates were then averaged by group, and smooth curves were drawn through the points established with the aid of a French curve. Thus the final curves were representative of the average shapes of the path walked by the groups selected for analysis.

In addition, analyses of the data were made to determine general patterns of veer, consistency of the direction of veer, and the direction of veer relative to handedness and sex. One-way analyses of variance were used to assess the effects of sex and handedness upon the amount of rotation occurring at different distances along the path walked.

This measure of angular rotation was decided upon, because it seemed to most accurately describe the pathways taken, and was a measurement relatively independent of the size of the grid system. It was found in a brief pilot study, prior to this investigation, that while perhaps more accuracy might be achieved by laying out a grid having

smaller squares, taking into consideration the walking speed of the
subjects, and the speed with which an experimenter could accurately
observe and mark the pathway on a small chart, the most practical
size of the grid would be in squares ten yards by ten yards. Inter-
observer reliability, in subsequent studies, based upon the plottings
of two experimenters observing the same fifty subjects, exceeded + .9.

RESULTS

(1) Individuals deprived of auditory and visual cues, when asked

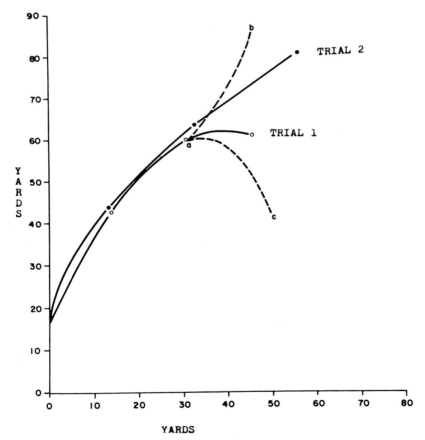

FIGURE 22-1. Average pattern walked by the total subjects on trials one and two.
Key: _____ hypothetical spread of subjects' pathways after walking
200 feet.

to walk a straight line do not follow a straight path but rather veer or deviate in some way from a straight line (Fig. 22-1).

(2) Subjects on the average walked pathways which spiraled inward rather than pathways which simply veered or circled. Increases in the amount of rotation for both trials 1 and 2 and for both trials combined at 100, 200, and 300 feet are shown in Tables 22-II and 22-III. The amount of rotation appeared to increase with the distance walked by the subjects. The most pronounced rotation occurred earlier in the first trial (between 200 and 300 ft.) than in the second trial (300 and 400 ft.).

TABLE 22-I

MEAN ANGULAR ROTATION OF ALL SUBJECTS AT
100, 200, 300, AND 400 FEET

Distance Traveled	N	*Trial One* Mean	SD
100 ft.	97	31.28°	13.51
200 ft.	97	40.33°	21.80
300 ft.	36*	77.21°	49.82
400 ft.	17*	77.80°	25.80
Distance Traveled	N	*Trial Two* Mean	SD
100 ft.	100	27.28°	22.43
200 ft.	100	32.51°	21.59
300 ft.	30	42.91°	22.92
400 ft.	44	92.90°	45.70
Distance Traveled	N	*Combined Trials* Mean	SD
100 ft.	197	29.25°	18.58
200 ft.	197	36.21°	21.69
300 ft.	66	66.25°	39.88
400 ft.	21	80.68°	30.60

* After traveling 200 ft., only 36 of the subjects remained on the graph; only 17 remained on the graph for 400 ft. Thus the rotational measures do not reflect the rotation of all subjects for all distances, and if available, their scores would have probably indicated a more marked spiraling tendency than is presented in the data above.

(3) Thirty subjects (28.6%) spiraled to the right on two consecutive trials, while twenty-five spiraled twice to the left (23.6%). Thirty additional subjects spiraled in opposite directions in their two trials, while an additional twenty produced patterns which zig-zagged and were difficult to classify as homotropic or heterotropic.

(4) There was no significant tendency for individuals to spiral in the same direction as their dominant hand, or in the direction of their

TABLE 22-II

COMPARISONS OF $\overline{X}$ ANGULAR ROTATION OF GROUPS CLASSIFIED AS TO SEX AND HANDEDNESS (M_r, M_l, F_r, F_l): TRIAL 1

	Sum of Squares	df	$\overline{X}$ Square	F
Distance—100 ft.				
Between	1,602.0	3	534.00	.58
Within	94,542.0	103	917.88	
Total	96,144.0	106	———	2.70*
Distance—200 ft.				
Between	3,847.2	3	1,282.4	1.40
Within	88,947.4	97	916.98	
Total	92,794.6	100	———	2.70*
Distance—300 ft.				
Between	7,819.6	3	2,606.53	1.01
Within	88,068.3	34	2,590.24	
Total	95,887.9	37	———	2.92*
Distance—400 ft.				
Between	3,792.1	3	1,264.03	2.59
Within	5,859.6	12	488.3	
Total	9,651.7	15	———	3.49*

* Significant at .05 level of confidence.

TABLE 22-III

COMPARISONS OF $\overline{X}$ ANGULAR ROTATION OF GROUPS CLASSIFIED AS TO SEX AND HANDEDNESS (M_r, M_l, F_r, F_l): TRIAL 2

	Sum of Squares	df	$\overline{X}$ Square	F
Distance—100 ft.				
Between	312.8	3	104.27	.166
Within	64,784.6	103	628.98	
Total	65,097.4	106	———	2.70*-
Distance—200 ft.				
Between	299.9	3	99.97	.205
Within	47,269.3	97	487.31	
Total	47,569.2	100	———	2.70*-
Distance—300 ft.				
Between	538.3	2	269.15	.302
Within	26,729.9	30	890.99	
Total	27,318.2	32	———	2.92

* Significant at .05 level of confidence.

dominant leg. In 56.8 percent of the trials, the subjects spiraled in the same directions as their dominant hand, while in 43.2 percent of the trials, subjects veered in the opposite direction.

(5) Based upon analyses of variance of the amount of veer occurring at each of 100-feet, 200-feet, 300-feet and 400-feet distances, no

significant differences were found in the amount of veer in the spiraling patterns of groups classified as to sex and hand dominance (M_r, M_l, F_r, F_l). (See Table 22-II.) That no such differences exist is further indicated by the very similar patterns of veer between males and females and between right-handed and left-handed subjects shown in Figures 22-2 and 22-3.

(6) Overall the subjects were found to deviate .83° per thirty-inch stride, or 33.87° per 100 feet of travel on the pathways. The most marked spiraling occurred on the first trial (43.98° of rotation per

TABLE 22-IV

INTERGROUP COMPARISONS, BASED UPON THE MEAN ROTATION AT 100 FEET ON TRIAL 1

Groups	N	Mean	SD	σ_M	σ_{diff}	M_1-M_2	t
Males	76	31.80	28.90	3.34	7.20	8.70	1.02*
Females	31	40.50	34.90	6.37			
Right Handed	91	33.80	32.10	2.65	4.01	3.50	.87*
Left Handed	16	37.30	23.20	2.45			
Veered Left on Both Trials	27	35.90	35.20	6.90	9.18	0.40	.04*
Veered Right on Both Trials	19	36.30	25.70	6.06			
Heterotropic Veerers	39	27.90	23.30	3.78	5.90	5.99	1.02*
Homotropic Veerers	46	33.89	30.45	4.54			

* Not significant at .05 level.

TABLE 22-V

INTERTRIAL COMPARISON OF DIFFERENCES IN ANGULAR ROTATION AT 100, 200, 300, AND 400 FEET

	M	SD	σ_M	σ_{diff}	M_1-M_2	t
Trial 1, at 100 ft.	31.28	13.51	1.37	2.73	4.00	1.46
vs Trial 2, at 100 ft.	27.28	22.43	2.36			
Trial 1, at 200 ft.	40.33	21.80	2.23	3.18	7.82	2.46*
vs Trial 2, at 200 ft.	32.51	21.58	2.27			
Trial 1, at 300 ft.	77.21	49.82	8.42	9.43	34.30	3.64**
vs Trial 2, at 300 ft.	42.91	22.92	4.25			
Trial 1, at 400 ft.	77.80	25.80	6.45	23.73	15.10	.64
vs Trial 2, at 400 ft.	92.90	45.70	22.85			

* Significant at .02
** Significant at .01

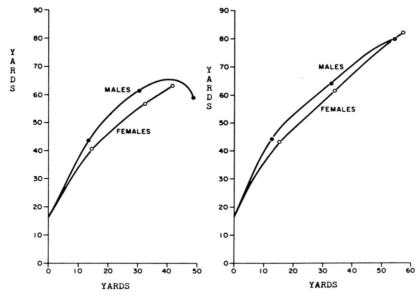

FIGURE 22-2. Average pattern walked by females and males on trial 1 (left) and trial 2 (right).

100 feet of "forward" travel), whereas on the second trial rotation per 100 feet was 31.98° (p = .001).

(7) Rotational measures obtained at proximal points on the pathways were more closely related than those at widely separate points. For example, moderately high intercorrelations were obtained on the first trial between rotation at 100 and 200 feet (+ .72, significant at .05) and rotation at 200 and 300 feet (+ .85, significant at .05) whereas between 100 and 400 feet, rotational measures were not highly correlated (+ .21).

(8) Intertrial correlations based upon rotation at 100 feet reached only +.157. In addition the marked variation of the scores was indicated by the high standard deviations of each group of rotational measures, based on the increase in angular rotation, and remained roughly 60 to 75 percent of the mean scores (Table 22-I).

DISCUSSION

Several methodological problems will be corrected in future studies. For example, leading the subjects back to the original starting point by the shortest route following their initial trial gave most of them

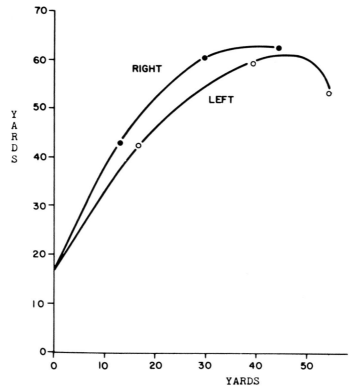

FIGURE 22-3. Average pattern walked by right-handed and left-handed subjects on trial 1.

a clue as to the direction and amount of rotation they evidenced on the initial trial. Therefore a large percent of those evidencing heterotropic veering patterns may have been overcompensating for their first trial's efforts. Similarly, the decrease in angular rotation of the second trial was probably a reflection of the knowledge the subjects gained of their pattern in the first trial.

Further measurement problems occurred as some subjects completed only 100 feet on the pathway before circling sharply off at the baseline; others completed 200 or 300 feet, while others completed a full circle usually in so far as at 200 feet. For example, they excluded the rotation which might have been recorded by subjects who had already left the grid after traveling only 100 feet. It is intended in future studies to start the subjects near the center of a circular pattern, so as to allow them the same distance from their starting point to the ouside edge of the grid pattern regardless of the direction they may take after being released.

After plotting the curves, it became apparent that the locations of the mean points established at 300 feet were distorted. Their location represented a mean of two markedly divergent pathways which the subjects seemed to follow after walking 200 feet. (Fig. 22-1). About one-half of the subjects continued to spiral, while the other half seemed to straighten out, and some even began to veer in the opposite direction. (See dotted lines on Fig. 22-1.) This marked variability in rotation taken after 200 feet was also reflected in the high standard deviations computed at these points (Table 22-I).

It is thus believed that in future studies a four-part analysis will be carried out, and exact mathematical formulas will be computed, based upon this classification system, objectifying the shape of these curves. The four classifications apparent in the data included (1) subjects veering left, (2) subjects spiraling left, (3) subjects veering right, and (4) subjects spiraling right. Essentially, therefore, about one-half of the subjects continued to spiral, while the other half walked a path progressing away from the initial straight line at almost constant angle once the 200-foot mark was passed.

This spiraling tendency appears to be another instance of the asymmetrical nature of man's action system. While it is apparently not related to hemispheric dominance as evidenced in arm and leg use, it may perhaps be an important but independent factor within the dominance spectrum. The problems relative to determining causality appear to be in discovering the nature and the location of the neural structures creating this imbalance.

The tendency of track athletes, basketball, and football players to move more effectively in one direction than in another, i.e. to "hit" over left tackle or to cut sharply for the basket from the right instead of the left, is influenced by the basic directional tendencies the individual possesses as he moves his entire body through space.

CONCLUSIONS

When humans are deprived of visual and auditory cues and requested to walk a straight line, they spiral at the rate of 33.87° per

100 feet of progress. The direction of the spiral is almost equally divided between the tendency to move to the left and the tendency to move to the right. Sex and reported hand dominance are neither predictive of the amount nor of the direction of veer evidenced by the subjects.

REFERENCES

1. BANERJEE, M. N.: Blindfold description of distance. *Indian J Psychol, 3*:95-99, 1928.
2. D'OLIVERIA, E. J.: Place of the pilot in formation flight. *Rev Med Lat Amer, 24*:1232-35, 1939.
3. LUND, F. H.: Physical asymmetrics and disorientation. *Amer J Psychol, 42*:51-62, 1930.
4. ROUSE, D. L., and WORCHEL, P.: Veering tendency in the blind. *New Outlook for the Blind, 49*:115-18, 1955.
5. SCHAEFFER, A. A.: Spiral movement in man. *J Morphol, 45*:293-398, 1928.

Chapter 23

IMMEDIATE AFTEREFFECTS OF OVERLOAD ON RESISTED AND NONRESISTED SPEEDS OF MOVEMENT*

Richard C. Nelson and Ward Lambert

INTRODUCTION

RECENT INVESTIGATIONS[1, 3, 4, 5, 6] of the immediate effects of increased resistance (overload) upon physical performance have indicated conflicting results. The inclusion in these studies of different movements as well as a variety of types and levels of overload may in part explain the inconsistencies in findings. Further, these previous experiments have not attempted to evaluate the perceptual aftereffects associated with postoverload performance, and consequently no comparison could be made between actual and perceived performances. Nofsinger[4] utilized the speed of nonresisted elbow flexion as the performance criterion in which three levels of overload were applied. The overloads had no statistically significant effect upon subsequent speed of movement, but a *kinesthetic illusion* of increased speed was apparently created, as all subjects stated they *felt faster* during postoverload trials. The use of a nonresisted movement and the lack of test replication limits the interpretation of these findings.

STATEMENT OF THE PROBLEM

The present experiment was designed to evaluate the effects of overload upon speed of both resisted and nonresisted elbow flexion. An

* R. C. Nelson and W. Lambert. Immediate aftereffects of overload on resisted and nonresisted speeds of movement. *Res Quart Amer Ass Health Phys Educ, 36*: 1965, 296-306. Reproduced here with the permission of Professor Richard C. Nelson and the American Association for Health, Physical Education, and Recreation. The writers wish to express their appreciation to Dwight Scott for his assistance in the collection of data.

analysis was made of the recorded subjective estimates of the post-overload performance.

Specifically, the hypotheses tested for both resisted and nonresisted movements were as follows: (1) that the application and removal of overload would lead to an immediate increased speed of movement, and (2) that a perceptual aftereffect would be generated which would cause the experimental postoverload trials to *feel faster*.

METHODOLOGY

Subjects and Experimental Design

This study was conducted in the air-conditioned research laboratory at the University of Maryland during June and July 1964. The nineteen male subjects included two faculty members and seventeen physical education graduate and undergraduate students. They ranged in age from twenty-one to thirty-seven years, with a median age of twenty-five years.

The investigation was conducted in two phases. The first phase involved the measurement of static elbow-flexion strength at an angle of 135° on four different days. During these sessions the subjects practiced on the speed-test apparatus and were oriented to the experimental test conditions.

In the second phase two elbow-flexion speed tests were employed. One utilized only the resistance of the forearm and the metal bar to which the arm was attached (nonresisted), and the other included an additional 10 percent of the subjects' strength score (resisted). The selection of 10 percent was based on previous experimental work, which had indicated this to be a moderate resistance, reducing the speed of movement about one fifth. The overload for both movements was established at 20 percent of the subjects' strength score. This overload was chosen because it was representative of those used in the study by Nofsinger.[4] Control conditions were included for both tests, resulting in four test conditions. These conditions were designated as follows: A—nonresisted control; B—nonresisted experimental; C—resisted control; and D—resisted experimental. The subjects, who were tested under all four conditions, served as their own controls. They performed under only one test condition each day.

One complete test cycle which included all four conditions was completed during each of three successive weeks.

The writers felt that replicating the complete experiment three times would increase the reliability of the results. All twenty-four possible arrangements of the four conditions were assigned at random to the subjects during the three weeks. Thus all test conditions were represented each test day while each subject followed a different test sequence each week.

Test Apparatus and Timing Device

The apparatus developed by Nofsinger[4] and modified by Fahrney[2] was used for both strength and speed testing (see Fig. 23-1). It consisted of a twenty-one-inch axle mounted on ball bearings with a lever arm attached to one end of the axle and a sprocket wheel attached to the other end. The axle and its components were mounted on a table forty inches high. An adjustable stool was attached to the table by means of wooden supports. A wooden handle was secured to the lever arm so that its center was positioned eight and one-half inches from the end of the axle. Thus each subject's arm contacted the handle at a spot below his wrist. The handle rested on a block of wood which elevated the forearm 10° from the hoizontal. Positioning the upper arm on a resting pad placed on the front edge of the apparatus caused a decrease of 5° at the elbow. As a result of these two factors, the elbow was positioned at an angle of 165° when in the starting position. A strap on the handle stabilized the subject's arm during testing. A force of only four pounds, applied at an angle of 90° to the lever arm, was necessary to raise the lever arm from a resting position of 10° from the horizontal. Thus, the lever arm was a slight, constant, but relatively unimportant factor in speed and strength testing.

The weights for the resisted movement were strung on a cable and joined to the sprocket by a link chain. The overload, which was 20 percent of the individual's strength score, was placed in a canvas bag also clamped to the link chain. This made it possible to apply and remove the overload quickly and easily. It should be noted that, as the sprocket rotated, the effective resistance to the movement remained at a right angle and was therefore constant through the range of motion.

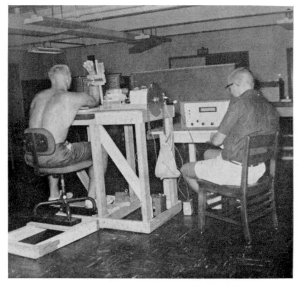

FIGURE 23-1. Test apparatus (a—subject, b—recorder, c—Beckman Counter, d—weight bag).

The timing apparatus consisted of two photocell circuits, one to activate and the other to stop the timer. A Beckman Counter (Model No. 8350) was used to measure the time interval to the nearest .00001 second. The light beams to the photocells were interrupted by the wooden arm when the lever arm was rotated upward 5° from the starting position. Thus the first 5° of movement were not included in the recorded time. The counter was triggered to stop when the lever bar had rotated 85° from the position of the first photocell. Thus the timed portion of the movement was from 160° to 75° at the elbow.

The recorded *time* was used to represent *speed* of movement, since the angular distance of 85° was the same for all subjects. A shorter time interval, of course, was indicative of a faster movement. It should be stressed that the movement times represented angular, not linear velocities.

MEASUREMENT OF STRENGTH

The apparatus in Figure 23-1 was modified slightly to permit the testing of elbow-flexion strength at an angle of 135°. The subject was seated on an adjustable stool with his right elbow placed in the designated position and his forearm attached to the rotating lever arm. The lever arm was prevented from going beyond a position of 135° by a cable which was attached to the arm. This cable, which formed a 90° angle with the lower arm, was attached to a modified Stoelting grip dynamometer which in turn was anchored securely to the floor. The dynamometer, which was read to the nearest ½ k., was calibrated twice each day by hanging from the dynamometer cable selected, accurately measured weights.

The subjects completed their maximal efforts spaced forty-five seconds apart on each of four days. Since the first day was considered practice, the data for that day were not used. The mean of the three trials was used to represent the strength score for each day. The mean of the three daily means was used as the strength score for the establishment of individual resistances and overloads used in the second phase of the study. Table 23-I contains the descriptive statistics and reliability coefficients for the strength data.

TABLE 23-I

DESCRIPTIVE STATISTICS AND RELIABILITY COEFFICIENTS
FOR STRENGTH TESTS (N = 19)

Test day	Mean (k.)	S.D.	r	Correlated t
1	32.1	6.5	0.90 (day 1 vs. 2)	0.89 (N.S.)
2	32.8	6.8	0.92 (day 1 vs. 2)	1.60 (N.S.)
3	31.8	6.6		

Test Procedure

The general test protocol was the same for all four test conditions. The subject reported to the laboratory ten minutes in advance of his scheduled time to fill out a questionnaire concerning amount of sleep, exercise, and diet, during the previous twenty-four hours. He then entered the test room and was seated at the apparatus which had previously been adjusted. The right arm was strapped to the handle and final adjustments in position were made. The subject was briefed on the test condition under which he was to perform.

Two investigators were present during all testing sessions. One served as the recorder while the other manipulated the weights during the application and removal of the overload and caught the weights at the termination of each resisted flexion movement. The recorder gave a preliminary signal of "O.K." prior to each flexion movement. The subject did not respond immediately upon hearing this command but rather moved under his own initiative, usually within one or two seconds thereafter. Reaction time was not recorded or considered in this study.

The subject performed six preoverload trials at ten-second intervals, which were followed by a thirty-second rest. During this rest period the overload was attached to the chain if the test condition was B or D. Under A and C, the two control conditions, no overload was applied. The subject next performed five overload trials, after which the overload, if used, was removed. The six postoverload trials began ten seconds after the last overload trial and continued at ten-second intervals. Previous experimentation indicated that six trials provided sufficient individual trial replication and yet avoided the problems of fatigue and boredom associated with an excessive number of trials. The decision to use five overload trials was somewhat arbitrary, since a prior study[4] had employed only three. It was felt that five trials would provide sufficient repetition to satiate the movement. Unfortunately, no other previous experiments were found which dealt specifically with this problem. Table 23-II contains the test sequence with the designated amounts of resistance under each test condition.

The experiment was replicated three times, thus making it possible

TABLE 23-II
TEST SEQUENCE AND LEVELS OF RESISTANCE

Condition	Preoverload (6 trials)	Overloads (5 trials)	Postoverload (6 trials)
A (Control)	nonresisted	nonresisted	nonresisted
B (Experimental)	nonresisted	20% load	nonresisted
C (Control)	resisted[a]	resisted	resisted
D (Experimental)	resisted	30% load[b]	resisted

[a] 10 percent of static strength was used as resistance.
[b] The 30 percent included 10 percent resistance and 20 percent overload.

to examine thoroughly the resisted and nonresisted speed-of-movement reliabilities, including within-days, between-days, and between-weeks. The pretrials under A and C were identical to the posttrials, making it possible to calculate the within-day reliability coefficients. Between-days reliability was based on the pretrials for A and B (nonresisted)

TABLE 23-III

RELIABILITY COEFFICIENTS AND CORRELATED t RATIOS FOR
RESISTED AND NONRESISTED MOVEMENT TIMES (N = 19)[a]

Within Day	*Week 1*		*Week 2*		*Week 3*	
	r	t	r	t	r	t
Nonresisted	0.82	1.24	0.80	0.41	0.94	0.52
(A pre-post)						
Resisted	0.90	0.57	0.88	0.44	0.95	0.20
(C pre-post)						
Between Days						
Nonresisted	0.71	1.37	0.83	0.27	0.87	1.06
(A pre-B pre)						
Resisted	0.71	0.98	0.50	0.28	0.83	0.90
(C pre-D pre)						

Between Weeks	Weeks 1 vs 2		Weeks 2 vs 3	
	r	t	r	t
Nonresisted				
A Pre	0.77	0.67	0.86	1.54
B Pre	0.61	0.84	0.78	2.81[b]
Resisted				
C Pre	0.57	2.69[b]	0.64	0.24
D Pre	0.54	1.62	0.58	0.66

[a] Individual scores based on mean of six trials.
[b] Statistically significant at the .05 level with 18 degrees of freedom.

and for C and D (resisted). Table 23-III includes the reliability
coefficients and correlated t ratios.

RESULTS

Nonresisted Movement

The data for conditions A and B were analyzed independently of
those for C and D. Since it was desirable to account for differences in
preoverload scores when evaluating the postoverload scores, the analysis
of covariance seemed to be the most appropriate statistical test to
employ. The preoverload scores were designated the control or independent variable, while the postoverload scores were considered the
dependent variable. The means of the six preoverload trials and the
six postoverload trials were used for each subject under each test
condition.

Tables 23-IV and 23-V contain the results for the nonresisted and
resisted movements respectively.

The only statistically significant *F* ratio in Table IV was for individuals. This significant difference was to be expected in this type of

TABLE 23-IV

SUMMARY OF COVARIANCE ANALYSIS OF DATA ON NONRESISTED
SPEED OF MOVEMENT

Source	D.F.	S.S.	M.S.	F
Total	112	0.003095		
Weeks	2	0.000066	0.000033	1.65[b]
Conditions	1	0.000022	0.000022	1.10[b]
Individuals	18	0.001177	0.000065	3.25[b, c]
Weeks x conditions	2	0.000012	0.000006	.27[a]
Weeks x individuals	36	0.000603	0.000017	.77[a]
Individuals x conditions	18	0.000434	0.000024	1.09[a]
Error (W x C x I)	35	0.000781	0.000022	
Pooled estimate				
(Error plus interactions)	91	0.001830	0.000020	

[a] Tested against error mean square.
[b] Tested against pooled mean square.
[c] Statistically significant at the .05 level.

TABLE 23-V

SUMMARY OF COVARIANCE ANALYSIS OF DATA ON RESISTED
SPEED OF MOVEMENT

Source	D.F.	S.S.	M.S.	F	P
Total	112	0.003072			
Weeks	2	0.000169	0.000085	4.25[b]	<.01
Conditions	1	0.000056	0.000056	2.43[c]	N.S.
Individuals	18	0.001370	0.000076	3.30[b]	<.01
Weeks x conditions	2	0.000019	0.000009	1.00[a]	N.S.
Weeks x individuals	36	0.000725	0.000020	2.22[a]	<.05
Individuals x conditions	18	0.000406	0.000023	2.56[a]	<.01
Error (W x C x I)	35	0.000327	0.000009		

[a] Tested against error mean square.
[b] Tested against weeks x individuals interaction mean square.
[c] Tested against individuals x conditions interaction square.

experiment inasmuch as a relatively wide range of movement times was represented. The fact that all three interactions were not statistically significant indicated that the individuals followed somewhat similar patterns of performance with respect to conditions (I X C) and across weeks (I X W) and that the group response under each condition was uniform during the three weeks of testing (W X C).

The nonsignificant F ratios for weeks and conditions indicated that the subjects responded in a similar manner across all three weeks and that the application and removal of the overload to the nonresisted movement had no significant effect upon speed of movement when compared with the control condition. Table 23-VI, which shows the group preoverload and postoverload means for all conditions during

TABLE 23-VI
PREOVERLOAD AND POSTOVERLOAD GROUP MEANS UNDER
FOUR TEST CONDITIONS (N = 19)

Condition	Week 1		Week 2		Week 3	
	Pre	*Post*	*Pre*	*Post*	*Pre*	*Post*
Resisted						
A	0.15737 [a]	0.15911(—) [b]	0.15851	0.15910(—)	0.16066	0.16121(—)
B	0.15987	0.15909(+)	0.15814	0.15729(+)	0.16200	0.16169(+)
Nonresisted						
C	0.19399	0.19424(—)	0.19940	0.20005(—)	0.20016	0.20144(—)
D	0.19595	0.19644(—)	0.20018	0.20297(—)	0.20185	0.20347(—)

[a] Means reported in seconds.
[b] The plus and minus indicate a tendency toward faster or slower post-overload times, respectively.

the three weeks, is included to assist the reader in the interpretation of these findings.

Resisted Movement

It is apparent from Table 23-VI that for the most part the resisted-movement results were strikingly different from the nonresisted (Table 23-IV). Two of the interactions (I X W and I X C) were statistically significant when tested against the error mean square. This suggested a lack of uniformity in performance among the subjects through the three weeks and between test conditions.

Because of the significant interactions, it was thought inappropriate to use the error term to test the main effects. As a result, mean squares of the weeks and of the individuals were tested against the individuals X weeks interaction, and in both cases the F ratios indicated a probability of less than .05. The significant difference in individuals was to be expected, while the differences in weeks was probably due to the lower group means during the first week as opposed to the second and third weeks (see Table 23-VI).

It was necessary to use the individuals X conditions interaction in the testing of the conditions mean square. Thus the effects of the overload without the influence of the interaction (I X C) could be ascertained. The F ratio of 2.43 for test conditions was not significant (.05 level). This denoted the lack of a significant difference in speed of resisted elbow flexion under the experimental condition (overload) as compared to the control.

Comparisons Between Pre-Overload and Post-Overload

The covariance analyses of test conditions reflected the performance of the subjects as a group. The writers felt it important to examine the individual differences between preoverload and postoverload for later use in the interpretation of the subjective responses. The mean preoverload score was compared with the mean postoverload score for each subject under each condition during all three experimental replications. Because of the precision of measurement, no subject had identical preoverload and postoverload mean scores. It was possible, then, to categorize all postoverload scores as faster or slower than preoverload scores. These were tabulated and statistically analyzed using the sign test (see Table 23-VII).

TABLE 23-VII

NONPARAMETRIC ANALYSIS OF INDIVIDUAL PREOVERLOAD
POSTOVERLOAD MOVEMENT TIMES

Week	Condition							
	A		B		C		D	
	F[a]	S	F	S	F	S	F	S
1	8	11	10	9	8	11	11	8
2	9	10	9	10	9	10	7	12
3	10	9	11	8	7	12	8	11
Totals	27	30	30	27	24	33	26	31
Sign test probabilities[b]	.69		.69		.23		.51	

[a] The F and S represent faster and slower postoverload than preoverload mean times, respectively.
[b] Sign tests using the totals within each condition revealed nonsignificant differences.

The high probabilities (.23 to .69) derived from the sign test indicated that neither the experimental nor control procedures significantly altered the speed of movement.

Analysis of Perceptual Aftereffects

Examination of the differences in preoverload and postoverload performance (Table VII) shows a slight tendency for the subjects to be slower under conditions A, C, and D and faster under condition B. The nonsignificant sign-test results, however, indicated that these variations were due to sampling error (chance fluctuation). It could be assumed, then, that the frequency of the subjective responses of *slower, no change,* and *faster* would be approximately the same under all test conditions. Since these subjective responses represented noncontinuous frequency-type data, the writers chose to use the chi-square test to evaluate the tabulated data for both the resisted (A and B) and non-resisted (C and D) movements. Table 23-VIII incorporates the observed and expected frequencies and the computed chi-square values. The highly significant results ($X^2 = 46.99$ and 60.34) signify a marked difference in frequencies under the control as opposed to experimental conditions. It is apparent that this is due to the shift toward the response *faster* under conditions B and D. If it is recalled that the variance analyses and sign test indicated no significant difference in performance, it is evident that a kinesthetic illusion of increased speed was manifested following the removal of the overload.

TABLE 23-VIII

CHI SQUARE TESTS OF SUBJECTIVE RESPONSES FOR
RESISTED AND NONRESISTED MOVEMENTS

Subjective responses	Condition					
	Nonresisted			Resisted		
	A—Control Observed	Expected	B—Experi- mental Observed	C—Control Observed	Expected	D—Experi- mental Observed
Faster	7	29	51	7	26	45
No change	41	23.5	6	37	24	11
Slower	9	4.5	0	13	7	1
χ^2		60.34[a]			46.99[a]	

[a] Statistically significant beyond the .01 level.

DISCUSSION

The nonsignificant difference between control and experimental conditions for the nonresisted movement supports the findings of Nofsinger.[4] In his study three levels of overload (15, 30, and 45% of flexion strength) were applied to a nonresisted elbow flexion movement. Only the 15 percent overload condition led to a faster post-overload performance, although this was not significantly different from the preoverload performance. The experimental condition for the nonresisted movement in this study also indicated a slight (but not significant) improvement. This similarity is probably fortuitous and is mentioned here only as an experimental observation.

The resisted movement as executed in this study was subject to considerable variability in performance. The low reliability coefficients and high correlated *t*-ratios indicated lack of uniformity in individual as well as group performance. The statistically significant interactions of individuals X weeks and of individuals X conditions added further evidence of this. Fatigue may have affected the subjects to greater or lesser degrees, particularly under the experimental condition. It is possible that it is necessary to further replicate the test before more consistent results can be obtained.

The results of the chi-square analyses of the subjective estimates of performance during postoverload trials clearly indicated the presence of a kinesthetic illusion of increased speed. The experimental techniques in this investigation were not sufficiently refined to determine the cause of this perceptual aftereffect. The writers offer the following possible explanations, based primarily on subjective experimental observations.

The first is based on the assumption that the motor unit activity (and muscular force applied) was approximately the same during preoverload and postoverload trials. This being so, the subject may in fact have been comparing the speed of the postoverload trials with the overload trials instead of with the preoverload trials. The subjects may have been unable to remember what the preoverload trials felt like. If the subjects were making this comparison, their responses of *faster* were for the most part correct.

It could be that a change in the co-contraction pattern of the flexors and extensors of the elbow caused the alteration in perception. It appeared to the writers that the subjects tended to move further through the range of motion during the first and second trials after the removal of the overload. This could be due to a more forceful contraction of the flexors without a corresponding increase in force of the antagonists (primarily the triceps), which are responsible for stopping the movement. On the other hand, the extensors could have responded slightly later, thereby allowing the flexion movement to continue beyond the usual stopping point. The use of EMG techniques in future experiments could help clarify this point.

From the practical standpoint these results cast doubt upon the assumed beneficial immediate effects of the application and removal of an overload. Such practices as swinging three bats, wearing ankle and wrist spats, and practicing various sports movements while wearing a weighted vest probably bring about no improvement in subsequent performance. It is possible that the associated kinesthetic illusion, if present, may prove to be an aid to performance. However, further research is necessary before this question can be clarified.

CONCLUSIONS

Within the experimental limitations of this investigation, the following conclusions appear warranted:

(1) The application and removal of an overload to both resisted and nonresisted movements has no effect upon the speed of these movements.

(2) A perceptual aftereffect in the form of a kinesthetic illusion of increased speed is created by the overload when applied to resisted and nonresisted movements.

REFERENCES

1. BISCHKE, R. G., and MOREHOUSE, L. E.: Specificity of warming up procedures. Unpublished material cited by L. E. Morehouse and John M. Cooper in *Kinesiology*. St. Louis, C. V. Mosby, 1950.
2. FAHRNEY, RICHARD A.: The effects of progressive resistive exercise upon speed of flexion and resisted elbow flexion. Unpublished master of arts thesis, U. of Maryland, 1964.
3. MURRAY, JOHN A.: The effect of muscular preset on performance in certain selected activities. Unpublished master of science thesis, Pennsylvania State University, 1959.
4. NOFSINGER, MICHAEL R.: The immediate effects of resistance exercise upon subsequent speed of movement. Unpublished master of arts thesis, U. of Maryland, 1963.
5. STOCKHOLM, ALAN: The immediate effects of increased resistance on physical performance. Unpublished master of arts thesis, U. of Maryland, 1962.
6. VAN HUSS, WAYNE D., and Others. Effect of overload warm-up on the velocity and accuracy of throwing. *Res Quart Amer Ass Health Phys Educ, 33*:472-475, 1962.

Chapter 24

ATHLETIC PARTICIPATION AND PERCEPTUAL AUGMENTATION AND REDUCTION*

E. DEAN RYAN AND ROBERT L. FOSTER

INTRODUCTION

RECENTLY A significant relationship was found between the ability of an individual to tolerate pain and the type of athletic activity in which he chooses to participate (Ryan & Kovacic, 1966). Contact athletes (football players and wrestlers) tolerated more pain than noncontact athletes (tennis players and golfers), and the noncontact athletes in turn tolerated more pain than nonathletes. It was hypothesized that this relationship might have been due to differences in a general perceptual characteristic of "augmenting" or "reducing" sensory inputs. Petrie and associates have shown that certain individuals appear to consistently reduce the intensity of their perceptions, while other individuals tend to consistently augment the intensity of perception (Petrie, 1960). Augmentation and reduction have been estimated by measuring the change in kinesthetically perceived size after stimulation. The subjects match the width of a standard bar which is felt with one hand, with an area on a tapered bar which is felt with the other hand. A large (or smaller) block is then rubbed. Thereafter, the original test bar is again equated with the tapered bar, and the difference between the two subjective estimations is measured. Those individuals who tend to consistently reduce after stimulation have been shown to be more extroverted than those who augment (Eysenck, 1957), than those who are more tolerant of pain (Petrie, Collins, & Phillips, 1960), less tolerant of sensory deprivation (Petrie

* E. D. Ryan and R. Foster: Athletic participation and perceptual augmentation and reduction, *J Abnorm Psychol,* 6:1967, 472-476. Copyright (1967) by the American Psychological Association, and reproduced here with permission of Professor E. Dean Ryan and the American Psychological Association.

et al., 1960), more mesomorphic (Wertheimer, 1955), and who judge time as passing more slowly than the augmenters (Petrie *et al.*, 1960). In addition, significantly more reducers were found in a delinquent group and significantly fewer augmenters than would be expected by chance (Petrie, McCulloch, & Kazdin, 1962). Petrie suggested that these differences are partially due to the tendency to reduce or augment the perceptual intensity of stimulation in general. Any change in the intensity of stimulation may cause subsequent stimulation to appear subjectively less intense for the "reducer" and more intense for the "augmenters."

All of the characteristics of the reducer, the tolerance of pain, intolerance of sensory deprivation, mesmorphy, extroversion, and to an extent the characteristics of the delinquent, have frequently been associated with athletic groups. It may be that the subjective reduction of sensory stimulation is associated with the choice of activities a child engages in. If indeed, the reducers suffer from lack of stimulation as suggested by Petrie *et al.* (1962), then they would need change, movement, speed, and possibly body contact, rather than sedentary pursuits. Conversely, it may be that the type of activity an individual engages in influences his perceptual pattern, thus encouraging augmentation or reduction.

This study was designed to investigate the relationship between a general perceptual pattern of augmentation and reduction in groups differing in athletic interests. It was hypothesized that groups participating in contact sports would possess the perceptual pattern of the reducer and thus reduce most in their estimation of kinesthetically perceived size, have faster reaction times, faster movement times, judge time as passing slower, and would tolerate most pain. Groups not interested in athletics would possess the perceptual characteristics of the augmenter, and thus reduce less in their estimation of kinesthetically perceived size, have slower reaction times, slower movement times, judge time as passing faster, and tolerate less pain. Groups participating in noncontact sports would tend to fall between the other two groups on all tests.

METHOD

Subjects

A questionnaire was administered to male high school students. They were asked their likes, dislikes, hobbies, and recreational pursuits.

On the basis of these answers three groups of subjects were selected. Group I was composed of boys who expressed a liking for certain athletics and were at the same time actually participating in contact sports (football or wrestling), Group II of boys who expressed an interest in noncontact sports and were also participating *only* in non-contact sports (golf, tennis, track), and Group III of boys who had expressed a dislike for athletics and were inactive as far as sports were concerned.

Letters were sent to parents requesting permission for sons to participate in an experiment dealing with perception. It was indicated that one of the tests would be a measure of pain tolerance. To obtain twenty subjects in each group it was necessary to contact twenty-two contact athletes, twenty-six noncontact athletes, and twenty-six non-athletes. The subjects assumed they had been randomly selected, and were unaware that athletic participation was a factor or that the experiment was in any way related to the questionnaire administered earlier.

Apparatus

(1). *Reaction times.* The reaction-time apparatus consisted of a small base with a sixteen-inch upright. On the upright were mounted in a vertical position two small neon lights and a microswitch. A second microswitch was located in the base of the reaction timer. The upper light was amber in color and served as the ready signal. The experimenter could vary the ready period from one-half to four seconds. The onset of the lower green light, which served as the stimulus, activated two standard electric timers. The first timer was stopped as the subject's finger moved from the upper microswitch, and the second timer stopped as the microswitch mounted in the base was touched. Reaction time was read directly from the first clock; movement time was computed by subtracting the time of the first clock from that of the second.

(2). *Pain tolerance.* An adaptation of Poser's mechanical stimulator was used (Poser, 1962). A single plastic, aluminum-tipped football cleat was secured to a curved fiber plate and fitted to the leg. The cleat was placed against the anterior border of the tibia, midway between the ankle and the knee. The sleeve of a standard clinical sphygmomanometer was used to secure the cleat firmly in place.

Cleat pressure against the tibia was induced by inflating the armlet at a slow constant rate (approximately 5 mm of mercury per second) until the subject indicated verbally that he was no longer willing to endure the pain. Pressure was immediately released by deflating the cuff. The data were recorded in millimeters of mercury.

(3). *Augmentation and reduction.* The apparatus used to measure augmentation and reduction was an adaptation of the kinesthetic aftereffect apparatus, originally described by Koehler and Dinnerstein (1947). The variable consisted of a wedge-shaped piece of hardwood, thirty inches long, one inch thick, 4.0 inches at the wide end, tapering to .5 inch at the narrow end. To maintain parallel alignment of the fingers, a sliding finger guide was fixed atop the wedge. Two hardwood blocks with parallel sides, ten inches long and two inches thick, served as the standard bar and the stimulation bar. The standard bar was 1.5 inches wide and the stimulation bar 2.5 inches wide.

All subjects were tested individually and in a random order. The subject was told he would be given five different tests and was instructed to do as well as possible on each one. The sequence was the same for each subject, that is, reaction time, two-minute time estimation, twenty-second time estimation, pain tolerance, and the kinesthetic measures of augmentation and reduction.

At the conclusion of the reaction-time test the subject was asked to sit quietly with his hands resting in his lap. He was asked to judge a two-minute period. When the subject thought two minutes had elapsed he would say, "time." This was repeated four times. No knowledge of results was given. The scores reported are the mean of the four trials.

Next, the subject was given a stopwatch and asked to duplicate the time interval demonstrated by the experimenter. The experimenter, holding the watch so the face was not visible to the subject, started his watch and let it run for twenty seconds. The subject, holding his own watch with the face down, was told to duplicate the time between the two clicks. This was done four times, each for a twenty-second period, with the mean of all trials used for comparison.

At the completion of the twenty-second test the subject was told his tolerance to pain would be measured, wherein he should make an effort to stand as much pain as possible. The pressure cleat was applied, and the subject was informed that pressure to the leg would be increased gradually and terminated when he could tolerate no more. The subject was unable to see the mercury column. After the first trial the experimenter commented that the score was considerably lower than the average of the group tested, and the subject was asked to take the test a second time, doing better if possible. The cleat was lowered one inch and a second trial was given.

Then the subject was blindfolded. He was instructed to grasp the standard bar between thumb and forefinger of the dominant hand and find the point that felt equal on the wedge-shaped comparison bar grasped identically in his other hand. Four base-line measurements were taken, alternating ascending and descending trials, that is, starting from the narrow end of the wedge on Trials 1 and 3 and from the wide end on the others. The standard bar was held in the subject's dominant hand during this testing period. The subject was then given the wider test block and instructed to rub with his preferred hand at a constant rate for ninety seconds. He then equated the perceived equivalent width of the original test block on the tapered bar. Again four measurements were taken, alternating ascending and descending trials, with the standard bar being held as in the original base-line measurements. This procedure was repeated for a second ninety-second trial and finally for a 120-second trial.

RESULTS

The results are presented in Tables 24-I and 24-II, with all means other than movement time being in the predicted direction. To test the significance of the difference between groups on each test a simple analysis of variance was used.

Augmentation and Reduction

There was no differences between groups in judging the width of the test bar prior to stimulation, with the contact athletes judging the 1.5 inch comparison bar as 1.67 inches, the noncontact as 1.69 inches, and the nonathletes as 1.66 inches. After ninety seconds of stimulation all three groups subjectively reduced the size of the comparison bar, although the difference between groups was not significant (Table

24-II). By 180 seconds of stimulation both athletic groups had increased the amount of reduction, while the trend for the nonathletic group had reversed, that is, they judged the comparison bar as being wider than after ninety seconds of stimulation. At this stage the difference between groups approached the .05 level of significance, $F\ (2,57) = 3.13$, $p < 3.15$. By 300 seconds of stimulation the difference between groups was quite pronounced, the estimation of width being .258 inch less for the contact athletes than before stimulation, for noncontact athletes .213 inch less, and for the nonathletes, .095 inch less. This difference was significant beyond the .01 level, $F\ (2,57) = 6.94$.

Reaction Time and Movement Time

Reaction times and movement times reported are the mean of all twenty trials. While the mean reaction times for the three groups were in the predicted direction, with the contact athletes fastest, noncontact athletes next, and the nonathletes slowest, the difference between the three groups was not significant, $F\ (2,57) = 1.61$ (Table 24-I). For movement time no trend was apparent, and mean scores were so similar that no test of significance was necessary.

Time Estimation

The differences between groups in estimation of 120 seconds was

TABLE 24-I

TIME MEASURES FOR ATHLETIC SUBGROUPS

Test	Contact Athletes	Noncontact Athletes	Nonathletes	F
Mean RT (sec.)	.201	.208	.213	1.61
Mean MT (sec.)	.117	.123	.117	—
Mean estimates of 120 sec.				
Trial 1	96.55	111.50	114.90	
Trial 2	101.95	119.35	122.50	
Trial 3	110.85	119.90	125.00	
Trial 4	104.90	125.20	126.85	
Mean of 4 trials	103.56	119.09	122.26	19.19**
Mean estimates of 20 sec.				
Trial 1	18.05	21.15	21.75	
Trial 2	19.30	20.10	21.65	
Trial 3	18.50	21.15	21.20	
Trial 4	17.40	20.50	21.40	
Mean of 4 trials	18.31	20.73	21.50	12.86**

** $p < .01$.

TABLE 24-II

DIFFERENCES IN KINESTHETIC SIZE PERCEPTION AND IN PAIN TOLERANCE
FOR ATHLETIC SUBGROUPS

	Contact Athletes	Noncontact Athletes	Nonathletes	F
Mean change in kinesthetically perceived size after stimulation				
90-sec stimulation	—.110 in.	—.108 in.	—.103 in.	*ns* *
180-sec stimulation	—.168	—.173	—.065	3.13*
300-sec stimulation	—.258	—.213	—.095	6.94**
Mean pain tolerance (mm/Hg)				
Trial 1	286.75	231.00	207.50	14.27**
Trial 2	298.00	251.00	230.75	13.78**

* $p < .06$.
** $p < .01$.

highly significant, $F(2,57) = 19.19$, with the contact athletes reducing the period by 16.44 seconds, the noncontact athletes underestimating by only 0.91 second, and the nonathletes enlarging by 2.26 seconds (Table 24-I). When duplicating a twenty-second period the trend was the same, with the contact athletes reducing 1.69, the noncontact athletes enlarging 0.73 second, and the nonathletes enlarging 1.50 seconds. The difference between groups was highly significant, $F(2,57) = 12.86$ (Table 24-I).

Pain Tolerance

On Test I the amount of pressure the three groups were willing to tolerate was in the predicted direction; the difference between groups being highly significant, $F(2,57) = 14.27$. The group of contact athletes tolerated 285.75 millimeters of mercury, the noncontract athletic group 231.00, and the nonathletic group, 207.50. On the second trial, after being individually informed they had done poorly, all three groups improved, with the contact athletic group averaging 298.00 millimeters, the noncontact athletic group 251.00, and the nonathletic group, 230.75. The difference between groups was highly significant, $F(2,57) = 13.78$ (Table 24-II). It was impossible to make a meaningful comparison of the amount of change each group made from Trial 1 to Trial 2 as the mercury column on the sphygmomanometer only read to 300 millimeters. It should be noted that the mean score on Trial 2 for the contact athletes was 298 millimeters of mercury.

Of the twenty contact athletes tested, sixteen withstood the maximum pressure, while each of the remaining four subjects tolerated 290 millimeters. Of the noncontact athletes five tolerated the maximum pressure, while three nonathletes tolerated the maximum.

Comparison of Extreme Augmenters and Reducers

Due to the large individual differences apparent within each group, and because Petrie's work has dealt primarily with extreme augmenters and reducers, an analysis was made of the fifteen subjects making the least reduction in their estimation of kinesthetically perceived size after 300 seconds of stimulation and the fifteen subjects making the greatest reduction, regardless of their athletic background. The results shown in Table 24-III parallel and substantiate the work of Petrie. There was no difference between groups in reaction time and movement time, but all other differences were in the predicted direction and highly significant. Of the extreme reducers, seven were contact athletes, six noncontact athletes, and two nonathletes. Of the extreme augmenters, eleven were nonathletes, one noncontact athlete, and three contact athletes.

TABLE 24-III

COMPARISON OF EXTREME AUGMENTERS AND REDUCERS AFTER
300 SECONDS OF STIMULATION[a]

Test	*Reduced Most*	*Reduced Least*	*t*
Kinesthetic estimation	—.380	+.018	
RT	.21 sec.	.21 sec.	0.45
MT	.12 sec.	.12 sec.	0.97
Time estimated 20 sec.	19.48 sec.	21.72 sec.	3.60**
Time estimated 120 sec.	105.96 sec.	126.66 sec.	4.30**
Pain tolerance 1	267.64 mm/Hg	223.98 mm/Hg	3.55**
Pain tolerance 2	280.31 mm/Hg	245.31 mm/Hg	3.41**

[a] N = 15 for both groups.
** $p < .01$.

DISCUSSION

The results of this study clearly support Petrie's theory of a generalized tendency for certain individuals to consistently reduce or diminish their perception of stimulation and for others to consistently augment or enlarge perceptions. The contact athletes showed the characteristics of the reducer, making the greatest subjective reduction of kinesthetically perceived size after stimulation, tolerating most pain, and consistently judging time as passing more slowly, than did groups composed of noncontact athletes or nonathletes.

While differences in pain tolerance could be explained by simply assuming athletes were more motivated to withstand pain, time estimation and estimation of kinesthetically perceived size are less amenable to changes in motivation. No amount of conscious effort should induce a naive subject to vary time or kinesthetic sensitivity in one direction or another. One other point should be noted. During the testing period the experimenter was aware of the subject's classification. Since procedures were standardized for each test it is unlikely that the results could be attributed to experimenter bias. The point remains, however, that this must be considered as a possible source of error.

The usual response in estimating kinesthetically perceived size is for subjects to reduce the perceived size of a test block after stimulation with a larger block, and to enlarge the perceived size of a test block after stimulation by a smaller block. Petrie has suggested, however, that "the reducer will tend to reduce even if he is stimulated for equal amounts of time with a block that is larger than the test object and a block that is smaller than the test object; that is to say, the total effect is for him to reduce (Petrie, Holland, & Wolk, 1963)."

The opposite relation holds for the augmenter, who will regularly tend to enlarge his estimate of size. In this study only large block stimulation was used, thus minimizing the chances of finding augmentation. In spite of this, however, 30 percent of the nonathletic group augmented in the kinesthetic estimation of size. It should be noted further that the nonathletic group, or the augmenters, consistently overestimated time.

Two inconsistencies in experimental method employed by Petrie and by this study should be noted. First, studies by Petrie have employed only ascending trials on the tapered bar, that is, the subject always started from the smaller end of the bar. In the present study, alternating ascending and descending trials were used. Dinnerstein *et al.* (1962), studying groups that differed in pain tolerance, found no difference in figural aftereffects when using alternating ascending and descending trials, but found significant differences when only ascending trials were analyzed. Thus it would be expected that even greater differences would be found between athletic subgroups if methods used by Petrie had been followed. Second, Petrie suggests a minimum of forty-five minutes rest before the kinesthetic test is administered. "Such a resting period is essential in order to allow the wearing off of the effect of whatever the subject may have been handling prior to testing (Petrie *et al.,* 1962)." In the present study approximately thirty minutes elapsed from the end of the reaction-time experiment to the start of the kinesthetic test. For approximately five minutes of this period the subject held a stopwatch in his preferred hand, pressing with his thumb four times. Whether the stimulation of the reaction-time test, followed by only thirty minutes of rest, had an effect on kinesthetic sensitivity is problematical. However, in light of the fact that there were no differences between groups in judgment of width prior to stimulation it would appear that differences due to time would be negligible.

The similarities between the perceptual characteristics of the contact athlete and the juvenile delinquent should be noted, and as Petrie points out, education of these individuals needs to make allowance for their vulnerabilities and strengths. Both groups appear to need stimulation, movement, and change instead of more sedentary activities. It would be expected that confinement and restriction of movement in the typical classroom would be less conducive to good study habits for the reducer than for the augmenter. Thus, an entirely different pedagogical approach would be desirable for the opposing perceptual types. Further, it would seem that a program of vigorous activity might provide a socially acceptable means of relieving sensory monotony and thus reduce the need for less desirable stimulation.

REFERENCES

1. DINNERSTEIN, A. J.; LOWENTHAL, M.; MARION, R. B., and OLIVO, J.: Pain tolerance and kinesthetic aftereffect. *Perceptual and Motor Skills,* 1962, *15,* 247-250.

2. EYSENCK, H. J.: *The dynamics of anxiety and hysteria.* London, Routledge & Kegan Paul, 1957.

3. KOEHLER, W., and DINNERSTEIN, D.: Figural aftereffects in kinesthesis. In A. Michotte (Ed.): *Miscellanea Psychologica.* Paris, Libraire Philosophique, 1947. Pp. 196-220.

4. PETRIE, A.: Some psychological aspects of pain and the relief of suffering. *Ann of the New York Acad of Science,* 1960, *86,* 13-27.

5. PETRIE, A.; COLLINS, W., and SOLOMON, P.: The tolerance for pain and sensory deprivation. *Amer J Psychol*, 1960, *73*, 80-90.
6. PETRIE, A.; HOLLAND, T., and WOLK, I.: Sensory stimulation causing subdued experience: Audio-analgesia and perceptual augmentation and reduction. *J of Nervous and Mental Disorders*, 1963, *137*, 312-321.
7. PETRIE, A.; McCULLOCH, R., and KAZDIN, P.: The perceptual characteristics of juvenile delinquents. *J of Nervous and Mental Disorders*, 1962, *134*, 415-421.
8. POSER, E. G.: A simple and reliable apparatus for the measurement of pain. *Amer J Psyhol*, 1962, *75*, 304-305.
9. RYAN, E. D., and KOVACIC, C. R.: Pain tolerance and athletic participation. *Percept Motor Skills*, 1966, *22*, 383-390.
10. WERTHEIMER, M.: Figural aftereffect as a measure of metabolic deficiency. *J of Personality*, 1955, *24*, 56-73.

PART NINE
PERSONALITY DYNAMICS

Chapter 25

MASCULINE INADEQUACY AND COMPENSATORY DEVELOPMENT OF PHYSIQUE*

ROBERT G. HARLOW

T HIS PAPER WILL PRESENT the results of a comparison of projective test performance between a group of weightlifters and a control
group of nonweightlifting athletes. The study was made to test certain
propositions initially derived with the aid of psychoanalytic theory.
The results have implications for Freudian theory, for projective testing, and for characterizing weight men.

INTRODUCTION

A decade ago most psychologists would probably have concluded
that a union of psychoanalytic theory and controlled research was impossible. Two circumstances were primarily responsible for this.
Reliable methods of research were not applicable, and Freudian theory
lacked both clarity and formal consistency. It did not have the co-
ordinating and operational definitions necessary to provide reliable
interaction with empirical data. Hence, it is easy to understand why
Sears, after a comprehensive survey of psychoanalytic research, would
conclude:

> Few investigators feel free to accept Freud's statements at face value.
> The reason lies in the same factor that makes psychoanalysis a bad
> science—its method. Psychoanalysis relies upon techniques that do not

* R. G. Harlow. Masculine inadequacy and compensatory development of
physique, *J Personality, 19*: 1951, 312-323. Reproduced here with permission of
the author and publisher. The author is greatly indebted to Dr. Gardner Lindzey
for his advice and encouragement during this study. An acknowledgment must also
be made to Bruce Harriman, who scored the samples of the protocols, on which the
reliability coefficient was computed.

[271]

admit of the repetition of observation, that have no self-evident or denotative validity, and that are tinctured to an unknown degree with the observer's own suggestions. These difficulties may not seriously interfere with therapy, but when the method is used for uncovering psychological facts that are required to have objective validity, it simply fails. [9, p. 133]

Today a somewhat different conclusion might be reached. While Freudian theory remains in much the same unsatisfactory state, means for measuring many psychoanalytic concepts have greatly improved. In particular, projective tests provide a flexible and reasonably sensitive medium for obtaining evidence of the ability of Freudian psychology to predict general behavior. These techniques have proved sufficiently reliable to satisfy most experimentalists, and at the same time answer the clinicians' demand for psychological meaning.

Of particular interest to this paper is a recent study ingeniously devised and executed by Gerald Blum.[3] Using an unvalidated projective technique, Blum showed a close correspondence between his findings and Freudian theory. The chief shortcoming of his research was that he did not derive the relationships between his data and psychoanalytic theory until the actual data had been studied. The lack of internal consistency in Freudian writings suggests that selective factors may have implicitly operated to swell the agreement between his empirical data and psychoanalytic theory.

This study differs from Blum's in that it employs measuring instruments which are partially validated and propositions which were stated in advance of the empirical investigation. The aim was to employ Freudian theory in such a way that not only was there a possibility for the theory to account adequately for the data obtained, but also that there was an equal possibility for the theory to be wrong or inadequate. The investigation was directed not at testing salient areas of Freudian theory, but rather at verifying the statements which Freudian theory would make concerning a particular group.

DERIVATION OF EMPIRICAL PROPOSITIONS

Observation of the characteristic behavior of weightlifters suggested an abnormal accentuation of certain customary signs of masculinity. Thune, in the only other available study, using a personality inventory, concluded, "Basically the YMCA weight lifters would appear more shy, lacking in self-confidence, and more concerned with body build. On the other hand, the lifting group wants to be strong, healthy and dominant to be more like other men." [11] This deviation from normal was so extreme and so consistent that the existence of a reaction formation was suspected.

Since the male, in almost all societies, is the sex expected to be strong and dominant, the given physical sex differences can easily become a symbol for male superiority. It follows that the more highly developed are the secondary masculine characteristics, the more manly the individual is often considered. The hypothesis growing out of these observations was that, in general, the weightlifter is characterized by excessive anxiety concerning his masculine adequacy; that his weightlifting and subsequent strength and physique development are attempts to demonstrate both to himself and to others his male potency. From this generalized assumption the author attempted to predict, within a psychoanalytic frame of reference, the characteristic ways in which this population would deviate from a control population of nonweightlifting athletes.

One of the most important considerations is the changing family structure, and process of socialization in our culture. While in most societies the father plays an important role in training the children, in ours his role has become almost vestigial. As Mead points out,[5, p. 265] "Probably the only way a son is inevitably like his father (in our culture) is in his essential maleness." The role of the mother, however, is much stronger. Parsons states,[8, p. 257] that our kinship system throws children of both sexes overwhelmingly upon the mother as the emotionally significant adult. Since the principal identification is made with the parent who is felt to give the decisive prohibitions, it is she who will be the primary identification figure. For a son, this situation is complicated and confusing. Because of this major part played by females in the identification process, many aspects of the feminine pattern become incorporated in the boy. Fenichel says[4, p. 506] "The result is that men today have to contend far more than formerly with feminine traits within themselves." They are to become men, and yet have within them much of a feminine superego. Those men who feel that they must reject this introverted femininity are forced to react strongly to counterbalance these tendencies. One of the most obvious reactions is development and accentuation of the secondary male physical characteristics—strength and physique, which clearly differentiate their male possessor from women.*

A frequent result of feminine identification by males is homosexuality. Fenichel points this out when he says that the probability of homosexual orientation increases the more a boy tends to identify with the mother. With this would go fewer heterosexual impulses. Here again Fenichel comments,[4, p.337] "The man with an unconscious feminine orientation may likewise avoid exercising his sexual functions because of anxiety. That means . . . that the same factors which make the man homosexual make him impotent toward women." However, because weight men are openly striving to prove themselves extremely masculine, the overt display of homosexuality would be expected to be rare. Nevertheless, both more homosexual impulses and fewer heterosexual impulses should be observed latently in weight men than in a control population.

It would also be predicted that weight men would show more hostility toward both males and females than do nonweight men. Toward women, because the weight man's relatively feminine superego, which he rejects, hinders his adequate adjustment in a society which puts a high premium on masculinity. This would probably be patricularly directed toward the mother—as the primary obstacle to successful adjustment. He would be expected to be hostile toward males for being what he longs to be, and yet feels he cannot achieve. This would be directed particularly against the father as a consequence of his failure to provide himself as an adequate model or identification figure.

Narcissism in weight men may be predicted directly from the initial hypothesis of inadequacy feelings. The fact that they feel insecure would lead, as a counterbalance, to increase in self-love and esteem. In order to maintain a relatively stable ego structure in the face of failure, they must develop a strong personal conception of their own

---

* This discussion might explain, in part, the rapid rise in interest in weight training in this country. David Willoughby, California Institute of Technology, anthropometrist and authority on weightlifting, estimates that at present there must be at least a million men interested in weight training in this country, whereas thirty years ago they could be counted in the hundreds.[12] Thune [11] also mentions the increase in interest in weight training in America.

worth and value. Alexander supports this when he says,[1, p. 116] "Reaction to frustration and repudiation in love leads to compensatory increases in narcissism." By turning his emotions inward, the narcissist becomes in a sense a measure of his own worth. In weight men enhancement of the self takes the specific form of development of an extremely masculine physique. The exhibitionism of physique contests, in which weight men frequently participate, in part supports this viewpoint.

Fewer heterosexual impulses in weight men might also be predicted to develop from their narcissism as well as from their feminine identification. This is derived originally from their feelings of masculine inadequacy which necessitate a compensatory self-overevaluation. Weight men have built a picture of themselves as successful, virile, and masculine. Because they are still not completely sure of their manliness, however, they fear to put it to the test. Rejection or impotency would be a difficult blow from which to recover. Hence, these men will probably show more rejection of, and aggression toward, women than a control population of non-weight-training athletes. Homosexual objects, on the other hand, occupy a different status. Alexander speaks of homosexuality as narcissistic identification.[1] The narcissist sees as a worthy love object only a person similar to himself. "This explains," says Fenichel,[4, p. 337] "the intimate relationship between homosexuality and narcissism." Margaret Mead has expressed the same sentiment when she writes that male homosexuality is often a search for as much maleness as possible.[5] Male companionship is desired for its masculinity. It is what the weight men crave, and feel they need to complete their nature.

Psychosomatic research suggests further the compensatory nature of weight training. Males in our society who have strong drives toward dependency, who want to rely on others and assume a feminine role, are often prone to strive against these feelings by reacting strongly. Alexander, in his discussion of the underlying desires for rest and comfort, in the lives of otherwise assertive and competitive men, concludes, "There are strong dependency tendencies against which the outward assertiveness and responsibility constitutes a reaction formation. The patients feel ashamed of their dependence and want to fit the American masculine pattern.[2] If a male is to fit well into society, he must assume a strong, dominant role. Those who do not feel this desire are in a dilemma. Either they must settle into a submissive role and be considered failures by most of society, or they must somehow react against this feeling. Weight men appear to be attempting to prove to themselves and society that they are not dependent and submissive. Since weight training is rooted in anatomy—only the strong, the male can participate—it is particularly well-suited for the expression of what is biologically and culturally accepted as masculine. However, in doing this, specific conflicts are aroused in the individual; those between *autonomy/compliance,* and *collapse/counteraction.* In addition, he would be expected, because of the great effort expended, to look on the environment as hostile or insecure, to show more inadequacy in coping with it, and to show greater needs for mastering it.

Basic to psychoanalytic theory is the belief that the early life of an individual plays an extremely important role in his later development. Because of this, it would be predicted that weight men would show more evidence of insecurity, hostility, and feelings of inadequacy as a child than do the nonweight men. It would also be expected that, because of both their long standing insecurity and the felt hostility of the environment, the weight men would have more feelings of rejection. Lastly, since all of these predictions have been grouped under the broad heading of masculine inadequacy, it would be predicted that weight men would be much more sensitive and responsive to male signs and symbols than are nonweight men.

Summarizing the preceding discussion of the weight man in contemporary society, the author suggested that the weight man differs from the nonweight man in that he is, in general, characterized by:

(1). Abnormally acute feelings of masculine inadequacy.
(2). Exposure from early in life to a depriving and frustrating environment.
(3). A failure to identify with an adequate male object.
(4). An excessive amount of narcissism.
(5). Underlying dependency feelings.

For each of these general characterizations specific hypotheses were derived and tested.

PROCEDURE

To test the hypotheses stated above, two sets of twenty subjects were selected—an experimental group of weight men and a control group of nonweightlifting athletes. Two projective tests (the Thematic Apperception Test and the Sentence Completion Test) were administered to these men and the groups compared on certain variables.

Subjects

(1) *Experimental group.* The main considerations in the selection of an experimental group of weight men were availability and representativeness. With this in mind the place selected for the bulk of the study was a leading gymnasium in Boston. This was centrally located and drew from all portions of the city.

Sixteen subjects were obtained there, the remaining four were members of the undergraduate body of Harvard University. Thus, twenty men made up our experimental population. The primary criterion for this group was that it have an enthusiastic interest in weight training.

(2) *Control group.* In selecting the control population the attempt was to secure subjects who were comparable to the experimental subjects as far as age, education, socioeconomic status, and general interest in athletics were concerned. In other words, the criterion for the control group was that it must be similar to the experimental group, with the specific exception that it have no interest in training with weights. Thus, sixteen non-weight training members of the gymnasium were selected as a control group (primarily basketball or volleyball players); the remaining four were athletically minded Harvard undergraduates.

Measures

(1) *Thematic Apperception Test.* Six cards, 20, 6BM, 13MF, 18BM, 7BM and 4 from Murray's revised test series[7] were selected as likely to evoke material pertinent to the hypothesis to be tested. The variables were drawn from Murray's list of needs and presses[6] from certain mimeographed material of the Harvard Psychological Clinic,

and were in part devised to fit the specific hypotheses. Some of Murray's individual variables were combined into one category, since their separation did not seem necessary for our purposes. The complete list of variables for this test as well as for the Sentence Completion Test are contained in Table 25-I.

TABLE 25-I

t-TESTS OF DIFFERENCE BETWEEN MEANS OF EXPERIMENTAL
AND CONTROL GROUPS

	TAT *t*	Sentence Completion *t*
I. Feelings of masculine inadequacy		
1. Concern about masculine symbols	....	5.56*
II. Exposure from early in life to a depriving and frustrating environment		
1. Insecurity and inadequacy as a child	....	1.18
2. Hostility in environment	3.82*	
3. Feelings of rejection	3.40*	1.99*
III. Failure to identify with adequate male figure		
1. Hostility toward mother	1.74*	3.34*
2. Hostility toward father	.79	.456
3. Inability to cope with environment	3.51*	
a. Social inadequacy	....	2.64*
b. Physical inadequacy	....	1.27
IV. An excessive amount of narcissism		
1. Narcissism	6.10*	4.02*
2. Aggression toward women	1.55	1.37
3. Heterosexual impulses	1.85*	2.94*
4. Homosexual impulses	2.22*	2.49*
V. Underlying dependency feelings		
1. Dependency feelings	2.21*	
2. Reaction formation	2.34*	
3. Conflict-autonomy/compliance	2.07*	
4. Conflict-collapse/counteraction	2.36*	
5. Need for mastering a situation	.54	

* Significant at the .05 level.

(2) *Sentence Completion Test.* With Murray's and MacKinnon's test as a base[10] a twenty-three item sentence completion test was constructed. Some of the items were identical to those of Murray and MacKinnon, and others were designed specifically for the study. Most of the categories scored were the same as those in the TAT. However, several subtractions were made, because the items could not be judged in the Sentence Completion Test, or were thought to be too difficult to judge. One of the items in the TAT was broken down into two parts for the Sentence Completion Test. Also, categories were added since they seemed to be particularly applicable for this test.

The testing was done individually, with the subjects being given the option of writing their own stories for the TAT or dictating them. Six weight men and two nonweight men elected to write their own stories. All of the subjects filled in their own Sentence Completion Test.

The scoring was done on a four-point scale, possible assignments running from 1 to 4. The variables scored were stated in such a way that the higher the rating of a weight man on any variable, the closer he would conform to the hypothesis. All names were deleted from the papers and all the ratings were done blind.

Statistical Treatment

All ratings were assumed to represent scale scores, and a *t*-test of differences between means of the experimental and control groups was made on each of the variables. A one-sided test of significance was employed, since the direction of the expected difference was, in all cases, predicted in advance. The .05 level of confidence or a *t* of 1.65 was selected as the point at which the null hypothesis would be rejected.

In addition, twelve randomly selected protocols from both the TAT and the Sentence Completion Test were given to an outside observer

TABLE 25-II
INTER-EXPERIMENTER RELIABILITY COEFFICIENTS

Category	TAT	Sentence Completion
Narcissism	.817	.849
Aggression toward women	.842	.832
Feelings of rejection	.623	.692
Heterosexual impulses	.858	.650
Homosexual impulses	.790	.794
Hostility toward mother	.863	.555
Hostility toward father	.712	.832
Inability to cope with environment	.892	
Social inadequacy	....	.772
Physical inadequacy	....	.523
Dependency	.681	
Hostility in environment	.876	
Need for mastering a situation	.874	
Conflict-autonomy/compliance	.849	
Conflict-collapse/counteraction	.695	
Reaction formation	.929	
Concern about masculine symbols	....	.628
Insecurity and inadequacy as a child	....	.592

for rating. At the time he was scoring the tests, not only did he not know their authors, but he was also unfamiliar with the hypotheses of this study. Reliability coefficients (Table 25-II) were computed for each variable; thus a check was provided for the accuracy of the ratings.

DISCUSSION

Deductive Power of Psychoanalytic Theory

The potential power of psychoanalytic theory as a predictive tool is the most striking impression gained from this study. All of the results were in the predicted direction, and all but seven (including both tests) were significantly so. That Freudian theory is still crude, however, is apparent in the gross way in which the empirical propositions were derived. Such haziness provides, for the *after-the-fact* interpreter, a convenient means for explaining contradictory data. The same ambiguity for the researcher, on the other hand, serves to frustrate attempts to derive adequate empirical propositions. No satisfactory test of the utility of psychoanalytic theory can be provided without greater conceptual clarity and a more exact statement of the relationship which exists between the various elements of the theory.

Considering this difficulty in deriving empirical propositions, it is impressive that in every case the relationships actually observed were correctly predicted. This was true despite the probable attenuation of the measures and the close similarity of the groups. Furthermore, with over a dozen propositions, the probability by chance of predicting all correctly is very small. Taking these things into consideration, this study thus provides imposing evidence of the ability of Freudian theory to deal with specific behavior patterns. Since psychoanalytic theory provided verifiable statements in this particular situation, it is likely that it will produce verifiable statements in other behavior areas. This follows especially, since Freudian theory was originally directed toward behavior which, superficially at least, bears little resemblence to the behavior under study.

Sensitivity of Projective Technique

It may seem illegitimate to attempt in the same study to validate both theoretical relationship and the instruments used in determining these relationships. In the one case we assume the adequacy of the instruments and inquire as to the relationship. In the other we assume the empirical relationships and inquire as to the sensitivity of the measure in detecting them. Though both cannot be assumed simultaneously, nevertheless, there is some sanction for testing both propositions in a single study. In the present case we assumed the adequacy of the instruments we employed. This meant that in the event of rejection of the hypotheses, we should have had to blame the theory rather than the empirical measures. In every case, however, the theory predicted correctly. In order for this to have occurred, the instruments must have measured accurately. Thus, we have initially assumed the adequacy of the measures and then, in the course of the study, have received additional evidence supporting this assumption.

Accepting this reasoning, there is obtained impressive evidence of the sensitivity to certain psychological variables of these two projective techniques. It is apparent that each of the instruments clearly differentiates between these two groups of known behavioral differences. Equally important is the close agreement between the measures. Of the categories scored on both tests, those that are significant are significant on both; those that are not significant are not significant on either test.

Characterization of Weight Men

The initial assumptions seem well borne out by the empirical data. This study would suggest that the following main characteristics distinguish the weight man from the nonweight man. The former has significantly greater feelings of masculine inadequacy. He appears decidedly more concerned with establishing his maleness, is more narcissistic than the nonweight man. He has fewer heterosexual impulses and shows more homosexual tendencies. Significantly, more hostility feelings are directed toward the mother and toward the environment at large, and, at the same time, the weight man shows evidence of inability to cope successfully with his environment. Feelings of rejection are prominent. He seems to be characterized by strong feelings of dependency and shows stronger compensatory needs than does the nonlifter.

In short, weight training seems to be an attempted solution for feelings of masculine inadequacy and inferiority. These men have identified the male ideal with a type of physique which is generally considered the antithesis of femininity. They attempt, by overtly assuming an extremely masculine role, to deny any passive or feminie feelings. Weight training may be looked on as answering a definite need and serving a specific function in the adjustment process of many individuals in our society.

SUMMARY AND CONCLUSIONS

The performances of twenty weightlifters and a control group of twenty non-weight-training athletes on two projective techniques (the TAT and the Sentence Completion Test) were compared on certain variables deduced with the aid of psychoanalytic theory. Significant differences were found between the groups on thirteen of the eighteen variables, and all of the results were in the predicted direction.

Three main conclusions were suggested by this study. They are as follows:

(1). That psychoanalytic theory is potentially a powerful predictive tool.

(2). That certain projective techniques, the TAT and Sentence Completion test, both are sensitive to certain variables and also show close correspondence in their ratings on individual variables.

(3). That there is a personality pattern which is, in general, characteristic of weight men.

REFERENCES

1. ALEXANDER, FRANZ: *Fundamentals of Psychoanalysis.* New York, Norton, 1948.
2. ALEXANDER, FRANZ: The influence of psychological factors upon gastro-intestinal disturbances. *Psychoanal Quar,* 1934, *3,* 501-539.
3. BLUM, GERALD: A study of the psychoanalytic theory of psychosexual development. *Genet Psychol Monogr,* Feb. 1949, *39,* first half.
4. FENICHEL, OTTO: *The Psychoanalytic Theory of the Neurosis.* New York, Norton, 1945.
5. MEAD, MARGARET: *Male and Female.* New York, Morrow, 1949.
6. MURRAY, H. A.: *Explorations in Personality.* New York. Oxford U P, 1947.

7. MURRAY, H. A.: *Thematic Apperception Test Manual.* Cambridge, Harvard 1943.
8. PARSONS, TALCOTT: Certain primary sources and patterns of aggression in the social structure of the western world. In: *Essays in Sociological Theory, Pure and Applied.* Glencoe, Free Press, 1949.
9. SEARS, ROBERT: *Survey of Objective Studies of Psychoanalytic Concepts.* New York, Social Science Research Council, 1942.
10. STEIN, MORRIS: The use of the sentence completion test for the diagnosis of personality. *J Clin Psychol,* 1947, *1,* 47-56.
11. THUNE, JOHN B.: Personality of weight lifters. *Res Quart Amer Phys Educ Ass, 20,* No. 3, 1949.
12. WILLOUGHBY, DAVID: Personal letter, Sept. 8, 1949.

Chapter 26

AGGRESSION IN BOXERS AND WRESTLERS AS MEASURED BY PROJECTIVE TECHNIQUES*

Burris F. Husman

INTRODUCTION

IN THE PAST few decades there has been considerable research devoted to the validation of sports and other physical education activities as educational tools. Much of this research has been physiologically and kinesiologically oriented; little has dealt with the psychological aspects of physical education.

PROBLEM

The problem of this research was to study the aggression of college boxers and wrestlers before, after, and during the season; and before and after a contest. Specifically, the present research was designed for the following reasons:

(1) To compare the aggression of boxers and wrestlers with each other, a control group (composed of cross-country participants and nonathlete college students), and with a normal population.

(2) To determine the effects of a season of competition and one emotionally charged match upon the aggression of the combative sport participants.

(3) To shed further light upon the frustration-aggression theories proposed by Dollard et al.,[2] thus determining if sport participation

* B. F. Husman. Aggression in boxers and wrestlers as measured by projective techniques. *Res Quart Amer Ass Health Phys Educ, 26*: 1955, 421-425. Reproduced here with the permission of the author and the American Association for Health, Physical Education, and Recreation. This study was submitted in partial fulfillment of the requirements for the Ed.D. degree at the University of Maryland under Warren R. Johnson.

lowers the aggression (Cathartic Theory) or if it increases the aggression (Circular or Interaction Theory).[5]

(4) To appraise the projective technique (a series of psychological tests, in which the subject is caught off guard, responds to an unstructured stimulus, and in so doing, divulges information about himself which he does not know or is not willing to admit)[1] as a tool for probing the personality traits of sport participants.

PROCEDURE

The Rosenzweig Picture-Frustration Study,[8] six selected pictures from Murray's Thematic Apperception Test,[6] and a twenty-item Sentence Completion Test [10, 11] were administered to nine college boxers, eight wrestlers, nine cross-country runners, and seventeen control subjects under the following conditions:

(1) Preseason (T_1)—a week or more prior to the official opening of practice for each sport.

(2) Precontest and midseason (T_2)—about half-way through the season and less than two days prior to an intercollegiate match.*

(3) Postcontest (T_3)—less than two days following an intercollegiate match.

(4) Postseason (T_4)—one week or more following cessation of practice and the last intercollegiate match of the season.

The Rosenzweig P-F Study was scored for direction of aggression and type of reaction, as prescribed by Rosenzweig.[9] Six of the eleven Rosenzweig scoring factors were analyzed in the results of this research. They were as follows:

(1) Extrapunitiveness—where the aggression is employed overtly and directed outwardly toward the environment.

(2) Intrapunitiveness—where the aggression is turned by the subject upon himself.

(3) Impunitiveness—where the aggression is evaded in an attempt to gloss over the frustration.

(4) Ego defense—where the ego of the subject predominates.

(5) Extrapunitive ego defense—where the subject aggresses extrapunitively to protect his ego.

---

* The cross country participants were not tested prior to and after a contest.

(6) Superego—where there is some accusation, charge or incrimination of the subject by someone else.

The Thematic Apperception Test (TAT) and the Sentence Completion Test (SCT) were scored for overall intensity of aggression by counting and rating the severity of the aggressive words expressed [4] and for direction by determining if the aggression was turned toward some person other than the hero (extrapunitive aggression) or toward the hero (intrapunitive aggression).

Reliability of scoring was established for each of the three tests employed. An 85 percent agreement was obtained between the author and an independent scorer (who had previously worked with Rosenzweig) on the scoring of the Rosenzweig P-F Study. On the Thematic Apperception Test and the Sentence Completion Test, correlations were obtained between the author and an independent scorer on the scoring factors, these correlations being .90 for the factors of overall intensity and extrapunitive aggression and between .60 and .77 for intrapunitive aggression.

TREATMENT OF THE DATA

The t-test was utilized to determine if a significant difference existed between the means of the scoring factors.[3] The means of the boxers were compared with those of the wrestlers, cross-country runners, and control subjects on all four test situations (T_1, T_2, T_3, and T_4). Likewise, the means of the wrestlers were compared with those of the cross-country runners, and control subjects; and the means of the cross-country runners were compared with those of the control group.

Comparisons were also made between the means of each of the groups on the various test situations (T_1, T_2, T_3, and T_4), to study the effects of one contest and the season upon aggression.

RESULTS*

Significant differences between means at the 5-percent level of confidence or better indicated the following:

* Because of the large number of comparisons made, it is impossible to present the results of this study in brief tabular form. They have been presented in both tabular and graphical form in the author's dissertation, and are available for study by writing the author.

(1) The boxers possessed less overall intensity of aggression than the wrestlers, cross-country runners, and the control group as measured by the Thematic Apperception Test. The *t*'s were 2.92, 3.40, and 2.89 respectively, all being significant at the 1-percent level of confidence or better with 25 degrees of freedom.

(2) The Rosenzweig Picture-Frustration Study and the Sentence Completion Test (SCT) indicated that the boxers had less tendency than the cross-country runners and the control subjects to express their aggression outwardly (extrapunitiveness), and that the boxers tended to blame themselves more for their frustrations or to gloss over their frustrations so that no person or object was to blame. Five *t*'s, all significant beyond the 5-percent level of confidence, indicated this. The Thematic Apperception Test, however, indicated the boxers to possess less intrapunitive aggression than the wrestlers, cross-country runners, and the control subjects. It was thought that the author's method of scoring intrapunitive aggression on this test may have been inadequate. This is partially verified by the low correlations obtained between the author and an independent worker on this scoring factor.

(3) The cross-country runners tended to aggress outwardly (extrapunitively) more than the boxers to protect their egos. The mean score of the boxers was 6.1 and that of the cross-country participants 9.8. The t between these two means was 3.38; a *t* of 2.90 being significant at the 1-percent level of confidence with seventeen degrees of freedom.

(4) On T_2 and T_4, the cross-country runners possessed more ego defense than the boxers. The *t*'s were 3.38 and 3.10 respectively; a *t* of 2.90 being significant at the 1-percent level of confidence.

(5) A *t* of 2.56 indicated that the boxers, after the contest (T_3), possessed more superego than the control group. A t of 2.06 with 25 degrees of freedom was required to establish confidence at the 5-percent level. It would be expected that the boxers would score higher on the trait superego after the contest, since superego purports to assess the subject's guilt feelings for his overt action.

(6) The cross country runners were more extrapunitive and less impunitive than the control group. A *t* of 2.98 on T_4 was significant at the 1-percent level of confidence, indicating the runners to be more extrapunitive; and a *t* of 2.50 on T_2 indicated that the control subjects

were more impunitive. A t of 2.79 was significant at the 1-percent level of confidence and a t of 2.06 was significant at the 5-percent level, with 25 degrees of freedom.

(7) By comparing Rosenzweig's trait of superego between the cross-country group and the control group, a t of 2.53 was computed on T_4, which indicated that the runners possessed more superego than the control group. Again a t of 2.06 was needed to establish the 5-percent level of confidence. This significant difference between the cross country runners and the control group may be explained by noting that the cross-country runners were more extrapunitive (see item 6 above)—thus aggressing against persons and objects in the environment more than the control group. Therefore, one would expect them to feel more guilty over their actions than the control subjects.

In addition to the significant differences described above, some non-significant differences seemed to suggest tendencies in and among the groups.

(1) The boxers apparently possessed more of Rosenzweig's trait—superego—than the normal population.* [7] The boxers' mean seemed to decrease after the season, and approached that of the normal population.

(2) Indications were that an emotionally charged contest tended to lower the extrapunitiveness, ego defense, and extrapunitive ego defense means of the participants.

(3) A combative contest tended to have the effect of causing the participants to turn their aggression inwardly.

(4) A season of participation tended to increase the aggression of the participants as measured by the TAT.

(5) A season of participation caused the Rosenzweig scoring factors of extrapunitiveness, intrapunitiveness, and superego to decrease for the boxers and cross-country runners.

(6) The results of this research tended to substantiate both the cathartic and circular theories of aggression.

(7) Of the twenty-three significant differences found in this research, thirteen were found by analyzing the TAT data. On this basis, the TAT seemed to be the best instrument for assessing aggression.

---

* The normal population here refers to the population used by Dr. Saul Rosenzweig in norming the Rosenzweig P-F Study.

(8) The TAT may be scored objectively by counting the frequency of aggressive words and rating their intensity.

CONCLUSIONS AND RECOMMENDATIONS

The results of this study indicated that the aggression of boxers was significantly different from that of the wrestlers, cross-country runners, and control subjects. The boxers possessed less overall intensity of aggression, were less extrapunitive and more intrapunitive and impunitive than the other subjects. The cross-country runners were more extrapunitive and less intrapunitive and impunitive than the control subjects.

Trends in the data which were not significant indicated that a season of participation tended to increase the aggression of the participants as measured by the Thematic Apperception Test, while a season of participation tended to lower the Rosenzweig scoring factors of extrapunitiveness, intrapunitiveness, and super-ego. An emotionally charged contest tended to lower the Rosenzweig scoring factors of extrapunitiveness, ego defense, and extrapunitive ego defense, and seemed to cause the participants to turn their aggression inwardly.

This research tended to substantiate both the cathartic and circular theories of aggression and indicated that the projective technique is useful in this type of research. Future studies might well be conducted using the TAT or Rosenzweig P-F to study aggression throughout a season or before and after a contest. The sport situation presents an unusual opportunity for analysis of personality traits. In sports, real life situations exist which offer physical educators and psychologists an ideal environment in which to conduct research.

REFERENCES

1. CLARK, R.: A method of administering and evaluating the thematic apperception test in group situations, *Genet Psychol Monogr, 30*:3-55, Aug. 1944.
2. DOLLARD, J.; MILLER, N. E.; DOOB, L. W.; MOWRER, O. H., and SEARS, R. R., *et al.*: *Frustration and Aggression.* New Haven, Yale University Press, 1939.
3. GUILFORD, J. P.: *Fundamental Statistics in Psychology and Education.* New York, McGraw, 1950. 633 pp.

4. LINDZEY, GARDNER: An experimental test of the validity of the Rosenzweig picture frustration study. *J of Personality, 18*:315-320, Mar. 1950.

5. MORLAN, GEORGE K.: A note on the frustration-aggression theories of Dollard and his associates. *The Psychological Review, 56*:1-8, Jan. 1949.

6. MURRAY, HENRY A., M.D., and Staff of Harvard Psychological Clinic: *Thematic Apperception Test Manual.* Cambridge, Harvard U, 1943. 20 pp.

7. ROSENZWEIG, SAUL: Revised norms for the adult form of the Rosenzweig picture-frustration study. *Journal of Personality, 18*:344-346, Mar. 1950.

8. ————, The picture association method and its application in a study of reactions to frustrations. *Journal of Personality, 14*:3-23, Sept. 1945.

9. ————; FLEMING, EDITH, and CLARK, HELEN J.: Revised scoring manual for the Rosenzweig picture-frustration study. *Journal of Psychology, 24*:165-208, Oct. 1947.

10. STEIN, MORRIS: The use of a sentence completion test for the diagnosis of personality. *Journal of Clinical Psychology, 3*:47-56, Jan. 1947.

11. SYMONDS, P. M.: The sentence completion test as a projective technique. *J Abnorm Psychol, 42*:320-329, July 1947.

Chapter 27

EFFECTS OF A COMBATIVE SPORT UPON PERSONALITY DYNAMICS AS MEASURED BY A PROJECTIVE TEST*

Warren R. Johnson and Daniel C. Hutton

INTRODUCTION

It is rather generally assumed that sports provide an outlet for powerful emotions which are accumulated in the course of daily living;† and thus we speak of the *cathartic* value of sports in something of the sense intended by Aristotle when he first applied the term to what he considered to be the psychologically cleansing effect of tragic drama. Presumably, the personality *displaces* or redirects pent-up aggressions and other powerful emotions and vents them harmlessly in the controlled and socially acceptable drama of athletic competition.[8, 13]

Taking another point of view, it may be argued that the cathartic effect of tragic drama derives from the frank portrayal of the culturally forbidden and violent, *and* from the terrible punishments of the transgressors. In contrast, however, sports are necessarily hemmed tightly round with rules and restrictions which prevent a truly cathartic release of the emotions. And lacking punishment for overtly expressed aggressions, the aftermath of violent sports may be strong guilt feelings.[7, 8, 15] Lemkau has commented on one aspect of this possibility:

* W. R. Johnson and D. C. Hutton: Effects of a combative sport upon personality dynamics as measured by a projective test. *Res Quart Amer Ass Health Phys Educ, 26*: 1955, 49-53. Reproduced here with the permission of Professor Warren R. Johnson and the American Association for Health, Physical Education, and Recreation.

† "And so man encountering threats must continue to fear and fear and hate and hate. Opportunities to give vent to both are severely restricted in our civilized lives, and so fear and hate are turned against things other than those for which they were originally intended." (Dr. G. S. Stevenson, Medical Director, The National Assoc. for Mental Health, Inc. See Ref. 24.)

I am a little skeptical, I must admit, about whether athletics are really
an outlet for aggressive feelings. It seems to me that the controls involved
in game rules are so complete that there is some doubt whether basic
aggression would be released in such a controlled situation. I would
rather at this moment at least, say that it is a release for the drive to
physical activity which certainly is not the same as aggression.[12, p. 17]

One might further argue that the very restrictions and rules which
define and order some sports so frustrate the venting of emotion that
the immediate and perhaps ultimate effect is heightened, rather than
lowered, aggressive feelings.[7, 14, p. 9ff] Some of the savage outbursts of
fist fighting in such sports as basketball and ice hockey might be
evidence in support of this possibility.

None of the points of view on this subject of aggression and aggression reduction in sports have been supported by an accumulation of
experimental data. More significantly, we have as yet very little
information on the much broader question of the effects of the competitive sports experience upon personality dynamics in general.

THE EXPERIMENT

An exploratory experiment was conducted in the hope of learning
something of how participation in a violent sport affects the dynamics
of personality. Wrestling was selected because of its combative nature
and because it has been found to be associated with exceptional emotional stress.[10]

The Personality Test

A projective personality test was utilized in the hope of penetrating
into some of the more subtle and usually inaccessible aspects of personality functioning.* Buck's House-Tree-Person test of *total personality*[3, p. 1] was selected as being reasonably well suited for use in this
initial inquiry because it seems to reflect the impact of strong emotion upon personality, and because the commonplace task it requires—
drawing a house, a tree, and a person with crayons—has been found
to be unlikely to give rise to blockages and refusals to be tested when
subjects are in an emotionally disturbed state.[5, p. 118]

---

* For a brief discussion of projective test theory, see the *Res Quart Amer Ass
Health Phys Educ,* Dec. 1954, p. 484.[11]

Limitations of the Test

Attention is directed to the fact that although the H-T-P has been established as a promising clinical test, it shares the limitations characteristic of projective tests, especially when used for experimental rather than clinical purposes. (See Ref. 1, p. 29ff and Ref. 17.) Moreover, some aspects of the H-T-P remain on questionable grounds in terms of certain of Buck's theoretical premises, and being a relatively new test its potentialities and limitations are not fully understood. (See Ref. 2, Vol. II, P. 180, and Ref. 6, P. 47.) Although the H-T-P yields various objectively derived scores, its full evaluation, like a medical diagnosis, rests to a considerable extent upon the clinical insight of the evaluator—upon his subjective interpretation of signs. It is for this reason that supporting evidence is not presented in the section of this paper on Results.

Conditions of the Research

The H-T-P test was administered to eight members of a college varsity wrestling team under three conditions: Condition I—approximately three weeks prior to the first intercollegiate match of the season to establish a *normal* personality evaluation for each wrestler; Condition II—four to five hours prior to the first interschool match of the season to determine the influence of anticipatory stress upon personality dynamics; and Condition III—the morning after the competition.

Test Evaluation

The tests were evaluated quantitatively and qualitatively in accordance with the prescribed procedures.[3, 4, 5] The psychologist who handled this phase of the work (and who had helped to develop the H-T-P technique) dealt with each test as though it were a clinical protocol.

DISCUSSION

Since the test in all three conditions of the research amounted to drawing a house, a tree, and a person, it was to be expected that subjects would not make identical drawings in each repetition of the test—therefore the three sets of tests would necessarily differ regardless of whether or not personality dynamics had actually undergone change due to the athletic experience. However, if no intervening experience had altered personality dynamics markedly between any two tests, there would be no reason to expect systematic changes in drawings which have been found to be indicative of some personality disturbance.

For a somewhat oversimplified example, let us suppose that in Condition I, subject A draws a path containing a few small circles to suggest pebbles, but that in Condition II (prematch) when drawing a similar path this subject draws pebbles until the path is literally covered with tiny circles. Now if this were an isolated occurrence in the drawings of Condition II, perhaps no great meaning would be attached to it; but if other parts of the house picture and the tree and person pictures also reflect a monotonous detailing of trivia, the test evaluator might well have reason to suspect compulsive behavior —which is a common reaction of personality when in a state of anxiety.[16, p. 291ff] Let us further suppose that in Condition III there is a return to something like the pattern of Condition I, that is, restored concern for *significant* detail work and for the integrity of the picture as a whole; and if this tendency is reflected in the tree and the person as well, one might assume that the personality is no longer reflecting anxiety in compulsive behavior.

The evaluation procedure of this research left something to be desired in that it was not possible for the evaluator to approach the tests in complete ignorance of the research purpose or plan. However, he did not know what type of sport was involved or between which two tests the intervening experience had occurred. Moreover, he had virtually no interest in or contact with athletic sports, nor had he had occasion to form specific opinions as to the effects of sports competition upon personality dynamics.

FINDINGS

Analysis and comparison of the tests revealed several group tendencies from condition to condition, outstanding among which were the following.

(1) In Condition II (prematch), the level of functioning intelligence of the group dropped from an estimated high average (mean IQ of 110) to low average (mean IQ of 92). There were strong

indications of heightened anxiety, and increased neurotic tendencies were noted, including compulsiveness and markedly heightened body consciousness. Aggressive feelings were much more in evidence, but the subjects showed an increased tendency to hold these feelings within strict controls and to direct them inwardly (*intrapunitive aggression*) rather than against persons or things in the environment (*extrapunitive aggression*).

(2) In Condition III (postmatch), functioning intelligence returned to or near its Condition I levels. The neurotic tendencies noted in Condition II were no longer in evidence. Aggressive feelings were greatly reduced, in most cases to levels below Condition I, whether or not the subjects had won in their matches.

Certain observations were made as to the characteristics of the group under *normal* conditions (Condition I). The subjects were described as evidencing a greater degree of aggressiveness or pent-up feelings of hostility than is ordinarily found. Seven of the subjects seemed to have little difficulty expressing their aggressive feelings in their drawings. One subject seemed disturbed by his own feelings of aggression and tended to direct them towards himself rather than outwardly.

Observations were also made regarding the characteristics (in Condition I) of three wrestlers of exceptional ability, one of whom was not a member of the experimental group. (The test evaluator was not informed as to the ability of these subjects.) All three were extremely aggressive, gave evidence of exceptional *drive* to be successful, and had strong feelings of self-assurance. They also gave evidence of more generalized and more conscious anxiety than is common. The *constriction of personality* (e.g. lowered functioning intelligence and increased neurotic signs) that was so apparent in the rest of the group in Condition II was considerably less in evidence in the two outstanding wrestlers.*

SUMMARY AND CONCLUSIONS

Eight college wrestlers were tested with the H-T-P projective test of personality under three conditions: before the wrestling season

---

* The observations of the exceptional personality traits of the outstanding wrestlers suggested a subsequent study of athletic champions in which two projective tests were used, the Rorschach as well as the H-T-P. (See Reference 11.)

(assumed to represent a *normal* measure for each subject); four to five hours before the first intercollegiate match of the season; and the morning after the competition. Interpretation of the tests revealed several group tendencies from condition to condition, outstanding among which were as follows: decrement of functioning intelligence; increased aggressive feelings (especially intrapunitive); increased neurotic signs in the before match condition; and a return to approximately the status of Condition I except for considerably less aggressive feelings in Condition III.

The experiment was frankly exploratory, the intention being to determine whether the projective technique is a promising tool for studying the effects of athletic competition upon personality dynamics. In spite of certain obvious weaknesses in research technique, the results of the study seemed encouraging to the present writers, and have led to work in similar veins.[9, 11]

The present research indicates that the subjects experienced something of a cathartic effect whether or not they won; however, this should certainly not be taken to invalidate Lemkau's argument in relation to sports in general. Findings in Condition II (prematch) seemed interesting in that they suggested the extent and nature of personality disturbance, referred to as *general constriction of personality* by the clinician, involved in anticipating a combative (but relatively very safe) sport.

The researchers concluded that the projective test technique is deserving of further study as a means of evaluating the effects of sports competition upon the dynamics of personality at all age levels.

REFERENCES

1. ANDERSON, H. H., and ANDERSON, G. L.: *Introduction to Projective Techniques.* New York: Prentice-Hall, 1951.

2. BROWER, D., and ABT, L. E.: *Progress in Clinical Psychology,* Vol. I & II. New York, Grune and Stratton, 1952.

3. BUCK, J. N.: *Administration and Interpretation of the H-T-P Test,* Proceedings of the H-T-P Workshop, Veterans Administration Hospital, Richmond, Virginia, 1950.

4. BUCK, J. N.: The quality of the quantity of the H-T-P, *J of Clinical Psych,* 7:352-356, Oct. 1952.

5. Buck, J. N.: The H.T.P. scoring manual, monograph supplement No. 5. *J of Clinical Psych,* Oct. 1948.

6. Buros, O. K.: *The Third Mental Measurement Year Book.* New Brunswick, Rutgers, 1949.

7. Dollard, J., and N. E. Miller, et al.: *Frustration and Aggression.* New Haven, Yale, 1939.

8. Gardener, G. E.: Recreation's part in mental health. *Recreation,* Jan. 1952.

9. Husman, B.: *An Analysis of Aggression in Boxers, Wrestlers, and Cross Country Runners as Measured by the Rosenzweig P-F Study, Selected TAT Pictures, and a Sentence Completion Test.* Doctoral dissertation, U of Maryland, 1954.

10. Johnson, W. R.: Emotion revealed in two types of athletic contests. *Res Quart Amer Ass Health Phys Educ, 20:*72-79, March 1949.

11. Johnson, W. R.; Hutton, D. C., and Johnson, G. B., Jr.: Personality traits of some champion athletes as measured by two projective tests: Rorschach and H-T-P. *Res Quart Amer Ass Health Phys Educ, 25:*484-485, Dec. 1954.

12. Lemkau, P. V.: Quotation in *Desirable Athletic Competition for Children.* Washington, D. C., Amer Ass for Health, Phys Ed and Recreation (NEA), 1952.

13. Menninger, W. C.: Recreation and mental health. *Recreation,* 1948.

14. Stevenson, G. S.: *Introduction to L. Freeman's Fight Against Fears.* New York, Crown, 1951.

15. Stone, A.: The Catharsis theory of aggression. *Lab Bull* (Laboratory of Social Relations, Harvard), *2:*9-13, June 1950.

16. White, R. W.: *The Abnormal Personality.* New York, Ronald, 1948.

17. Zubin, J.: Objective evaluation of personality tests. *Amer J Psychiat, 107:* 569 ff., Feb. 1951.

Chapter 28

DISCRIMINANT FUNCTION AND HIERARCHIAL GROUPING ANALYSIS OF KARATE PARTICIPANTS' PERSONALITY PROFILES*

Walter Kroll and B. Robert Carlson

INTRODUCTION

The sport of karate has been experiencing widespread growth throughout the United States. Although originally practiced as a method of unarmed self-defense, the current popular emphasis of karate is upon physical fitness, self-confidence, and mental control training. This seems a reasonable position since combat activities are usually thought of as providing opportunities for the display of prowess and masculinity, development of self-confidence, and a release of tension with sublimation of aggressive impulses. Unfortunately very little is known concerning personality factors in combat activities. A recent review of personality studies in wrestling,[9] for example, reported few distinguishing characteristics for amateur high school and college wrestlers.

It seems clear that definition of personality characteristics of individuals initially selecting and subsequently realizing successful and satisfying experiences in various physical activities is needed. In the same manner, studying the effects that such experiences may have upon participants and whether or not successful participation can be linked with personality factors needs concurrent emphasis. Such information is not only desirable in affording a sound basis for curriculum decisions in physical education but in the prescription of

* W. Kroll and B. R. Carlson: Discriminant function and hierarchial grouping analysis of karate participants' personality profiles. *Res Quart Amer Ass Health Phys Educ, 38*:1967, 405-411. Reproduced here with the permission of Professor Walter Kroll and the American Association for Health, Physical Education, and Recreation.

[298]

physical activity as a therapeutic adjunct as well. Both Davis[4] and Layman[6] cite the need of understanding the psychological significance of activity as well as the needs of the psychiatric patient.

Karate has several advantages, differing in importance, to offer as a physical education activity and/or therapeutic adjunct in psychiatry: (1) women can paritcipate in karate; (2) as a method of self-defense karate may be considered superior to amateur boxing or wrestling; (3) karate effectively develops certain muscular strengths;[10] and (4) the emphasis upon wholesome character attributes and etiquette rituals is desirable in attempts at amelioration of asocial tendencies.

PURPOSE

The purpose of this study was to investigate the personality profiles of amateur karate participants.

PROCEDURES

During the spring of 1965 a karate tournament and clinic was conducted with teams representing five karate clubs from several college and athletic groups. Competition was held for various belt classifications. One of the authors administered Form A of the Cattell sixteen personality factor questionnaire, or 16 PF test.[1] The 16 PF test is purported to measure the main dimensions of personality; it is soundly based on extensive research, is recognized as one of the better personality inventories, and has been translated into several foreign languages.

The total sample consisted of seventy-one subjects divided into three criterion groups dependent upon belt classification level and experience. The advanced group (N = 17) was comprised of karate participants possessing black, brown, yellow, or blue belts, and having had more than one year of experience. The intermediate group (N = 25) consisted of green belt participants with more than six months of experience. The novice group (N = 29) was composed of white belt participants with six months or less of experience. Classification of criterion groups in this manner afforded the means to consider the possibility of a trend in personality characteristics from novice to advanced. It provided opportunity for a cross-section view of personality profiles for participants initially selecting the activity (novice), and for those continuing on in the activity with apparent satisfaction and success (intermediate and advanced).

Following test manual recommendations, raw test scores were used in the analysis. Mean raw scores for group profile factors were converted into standard ten scores, or stens, for comparison purposes, using norm tables for college age males. The analysis procedure employed was a multiple discriminant analysis[2] which determines whether criterion groups can be distinguished from each other using the entire profile simultaneously. A multivariate technique, multiple discriminant analysis considers individual variability about group means, group variability on profile components, and the interrelationships between all profile components. A hierarchial grouping analysis[11] was subsequently employed as a check on suitability of classification criteria.

RESULTS

Table 28-I summarizes the results of the multiple discriminant function analysis and presents group sten scores on profile components as well as separate univariate F tests. Wilks' lambda was used to test the hypothesis that the three karate groups demonstrated similar sixteen PF test profiles. Wilks' lambda was .593 ($F = .991$, $p = .49$) and the multivariate, generalized null hypothesis that no differences existed in group profiles was regarded as tenable. Using Rao's[8] technique, neither one of the two possible discriminant functions was significant. None of the univariate F tests for the sixteen profile components reached the level required for significance.

As with any arbitrary selection of criterion groups, issue may be taken with the criteria for classification. In the present situation, for example, the following might be contended: (1) belt level and length of participation were inappropriate; (2) satisfaction and success are unrelated; (3) length of participation is unrelated to either success or satisfaction. Indeed, there can be any number of objections raised against any scheme proposed for classification.*

---

* Agreeing upon appropriate criteria with which to form criterion groups remains a thorny issue. Typically, critics of criterion group selecton are proficient in pointing out deficiencies but fail to acknowledge that amelioration of cited deficiencies only results in a classification scheme with another set of deficiencies. The task is not to enumerate deficiencies, which are often self-evident, but to suggest a better method of classification.

TABLE 28-I

DISCRIMINANT ANALYSIS, UNIVARIATE F TESTS, AND 16 PF
PROFILE STEN SCORES OF KARATE PARTICIPANTS

Profile Component	Advanced (N = 17)	Mean stens Intermediate (N = 25)	Novice (N = 29)	F	p
A	5.6	5.0	6.0	2.83	.07
B	6.1	6.1	6.2	.05	.96
C	5.4	5.7	5.7	.20	.82
E	5.8	5.8	5.9	.03	.97
F	6.1	5.3	5.3	1.31	.28
G	6.0	6.7	6.4	1.42	.25
H	5.6	5.2	5.4	.39	.68
I	6.0	5.2	5.8	1.02	.36
L	6.3	4.8	5.3	2.24	.11
M	5.8	5.8	6.2	.33	.72
N	5.7	5.5	5.8	.25	.78
O	5.8	5.3	5.8	.43	.65
Q_1	6.4	6.0	5.8	.29	.75
Q_2	6.3	7.0	6.5	1.40	.25
Q_3	5.8	5.7	6.0	.43	.65
Q_4	6.5	5.7	6.0	1.04	.36

	Percent of trace	X^2
Root 1	68.44	21.39, df = 17 Wilks' lambda = .593
Root 2	31.56	10.79, df = 15 F = .991, df = 32 and 106

In the present study the problem revolves around a total sample of seventy-one karate participants and the question of personality profile differences when the sample is subdivided into criterion groups. The criteria upon which the sample is to be subdivided must effect similar, but mutually exclusive groups. The criteria of belt level and length of participation were used, but as discussed previously these criteria might be inappropriate.

Under this state of affairs, there exists a sample of seventy-one personality profiles to be grouped into mutually exclusive sets upon the basis of some appropriate criteria. If differences in personality profiles between groups result, the cause would likely be ascribed to differences between groups as reflected in the classification criteria. Then the only problem remaining would be to settle upon the appropriateness of the criteria. Too often this results in an endless conflict of unsuitable alternatives.

Rather than selecting a set of criteria first and then assessing the possibility of profile differences between groups, it is possible to first form mutually exclusive and optimally homogeneous groups and then consider criteria for classification. If between group differences result,

a search for appropriate criteria with which to explain group membership could be undertaken. If no such criteria can be found, or if no
between-group differences result on profiles clustered for optimally
homogeneous groups, it might be concluded no such criteria exist.

Ward [11] has provided a technique which reduces the number of
groups from N to $N-1$, $N-2$, ... 1, where N represents the
original number of groups. In the present case, N equals the number
of subjects—71. Called hierarchial grouping, the objective is to reduce
the number of groups in an iterative fashion by forming groups so that
optimal homogeneity on profile measures results. This is achieved by
minimizing the sum of squared deviations about the group mean for
each profile variable within each group, and for all groups simultaneously. A profile of n-scores is considered as occupying an n-dimen-
sional orthogonal space. By analytic geometry a distance measure
between any pair of profiles, A_1, B_1, ... Z_{n_1} and A_2, B_2, ... Z_{n_2} is

$$D = \sqrt{(A_1 - A_2)^2 + (B_1 - B_2)^2 + \ldots + (Z_{n_1} - Z_{n_2})^2}$$

The seventy-one sets of profiles were subjected to hierarchial grouping analysis. Individual profile components were standardized to avoid
overloading of the criterion (total within-groups variance) due to
differences in raw score distributions. Profile components were thus
weighted equally. This, of course, has the result of weighting any
common factors that appear in the separate profile components. As
Cronbach and Gleser [3] propose, however, this is frequently desirable
since such common factors are of practical significance.

Figure 28-1 presents the increase in total within-groups variance
(TWGss) with each iterative reduction from N groups to one group.
Relative homogeneity of the groups formed can be assessed by noting
the increase in TWGss at various levels of the reduction process. The
increase in TWGss as the number of groups is reduced from seventy-
one to seventy (TWGss $= 23.0$) up to a reduction from twenty-
eight to twenty-seven groups (TWGss $= 98.95$) is less than 100 for
each iterative reduction in the series. The increases from twenty-six
down to twelve groups are also relatively small, but when the reduction process goes past ten hierarchial groups TWGss increases are
marked.

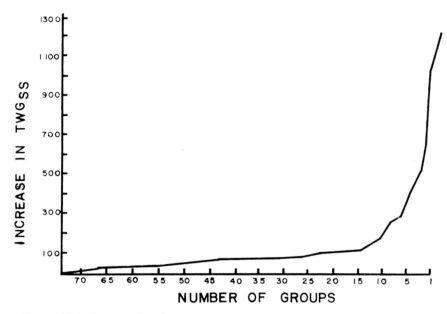

FIGURE 28-1. Increase in within-groups variance as a result of iterative reduction of hierarchial groups.

The sharp increases in TWGss with each iterative reduction beyond ten hierarchial groups indicates a considerable loss in classification accuracy—i.e. the relative cost in terms of optimal homogeneity as reflected in total within-groups variance is high when hierarchial groups are reduced past ten. Such information suggests that groups rapidly lose profile similarity when reduced past ten, and it may be inappropriate to consider less than ten hierarchial groups for efficient classification.

Inspection of group membership for ten hierarchial groups suggested no meaningful pattern of possible criteria for membership. No criterion or set of criteria could be postulated as a classification scheme to explain why particular group memberships resulted. Criteria considered were age, height, weight, belt level class, college vs athletic club membership, and length of participation. As the number of hierarchial groups decreased from ten, attempts at postulating criteria for membership became even more unsuccessful.

It seemed reasonable to conclude that forming optimally homogeneous groups on the basis of 16 PF test profiles failed to suggest meaningful criteria for classification purposes. There was no suggestion of a personality profile pattern linked to the possible criteria considered. The marked loss in optimal profile homogeneity as iterative reduction went past ten hierarchial groups indicated lack of evidence for a characteristic personality profile of karate participants.

DISCUSSION

The findings are compatible with the results of comparable studies using the 16 PF test done on swimmers[7] and on wrestlers.[5] Parsons[7] studied thirty-five swimmers of national championship caliber in Canada. When comparison was made of profile components for eleven swimmers chosen for international competition with the remaining twenty-four swimmers, no significant differences resulted. Similarly, three groups of amateur wrestlers representing superior, excellent, and average level of wrestling achievement demonstrated no 16 PF profile differences using multiple discriminant analysis.[5] Both of these studies, however, found differences when criterion groups were compared with norms for corresponding populations. Parsons found significant differences on fifteen of the sixteen profile components, and it was suggested that wrestlers exhibited a departure from average on Factor I, indicating toughmindedness and masculinity.

When sten scores for karate groups were compared with norm values no meaningful departures were noted. According to Cattell,[1] only sten scores of four and lower or seven and higher indicate definite departure from average. Thirty-four of the forty-eight group sten scores in Table I fell within the normal limits of five and six ($.25\sigma$ on either side of the mean). Only one sten score reached 7.0 (Factor Q_2 for the intermediate group), and the lowest sten score was 4.8 (Factor L for the intermediate group). Since the order of scores by criterion groups on these two factors (Q_2 and L) demonstrates no collinearity, it seems unreasonable to attach much significance to these two events. If the groups had shown a monotonic increase or decrease on either of these factors by levels of karate success, the factors might have suggested existence of some pattern. Even then the question of probability due to multiple F tests would force such an interpretation into the penumbra of speculation.

The karate groups were quite homogeneous on Factor B (intelligence), but this is a likely result when the criterion groups are composed primarily of college students and/or college graduates. A similar result occurred in the study done on amateur wrestlers.[5] Unlike amateur wrestlers, karate groups demonstrated average values on Factor I (tough-minded versus tender-minded). Since wrestling and karate are both individual combat activities one might have expected similarity on Factor I, but this did not occur.

SUMMARY AND CONCLUSIONS

Three criterion groups of karate participants were studied representing advanced (N = 17), intermediate (N = 25), and novice (N = 29) classifications. Multiple discriminant analysis revealed no significant profile differences between criterion groups. None of the univariate F tests on the sixteen profile components were significant, and the sten scores fell generally within normal values. A hierarchial grouping analysis failed to suggest meaningful criteria for alternative classification criteria.

Based upon the results of the 16 PF test secured on karate participants, it would seem there are no profile components or patterns which differentiate between (1) levels of karate participation and proficiency, or (2) karate participants and the normal population.

REFERENCES

1. CATTELL, RAYMOND B., and STICE, GLEN F.: *Handbook For the Sixteen Personality Factor Questionnaire.* Champaign, The Institute for Personality and Ability Testing, 1957.
2. COOLEY, WILLIAM W., and LOHNES, PAUL R.: *Multivariate Procedures for the Behavioral Sciences.* New York, Wiley, 1962.
3. CRONBACH, L. S., and GLESER, GOLDINE C.: Assessing similarity between profiles. *Psychol Bull, 50*:456-73, 1953.
4. DAVIS, JOHN E.: *Clinical Applications of Recreational Therapy.* Springfield, Thomas, 1952.
5. KROLL, WALTER: Sixteen personality factor profiles of collegiate wrestlers. *Res Quart Amer Ass Health Phys Educ, 37*:49-57, 1967.
6. LAYMAN, EMMA M.: Physical activity as a psychiatric adjunct. In Warren R. Johnson (Ed.): *Science and Medicine of Exercise and Sports.* New York, Harper, 1960.
7. PARSONS, DAVID R.: *Personality Traits of National Representative Swim-*

mers—Canada, 1962. Unpublished master's thesis. U of British Columbia, 1963.

8. RAO, C. R.: *Advanced Statistical Methods in Biometric Research.* New York, Wiley, 1952.

9. RASCH, PHILIP J., and KROLL, WALTER: *What Research Tells the Coach About Wrestling.* Washington, D. C., AAHPER, 1964.

10. RASCH, PHILIP J., and O'CONNELL, EUGENE R.: TPS scores of experienced karate students. *Res Quart Amer Ass Health Phys Educ, 34*:108-10, 1963.

11. WARD, JOE H., and HOOK, MARION E.: Application of an hierarchial grouping procedure to a problem of grouping profiles. *Educ & Psychol Measmt, 23*:69-81, 1963.

Chapter 29

PSYCHOLOGICAL CONSISTENCIES WITHIN THE PERSONALITY OF HIGH-LEVEL COMPETITORS*

BRUCE C. OGILVIE

INTRODUCTION

LONGITUDINAL STUDIES of the potential effect of high-level competition upon the character formation of youthful competitors in sports cannot be found in the literature of psychology or physical education. In a recent study of age-group swimmers, trends for both boys and girls of ages between ten and fourteen appeared to be so consistent that it becomes possible to engage in more intelligent speculation about the effects of competition upon personality. The data, presented in cross-sectional form, will have to be interpreted with caution because of the highly select sample that they represent.

My research interest in the area of athletic personality, motivation, and the possible effects on character formation of competition has developed from extensive clinical experience with problem athletes. During a period of years, athletes from every sport representing every level from age-group competition through high school, college, and professional teams have been referred because of psychological problems. The range of these problems and the psychological conflicts associated with competition have covered the entire spectrum of emotional disorder. The variety of somatic complaints and the severity of emotional reactions to the stress of high-level competition have at times given me serious doubts as to the value of athletic competition. In the role of consultant psychologist to competitors who responded with such a wide range of negative reactions to the stress of college,

  * B. C. Ogilvie: Psychological consistencies within the personality of high-level competitors. *JAMA, 205*:156-162, 1968. Reproduced with permission of the Editor of the *Journal of the American Medical Association* and the author.

professional, and even Olympic competition, I have encountered serious questions which have forced me to make a critical analysis of the values in sports.

METHODS OF STUDY

Sociometric and psychometric studies have been designed to measure a number of practical and academic questions. A significant number of investigators have directed their attention to determining the contribution that games, recreation, and competition have made to the socialization process. Other investigators have directed their energies toward determining the contribution of athletic participation to personality and character formation.[1] More recently there has been considerable emphasis upon the identification of the personality variables that can be found to relate significantly to athletic achievement. The selection of criterion groups of athletes, such as those who have sufficient talent to participate in professional sports or to represent the United States, or their own country, in the Olympic Games, does permit reliable statements about the personality of the successful athlete. The comparison of athlete to nonathlete at the various levels of competition has provided a limited understanding as to the character structure of those who retain an interest in continuing in athletics.

The variety of objective personality questionnaires used to investigate athletic personality includes those instruments that have been used most frequently for selection of personnel in business or industry. They include the Minnesota Multiphasic Personality Inventory (MMPI),[2] the California Personality Inventory (CPI),[3] the Edwards Personal Preference Schedule (EPPS),[4] the Maudsley Psychological Inventory (MPI),[5] and the Cattell 16 PF IPAT (16PF).[6]

RESULTS

There is high predictability that athletic skills and high motor ability are significantly related to peer acceptance at the onset of adolescence. The evidence from the studies of the highly select group swimmers at the nationally renowned Santa Clara Swim Club reinforces the need for caution about the relationship between high motor ability and personality. The criteria for acceptance as a member, as determined by Coach George Haines, seem to this investigator to be the most stringent that have been observed anywhere in the western world. When the entire team is separated by sex and age grouping, the cross-sectional analysis suggests that, when common personality traits are examined, the relationship between personality and competition becomes less clear. When we control for sex differences and level of competition, we find that boys and girls become much more similar between the ages of ten and fourteen years of age.[7] The ten-year-old boys were on the cool, reserved, introverted end of the scale, while those swimmers who remained in an extremely competitive training program until fourteen years of age measured more warmhearted, outgoing, and extraverted. There was a shift toward greater emotional stability and higher conscious development from ages ten to fourteen years. The populations of boys showed an extreme increase for the personality dimensions self-assertion, independence, and aggression.

This has some theoretical interest based upon the study of the United States 1964 Olympic swimming team. This trait tended to distinguish the medalist from the nonmedalist Olympic competitors.[8] The most significant shift with age occurred for the personality dimension sober-serious vs happy-go-lucky surgency. In that this trait correlates most significantly with the dimension extraversion-introversion, one is forced to respect the possible contribution of this trait of personality to continued competition. These young men moved toward increased emotional stability with increased age. This finding has considerable significance in the light of the most recent finding for the relationship between anxiety control and emotional stability. The highest correlation found within an entire university basketball league for the personality trait included in the 16PF was between anxiety and emotional stability. Criticism can be leveled at the cross-sectional comparison method of analysis because it is not possible to separate attenuation factors from personality changes as a reflection of trait conditioning during competition training.

These data support the generalization that increased control of anxiety, self-control, self-assurance, self-assertiveness, tough-mindedness, and extraversion all increase with age. These highly select young male competitors appear to possess the personality traits that have been demonstrated to be most descriptive of world-class athletic competitors. The data for the young females with mean ages of ten and fourteen years lends considerable support for the foregoing conclusion. They moved toward a more outgoing, warmhearted selection of women with increased age, but do not reach the level of young males for this trait. In terms of national norms there was a tendency for the girls to be more intelligent, more emotionally stable, have higher conscience development, become more tough-minded, more individualistic, more self-disciplined, and slightly less anxious and tense.

In the absence of longitudinal data, profile comparisons have been made with those of Rushall [9] who published the only study reporting findings for Indiana age-group swimmers. It is not possible to estimate the level of selectivity of these youthful competitors in relation to the Santa Clara Swim Club, but the fact that they represent an area so close to the nationally known Dr. James Councilman does suggest that they would be a highly select group. The Indiana girls (43) tended to be more outgoing, more individualistic and more self-sufficient. SCSC girls (53) tended to be more intelligent, more emotionally stable, less excitable, more self-assertive, more venturesome-bold, more individualistic, slightly more self-assured, and slightly more tough-minded. These two groups of swimmers were very similar for the personality traits phlegmatic vs excitable, happy-go-lucky vs sober, venturesome vs shy, group dependence vs self-sufficiency, and undisciplined vs self-controlled. Reviewing the same dimensions for boys, the differences in profiles indicated that SCSC (47) were more emotionally stable, more venturesome, more controlled — self-disciplined, more relaxed — less tense. Indiana boys (27) were more excitable, more tough-minded, and more happy-go-lucky. Slight differences favored SCSC boys for the traits intelligence, self-sufficiency, and outgoing-warmhearted. In the absence of adequate control data based upon samples of youngsters, mean age fourteen years, who are not as highly select as these swimmers, these comparisons do support the notion that those who remain in highly competitive programs share many personality traits in common. There will be differences with regard to the degree to which these traits are found to be present within groups who are matched for age, but no critical statement can be made until some effort is made to control for the degree of selectivity of youthful competitors. Independent of all the possible qualifications, these data suggest that there is a movement toward extraversion with age for males but less so for females.

Cross-cultural data as reported by Kane[10] for British female subjects decreases the probability of the general statements that can be made with respect to the female who attains a high level of athletic achievement. In his published studies of two small samples of British Olympic sportswomen, including swimmers and athletes, he reported a similarity coefficient of 0.85. These women were remarkably similar in personality structure. They were outgoing-warmhearted, happy-go-lucky, and high for the trait of extraversion. They were low on emotional stability, conscience development, high in anxiety with higher than average resting levels of anxiety. Kane compared these Olympic females with a sample of British women physical educators, many of whom had been outstanding sportswomen. The two samples were found to be quite similar. The physical educators were happy-go-lucky, low on self-assertion, low for emotional stability, tended to be apprehensive-worried, tended toward high resting levels of anxiety, and were significantly extraverted.

There seems to be considerable support from 16PF data that cross-cultural differences exist for certain personality traits which are particularly evident for female comparisons. Cultural differences do prevail for males but seem to be much more a manifestation of sports specific differences as comparisons of track and team sports such as basketball.[11] A profile comparison of Rushall's highly successful university swimming team and the highly successful San Jose State women's swimming team supports the conclusion that United States competitors share many more personality traits in common independent of sex. These two teams with exceptional records were quite similar in terms of mean profiles. The Indiana males were slightly brighter, and slightly more outgoing. The college women were much more venturesome-bold, more experimental, lower in resting level of anxiety, and less tense. Both samples would be described as outgoing, bright, emotionally stable, self-assertive, happy-go-lucky, high conscience development, tending toward tough-mindedness and self-sufficiency. They were also similar in that they were slightly distrustful of others, tended to be wrapped up in inner urgencies, and tended to follow their own urges. These two samples which are matched for age, level of competition, and educational level offer support for trait similarity. The cultural differences between United States and British females received further support when British women in team sports were compared with American female competitors.[10] In general, British Olympic swimmers and team athletes were more outgoing-warm-hearted and tended to be more extraverted. United States females tended to be more reserved-cool, slightly more self-assertive, venturesome, tough-minded, self-sufficient, and much less anxious and tense. These women share many common traits of personality, but the differences in emotional stability, conscience development, and resting level of anxiety would probably prove to be significant differences for a sample of this size.

The reliability of our statements about the personality structure of successful athletes has been greatly reduced by our failure to control for such factors as culture, educational level, age, and sex. Of particular significance to this review has been the failure to control for team vs individual sport. There is a growing body of evidence that sports specificity with regard to certain traits of personality can be predicted. Peterson[12] compared the personality structure of women-team vs women-individual sports. She tested 156 Amateur Athletic Union and US Olympic women, using the 16PF. The thirty-eight individual sports women represented swimming, diving, riding, fencing, canoeing, gymnastics, and track. The fifty-nine team women represented the 1964 Olympic volleyball team and ten AAU basketball women. Women individual competitors were found to be significantly more dominant, aggressive, venturesome, self-sufficient, and more experimental. Team sportswomen were significantly more tough-minded and shrewd-worldly-wise. When the San Jose State women swimmers were compared with these two high-level competitors, they were found to lie between the team and individual sportswomen or achieve a profile that was identical to individual sportswomen. They differed most from the team sportswomen on the traits self-assertion, venturesomeness, inner urgencies, forthrightness, experimenting, self-sufficiency, and resting tension. Had these women been combined into a single sample without regard to team vs individual sport distinctions, the most reliable description would be as follows: These ninety-seven women are cool-reserved, bright, emotionally stable, self-opinionated, venturesome and tough-minded. They appear to be similar to the general population for the traits sober vs happy-go-lucky, conscience development, placid vs apprehensive, and casual vs controlled. It does seem that US sportswomen share many more traits in common with those found for both British and US sportsmen. These women tend to be no-nonsense types of persons who are emotionally stable, assertive, socially bold, and possess reasonable self-control. They are independent and possess the qualities that incline them toward leadership roles. As reported previously, the similarity of psychological profile greatly increases for sportswomen, even for the British, when they were separated on the basis of international achievement.[13] Even though these were very limited samples, the fact that the personality profiles were almost identical with that for the US women does offer further support for the relationship between certain traits and athletic achievement.

When the most restrictive standards are applied in order to establish the highest order of criteria for athletic success, the significance of specific personality traits does receive considerable empirical support. A number of investigations can be used to substantiate the relevance of these traits in terms of how they may actually contribute to the attainment level of athletic success. The 1964 Olympic male swimmers were divided into gold medalists and non-gold-medalists in order to establish the highest possible criteria for excellence in swimming. Important trends appeared, none of which achieved statistical significance. The medalists tended to separate themselves for the traits emotional stability, self-sufficiency, self-assurance, self-control, self-discipline, and liberality of thinking. On the basis of second-order factors, they tended to be lower in anxiety, lower in neuroticism, more independent, and slightly better able to handle emotional stress. When Kane separated his world-class tennis women from tournament-level women, he found them to be more emotionally stable, higher in ego strength, higher in self-confidence, and with lower resting levels of anxiety. Returning to the data for age-group swimmers, I believe that the observed changes of personality structure from the ages of ten years to fourteen years offer some empirical support for the predictions that could be made in respect to personality and athletic success. The changes observed cannot be attributed to character formation, as conditioned by competition, but must be accepted as the interaction of a number of variables, which can only be identified at the termination of the longitudinal study. The shifts that are consistent both for boys and girls are that both become more outgoing-warmhearted and more emotionally stable, have increased conscience development and increased tough-mindedness, become more forthright, have increased self-control, and moved from high resting tension to low levels of tension.

REVIEW OF THE MOST SIGNIFICANT PERSONALITY TRAITS

An examination of the limited data available when a common measure of personality such as the IPAT 16PF is applied does permit a more rational speculation about the relationship between athletic achievement and personality. Admittedly, there is insufficient empirical data to support the generally held philosophy that competitive sports, in some way, make a positive contribution to character formation. There is considerable evidence from the data now being analyzed, based upon large samples of members of the coaching fraternity, that athletic competition may limit personal growth in other areas.[14] The probability is very high that we have only succeeded in collecting data for those individuals whose character formation was such that they could endure the stress and strain necessary for high-level achievement in athletics.

The traits reviewed and found significant in various studies do not assume a clear hierarchial order. It seems reasonable, therefore, that parental and educational emphasis be placed upon the following traits if our concern is with the development of physical excellence: emotional stability, tough-mindedness, conscientiousness, controlled self-discipline, self-assurance, relaxed low-tension level, trusting—free of jealousy, and for males, increased outgoing personality.

Emotional Stability

In terms of logical expectations, many studies consistently support the significant contribution of emotional stability to athletic success as well as coaching success. It would be unusual if this were not the case, in that for every other area of investigation where human achievement has been the focus, these factors have consistently been found to be positively related. The exception is in relation to cross-cultural differences for women competitors. The generalization holds true only when we apply rigid standards of excellence, such as rating as an international-class athlete. This trait may be characterized as facing reality calmly, avoidance of emotional upset, learning to control feelings, avoiding feelings that might interfere with problem solving, refusing to retreat to childish less-mature solutions for conflicts. There are few areas of human commitment that have the potentiality for reinforcing life's realities as would be found in high-level competitive athletics. The very nature of sport demands that one place his ability before the public eye, which results in an awareness of one's failings in a way that is inescapable. Unconscious denial of failure or unconscious fear of placing one's talent on the line can rarely be used as an adequate defense against reality. The *moment of truth* is axiomatic in the life of the great competitor. Therefore, it was to be expected that those who remain, and those who excell would have a higher than average potential for coming to grips with reality. To be a winner it is essential that failure to achieve or failure to realize the coach's goals be accepted as a personal responsibility, which of course demands emotional strength. Successful athletes are achievement-oriented people and derive personal satisfaction from their striving. High achievement needs are based upon personal attitudes about the probability of success vs failure associated with each investment of self. All things considered, he is at his very best when the odds are slightly against him. Ambitious people derive slight joy, if any, when their ability remains uncontested. The great athletes that I have interviewed do not dwell upon their losses, but concentrate upon that part of their performance that limited their excellence.

Tough-Tender-Mindedness

The trait tough-tender-mindedness, as defined by Cattell,[15] contains a number of tendencies that become polarized within the personality structure of the individual. At the tender end of the continuum would be the person who is demanding, impatient, dependent, gentle, sentimental, imaginative, easily anxious, and likes to be with people. At the tough-minded end of the continuum would be the person who is

emotionally mature, independent-minded, and possesses a hard realistic outlook. This person overrides his feelings, is not fanciful, does
not show anxiety, and is self-sufficient. Cattell reports that this trait is
culturally determined; therefore, it seems essential that we examine
the behavioral expectancies associated with the tendencies of an individual to fall at one or the other of the extremes of this trait. Cattell
described the tender-minded person as being basically involved in
"imaginative escapism or even an undisciplined mind," while the
tough-minded takes a cold, realistic appraisal of the facts and does not
allow himself to become involved in sentimental overreaction. On the
positive side, tender-mindedness is related to creativity, but it has also
been shown to be strongly associated with neuroticism. We have collected data upon over 10,000 athletes ranging from high school
through the most select professional athletes such as those found in
sports car racing. The licensed race driver sets the standard for tough-
mindedness, followed very closely by three separate samples of driver
trainees tested in 1966, 1967, and 1968. One might anticipate that
the individual who is accelerating from 0 mph to 180 mph while in
a crowd of thirty-two other cars, each of whom is seeking to enter
a course turn that can only accommodate a single car, must possess
a high degree of hard-headed realism. This trait is also one of the
most pronounced in the personality of professional coaches. The
capacity to endure the stress associated with the press, fan, and owner
reactions to their administration, while retaining the capacity to make
hard-headed decisions essential for achieving their goals, would seem
to make this trait a prerequisite for tenure.

The consistency with which one can predict the increased probability of tough-mindedness as being significantly related to athletic
ability and athletic achievement, received support from even the
more limited data available for sportswomen. The relationship between this trait and athletic achievement received support from factor
analytic studies of national level competitors and was also related to
team success. Some reservations might arise as to the virtue of offer-
ing social rewards for the reinforcement of the behaviors that would
eventually contribute to tough-mindedness. The balance provided by
the presence of other positive traits seems, at this level of investigation, to be an important control over the exaggeration of any single
personality trait.

Conscientiousness

The trait of conscientiousness is of particular significance in terms of acting as a control or suppressor of tough-mindedness. Conscientiousness is also relevant in terms of the other seven traits that have been selected for emphasis. Cattell [15] described the person at the negative end of the pole as being a quitter, fickle, frivolous, immature, relaxed, indolent, neglectful of social chores, and changeable. The positive end of the pole would be the person who is conscientious, persevering, staid, and rule-bound. The author uses this trait as being synonymous with superego formation. To quote Cattell, "It has much to do with persistence in super-personal goals and ideals, and with attempts to exercise powerful self-control." This trait is low in sociopaths but high in face-to-face leaders. The polls show that fairmindedness in a leader is one of the primary demands of followers. Neither the investigations reviewed nor the strong support within our numerous studies would permit a general statement relating to cause and effect. This personality attribute has received more social comment than any other athletic trait in that every appeal to youth, every address at an awards banquet, and every philosophy of physical education, holds this trait out as a primary goal. Longitudinal studies are now in progress, but it will be five or six years before reliable statements can be made as to the relationship between athletic participation and conscience development. The only evidence was the magnitude of the change on this trait for youthful swimmers from ten to fourteen years of age. Should this finding receive confirmation, it would indicate that conscience development is the primary character trait in determining the probability of a youngster remaining in competitive swimming. It is not possible from cross-sectional analysis to attribute significance to the possibility that children with shallow superego structures gradually eliminate themselves from the stress of competition, or whether some positive reinforcement of character formation does occur. At the present, we must consider that an interaction of both these factors has accounted for the observed improved sense of responsibility on the part of the children. The relative contribution of other traits of personality, such as persistence and emotional stability, to this dimension must contribute in some way to the attenuation of this sample of swimmers from the age of ten to fourteen years. We cannot state unequivocally that high-level athletic competition contributes to a refined conscience, but the evidence strongly supports the tendency for those with sensitive consciences to remain in highly competitive programs.

Self-Control

The trait self-control contains a number of interrelated personality variables. The person at the negative end of the continuum would be characterized as casual, careless of protocol, untidy, follows own urges, disregards orderliness, and has difficulty following through with a routine. At the positive end of the continuum is the person who is controlled, socially precise, self-disciplined, and in the extreme may even be compulsive. This person shows socially approved behavior and foresight which is characteristic of chosen leaders. Cattell uses the synonym *will power* as the most general descriptive label for this trait. This old-fashioned term seems, to this investigator, to retain the feeling meaning in terms of behavior expectancies. That we found so much empirical support by the use of psychometric devices seems to emphasize once again the necessary personal integrational forces which are essential in order that one may remain with the highest level of athletic competition. This was such a distinctive feature that it became predictive of both individual and team success. Hundreds of hours of interviews with some of the world's most outstanding athletes, both amateur and professional, resulted in one highly consistent spontaneous statement with reference to pride and achievement. In terms of psychological measurement, self-control would be one of the most significant contributors to this complex term *he has pride,* which is used so universally by great athletes to characterize other greats.

Tension Level

The trait relaxed vs tense has been shown to be related significantly to athletic achievement. The athlete at the positive end of the continuum is described as relaxed, tranquil, torpid, and unfrustrated. At the negative end of the scale, the athlete would be tense, driven, overwrought, and fretful. There is a growing body of evidence that self-control and low levels of tension interact positively to contribute to successful athletic performance. The relationship between low anxiety and team and individual success is consistent both for sportsmen and sportswomen. The licensed sports-car driver sets the standard for absence of tension, followed by the samples of driver trainees. The measurement of this trait for youthful competitors indicated that only the fourteen-year-old SCSC girls failed to improve over the ten-year-olds. The Indiana fourteen-year-old boys and girls appeared to be low average for the tense-relaxed dimension. The behavioral expectancies associated with the tense individual are a poor view of group unity, existing leadership, and orderliness. They tend to admit more common frailties, disagree more, are more susceptible to annoyance, have less confident assumptions of skill in untried performances, and tend toward hard-headed cynicism.

During a number of years as a consultant, I have found this trait to provide the most reliable insight that psychological threshold for stress has been violated.[16] The physical signs associated with this form of emotional tension and anxiety covered the broad spectrum of those found represented in clinical work with psychosomatic disorders of every description. The body of the competitor often spoke the language of fear with greater eloquence than could be verbalized by the individual. Performance, coordination, even of the motorically gifted, suffers dramatically when physiologic and psychological boundaries intersect.[16] Present research supports a growing concern with the teaching techniques of tension reduction which will enable each performer to master exaggerated forms of pre-event anxiety. Should future investigations continue to verify these initial findings, there are serious implications for teachers and coaches. Factor analytic studies offer strong support that anxiety is a unitary trait which has a distinctive hereditary base. Particular emphasis must be placed upon the significance of success and failure for those youthful competitors who rate high in resting levels of anxiety. There is empirical support that a curvilinear relationship is obtained for anxiety rising from eight and one-half years of age to fifteen and one-half and then dropping steadily to age thirty-five, followed by a slow rise to sixty-five years of age.[15] An important goal would be to provide the best emotional climate for the child as a learner, but greater emphasis must be placed upon individual differences with respect to this personality trait. The highly anxious must receive greater positive reinforcement during early phases of training for competition. It is this investigator's studied experience that the coach can be taught how to condition his athletes in the most wholesome techniques for the containment of anxiety.

Self-Assuredness

The trait self-assured vs apprehensive-worried, received much empirical support at every level of competition for both males and females. The limited data for age-group swimmers offered more support for SCSC boys and girls, although Indiana boys and girls appear at least average for this trait. The positive end of the continuum described the athlete as confident, adequate, cheerful, and serene. At the negative end would be the depressed, excessively guilt-prone, easily upset, and even phobic athlete. The behavioral expectancies for the individual measuring high in apprehension appear clinically as some form of depression. This form of intropunitiveness can assume the character of a *free-floating anxiety reaction.* These individuals respond to unbearable stress by expressing serious doubts about their ability and utilizing some self-punishing form of defense in order to displace the real tension. The very nature of competition acts as such a reality reinforcer that the opportunity to rationalize failure becomes increasingly more difficult. The highly consistent relationship between self-assurance and attained level of athletic competition seems almost too obvious. The challenge in how to use athletics as a creative positive force in the lives of youth is very great; unfortunately, serious investigation of the means to produce such ends has received little attention.

Trustfulness vs Suspicion

The trait trusting vs suspicion may seem to be one of the most unexpected findings contained in this review. Past research using other psychometric devices has contributed to a personality dimension which we have labeled *coachability.*[17] This is the tendency to be open to teachers and authorities and have a basic respect for the instruction of others. Cattell [15] defines the positive end of this trait as a tendency to be trusting, adaptable, free of jealousy, and to have an ease in getting along with others. The negative end would be the person who is suspicious, self-opinionated, and hard to fool. The behavioral expectancies would be slowness in making friends, a tendency to feel superior to others as a defense, and an extreme tendency to brood and be irritable. The finding that successful coaches and athletes move toward the trusting end of the scale is consistent with their proclivity for making quick adjustments. This also supports the previous trait with respect to their increased capacity for accepting personal responsibility for their achievement. The tendency to project negative feelings or attitudes upon others would certainly reduce ones capacity to learn. The athlete with a paranoid attitude toward life has presented a very special challenge to both the coach and the team. During the past fifteen years we have experimented with recommended handling programs for athletes who fall at the extreme of the suspicious end of the scale. The delicate balance that must be established between the athlete and coach has been a particular problem, but individual cases of success have offered us much encouragement that open communication can be achieved.

Outgoing vs Reserved Personality

The final trait outgoing vs reserved seems to be much more predictive of highly successful male competitors and British females. The literature does suggest a movement from introversion towards increased extraversion but not to the same degree that is found for males. At one end of the scale we have the outgoing, warmhearted, good-natured, cooperative, attentive to people, soft-hearted, and adaptable. The other pole would be the person who is critical, grasping, obstructive, cool, aloof, hard, precise, and rigid. Behaviorally one moves toward others and social participation or, conversely, away from others with a desire to be alone. In the extreme the cool reserved person may even resent encroachment upon his self-security.

With the exception of race drivers and such individual events as distance runners, many studies support a tendency for successful male athletes to be on the warmhearted end of the scale. This is consistent for national level British women athletes who measured as extremely outgoing and warmhearted but this is inconsistent with our studies and those in the literature for U.S. sportswomen. There is perfect consistency that high-level female competitors who represent the U.S. tend to be cool, reserved, and less sociable. The movement for girls in age-group swimming away from the introversion end of the scale to decreased introversion by the time they are fourteen years of age has a number of possible interpretations. In the light of the cross-cultural consistencies for males that extroversion was related to continuation in athletics, two major questions evolve. First, cultural differences are quite apparent for women, with the extraversive traits contributing more to continuation for British women than for U.S. women. The data do suggest that extremely introverted U.S. females have a higher attenuation rate than do extraverted females. There is evidence that introverted children swimmers have a greater tendency to retain fears associated with past traumas centering around water and swimming experience. There is much evidence that reward and punishment conditioning effects are not independent of one's temperamental predisposition towards introversion or extraversion.

Cattell [15] reports that the sociable vs reserved factor was the most readily verified trait found within his voluminous research. He attributes to heredity the major contribution to this trait and holds the environment only slightly accountable for variation of this trait. It may be assumed, therefore, that attempts to condition young athletes towards extraversion would be both unwise and unnatural. It would be far more realistic to accept a wide range of individual differences for this trait and adjust our teaching to that form which is most compatible with the personality structure of the young competitor.

SUMMARY

There is insufficient evidence to conclude that high-level competition makes a positive contribution to personality. We can state with some degree of certitude that those who retain their motivation for competition will have most of the following personality traits: ambition, organization, deference, dominance, endurance, and aggression. There will be fewer introverted types by adult-level competition. Emotional maturity will range from average to high average and be complemented by self-control, self-confidence, tough-mindedness, trustfulness, intelligence, high conscience development, and low levels of tension. Such traits as autonomy, exhibitionism, and affiliation prove to be less general.

REFERENCES

1. CRATTY, B. J.: Personality and performance, in *Psychology and Physical Activity*. Englewood Cliffs, Prentice-Hall, 1968, pp. 15-25.

2. HATHAWAY, S. R., and McKINLEY, J. C.: *Minnesota Multiphasic Personality Inventory* (manual). New York, Psychological Corporation, 1951.
3. GOUGH, H. G.: *California Psychological Inventory.* Palo Alto, Consulting Psychologist Press, 1957.
4. EDWARDS, A. L.: *Edwards Personal Preference Schedule* (manual). New York, Psychological Corporation, 1954.
5. EYSENCK, H. J.: *Manual of the Maudsley Personality Inventory.* London, U of London, 1959.
6. CATTELL, R. B., and EBER, H. W.: *Handbook for the 16 Personality Factor Questionnaire.* Illinois, Institute for Personality and Ability Testing, 1957.
7. OGILVIE, B. C.: The unanswered question: Competition and its effects upon femininity. *Swimming Tech, 4*:83 Oct. 1967.
8. OGILVIE, B. C.; TUTKO, T. A., and YOUNG, I.: Comparison medalist, non-medalists, olympic swimmers, in Antonelli, F. (Ed.): In *Proceedings of the First International Congress on Sports Psychology.* Rome, 1965, pp. 201-209.
9. RUSHALL, B. S.: Personality profiles and a theory of behavior modification for swimmers. *Swimming Tech, 4*:66-71, 1967.
10. KANE, J. E., and WARBURTON, F. W.: Personality relates to sport and physical ability, in *Reading in Physical Education.* London, Physical Education Association, 1966.
11. OGILVIE, B. C., and TUTKO, T. A.: What is an Athlete? In *Encyclopedia of Sports Medicine.* New York, McGraw. To be published.
12. PETERSON, S. L.; WEBER, J. C., and TROUSDALE, W. W.: Personality traits of women in team vs women in individual sports. *Res Quart Amer Ass Health Phys Educ, 38*:686-690, 1967.
13. OGILVIE, B. C.: Personality profile of successful coaches, in A. J. Ryan, (Ed.): *Proceedings of Sports Injury Clinic,* Madison. U. of Wis, 1965.
14. OGILVIE, B. C., and TUTKO, T. A.: Self image and measured personality of coaches, to be read before the Second International Congress of Sports Psychology. Washington, DC, November, 1968.
15, CATTELL, R. B.: *The Scientific Analysis of Personality.* Baltimore, Penguin, 1965.
16. OGILVIE, B. C.: Model for general psychological adaptation. *Track Tech, 14*:428-429, 1964.
17. OGILVIE, B. C., and TUTKO, T. A.: *Problem Athletes and How to Handle Them.* London, Pelham Books, 1966.

Chapter 30

PERSONALITY TRAITS OF WOMEN IN TEAM SPORTS VS. WOMEN IN INDIVIDUAL SPORTS*

Sheri L. Peterson, Jerome C. Weber, and William W. Trousdale

INTRODUCTION

It would be to the obvious benefit of the physical educator and athletic coach if it were possible to identify specific personality factors that are associated with individuals who tend to favor one type of sports participation as opposed to another. However, that such identifying characteristics exist remains to be more fully substantiated. Cofer and Johnson[5] state that "Although there is a growing research literature dealing with the personality traits of various types of athletes, studies have not been done which justify generalization as to specific identifying characteristics of groups."

PURPOSE

The purpose of this study was to determine if there are any distinguishing personality traits of women who engage in team sports as opposed to women who engage in individual sports. It was hoped that this added knowledge concerning the personality traits of women athletes would facilitate the development of better physical education and athletic programs for women.

REVIEW OF LITERATURE

Booth,[1] using the Minnesota Multiphasic Personality Inventory,

* S. L. Peterson, J. C. Weber, and W. W. Trousdale: Personality traits of women in team sports vs. women in individual sports. *Res Quart Amer Ass Health Phys Educ, 38*:1967, 686-690. Reproduced here with the permission of Professor Jerome C. Weber and the American Association for Health, Physical Education, and Recreation.

[324]

found that varsity athletes were significantly lower in anxiety than nonathletes and freshman athletes, that varsity athletes and upper-class nonathletes were significantly more dominant than freshman athletes and nonathletes, that varsity athletes engaged in only individual sports were significantly more depressive than those engaged in only team sports, and that upper-class nonathletes were significantly more socially responsible than the other groups.

Duggan[6] found that women undergraduate physical education majors were less neurotic and more extroverted and dominating than nonmajors. Flanagan[7] found fencers to be more dominating than basketball players, volleyball players, and boxers, and more feminine than the basketball players. The badminton players were judged to be the most extroverted group and the volleyball players were the most emotionally unstable. Lakie[8] found no differences between athletes from state colleges, state universities, and private universities.

Neal [10] found that women athletes scored significantly higher on the Edwards Personal Preference Schedule variables of achievement, autonomy, affiliation, and nurturance than a control group of nonathletes. Sperling[12] compared nonathletes to varsity and intramural athletes and found the athletes scored higher in personality adjustment, ascendance, and extroversion, and lower in aesthetic appreciation and theoretical orientation.

Carter and Shannon[2] found high school athletes more socially adjusted than nonathletes. LaPlace[9] found major league baseball players had more self-discipline, initiative, and ability to get along with others than minor league players.

METHODS

The Sixteen Personality Factor Questionnaire (16 PF) was chosen because of its compatibility with the design of the study. Form A of the 16 PF was used for all subjects. The 16 PF is a personality questionnaire designed to "measure dimensions of human personality comprehensively, in young adults and adults. . . ." [3]

A total of thirty-eight women athletes were included in the individual sports group. This included all women of the 1964 United States Olympic teams who were willing to participate in the study. The sports in which these women competed were swimming, diving, riding, fencing, canoeing, gymnastics, and track and field.

A total of fifty-nine women athletes were included in the team sports group. This included all women of the 1964 United States Olympic volleyball team and the top ten 1964 women's AAU basketball teams who were willing to participate in the study.

After agreeing to participate in the study, each subject received a copy of Form A of the 16 PF test, completed it, and returned it to the authors. The tests were then scored and the raw scores were converted to sten scores which are standard scores on a ten-point scale. Scores above six and below four are considered to be a departure from the average in the factors on the 16 PF. The *t*-test was used to analyze differences between groups on each of the sixteen variables tested.

RESULTS

Sten scores for the individual and team women athletes were found to differ significantly at or beyond the .05 level on seven of the sixteen factors. The sten scores for both groups on each of the 16 factors are found in Table 30-I.

The factors measured on each of the items of the 16 PF were as follows:

Factor A—A high score indicates cyclothymia or a warm, sociable being vs a low score indicating schizothymia or an aloof, stiff person.

Factor B—A high score indicates a high level of general intelligence vs a low score indicating dullness.

Factor C—A high score indicates emotional stability or ego strength vs a low score which indicates emotional instability and emotional dissatisfaction.

Factor E—A high score indicates dominance, ascendance, or aggressiveness vs a low score which indicates submissiveness.

Factor F—A high score indicates surgency or enthusiasm vs a low score which indicates desurgency or seriousness.

Factor G—A high score indicates character or superego strength vs a low score which indicates a lack of rigid internal standards.

Factor H—A high score indicates parmia or adventurousness vs a low score which indicates threctia or shyness and timidity.

Factor I—A high score indicates premsia or sensitivity vs a low score which indicates harria or toughness and a high degree of real-isticness.

Factor L—A high score indicates pretension or a high degree of suspicion and jealousy vs relaxed security and acceptance as indicated by a low score.

Factor M—A high score indicates autia or introversion vs a low score which indicates praxernia or a great deal of practicality.

Factor N—A high score indicates sophistication vs a low score which indicates a lack of pretentiousness.

Factor O—A high score indicates timidity and insecurity vs a low score which indicates confidence and self-security.

Factor Q1—A high score indicates radicalism of temperament vs a low score which indicates conservatism of temperament.

Factor Q2—A high score indicates self-sufficiency vs a low score which indicates group dependency.

Factor Q3—A high score indicates a high self-sentiment formation or great control vs a low score which indicates poor self-sentiment formation or laxity.

Factor Q4—A high score indicates high ergic tension or a great deal of tension and excitability vs a low score which indicates low ergic tension or what is described as phlegmatic.

TABLE 30-I

COMPARISON OF STEN SCORES OF INDIVIDUAL SPORTS ATHLETES AND TEAM SPORTS ATHLETES ON FACTORS OF THE 16 PF

Factor	*I*	*t*	*Factor*	*I*	*t*
A	4.08	4.37	L	6.20	6.53
B	6.99	6.75	M	6.13	4.05[a]
C	6.63	5.96	N	5.00	5.96[a]
E	6.58	5.52[a]	O	5.01	5.33
F	5.37	5.08	Q_1	5.89	5.01[a]
G	5.60	5.91	Q_2	6.08	5.01[a]
H	6.49	5.41[a]	Q_3	5.43	5.58
I	5.20	3.77[a]	Q_4	5.12	5.18

[a] Significant at or beyond the .05 level.

The results indicate that women who are engaged in individual sports are more dominant and aggressive (E), adventurous (H), sensitive (I), imaginative (M), radical (Q1), and self-sufficient and resourceful (Q2) than women who are engaged in team sports. Individual sports athletes also appear less sophisticated (N).

CONCLUSIONS

The results of the present study indicate that women athletes engaged in individual sports are high in such personality traits as dominance, self-sufficiency, and impulsiveness. These women like to make their own decisions and may express dissatisfaction with group situations and their high premium on procedural rules. These women tend to be more independent minded, introverted, and self-absorbed than the team sports athletes. The individual sports athletes are self-assured and have a higher degree of emotional, artistic, and creative interests and enjoy attention. They are also more radical in their thinking and are less inhibited, which may be important in their ability to perform before others by themselves.

The team sports athletes show themselves to be self-sufficient but not as self-absorbed or introverted as the individual sports athletes. Team sports athletes are steady, practical, dependable, and interested in immediate issues. These women also show themselves to be self-reliant, responsible, and emotionally disciplined. The team sports athletes would tend to be less affected by fads, realistic, and tend to generate group solidarity. These women are higher in sophistication than individual sports athletes.

Both groups are a little more serious than the average and may have a tendency to express themselves less freely. These women are intellectually brighter, more conscientious, aggressive, and persevering than the norms for others of equivalent age and education. Socially, both groups tend to be somewhat cool and aloof.

REFERENCES

1. BOOTH, E. G., JR.: Personality traits of athletes as measured by the MMPI. *Res Quart Amer Ass Health Phys Educ, 29*:127-38, 1958.
2. CARTER, C. C., and SHANNON, J. R.: Adjustment and personality traits of athletes and non-athletes. *School Rev, 48*:115-19, 1940.
3. CATTELL, R. B., and EBER, H. W.: *About the 16 PF. Supplement to the handbook for the 16 PF questionnaire.* Champaign, The Institute for Personality and Ability Testing, 1957.
4. CATTELL, R. B., and EBER, H. W.: *The Sixteen Personality Factor Ques-*

tionnaire. Form A, 1962 edition. Champaign, The Institute for Personality and Ability Testing, 1957.

5. COFER, C. N., and JOHNSON, W. R.: Personality dynamics in relation to exercise and sports. In Johnson, W. R. (Ed.): *Science and Medicine of Exercise and Sports.* New York, Harper, 1960.

6. DUGGAN, A. S.: *A Comparative Study of Undergraduate Women Majors and Nonmajors with Respect to Certain Personality Traits.* New York, Columbia, University Press, 1936.

7. FLANAGAN, L. A.: A study of some personality traits of different physical activity groups. *Res Quart Amer Ass Health Phys Educ, 22:*312-23, 1951.

8. LAKIE, W. L.: Personality characteristics of certain groups of intercollegiate athletes. *Res Quart Amer Ass Health Phys Educ, 33:*566-73, 1962.

9. LaPLACE, J. P.: Personality and its relationship to success in professional baseball. *Res Quart Amer Ass Health Phys Educ, 25:*313-19, 1954.

10. NEAL, P.: *Personality Traits of United States Women Athletes Who Participated in the 1959 Pan-American Games, as Measured by the Edwards Personal Preference Schedule.* Unpublished master's thesis, U of Utah, 1963.

11. SAKOTA, J. M., and others: Test of significance for a series of statistical tests. *Psych Bull, 51:*172-74, 1954.

12. SPERLING, A. P.: Relationship between personality adjustment and achievement in physical education activities. *Res Quart Amer Ass Health Phys Educ, 13:*351-63, 1942.

PART TEN
PSYCHOPHYSIOLOGY

Chapter 31

PSYCHOGALVANIC AND WORD ASSOCIATION STUDIES OF ATHLETES*

Warren R. Johnson

INTRODUCTION

Although many phases of competitive athletics have been sub-jected to careful scientific investigation, very little has been done along lines of systematic exploration of the emotional aspects of such competition—in spite of the fact that most coaches recognize the importance of psychological fitness for optimal performance. The present study is the fourth in a series of *on the spot* studies by the present investigator designed to explore the emotional aspect of athletic sports contests.[2]

It must be acknowledged at the outset that emotion is one of the most difficult of all psychophysical phenomena to study—particularly when such a study is attempted in *media res* or in the midst of life situations rather than in the laboratory. At the present time neither the precise nature or function of human emotion is known; no one has yet succeeded in defining emotion in an entirely satisfactory way.[10] No one has succeeded in measuring emotion in such a way that he could state with confidence: "I am measuring emotion, *per se.*" Con-sequently, it is necessary to deal with the phenomenon indirectly in terms of indices and manifestations; it is also necessary to interpret findings cautiously and tentatively.[10]

PURPOSE OF THE STUDY

The concern of this particular study was focused upon the following considerations:

* W. R. Johnson. Psychogalvanic and word association studies of athletes. *Res Quart Amer Ass Health Phys Educ, 22:* 1951, 427-433. Reproduced here with the permission of the author and the American Association for Health, Physical Education, and Recreation.

[333]

(1) An attempt to ascertain something of the emotional intensity of the precompetition experience associated with certain winter sports.

(2) An attempt to compare the reactivity of the subjects to different types of critical word stimuli in the word association tests; i.e. to compare the athletes' reactions to both the psychosexual critical and the sports critical words.

(3) An attempt to compare the reactions of athletes in various sports to the word stimuli (i.e. to compare wrestlers with swimmers, etc.).

(4) An attempt to continue laying the basis for individual and group analysis along lines of emotional reactions which show promise of becoming of value for coaching and other educational purposes.[3]

(5) An attempt to evaluate the psychogalvanic and word association testing technique as a practical tool for determining the emotional response of athletes.

SUBJECTS OF THE RESEARCH

The Experimental Group

This group involved eighty-two college athletes in four winter season sports; i.e. twenty-four swimmers, twenty-four wrestlers, nineteen basketball players, and fifteen hockey players. These athletes were from such schools as Boston University, Harvard, M. I. T., Tufts, Williams, and Springfield. For purposes of this research an *athlete* was defined as an individual about to participate in an intercollegiate sports contest (i.e. within approximately one hour).

The Control Group

This group consisted of eighty-two college men of a general, athletic appearance but not athletes (as defined), between twenty and thirty years of age. This group was selected from a college population. (See Items 1 and 2 in Research Procedure.)

DISCUSSION OF THE TOOLS OF RESEARCH

There were two principal tools of the research, both of which are well-established psychological testing devices. A relatively large body of evidence may be cited as justification for using the psychogalvanic and word association techniques in studies of emotional reactivity—in spite of the fact that apparently neither has been used previously in this particular area.

The First Tool

A sensitive psychogalvanometer of a modified Wheatstone Bridge variety was especially designed and constructed for this research. This device conformed to the criteria established by such writers as Ruckmick.[8] A considerable amount of preliminary experimentation suggested most practical levels of sensitivity to be used in the investigation. The electrode arrangement was not unlike that frequently seen in certain so-called *lie detectors;* two 7 inch x 5 inch aluminum plates were so arranged as to take advantage of the peculiar palmar and finger-pad skin reactivity, which has been investigated and described by such people as Lund and Richter.[3, 7] In the interests of gaining the largest possible N and since gross changes were the primary objects of consideration, no effort was made to reduce the relatively minor effects of slight bodily movements or temperature and moisture variations on the electrode plates.[7, 8]

Although the precise physiological mechanisms involved in the electrodermal response are not known, the resistance encountered by the current as it passes through the pores of the palmar and plantar regions has been shown to vary with emotional disturbances.[3, 7, 8, 10] Used in conjunction with a properly constructed word association test, this electrical device has the advantage of indicating mechanically on the galvanometer a subject's reactions to each word in a series of stimulus words, some of which are important for determining extent and nature of emotional upset.

The Second Tool

Two types of word association tests were constructed in accordance with principles established by psychological research.

These word lists of twenty-four items each were somewhat shorter than those ordinarily employed in word association studies. For his purposes, Rapaporte used a short test composed of sixty words[6] and Luria used as few as thirty.[4] Time limitations in the present *on the spot* research dictated the short twenty-four-word test used, particularly since both Type I and Type II word lists (total of 48 words) were administered to all of the athlete group. Furthermore, the *proportion* of critical to indifferent words in the present lists was modeled after that of certain classical studies.[4, 6, 9]

Test I

In word association test Type I, six *critical* words of a psychosexual nature were interspersed among eighteen *indifferent* words. The critical words of this test were carefully selected after an analysis of word association tests of such writers as Jung, Luria, and Rapaporte. Thus, an effort was made to include a verbal representation for a "variety of areas of ideation, conflicts in which are likely to be prominent in the different types of maladjustments." [6, p. 13 ff.] All subjects in both experimental and control groups were given word association test Type I.

Test II

In word association Test II, six critical words pertaining to significant aspects of each sport were interspersed among the same eighteen indifferent words as in Test I.

Whereas in clinical word association testing, words of psychosexual connotation are used to determine areas of psychic conflict,[6, 9] in lie detection critical words are selected on the basis of their application to a specific situation, e.g. one involving some criminal act.[4] In the latter type, words are chosen which, presumably, will have guilt meaning only to those individuals with an intimate knowledge of the details of the crime. If, for example, a poisonous powder has been the instrument of murder, and only the actual murderer is aware of this fact, the word *powder* might be expected to be a highly emotionally charged (or cathexed)and thus critical word for the guilty person and an indifferent word for the guiltless suspects who are unaware of the implication of the word *powder*. It is likely that the guilty person's reaction to this word would occasion a considerable deflection or other change in the lie detection device being used.

In view of the above discussion regarding selection of critical words on the basis of their meaning in the immediate situation rather than on the basis of association with more basic conflicts, and since the control group (nonathletes) was by definition composed of individuals under no known stress and not particularly emotionally involved in the winter sports under consideration, word association Test II was not administered to the control group. It seemed highly probable that if one of the stimulus word lists would elicit exceptional reactivity from the control group, it would most likely be the list containing the psychosexual critical words. Preliminary testing seemed to confirm the apparent superfluity of administering Test II to the control group. Furthermore, the problems of time limitation and selection of qualified control group subjects in sufficiently large number made administration of Test II to this group impracticable. As has been pointed out earlier, the hypothesis which gave rise to word association list Type II (sports critical words) was comparable to that which explains modern lie detection work; both applications are contingent upon the *disturbed* state of the subject at the time of testing. In both the psychosexual (Type I) and other critical word tests (e.g. Type II) hyperreactivity has been demonstrated to be dependent upon the existence of a condition of stress on the part of the subjects.[4, 6, 9, 10] In this connection, it is of interest to note that in his classical word association studies of criminal and student inquisitions in Russia, Luria described the stress situation imposed on the subjects as provoking a "reaction similar in structure to that of the neurosis; it creates, as it were, a temporary actual neurosis, which is most distinct in those subjects already having a neuropathic disposition."[4, p. 75] Having studied the stress of many combative sport athletes just before they went into action, the present writer reasoned that the precontest emotional disturbance might in some instances be of sufficient intensity to approximate Luria's description of a *temporary actual neurosis*. If such were the case, it seemed reasonable that the psychogalvanic-word association technique would be applicable.*

In word association test Type II, for each of the four sports, coaches aided in the selection of six representative words which bore directly upon some vital factors in competition. For example, *foul shot* and

---

* For an analysis of disturbances in aviation combat personnel, cf. Grinker & Spiegel, *Men Under Stress*. Philadelphia, Blakiston, 1945.

the bench were used in the basketball list, and *take down* and *head lock* in the wrestling list. *Wall, table,* and *grass* are sample indifferent words that were used.

RESEARCH PROCEDURE

The Experimental Group

Both types of word association tests were administered to the eighty-two athletes within approximately one hour before their actual intercollegiate competitions. The testing was done in or near the athletes' dressing rooms as the individuals were preparing for the various competitions. The athletes had not eaten within one and one-half hours of being tested, had not exercised earlier in the day, and were not under known emotional stress caused by factors other than their sport.

Prior to testing, the athletes were told the general nature and purpose of the research. The subjects were seated comfortably in some comparatively secluded spot; brief instructions were given to them in which they were asked to rest their hands on the electrode plates, to restrict all bodily movements to a minimum, to keep their eyes closed in order not to be disturbed by other activities in the room, and to respond verbally to each of the investigator's stimulus words with the first word that came into their minds.[9] The combination of tests took approximately ten minutes to administer per subject.

Ideally, these same athletes would have been tested again when an athletic contest was not about to take place; thus, direct comparison could have been made on the same subjects between reactions under *normal* and precontest situations. However, since the athletes were from a number of universities, it was impossible under the circumstances to make further contact with them.

The Control Group

Because the athletic group could not be retested, a relatively large and grossly comparable control group was employed in an effort to ascertain something of the reactions to the stimulus words of individuals not in an excited state. The psychosexual word association test only was administered to the eighty-two controls—at times when the subjects were under no known emotional stress, had not exercised earlier in the day, and had not eaten within one and one-half hours. The same procedures were followed here as with the experimental group. In an effort to make the testing environment comparable to that of the athletic dressing room, the testing of this group was done in a large office in which there was ordinarily a considerable amount of activity.

TREATMENT OF THE DATA AND FINDINGS

The nearly 6,000 individual items were analyzed in such a way as to reveal extent of group reactions to each word. No effort was made in the direction of qualitative analysis of individual responses to the stimulus words. However, beyond a doubt, this aspect of the testing procedure played an important part in the quantitative reactions with which this research dealt.[9]

Table 31-I shows that in terms of the psychogalvanic response to word stimuli, the athlete group (precontest) had a considerably higher mean reaction to the stimulus words in both the psychosexual and sports critical word lists than did the nonathlete control group to the psychosexual list. Furthermore, the statistical treatment indicated that the mean differences (Ma-1 Mc-1; Ma-2 Mc-1) were true differences at high levels of confidence.

A graph was constructed showing the mean reactions of the groups from word to word of the word association lists. As may be seen in Figure 31-1, the precontest or *stress* situation gave rise to much greater psychogalvanic deflections in both the psychosexual and sports critical

TABLE 31-I

MEAN REACTIONS OF THE ATHLETE AND CONTROL GROUPS TO THE STIMULUS WORD LISTS

Group & Test Type	N	Mean Resistance $(R_n\text{-}R_1)$	Standard Deviation	t-test	Confidence Level
Athlete, type I	82	$M_{a\text{-}1} = 142$	130	$M_{a\text{-}1}M_{a\text{-}2} = 1.7$	9%
Athlete, type II	82	$M_{a\text{-}2} = 131$	72	$M_{a\text{-}2}M_{c\text{-}1} = 6.2$	under 1%
Control, type I	82	$M_{c\text{-}1} = 106$	31	$M_{a\text{-}1}M_{c\text{-}1} = 7.3$	under 1%

NOTE: Table I shows an analysis of the reactions of the athlete group (under pre-contest stress) for both test type I & II (psychosexual and sports critical words) and non-athlete control group for test type I (psychosexual critical words). 5,904 total test items.

TABLE 31-II

COMPARISON OF THE FOUR SPORTS IN TERMS OF REACTIVITY
TO BOTH THE SPORTS AND PSYCHOSEXUAL WORD LISTS

Sport	N	*Mean (ohms)* $R_n - R_1$
Basketball	19	210
Swimming	24	130
Wrestling	24	120
Hockey	15	120

NOTE: Table II shows the mean reactivity of the athletes tested to the psycho-sexual stimulus word list. The basketball group was reactive at a significantly higher level than the others.

words (words 4, 8, 11, 15, 20, and 23) than did the *undisturbed* condition in which the controls were tested. The indifferent words resulted in somewhat smaller deflections in the athlete group test Type I, than in the others.

In both graphic and statistical treatments, the nineteen basketball players stood out as being decidedly more reactive than the other

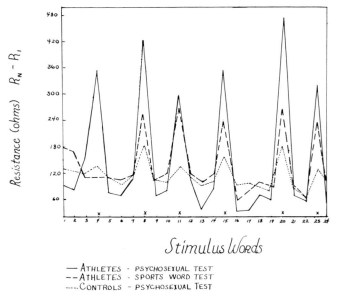

Stimulus Words

— ATHLETES - PSYCHOSEXUAL TEST
-- ATHLETES - SPORTS WORD TEST
.... CONTROLS - PSYCHOSEXUAL TEST

FIGURE 31-1. This shows the relative mean psychogalvanic deflections of the two athlete group tests and the control group test. Words 4, 8, 11, 15, 20, and 23 are the critical words in both the psychosexual and sports critical word lists.

athletes; i.e. at less than the 1 percent level of confidence. Tests of significance indicated that, except for basketball, none of the observed mean differences among wrestling, swimming, and hockey, were true differences at high levels of confidence.

CONCLUSIONS AND DISCUSSION

(1) In terms of the techniques of the present study, the precontest situation of the sports tested is evidently characterized by a tendency towards exaggerated psychogalvanic reactivity.* The athletes as a group were found to be very significantly more reactive to both types of critical word stimuli employed than were the controls who were under no known emotional stress. However, attention is called to the consideration that the *disturbed state* that so commonly characterizes the precontest situation is probably not detrimental to individuals who are comparatively free of profound personality disturbances. Indeed, within limits, varieties of emotional disturbance probably serve to improve neurological and endocrine integration for competitive action.[1]

(2) The athlete group reacted vigorously to both the psychosexual and sports critical words.

(3) In no case did men who are considered outstanding performers by their coaches react in an extreme manner.

(4) Only the basketball players stood out as being significantly higher in reactivity than the other athletes. This fact is not consistent with the writer's previous findings in which the individual and combative athletes were characterized by greater emotional disturbance as indicated by other types of physiological tests. The deviation of the basketball players may conceivably have been due to coaching techniques or to the personality structure of these particular subjects. In all events, taken individually, these athlete groups are obviously too small to justify conclusive interpretation.

(5) Evaluation of the technique. The psychogalvanic-word association technique is of experimental interest because it suggests something of the nature and extent of the psychophysical disturbance occasioned by athletic sports competition. Consequently, it may be said that such information contributes to a more precise understanding

---

* And thus, the precontest situation may, perhaps, be said to approximate Luria's definition of a *temporary actual neurosis*. [4, p.75]

of that phase of physical education which has to do with intercollegiate competition.

It is unlikely, however, that the present technique will prove of practical value as a coaching tool. Use of the apparatus and word lists requires a certain degree of technical investigation and practice, and in addition, the actual administration of the tests is time-consuming and exacting. Although the athletes themselves have almost invariably been extremely cooperative and very much interested in the research, the time of testing before competition is usually difficult for investigator and subject alike.

A great deal more research must be conducted with these techniques before psychogalvanic reactions to the stimulus words can be accurately interpreted in terms of their implications for championship personality structure and individual *readiness* for competition.

REFERENCES

1. ARNOLD, MAGDA: Physiological differentiation of emotional states. *Psychological Review,* 1945, *52,* 35-48.
2. JOHNSON, WARREN R.: A study of emotion revealed in two types of athletic contest. *Res Quart Amer Ass Health Phys Educ,* 1949, *20,* 72-79.
3. LUND, FREDERICK: *Emotions.* New York, Ronald, 1942.
4. LURIA, A. R.: *The Nature of Human Conflicts.* New York, Liveright, 1932.
5. MOLONEY, JAMES C.: Psychiatric observations in Okinawa Shima. *Psychiatry,* 1945, *8,* 391-99.
6. RAPAPORT, DAVID: *Diagnostic Psychological Testing.* Chicago, Year Bk., 1946.
7. RICHTER, CURT P.; WOODRUFF, BETHE G., *et al.*: Hand and foot patterns of low electrical skin resistance: Their anatomical and neurological significance: *J Neurophysiol, 6,* 417-24 (1943).
8. RUCKMICK, CHRISTIAN: *The Psychology of Feeling and Emotion.* New York & London, McGraw, 1936.
9. SCHAFER, ROY: A study of thought processes in a word association test. *Character and Personality. 13,* 212-27 (1945).
10. YOUNG, PAUL T.: *Emotion in Man & Animal.* New York, Wiley & Sons, Inc., 1943.

Chapter 32

RELATIONSHIP BETWEEN MOTOR
PERFORMANCE AND AROUSAL*

E. DEAN RYAN

INTRODUCTION

THE CONCEPT of an arousal continuum has been used recently to study motivation and emotion.[2, 5, 7, 11] It has been argued that behavior falls on a continuum of activation or arousal that extends from deep sleep at the low arousal end to excited or emotional states at the high arousal end with no distinguishable break between sleep or emotion. Overmotivated or emotional behavior is thus reflected as high arousal, and lethargic or phlegmatic behavior is reflected as low arousal. In reviewing this concept of arousal, both Duffy[2] and Malmo[6, 7] have indicated that the distinction between emotional and nonemotional behavior is superfluous and have tended to equate arousal with intensity of motivation.

The definition of arousal level has usually been in terms of certain physiological measures such as galvanic skin conductance (GSC), pulse rate, respiration, electromyographic (EMG), or electrocephalogram (EEG) recordings.

In a study of eyelid conditioning by Runquist and Ross,[8] subjects were classified on the bases of combined pulse rate changes and GSR responses to a weak air puff prior to testing, as either emotional or nonemotional. The emotional group performed at a higher level than the nonemotional group.

In a similar experiment, which included muscle tension as well as

* E. D. Ryan: Relationship between motor performance and arousal. *Res Quart Amer Ass Health Phys Educ, 33*:1962, 279-287. Reproduced here with the permission of the author and the American Association for Health, Physical Education, and Recreation. This study was supported in part by University of California Faculty Research Grant No. D79.

[343]

pulse rate and GSC, Runquist and Spence[9] compared eyelid conditioning performance of two groups selected on the basis of GSR and pulse rate responses to the unconditional stimulus during conditioning trials. The group classified as emotionally responsive gave significantly more conditioned responses than the group classified as nonemotional, thus confirming the earlier study. When subjects were divided into four groups on the basis of electromyograph responses to a single air puff trial, the curves of acquisition of the conditioned response rank ordered themselves on the basis of the EMG response, the group with greatest response having best performance.

Stennett[10] studied the relationship between performance in auditory tracking under four conditions of increasing incentive and two physiological measures of arousal (skin conductance and electromyographic recordings). The incentive conditions ranged from one in which the subject was under the impression that his scores were not being recorded to one in which his score determined whether or not he avoided a strong electric shock and earned bonus money of from $2 to $5. The most efficient tracking performance was associated with intermediate steepness of EMG gradients and intermediate levels of palmar skin conductance. With lower levels of physiological functioning, performance on tracking was inferior. Performance on tracking associated with extremely high physiological functioning was also inferior to tracking performance associated with moderate levels of physiological functioning.

These studies suggest that, at least up through moderate levels, increased arousal should be accompanied by improved performance. Thus, it would be expected that when factors affecting the level of arousal are held constant for all subjects, groups with higher levels of arousal should have superior performance to groups with lower arousal levels. The purpose of the present investigation was to test this expectation using scores on a gross motor task as the measure of performance and skin conductance as the measure of arousal.

METHOD

Apparatus

The motor task selected was balancing on a pivoted platform, usually called a stabilometer.[1] The stabilometer consisted of a platform

107 centimeters long and sixty-one centimeters wide, fastened to a crosswise pivot rod of heavy steel that turned on ball bearings. The platform was twenty-five centimeters above this center of rotation. The ball bearings were mounted in uprights at the sides of the platform which were firmly attached and braced to a large wooden base underneath. The range of motion was ±15° from the horizontal. A work adder recorded tilting movements of the platform on a dial that was scaled in 100 arbitrary units. Each scale unit represented 12° of back and forth platform tilting.

An electric timing clock, used to control the testing time, was arranged to stop automatically when either end of the platform was in contact with the base. This provision ensured that each thirty-second trial represented that much net time of actual balancing effort.

The subject stood on the raised pivoted platform in an erect position with his eyes open, facing sideways and straddling the pivot rod with one foot on either side of it. The distance between the feet was 38.1 centimeters center to center.

The task was to balance the platform, keeping it approximately level with a minimum of movement. Each subject was given twelve thirty-second trials, with a thirty-second rest period between each trial. The subject's score per trial was the total number of arbitrary movement units cumulated on the work adder for each thirty-second period. The nature of the task made previous practice on similar skills unlikely.

To measure the conductance of the skin, a microammeter circuit similar to one used by Harmon and Johnson[3] was employed.* A three-volt dry battery supplied the small electric current that flowed through the microammeter and the skin of the fingertips. Two six-millimeter silver electrodes, twenty-five millimeters apart, were imbedded 0.8 millimeter deep at the end of a plastic bar six millimeters thick, having the dimensions 300 millimeters x 50 millimeters. A metal weight secured to the end of the plastic bar brought the total weight of the electrodes and the bar to 220 grams. The plastic bar was hinged to a supporting stand. The subject being tested placed the right hand (palm up) on the electrodes from underneath, pushing

* The author wishes to thank F. M. Henry, University of California, Berkeley, for the design and construction of the apparatus to measure skin conductance.

up with the tips of the index and middle fingers to elevate the bar. This technique insured a constant pressure on the surface of the fingers. A calibration curve permitted direct conversion of readings on the microammeter to microhms of conductance.

Design

The subjects were forty male university students, all volunteers, from various areas of specialization. None had previous experience in performing on tasks similar to the stabilometer. It was explained that changes in skin conductance were being studied in relation to performance on the stabilometer. The technique of taking GSC was demonstrated. If questions were asked as to the purpose of skin conductance, the experimenter simply stated that the GSC was a measure of sweat gland activity. The resting GSC was taken and the subject was seated while the performance technique was explained and demonstrated. This was followed by a second measure of GSC. In those few cases where both readings were not the same, the subject was allowed to rest until the GSC stabilized. Skin conductance was recorded during the thirty-second rest period after each trial.

Subjects were urged to do as well as possible on all trials. It was hoped that this would produce the optimum level of arousal without overmotivating and thereby avoid the drop in performance found by Stennett and others in states of overarousal.

RESULTS

Several measures of conductance were made to determine which would be most useful in determining the relationship between arousal and motor performance. Subjects were ranked on the basis of: (1) initial conductance; (2) final conductance; (3) total change in conductance from rest to final trial 12; (4) conductance after trial 1; and (5) change in conductance from rest to trial 1. The highest twenty subjects in each of the five classifications were designated as high arousal, while the twenty subjects with the lowest conductance were designated as low arousal.

As most of the learning occurred during the first six trials, performance scores were broken into two groups of six trials each for analysis. Tables 32-I-32-V show that for all five classifications the trials effect was significant at the 1 percent level during the first six trials, but nonsignificant during the second six trials. The error term used was the mean square based upon the pooled interaction sums of squares for subjects by trials. These results permitted inspection of conductance and performance scores during learning as well as when a performance plateau had been reached.

Initial Conductance
(preexperimental)

The group mean performance and mean conductance scores are shown in Figure 32-1. Although performance of the high arousal

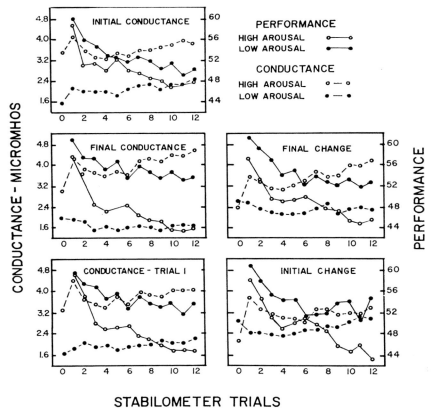

FIGURE 32-1. Mean learning and conductance curves for high arousal and low arousal groups.

TABLE 32-I

ANALYSIS OF PERFORMANCE SCORES BETWEEN HIGH AND LOW
AROUSAL GROUPS ON INITIAL CONDUCTANCE

Source	df	Trials 1-6		Trials 7-12	
		MS	F	MS	F
Groups	1	127.60	0.37	501.71	0.76
Subjects in the same group	38	344.80		656.25	
Trials	5	426.79	9.59[a]	36.47	1.34
T x G	5	16.24		10.59	
Pooled Subjects x T	190	44.51		27.27	
Total	239				

[a] $p < .01$

group appears to be superior to that of the low arousal, an analysis
of variance on these performance scores, summarized in Table 32-I,
indicates there is no significant difference in performance between the
two groups on trials 1-6 ($F = 0.37$) or on trials 7-12 ($F = 0.76$).
The mean square based upon variation between subjects in the same
group was used to test the significance of the difference between the
groups. The pattern of conductance for both groups, while differing
in absolute values, is quite similar.

Final Conductance
(after trial 12)

The pattern of conductance based on groups differing in final conductance is far different from that depicted in the first graph. The
low arousal group shows an apparent decrease in conductance while
the high arousal group displays the same initial change that was
evident in both groups in initial conductance. After dropping in conductance the high arousals show a marked gain in conductance as
performance continues. The low arousals, on the other hand, show
very little change of any kind.

Analysis of mean performance scores summarized in Table 32-II
show that high arousals perform significantly better than low arousals
on both trials 1-6 and trials 7-12 ($F = 8.98$ and 10.30). The differ-
ence between groups at trial 1, however, was not significant ($t = 1.24$). The interaction between trials and groups is significant on
trials 1-6, indicating that the high arousals progressed at a faster

TABLE 32-II

ANALYSIS OF PERFORMANCE SCORES BETWEEN HIGH AND LOW
AROUSAL GROUPS ON FINAL CONDUCTANCE

		Trials 1-6		*Trials* 7-12	
Source	*df*	*MS*	*F*	*MS*	*F*
Groups	1	2528.50	8.98[b]	5424.51	10.30[b]
Subjects in the same group	38	281.62		526.70	
Trials	5	426.80	13.45[b]	36.47	1.34
T x G	5	78.76	2.45[a]	13.59	
Pooled Subjects x T	190	31.74		27.19	
Total	239				

[a] $p < .05$
[b] $p < .01$

rate than did the low arousals. This can be observed from the graph of final conductance.

Total Change in Conductance
(preexperimental to trial 12)

The high arousal group consists of those subjects making the greatest total change in conductance, while the low arousals are those making the least total change. The conductance curves are similar to those depicted in final conductance, with the low arousals showing little or no change over the twelve trials. The high arousals, on the other hand, make a rapid change from resting to trial 1, then gradually decrease during the early learning stages, and as learning appears to slow down the conductance again begins to rise.

The summary of an analysis of variance of performance scores based on total change in conductance is presented in Table 32-III. The comparison of performance scores on trials 1-6 yielded an F of 5.49 which was significant at the 5 percent level, while performance scores on trials 7-12 yielded an F of 4.31, also significant at the 5 percent level, thus indicating that the high arousal group performed better than the low arousal group on both the first six trials and the last six trials. Although the groups differed in performance during the first six trials, there was no difference at trial 1 ($t = 1.92$, with $P = 2.02$ at the 5 percent level). The interaction of trials x groups was not statistically significant, indicating no difference in the curves

TABLE 32-III

ANALYSIS OF PERFORMANCE SCORES BETWEEN HIGH AND LOW
AROUSAL GROUPS ON TOTAL CHANGE IN CONDUCTANCE

Source	df	Trials 1-6		Trials 7-12	
		MS	F	MS	F
Groups	1	1669.54	5.49[a]	2593.84	4.31
Subjects in the					
same group	38	304.22		601.19	
Trials	5	426.79	12.94[b]	36.47	1.30
T x G	5	28.29		15.11	
Pooled Subjects					
x T	190	32.97		28.11	
Total	239				

[a] $p < .05$
[b] $p < .01$

during acquisition, that is, indicating that the two curves tend to remain parallel throughout the 12 trials.

Conductance After Trial 1

The high arousal group shows a sharp increase in conductance from the preexperimental state to trial 1, while the low arousal group shows little or no gain. The performance of the high arousal group obviously does not differ from the low arousal group at trial 1, and there was no significant difference between groups on trials 1-6 (Table 32-IV). As learning progresses, the curves separate until there is a significant difference between the groups on trials 7-12 ($F = 6.22$).

The interaction of trials by groups was significant for trials 1-6,

TABLE 32-IV

ANALYSIS OF PERFORMANCE SCORES BETWEEN HIGH AND LOW
AROUSAL GROUPS ON TRIAL ONE

Source	df	Trials 1-6		Trials 7-12	
		MS	F	MS	F
Groups	1	1071.04	3.35	3580.54	6.22[a]
Subjects in the					
same group	38	319.97		575.23	
Trials	5	406.25	12.78[b]	36.47	1.39
T x G	5	93.63	2.95[a]	11.91	0.45
Pooled Subjects					
x T	190	31.78		26.20	
Total	239				

[a] $p < .05$
[b] $p < .01$

indicating that the performance of the high arousal group improved
at a faster rate than that of the low arousal group.

Initial Change in Conductance
(preexperimental to trial one)

The graph of conductance scores for the high arousal group shows
the sharp increase in conductance from the resting state to trial 1 that
was evident in the high arousal group in all previous categories. The
low arousal group in contrast, decreases from the resting state to trial
1 and then makes very little change for several trials.

The mean performance scores appear to be superior for the high
arousals at every trial, with the greatest difference in performance
occurring during the last four or five trials. An analysis of variance
of these scores, as summarized in Table 32-V partially supports these
observations. For trials 1-6 the observed differences in performance
are not significant ($F = 2.07$ with 4.1 being required for significance
at the 5% level.) For trials 7-12, however, an F of 4.56 is significant,
indicating that the performance of the high arousal group is superior
to that of the low arousal group. Further, the interaction of trials
by groups, while not significant for the first six trials is significant
at the 1 percent level during the second six trials ($F = 5.07$). This
is shown clearly in the graph for initial change in conductance, with
the two performance curves running approximately parallel for the
first six trials then diverging, with the low arousals' performance level-
ing off, while the performance of the high arousal group continues to
improve.

TABLE 32-V

ANALYSIS OF PERFORMANCE SCORES BETWEEN HIGH AND LOW
AROUSAL GROUPS ON INITIAL CHANGE IN CONDUCTANCE

Source	df	Trials 1-6 MS	F	Trials 7-12 MS	F
Groups	1	638.44	2.07	2727.01	4.56[a]
Subjects in the same group	38	330.30		597.69	
Trials	5	430.23	27.23[b]	36.47	1.50
T x G	5	32.31	2.04	123.29	5.07[b]
Pooled Subjects x T	190	15.80		24.30	
Total	239				

[a] $p < .05$
[b] $p < .01$

DISCUSSION

The analyses of data as presented indicate that there is a relationship between arousal, as measured by skin conductance, and performance on a gross motor skill. All measures of arousal except initial conductance differentiate between groups, with the high arousal groups having performance superior to the low arousal groups.

The fact that initial conductance does not differentiate between groups in performance is not surprising. It should be remembered that the measure referred to as initial conductance was taken prior to testing. In fact, subjects had not been introduced to the task to be learned. Therefore, the initial conductance could not reflect the subjects' arousal to the specific task.

The importance of the change from the preexperimental state to the experimental state can be readily observed in the graphs. When grouped by any measure other than initial conductance, the high arousal groups show a sharp increase in conductance from the initial test to trial 1, while the low arousal groups show no such change. Performance measures based on conductance early in learning, while not significant for the first six trials, were significant for the last six. On the other hand, conductance taken later in performance reflected differences between groups in both the early stages of learning and later when performance had reached a plateau.

Whether the improved performance was due to increased arousal or whether increased arousal was due to improved performance is an open question. As Kendler[4] has pointed out, while performance has been assumed to be a function of arousal, just the opposite might be true. If arousal depended upon performance, we would expect differences in performance when one group exhibited a sharp increase in conductance over the other. On trial 1, however, when subjects were arbitrarily dichotomized on the bases of conductance, there were no significant differences in performance between high and low conductance groups. This can best be seen in the graph for *conductance —trial 1* (Fig. 32-1), although it is equally true in the other classifications (the largest t was 1.92 with $P = 2.02$ at 5% level). On the other hand, late in learning, the high arousal groups always had performance superior to the low arousal groups.

Thus, early in learning there were no differences in performance despite one group's showing sharp increases in conductance. As learning progressed, however, the group showing the sharp increase displayed performance superior to the group showing no increase in conductance. These results, while not conclusive, seem to indicate that arousal, as measured by skin conductance, precedes performance.

SUMMARY

Forty male subjects were tested on a motor learning task that involved twelve trials on a pivoted platform called a stabilometer. Each subject's GSC was taken before the introduction of the task and immediately after each of the twelve trials. Subjects were then dichotomized on the basis of: (1) initial conductance; (2) final conductance; (3) total change in conductance from rest to trial 12; (4) conductance after trial 1 and; (5) change in conductance from rest to trial 1. The twenty subjects with the highest GSCs in each category were placed in one group and the twenty subjects with lowest GSCs placed in a second group.

There was no difference in performance between groups when subjects were dichotomized on the basis of initial conductance. When subjects were divided on basis of conductance taken early in learning (conductance after trial 1 and change from rest to trial 1) there was no difference in performance between groups early in learning, but the group with higher conductance had superior performance late in learning. When dichotomized by conductance taken late in learning (final conductance and total change in conductance) the group with higher conductance had performance superior to the low conductance group both early and late in learning.

These results lend support to the concept of an arousal continuum as proposed by Duffy and Malmo. Further, these results, while not conclusive, seem to indicate that arousal precedes performance.

REFERENCES

1. BACHMAN, J. C.: Specificity vs. generality in learning and performing two large muscle motor tasks. *Res Quart Amer Ass Health Phys Educ, 32*: 3-11; March 1961.
2. DUFFY, E.: The psychological significance of the concept of arousal or activation. *Psychological Review 64*:265-75; September 1957.

3. HARMON, J. M., and JOHNSON, W. R.: The emotional reactions of college athletes. *Res Quart Amer Ass Health Phys Educ, 23*:391-98; Dec. 1952.

4. KENDLER, W. H.: Learning. *Annual Review of Psychology, 10*:43-79, 1959.

5. LINDSEY, D. B.: Emotion. In Stevens, S. S. (Ed.): *Handbook of Experimental Psychology,* New York, Wiley, 1951.

6. MALMO, R. B.: Anxiety and behavioral arousal. *Psychological Review, 64*: 276-87; September 1957.

7. MALMO, R. B.: Measurement of drive; an unsolved problem in psychology. In Jones, M. R. (Ed.): *Nebraska Symposium on Motivation,* Lincoln, U of Nebraska, 1958.

8. RUNQUIST, W. N., and ROSS, L. E.: The relation between physiological measures of emotionality and performance in eyelid conditioning. *J Exp Psychol 57*:329-32; May 1959.

9. RUNQUIST, W. N., and SPENCE, K. W.: Performance in eyelid conditioning related to changes in muscular tension and physiological measures of emotionality. *J Exp Psychol, 58*:417-21; June 1959.

10. STENNETT, R. G.: The relationship of performance level to level of arousal. *J Exp Psychol, 54*:54-61; January 1957.

11. WOODWORTH, R. S., and SCHLOSBERG, N.: *Experimental Psychology.* Revised edition. New York, Holt, 1954.

PART ELEVEN
SOCIAL PSYCHOLOGY

Chapter 33

RELATIONSHIPS BETWEEN SELECTED SOCIAL AND PHYSICAL FACTORS*

CHARLES C. COWELL AND A. H. ISMAIL

INTRODUCTION

PHYSICAL EDUCATION is concerned with the development of organic power and neuromuscular skills, but since the organism is an integrated totality, it is also concerned with what happens to human personality as a result of the achievement of these objectives. Observation of play behavior has diagnostic and guidance values to teachers and clinicians. Unsocial or antisocial behavior is and has always been an index of considerable importance in understanding personality deviations.

The purpose of this study was to determine the possible relationships between selected physical and social measures and to test some of the above assumptions for validity and significance.

PROCEDURES

All the data were collected on preadolescent boys with the exception of the data pertaining to football ability, which was secured from the Purdue University football freshmen of 1958-59.

Three instruments measuring social adjustment were utilized to obtain data on the social factor: the Cowell Personal Distance Scale;[4] the Cowell Social Adjustment Indexes (forms A and B);[4] and the Partridge Leadership Ballot.[9] Data pertaining to the physical factor were obtained by using three physical measures: the Purdue Motor Fitness Test;[15] the Cowell Athletic Aptitude Test;[15] and a nine-item criterion scale for measuring football ability developed by the authors.[5]

* C. C. Cowell and A. H. Ismail: Relationships between selected social and physical factors. *Res Quart Amer Ass Health Phys Educ, 33*:1962, 40-43. Reproduced here with the permission of Professor A. H. Ismail and the American Association for Health, Physical Education, and Recreation.

Pearson correlation coefficients were obtained between the social and physical measures, and these were investigated for significance by testing the null hypothesis and utilizing the Kendall formula.

Four independent studies were conducted for the purpose of meeting the stated objectives of the study. A summary of data from these studies is presented here.

(1) Reynolds[12] obtained a correlation coefficient of .414, significant at the 1 percent level of confidence, between the scores on the Cowell Personal Distance Scale and the scores on the Purdue Motor Fitness Test. His study involved eighty-three boys from ten to twelve years of age.

(2) Bossung[2] obtained the following correlation coefficients—.319, .314, and .322—significant at the 1 percent level of confidence, between the scores on the Purdue Motor Fitness Test and the scores on the Cowell Social Adjustment Indexes A, B, and A, B combined, respectively. In addition, correlation coefficients of .426, .430, and .443, significant at the 1 percent level of confidence, were obtained between the scores on the Cowell Social Adjustment Indexes and the scores on the Cowell Athletic Aptitude Test. His study utilized seventy-five boys aged twelve to thirteen.

(3) Edwards[6] obtained a correlation coefficient of .371, significant at the 1 percent level of confidence, between the Cowell Athletic Aptitude Test and the Cowell Personal Distance Scale. A correlation coefficient of .389, significant at the 1 percent level of confidence, was obtained between the scores on the Cowell Athletic Aptitude Test and those on the Partridge Leadership Ballot. The study covered eighty-one boys aged ten to twelve.

(4) Cowell and Ismail[5] obtained a correlation coefficient of .783, significant at the 1 percent level of confidence, between the scores on the Football Ability Scale and the scores on the Cowell Personal Distance Scale. Their study covered forty-five boys aged eighteen to twenty.

In summary, at the age levels noted, there were significant relationships or associations between the selected physical and social measures.

REVIEW OF LITERATURE

Other studies supporting these particular findings include the following:

Wells[18] found that various physical measures were significant, when related to personality traits. Reaney[11] tested more than 600 boys and girls on their ability to play certain games and on leadership ability and found that those who possessed high ability in playing games were also leaders of these games. Rarick and McKee[10] found that third grade children who attained a high level of motor proficiency tended to be more frequently well adjusted in school and personal relationships.

Betz[1] found low but significant relationships between several physical fitness classes and certain personality traits as measured by Cattell's 16-item Personality Factor Inventory. Cowell [3, 4] found that social adjustment ratings either by teachers or by classmates were positively and significantly related to physical education ability. Furthermore, *fringers* were less acceptable socially to other boys and girls as compared with active boys. Sperling[14] and Signorella[13] found significant differences in social adjustment between athletes and nonathletes.

Stogdill [16] found that height, weight, energy, health, and especially athletic prowess are all associated with leadership. Flowtow[7] and Ondrus[8] both found that members of athletic teams had higher social status than boys not able to make the team. Trapp[17] found that the process of social integration in a college football squad was positive and continued throughout three evenly spaced balloting periods of the football season.

DISCUSSION

Based on the findings drawn from this investigation, which are supported by similar results of other related studies, the following conclusions may be drawn:

For the age ranges studied, boys who score high on physical measures are likely to have leadership potentialities, to be accepted at close personal distance by their associates, and to be well-adjusted socially.

The findings (not reported here in full) further reveal that those engaged in team sports are likely to be accepted at closer personal distance than those engaged in more individual programs of motor fitness. In other words, it would seem that the personal distance index for an individual may be improved by shifting from generality to specificity, especially to team games. Apparently, each player tends to accept his colleagues at closer personal distance when all are members of a group working toward a common goal.

REFERENCES

1. BETZ, ROBERT L.: *A Comparison Between Personality Traits and Physical Fitness Tests of Males 26-60.* Master's thesis. Urbana, U of Ill, 1956.

2. BOSSUNG, RICHARD E.: *The Relationship Between Selected Physical and Social Behavior Measures.* Minor research project. Lafayette, Purdue, 1960.

3. COWELL, CHARLES C.: An abstract of a study of differentials in junior high school boys based on the observation of physical education activity. *Res Quart, 6*:129-36, December 1935.

4. ———. Validating an index of social adjustment for high school use. *Res Quart Amer Ass Health Phys Educ, 29*:7-18; March 1958.

5. COWELL, C. C., and ISMAIL, A. H.: *An Analysis of Selected Factors in the Study of A University Freshman Football Squad.* Paper delivered at the National AHPER Convention, Miami Beach, Florida, 1960.

6. EDWARDS, JOSEPH F.: *The Relationship Between the Cowell Athletic Aptitude Test and Some Selected Social Measures.* Minor research project. Lafayette, Purdue, 1959.

7. FLOWTOW, ERNEST A.: Charting social relationships of school children. *Elementary School J, 46*:498, 504, May 1946.

8. ONDRUS, JOSEPH: *A Sociometric Analysis of Group Structure and the Effect of Football Activities on Interpersonal Relationships.* Doctoral dissertation. New York U., New York, 1953.

9. PARTRIDGE, E. DeALTON: *Leadership Among Adolescent Boys.* New York. Columbia, 1934.

10. RARICK, LAWRENCE, and McKEE, ROBERT: A study of twenty third-grade children exhibiting extreme levels of achievement on tests of motor proficiency. *Res Quart Amer Ass Health Phys Educ, 20*:142-52, May 1949.

11. REANEY, M. JANE: The correlation between general intelligence and play ability as shown in organized group games. *Brit J Psychol, 7*:226-52, 1914.

12. REYNOLDS, THOMAS F.: *The Relationship Between the Cowell Personal Distance Scale and the Purdue Motor Fitness Test.* Minor research project. Lafayette, Purdue, 1959.

13. SIGNORELLA, MICHAEL: Social adjustment and athletic participation. Minor research project. Lafayette, Purdue, 1953.

14. SPERLING, A. P.: The relationship between personality adjustment and achievement in physical education activities. *Res Quart Amer Ass Health Phys Educ, 13*:351-63; October 1942.

15. Staff of the Department of Physical Education For Men. *Charting the Development of Intermediate and Junior High School Boys in Motor Fitness and Its Correlates.* Lafayette, Purdue, 1959.

16. STOGDILL, RALPH M.: Personal factors associated with leadership: A survey of literature. *J of Psychol, 25*:35-71; 1948.
17. TRAPP, WILLIAM G.: A study of social integration in a college football squad. Washington, D.C., *56th Annual Proceedings,* College Physical Education Association, 1953.
18. WELLS, HAROLD P.: *Relationships Between Physical Fitness and Psychological Variables.* Doctoral dissertation. Urbana, U of Ill, 1958.

Chapter 34

EFFECT OF SPECTATORS ON ATHLETES AND NON-ATHLETES PERFORMING A GROSS MOTOR TASK*

ROBERT N. SINGER

INTRODUCTION

THE PRESENCE or absence of spectators frequently has an effect upon performance. One of the outstanding qualities of the successful athlete is his ability to perform, and perform well, before numerous spectators. Whereas many individuals would find their performance of athletic skills hampered under the pressure and stress brought forth by the presence of spectators, the better athletes appear to be oblivious to their environment during a contest. Many athletes even demonstrate a superior effort under this pressure.

Perhaps athletes react more favorably under stress. Perhaps their motivation is increased. Then again, possibly they become conditioned to the crowds: they perform mechanically and effectively regardless of whether the stadiums or gymnasiums are filled or empty.

The question naturally arises—Is this performance trait transferrable to other situations? Are these individuals, after learning entirely new skills in privacy, able to perform in the same manner, with the same success, before an audience? Or is this quality specific only to the situation to which it was conditioned?

PURPOSE OF THE STUDY

It was the purpose of this study to compare the effect of spectator

* R. N. Singer: Effect of spectators on athletes and non-athletes performing a gross motor task. *Res Quart Amer Ass Health Phys Educ*, *36*: 1965, 473-482. Reproduced here with the permission of the author and American Association for Health, Physical Education, and Recreation.

presence on athletes and nonathletes performing a motor skill involving balance coordination. The skill was novel to both groups.

Secondarily, the study attempted to determine any difference between athletes and nonathletes in attaining skill in this task.

The study was limited to the following:

(1) The effect of spectators on male college athletes (representing selected sports) and nonathletes.

(2) The influence of a mixed audience—the experimenter, two staff members, two female secretaries, and one or two male undergraduate students.

(3) The reaction caused by the mere presence of the observers, not of anything they did or said.

(4) The effect of this group of spectators on these subjects when learning a specific gross motor skill: balancing one's weight on a stabilometer.

HYPOTHESES

It was hypothesized that the athletes would perform better in front of a crowd than the nonathletes. Previous experience in performing motor skills before people was assumed to have a positive transfer effect to the experimental situation of this study.

Secondly, it was predicted that the athletes would, in general, acquire greater skill and therefore display superior performance on the stabilometer throughout the experiment. Since body balance and position is a necessary factor for achievement in most sports, it was felt that this quality would carry over to the acquisition of the balancing skill required in this study.

REVIEW OF THE LITERATURE

Research is very sparse in this area of audience effect on performance. In an extremely early study, Triplett [12] had subjects perform a reel-winding task as well as in bicycle races. He found that the presence of others had various effects on the output of the subjects but nevertheless concluded that the bodily presence of another seemed to liberate latent energy and stimulate the performer to greater effort.

Gates [6] required his subjects to undertake a color-naming task and a vocabulary test in front of varying numbers of spectators. The audience changed from only the experimenter to a small group (4 to 6 persons) to an entire class. Effects of the alternate situations were found to differ with each individual.

Lazarus and others,[9] after reviewing research on verbal and perceptual motor-stressful situations, concluded that although a large number of studies indicate impairment of performance under psychological stress, other studies have obtained contrary results. Evidently, some subjects' performance will be impaired because of an emotional disturbance whereas others may be facilitated. Still others may not be affected at all.

Studies[4, 7, 14] have indicated that performing in groups provides better results than working individually. For instance, Abel[1] found that her subjects did better on a paper and pencil maze when working in pairs than alone. In these studies, however, knowledge was pooled and verbal assistance was desired and encouraged. The design of this study is such as not to permit any assistance or emotional expressions by the group of spectators observing the subjects.

Knowledge of a forthcoming stressful situation will evidently have deleterious effects on the performance of prestress tasks. In a recent study, Beam[3] had fifty-four subjects learn nonsense syllables before encountering such natural stressful situations as giving a simple oral report, appearing in a dramatic production before a large number of people, and taking doctoral preliminary examinations. All these events hampered the learning of nonsense syllables. Therefore precaution was taken in this investigation not to inform the subjects of the experimental condition they would ultimately have to face.

As to whether there is a general factor of resistance to stressful conditions, at least one investigation[10] did not find a significant relationship between two stress performance scores obtained on each subject attempting to achieve skill on the Dunlap hand-steadiness apparatus.

Ryan[11] utilized a stabilometer in order to discover the relationship between learning to perform a motor skill and such factors as intellectual capacity, intellectual achievement, motivation, and athletic ability. Each subject was given twelve trials lasting thirty seconds, each with a thirty-seconds rest pause in between trials. One of his findings was that varsity athletes did not perform any differently than the nonathletes on the balancing task.

After reviewing literature related to the problem under investigation in this study, Cratty[5] asks what the effect of an audience is on an athlete. Evidently, people in general react to stressful situations in various ways. The question as to whether selected individuals, familiar with the stress although not with the task, will perform any differently than randomly selected individuals, remains unanswered.

PROCEDURE

Apparatus

A stabilometer (Fig. 34-1) adapted from Bachman[2] and adjusted by Turvey,[13] was the instrument used in this study. A balance board, thirty-six by twenty-one inches, was placed between triangular supports

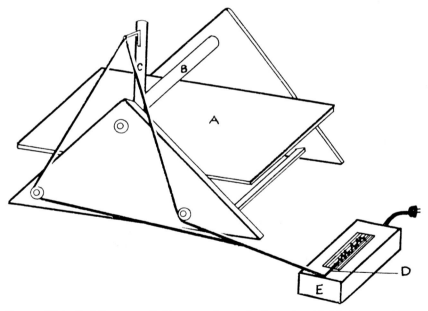

FIGURE 34-1. Stabilometer. Subject stands on platform A, with his feet straddling axle B. Lever arm C is attached to the platform. A cord extends from needle D to a point under the near pulley to and around the far pulley to the lever arm where it is firmly attached. Another cord extends from the lever arm, around the near pulley, and is also attached to the needle. The needle records the extent of movement of the platform on graph paper inserted in the electric kymograph (E).

and an axle passed ten inches above the board (platform). This height of the axle was considered to give the task a certain degree of difficulty.

An electric kymograph recorded the subject's balance skill. A string was attached to the ink-filled pen on the kymograph, passed under the first pulley to and around the far pulley, and attached at the top of the lever arm. The lever arm was connected to the platform. Another string was extended from the lever arm to and around the rear pulley and finally back to the pen. The pen recorded balance fluctuations on graph paper inserted in the kymograph. The extent of the individual's movement on the balance board corresponded to the line drawn on the kymograph, less movement resulting in a straighter line.

This graph paper moved at a rate of speed of twelve inches a minute, making it possible to calibrate evenly. A $10°$ range on either side of the point of equilibrium was determined and found acceptable as the desired maximum range of movement of the platform. Time on target in a particular period was determined through an accurate reading of the graph paper in the kymograph.

Task

The subject entered the room, received instructions, and stood on the horizontal platform, feet fourteen to sixteen inches apart, straddling the pivot rod axle. Each subject received ten practice trials of thirty seconds duration with thirty seconds rest intervals between trials. He attempted to maintain a balanced position as long and as often as possible during each trial.

The next day, each subject was given three more practice trials. Only the experimenter was present for these as well as the previous trials. However, after the three trials, six spectators, composed of male faculty members, male students, and female secretaries, entered the room. The subjects had not been informed that this situation would occur and were therefore totally unaware and unprepared for it.

After taking their seats in a semicircle close to and facing the subject, the spectators did not speak or smile but kept their eyes fixed on the performer. This procedure was followed because it was noted in a pilot study that when the spectators were allowed to speak and in general *act like normal spectators* there was inconsistency as to their reactions to the various performers. Each subject received three more trials with thirty seconds rest intervals on the stabilometer under this condition.

Subjects

The subjects were sixteen of Ohio State's better athletes, representing the following sports: basketball (4), baseball (2), track and field (1), gymnastics (1), tennis (4), golf (2), and wrestling (2). They were also physical education majors and were selected for this study not only because of their athletic attributes but for their accessibility as subjects as well. Sixteen nonathletes were selected from the required physical education classes. They had never competed on a high school or college varsity team, and were screened to make sure they had no past experience in performing before an audience, such as in the capacity of an actor, artist, etc.

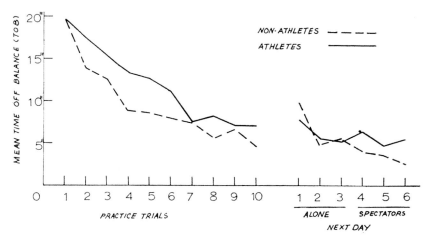

FIGURE 34-2. Performance comparison between athletes and nonathletes before and during presence of spectators.

Results

Table 34-I contains the mean scores and standard deviations for the athletes and nonathletes when practicing alone and when tested in front of spectators. The data are presented graphically in Figure 34-2. The number of seconds of each thirty seconds trial in which a

TABLE 34-I

MEANS AND STANDARD DEVIATIONS OF ATHLETE AND NON-ATHLETE
GROUPS WITH AND WITHOUT THE PRESENCE OF SPECTATORS

Groups		First day (practice trials)									
		1	2	3	4	5	6	7	8	9	10
Athletes	$\overline{X}$	19.88	17.63	15.40	13.38	12.78	11.16	7.84	8.19	7.31	7.28
	s	4.46	4.98	4.26	4.63	5.83	4.98	4.79	5.30	3.57	4.70
Nonathletes	$\overline{X}$	19.75	14.00	12.60	9.00	8.78	8.03	7.75	5.78	6.78	4.66
	s	4.44	4.72	5.21	4.97	5.24	4.62	5.37	5.06	4.71	3.85

Groups		Second day					
		Without spectators			With spectators		
		1	2	3	4	5	6
Athletes	$\overline{X}$	7.97	5.66	5.31	6.50	4.97	5.69
	s	4.71	3.43	3.71	4.10	3.31	4.73
Nonathletes	$\overline{X}$	10.03	5.22	5.66	4.25	3.81	2.78
	s	3.21	2.45	3.82	4.05	3.28	2.20

subject was not balancing within the predetermined range (TOB) has
been plotted. Therefore, the performance curves generally decrease
with each practice trial.

A two-factor analysis of variance with repeated measures (Table
34-II) was calculated for the ten practice trials each group received
the first day. The F ratio for factor B (practice trials) was significant
at the .01 level and indicates that each group improved throughout
the practice trials. The significant AB interaction (.05 level) indicates
that the rate of change during the trials differed for the two groups.
A *t*-test yielding a score of 1.75 on the tenth trial approached but
was not significant at the .05 level. A *t*-score is not presented for each
practice trial because it was believed that the reader would be mainly
interested in the end of practice difference.

TABLE 34-II

ANALYSIS OF VARIANCE OF PERFORMANCE DURING PRACTICE

Source of variation	df	SS	MS	F
Between subjects	31	4951.00		
A (athlete and nonathlete groups)	1	450.48	450.48	3.03
S's within groups	30	4500.52	150.02	
Within subjects	288	8337.37		
B (practice trials)	9	5731.32	636.81	6.81[a]
AB	9	181.49	20.16	2.16[b]
B x S's within groups	270	2524.56	9.35	

[a] Significant at the .01 level.
[b] Significant at the .05 level.

It can be observed, though, that throughout the ten practice trials the nonathletes performed at a greater level of skill than the athletes. Both groups began at the same skill level, but the nonathletes appeared to have had greater success in balancing afterwards. Intersport differences were not calculated because of the small number of athletes representing each sport.

Reliability coefficients were obtained for each group, using the second and third trials of the second day as criterion measures. The coefficient for the athletes was .84, while the coefficient for the non-athletes was .76. Although these are not exceptionally high figures, it must be acknowledged that it is not an easy task to be consistent on consecutive trials on such a delicate apparatus as the stabilometer. The performance scores for the athletes and nonathletes before and during the presence of spectators the following day were analyzed using a 2 x 2 x 3 factorial design with repeated measures. This method of analysis is described by Winer,[15] and the data is presented in Table 34-III.

TABLE 34-III

ANALYSIS OF VARIANCE OF PERFORMANCE BEFORE AND DURING THE PRESENCE OF SPECTATORS

Source of variation	df	SS	MS	F
Between subjects	31	1464.08		
A (athlete and nonathlete groups)	1	28.91	28.91	.60
S's within groups	30	1435.17	47.84	
Within subjects	160	1572.29		
B (spectator effect)	1	147.88	147.88	16.82[a]
AB	1	15.44	15.44	1.76
B x S's within groups	30	263.83	8.79	
C (trials)	2	217.61	103.81	16.63[a]
AC	2	67.10	33.55	5.38[a]
C x S's within groups	60	374.61	6.24	
BC	2	60.57	30.29	4.47[b]
ABC	2	19.27	9.64	1.42
BC x S's within groups	60	406.00	6.77	

[a] Significant at the .01 level.
[b] Significant at the .05 level.

The significant B factor indicates that the groups performed differently before the arrival of spectators from the way they performed during the spectators' presence. The significant effect due to trials (factor C) demonstrates that the means changed during the trials. The significant groups times trials (AC) interaction indicates that the rate of change during the trials differed for the two groups. The spectator effect times trials (BC) interaction was significant at the .05 level and indicates that the rate of change during the trials differed for both groups when balancing alone and when performing in front of spectators.

The presence of spectators had different effects on each group. Because of the extremely high between-subject error term, main effect A (athlete and nonathlete groups) could not be demonstrated to be statistically significant.

In order to determine which means were significantly different, a test on the difference between all possible pairs of means was made using Winer's[15] interpretation of the Newman-Keuls method. This multiple-range test and the data derived from this study is presented in Table 34-IV. The level of significance was set at the .05 level.

According to the Newman-Keuls test, the athletes did not perform any differently when the spectators arrived (trials 4, 5, 6) than on their third trial alone . The nonathletes reached a skill level on trials 5 and 6 which was significantly greater than that on their third trial. In general, the athletes were progressively improving until the arrival of the spectators, at which time they more or less reached a plateau. On the other hand, the nonathletes continually did better throughout the trials, regardless of the presence of the spectators.

A comparison between groups showed both to be approximately equal in skill at trials 2 and 3. However, on trial 4 (the first in front of the spectators) the nonathletes were significantly superior in performance. The difference was also significantly in favor of the nonathletes on trial 6.

The scores were also grouped and analyzed using a t-ratio. Trials 1, 2, and 3 composed the first block, while trials 4, 5, and 6 were included in the second block. The 5 percent level of significance yielded no differences between the athletes and nonathletes before the arrival of spectators (block 1 $= t$ of .46) and after the arrival of spectators (block 2 $= t$ of 1.28). No significant difference was found in the athletes between block 1 and block 2. However, a t-score of 1.98 satisfied the 1.98 ($df = 94$) level of significance in the nonathletes between the first and second block scores.

DISCUSSION

The first hypothesis was not confirmed: the athletes did not perform

TABLE 34-IV

NEWMAN-KEULS MULTIPLE-RANGE TEST ON ORDERED MEANS TO DETERMINE SIGNIFICANCE OF THE DIFFERENCES BETWEEN MEANS OF GROUPS BEFORE AND DURING THE PRESENCE OF SPECTATORS

						Ordered Means						
	1	2	3	4	5	6	7	8	9	10	11	12
	2.78	3.81	4.25	4.97	5.22	5.31	5.66	5.66	5.69	6.50	7.97	10.03
		1.03	1.47	2.19	2.44	2.53	2.88	2.88	2.91	3.72	5.19	7.25
			.44	1.16	1.41	1.50	1.85	1.85	1.88	2.69	4.16	6.22
				.72	.97	1.06	1.41	1.41	1.44	2.25	3.72	5.78
					.25	.34	.69	.69	.72	1.53	3.00	5.06
						.09	.44	.44	.47	1.28	2.75	4.81
							.35	.35	.38	1.19	2.66	4.72
								.00	.03	.84	2.31	4.37
									.03	.84	2.31	4.37
										.81	2.28	4.34
											1.47	3.53
												2.06
Rejection value (.05 level)		2.83	3.40	3.74	3.98	4.16	4.31	4.44	4.55	4.65	4.73	4.81
(Rej.) (S$_E$)[a]		1.19	1.43	1.55	1.67	1.75	1.81	1.86	1.91	1.95	1.99	2.02

[a] S$_E$ = .42.

more efficiently than the nonathletes during the presence of spectators. The nonathletes were statistically more efficient than the athletes on two of the three trials performed in front of people.

The athletes did not attain greater skill during practice on the stabilometer, and therefore the second hypothesis must be rejected. The nonathletes appeared to obtain greater and quicker insight into the problem and performed at a higher skill level throughout the practice trials. The tenth and last trial approached but did not yield a significant difference at the .05 level of significance. The differences between the groups were not significant on each of the ten practice trials, but nevertheless these differences were much greater than those found by Ryan.[11] He concluded that there was no difference in stabilometer performance between athletes and nonathletes.

One might apply these findings to Franklin Henry's Memory Drum theory.[8] The specificity with which we learn things appears to be verified by the inability of the athletes to transfer the balance needed for their specific sport to the task of this study and by their failure to perform a motor skill well in front of people even though they had successfully executed other motor skills before crowds on many previous occasions.

Possibly athletes are more sensitive to people watching them perform, and feel uncomfortable demonstrating a skill at which they are not extremely competent before a group. Interestingly enough, when questioned after their performances as to how they felt when they saw that an audience was going to watch them, the athletes generally stated that they were either not bothered or glad. The nonathletes, with the exception of one, admitted extreme nervousness. Some even said that their legs were shaking. Reported feelings and measured performance certainly did not appear to be closely related in this study.

CONCLUSIONS

On two of three trials in the presence of spectators, nonathletes performed on the stabilometer at a significantly higher level of skill than athletes. Nonathletes generally displayed superior performance to the athletes throughout the trials when practicing alone. However, these differences were not significant at the .05 level.

REFERENCES

1. ABEL, THEODORA M.: The influence of social facilitation on motor performance at different levels of intelligence. *Amer J Psychol, 51*:379-88, 1938.
2. BACHMAN, JOHN C.: Specificity vs. generality in learning and performing two large muscle motor tasks. *Res Quart Amer Ass Health Phys Educ, 32*:3-11, 1961.
3. BEAM, J. C.: Serial learning and conditioning under real life stress. *J Abnorm Soc Psychol, 51*:543-51, 1955.
4. BEASLEY, JULIANE: Comparison of the performance of individuals and three-member groups in a maze learning situation. *Percep Mot Skills, 8*:291-94, 1958.
5. CRATTY, BRYANT J.: Movement behavior and motor learning. Philadelphia, Lea and F, 1964.
6. GATES, G.: The effect of an audience on performance. *J Abnorm Soc Psychol, 18*:334-46, 1924.
7. GURNEE, H.: Maze learning in the collective situation. *J Psychol, 3*:437-43, 1937.
8. HENRY, FRANKLIN M.: Increased response latency for complicated movements and a "memory drum" theory of neuromotor reaction. *Res Quart Amer Ass Health Phys Educ, 31*:448-58, 1960.
9. LAZARUS, RICHARD S., DEESE, JAMES, and OSLER, SONIA F.: The effects of psychological stress upon performance. *Psychol Bull, 49*:293-317, 1952.
10. PARSONS, OSCAR A.; PHILLIPS, LESLIE, and LANE, JOHN E.: Performance on the same psychomotor task under different stressful conditions. *J Psychol, 38*:457-66, 1954.
11. RYAN, E. DEAN: Relative academic achievement and stabilometer performance. *Res Quart Amer Ass Health Phys Educ, 34*:185-90, 1963.
12. TRIPLETT, NORMAN: The dynamogenic factors in pacemaking and competition. *Amer J Psychol, 9*:507-33, 1897-98.
13. TURVEY, MICHAEL: Effect of environment change upon the recall of a gross motor skill. Unpublished master's thesis, Ohio State University, 1964.
14. WEYNER, NORMA, and ZEAMAN, D.: Team and individual performances on a motor learning task. *J Gen Psychol, 55*:127-42, 1956.
15. WINER, B. J.: *Statistical principles in experimental design.* New York, McGraw, 1962.

Chapter 35

GAME INVOLVEMENT IN ADULTS*

BRIAN SUTTON-SMITH, JOHN M. ROBERTS, AND ROBERT M. KOZELKA

INTRODUCTION

THE MOST COMMON explanation for individual differences in recreative interest is that they are the outcome of such nonpsychological factors as differences in wealth, group membership or ecologic opportunity.[2, 18] It is held here, however, that persistence in recreations of various sorts is linked with the expression of characteristic motives. Earlier papers[10, 11, 12, 15] have shown that when games of the three major classes of strategy, chance, and physical skill are examined cross-culturally they are systematically related to specific variables both in the sphere of child training and elsewhere in the general culture. Thus, games of strategy are related to obedience training and to cultural complexity, games of chance are associated with high responsibility training and a belief in the benevolence of the gods, and games of physical skill are related to an emphasis on achievement.

These relationships suggested a *conflict-enculturation* hypothesis of model involvement which stated [11, 12, 15] that conflicts induced by social learning in childhood and later (such as those related to obedience, achievement, and responsibility) lead to involvement in expressive models, such as games, through which these conflicts are assuaged and as a result of which a process of buffered learning occurs which has enculturative value for the competences required in the culture (such as acquiring the competitive styles of strategy, physical skill or chance). The same *conflict-enculturation* hypothesis will be cited in the discussion of game involvement in American adults.

* B. Sutton-Smith, J. M. Roberts, and R. M. Kozelka: Game involvement in adults. *J Soc Psychol, 60:* 1963, 15-30. Reproduced here with the permission of Professor Brian Sutton-Smith and The Journal Press. This investigation was supported by Public Health Research Grant MH 04161-03 from the National Institute of Mental Health, Public Health Service.

[374]

In an earlier publication,[11] the game relationships were based on cross-cultural comparisons and the findings from this source were then strengthened by using them as a basis for predictions within the United States (a technique termed subsystem replication). Thus it was held that girls who have higher obedience and responsibility training than boys would play more games of strategy and games of chance, while boys who have higher achievement training than girls would play more games of physical skill. These predictions were confirmed in the case of a sample of 1,900 Ohio school children. In an attempt to strengthen these findings even further, the present paper extends this subsystem replication to cover sex, economic, and occupational differences in the recreational involvements of national samples of adults.

The predictions for adult game preferences in the United States which have been derived from earlier studies are the following:

(1) Because games of strategy are associated cross-culturally with severe primary socialization, psychological discipline, high obedience training and complex cultures, they will be preferred in this culture by the persons who have had greater experience of such a child training pattern, that is, the higher status groups as compared with the lower, and women as compared with men.

(2) Because games of chance are associated cross-culturally with high routine responsibility training, punishment for the display of initiative, and a belief in the benevolence of the gods, they will be preferred in this culture by members of the lower status groups as compared with the higher and by women as compared with men.

(3) Because games of physical skill are associated cross-culturally with high achievement training, they will be preferred in this culture by the upper as compared with the lower status groups and by men as compared with women.

With respect to the third prediction the state of the literature does not permit the definite statement that the relationship between need achievement and status is a linear one.[3] There are some indications that upper middle groups may have as high an achievement motivation as the upper groups. Two cautionary points are necessary with respect to these predictions. First, there is no implication in this account that those adults who are highly involved in games need any awareness of the motivations associated with their preferred games. Phenomenologically they may enjoy playing and they like to win. Secondly, it is not claimed that all differences between status groups in game preferences can be explained in terms of the present categories of psychological motivation. Other variables of an historical and social psychological sort are certainly involved in recreational choice as a considerable literature attests.[4] The purpose here is to show, rather, that if the present psychological considerations are taken into account they can predict to major effects for which other more satisfactory general theoretical formulations do not exist.

METHOD

Three survey polls made in 1940 and 1948 were used in this study.* All polls provided tests for some or all of the above hypotheses. The polls are described briefly as follows:

(1) *The American Institute of Public Opinion* (Gallup) Poll of 1940 (U.S.A.—A.I.P.O. No. 187) in which 3,242 subjects were asked, amongst various questions of a political and recreative sort: "Which of the following games have you played in the last year?" The list included tennis and golf; bridge and checkers; bingo, craps, and dice. Tennis and golf are games of physical skill; bridge and checkers taken together constitute a combination category of chance and strategy; and bingo, craps, and dice are games of pure chance. Responses classified by sex and occupation were used in this study.

(2) *The Minnesota Poll, No. 53, 1948* in which 598 respondents were asked: "These are some questions dealing with recreation, that is, the things people do in their spare time for their own enjoyment. Which of these things do you like to do most in your spare time?" Responses to the items *doing miscellaneous sports* (which included fishing, hunting, bowling, football and baseball, golf, skating and swimming) and *watching sports contests* were analyzed by sex and level of education. While some of the above items are not games, it is assumed that dominance of physical skill games in this category is the major determinant of responses.

(3) *The Roper-Fortune Survey No. 73 of 1948* was a survey de-

* All data were made available through the facilities of the Roper Public Opinion Center at Williams College, Williamstown, Massachusetts.

voted completely to recreation. The responses of 3,008 subjects were classified in terms of sex, income, education and occupation. Subjects were asked which of several activities they most enjoyed doing in their spare time. The responses most relevant to this inquiry were those having to do with sports. These have been arranged in terms of activities involving direct participation (doing outdoor sports, going out for sports and other participant sports) and vicarious participation (watching sports, attending sports and listening to sports on radio). The very different levels of response in Table 35-III are due to the fact that Items 1 and 4 were provided by the questionnaire while Items 2, 3, 5, and 6 were written in by the respondents.

The use of the poll data to test the predictions was quite straightforward. The actual techniques used can be plainly inferred from the results presented below.

RESULTS

All the results from the first poll were in the predicted direction, which means that the findings from the cross-cultural study have now been replicated both with children and adults within the United States. As Table 35-I indicates the males who are assumed to have had higher achievement training than the females played more games of physical skill (tennis and golf) ($t = 2.78$, $p = < .01$).* The females who have had more obedience and responsibility training played more games of strategy and chance (checkers and bridge) ($t = 2.19$, $p = < .05$) and more games of chance (bingo, craps and dice) ($t = 2.23$, $p = < .05$) than the males.

The occupational differences are also in general accord with the predictions. The professional classes, whom it is assumed have had the highest achievement and obedience training, showed a greater interest in physical skill and strategy games than any of the other classes. For games of physical skill all differences are significant at $p = < .01$. For games of strategy, the differences between the professional classes and some of the intermediate groups (*viz.* clerks) were reduced, but the former still displayed a significantly greater preference for such games than all the worker groups (servants, skilled, unskilled

---

* All tests are *t*-tests and are based on the significance of the difference between the percentage of responses.

TABLE 35-I

A.I.P.O. POLL NO. 187. SEX AND OCCUPATIONAL RESPONSES
TO GAMES

Respondent group	N	Percentage of responses		
		Golf, tennis	*Bridge, checkers*	*Dice, craps bingo*
Males	2163	21	58	1.10
Females	1079	17	62	2.22
Professionals	289	49	74	.34
Proprietors	497	36	66	1.0
Clerks	539	35	72	.73
Skilled workers	254	21	54	.78
Servants	99	15	63	2.1
Semiskilled workers	377	14	52	3.4
Other unskilled	218	9	43	1.8
Farmers	652	7	53	1.6
Farm laborers	26	7	42	0

and semiskilled) ($p = < .05$). Again, as predicted, most of the worker categories in which responsibility and routine occupations were held to be characteristic showed a greater interest in games of chance than the professional group, although only the difference between the semiskilled worker group and the professional group was significant ($p = < .01$).

The second poll (No. 53) provided a more fitting test of the hypothesis concerning achievement and sports because the recreations mentioned are more general, and not necessarily those which would be associated in common expectation with higher status groups (as are golf and tennis). The sex difference is stronger in this case being significant both for doing sports ($t = 5.38$, $p = < .01$) and watching sports ($t = 6.36$, $p = < .01$). The tendency in the results was for the college educated to show more interest than the high school educated, who showed more interest than the grade school educated. None of these differences for engaging in sports were significant though they were all directional. Thus for the college incomplete group compared with the grade school group, $t = 1.93$ and for the combined college group compared with the grade school group, $t = 1.95$. All differences were greater for watching sports. Both combined college ($t = 3.75$, $p = < .01$) and combined high school groups ($t = 2.77$, $p = < .01$) manifested a significantly higher level of preference than the grade school group.

Table 35-III indicates that as in Tables 35-I and 35-II there was

TABLE 35-II

MINNESOTA POLL NO. 53, 1948. SEX AND EDUCATIONAL
RESPONSES TO SPORTS ITEMS

| *Respondents* | *N* | Percentage of responses | |
		Miscellaneous sports, fishing, hunting, bowling, football, baseball, golf, skating, swimming	*Watching sports contests*
Male	296	28	33
Female	302	11	12
College graduate	66	23	28
College (incomplete)	64	28	36
High school graduate	163	24	25
High school (incomplete)	106	15	23
Grade school	192	16	14

a tendency for higher status groups (education and income) to display a greater participant and vicarious interest in sports. The educational status index followed the predicted pattern most consistently with the college groups showing higher percentages than the grade school groups on all comparisons. Five out of six of the differences were significant at $p = < .05$ (Nos. 1, 2, 3, 4, 6), the other was directional (No. 5). The highest economic status group (A) had significantly higher percentages than the lowest economic status group (D) on two out of the six possible comparisons (Nos. 1 and 4). Two were directional (Nos. 2 and 3). The occupational extremes (professional vs factory wages) did not show any significant difference in favor of the professionals; in fact, factory wage workers evinced a significantly greater preference for attending sports (No. 4; $p = < .05$). Salary executives did show stronger directional preferences than factory wage workers on most of the items, though none of the differences were significant.

In sum, of the eighteen comparisons between the extremes in each status category (college *vs* grade school; economic A *vs* economic D; professional *vs* factory wage workers), seven favored the hypothesis, ten were nonsignificant and one was in a contrary direction.

DISCUSSION

The major predictions of this study have been confirmed. Both the cross-cultural findings and the smaller scale regional subsystem

TABLE 35-III

ROPER FORTUNE SURVEY NO. 73. RESPONSES TO RECREATIONAL ITEMS BY SEX, ECONOMIC STATUS, EDUCATIONAL STATUS, AND OCCUPATIONAL STATUS

Respondents	N	Direct Participation			Vicarious Participation		
		1 Doing outdoor sports	2 Go out for sports	3 Other partic. sports	4 Watching sports	5 Attend sports	6 Listen to sports on radio
Sex							
Male	1502	21	2.	6	26	4.4	3
Female	1506	6	.8	2	5	.8	.5
Economic							
Class A	185	18	1.1	4.8	19	1.1	2.1
B	702	13	1.7	7.7	19	4.4	1.8
C	1354	15	1.7	4.0	16	2.4	1.3
D	767	12	.5	2.3	11	1.8	2.3
Educational							
College	684	17	1.7	6.1	20	3.6	2.3
High school	1378	15	1.8	5.2	17	2.2	1.9
Grade 1-8	873	9	.4	1.7	11	2.6	1.0
Occupational							
A Professional	133	15	.7	10.6	20	4.5	5.2
B Proprietor	239	21	1.5	7.6	25	4.5	2.0
C Salary exec.	101	27	—	10.0	34	5.0	3.0
D Salary minor	285	17	4.2	5.5	23	2.4	1.0
E Factory wgs.	326	23	2.1	5.3	27	3.6	3.0
F Other wages	365	14	1.9	4.9	20	3.2	2.0
G Farm propr.	207	19	1.5	2.5	15	3.3	.9
H Farm wages	92	21	1.0	4.4	17	3.3	3.0
I Housekeeper	1048	7	.6	1.8	4	.6	.3
J Student	66	25	6.0	10.6	33	9.0	0.0

findings with children have now been replicated on these three national adult samples. Additional support for some of these empirical findings may be found in the studies reported by Caillois,[1] Clarke,[2] de Grazia[5] and White,[18] where they overlap with this inquiry. In the present study, games of strategy have been shown to be associated with women and higher status, games of chance with women and lower status, and games of physical skill with men and higher status. It will be recalled that these predictions have a basis in the hypothesized intervening psychological variables of obedience, responsibility and achievement training which were found to be related to games in the cross-cultural study. Thus in earlier studies, conflict over obedience induced by child training procedures was shown to be related to the presence of games of strategy on one level and cultural complexity on another.[10, 11] The same relationships were discovered to hold for the relative importance of strategic outcomes in tales.[12] Responsibility training was shown to be related to games of chance and a belief in the benevolence of the gods. Games of physical skill were related to achievement training. The fact that, cross-culturally, women generally have higher obedience and responsibility training led to the present predictions that in this culture also they would show more preference for games of strategy and chance than men. In addition, because men have higher achievement training it was predicted that they would prefer more games of physical skill than do women. The association of games of strategy with cultural complexity and of obedience training with higher social status led to the prediction that these games would be associated in this culture with higher social status. The association of games of chance with responsibility training, which involves menial and low level drudgery and routine activities, led to the prediction that these games would be preferred by persons of lower social status. Again the association of achievement with higher social status led to the prediction that persons of higher status would play more games of physical skill. All of the various findings support the *conflict-enculturation* hypothesis stated in the introduction.

Although the results of this study have followed the predictions with considerable consistency, there has been one important exception. The professional occupational group (Table III), failed to show a high percentage of response to interest in physical game activities. The other high status group (the salary executives) and a low status group (the factor wage workers), both showed significantly higher percentages of interest. One interpretation of this result is that the occupational status index is not as adequate an index of need achievement as are the economic and educational indices in which no such reversal of expectation occurred. Kaltenbach and McClelland,[7] using a sociometrically based criterion of perceived success, placed the occupational index as the least adequate criterion. In an earlier paper, however, the present investigators have taken another position which would seem to handle this exception more comprehensively. Thus in the earlier cross-cultural work it was discovered that the number of types of games in a culture is positively associated with achievement training.[11] It seemed reasonable then to view games as various types of achievement models, from which it was postulated that those who practice persistently at a particular game type should be rehearsing the success style that is involved in that model. Those persisting with games of strategy would be practicing a style in which success is contingent upon clever decision making (a strategic success style); those practicing games of physical skill would be practicing a style in which success is contingent upon a display of power, motor skill or courage (Potency); those playing games of chance would be practicing a style in which success is contingent upon the omnipotence of the player's luck (Fortunism). In a study with children,[15] in which a sociometric instrument based on these systilistic characteristics was used to predict intelligence, socioeconomic status, personality attributes and game preferences, it was found that those to whom a fortunist style was attributed by their peers tended to be more often seen as failures both by children and by teachers, and to be of lower intelligence and socioeconomic status; that those to whom a potent style was attributed were of high group status, were perceived of as good at sport, showed a higher preference for games of physical skill, but were of low intelligence; that those who were seen as strategists were also of high group status, were seen as not good at physical sports, preferred games of strategy, and were of high intelligence. These findings permit the formulation that achievement by high status persons may be differentiated into at least two types—that with a basis in power, and that with a basis in strategy.

In the high economic and educational status groups of Table 35-III, these two achievement styles are presumably mixed together. In the occupational section, however, it seems a differentiation has occurred by occupational group. Salary executives who show greater preference for physical skill games than professionals may be said to show a higher preference also for a power style than the professionals do, that is, if the earlier finding with children with regard to competitive styles and game choices can be safely extrapolated to this present data. The higher choice that professionals have for games of strategy (Table 35-I) is consistent with this interpretation. Further support for the formulation comes from a study by Veroff, Atkinson, Feld, and Gurin,[17] in which a T.A.T. measure of power and achievement was used in a nationwide sample. Analysis of the relationships between occupational groups and power (p. 23) shows a ranking somewhat similar to that shown above for the interest in physical sports (Tables 35-III). Salary executives and factory workers have a higher ranking than professionals on both power and physical sports interest. Conversely, the Veroff rankings on achievement are similar to those in Table 35-I for strategy. None of these parallels can be regarded as finally convincing, but the suggestion certainly follows that the present relationships might be further explicated in future research by the measurement of achievement which is differentiated in terms of strategy and power.

Although the *conflict-enculturation* hypothesis has been described in other publications,[11, 12, 15] it is relevant here to explicate the hypothesis in terms of its relationships to achievement motivation since this particular motivation has been given most attention in this paper. Discussion of the hypothesis in relation to obedience and responsibility, as well as to achievement, will be found elsewhere [11, 12, 15] and a much more elaborate treatment of the hypothesis will be forthcoming.

It will be recalled that games of all types have been shown to have some relationship to achievement training and that all games can be viewed as achievement models, particularly those which model achievement through power and skill. Games of pure physical skill (weight lifting, bowling) model only these last characteristics, but games of physical skill and strategy (boxing, football) model in addition the attributes of strategy.

The *conflict-enculturation* hypothesis involves a number of propositions, each of which will be stated abstractly below and then followed
by the relevant details. The first two propositions have to do with
conflict and include the concepts of conflict arousal, curosity, and
model involvement. The second two propositions are concerned with
enculturation and include the concepts of social learning and personality adjustment.

> 1-a. Conflict induced in children or adults by achievement train-
> ing arouses in them curiosity about those expressive models that
> contain a representation of winning and losing as a result of the
> application of power and skill.

The hypothesis holds that learning can produce conflicts (a balance
of approach and avoidance tendencies), which heighten an individual's interest in the variables which are involved in his conflict.
This is the familiar concept of conflict-induced drive.[19] The positive
and negative discipline which might be expected to underly such
approach-avoidance tendencies have been established in earlier research.[11] Thus playing games of physical skill was found in tribal cultures with a high frequency of achievement training, a high reward
for achievement, but at the same time high punishment for non-
performance of achievement. It would seem that children, seriously
limited in size, skill and power, yet motivated to achieve and anxious
about being able to do so, can seldom find in full scale cultural participation sufficient behavioral opportunities to adequately match
both their desire and their anxious incompetence. It is believed that in
childhood this achievement anxiety expresses itself most frequently as
a fear of failure. The contemporary psychological definition of achievement drive as competition against a standard of excellence, tends to
underplay the extent to which in childhood such an achievement
standard is usually part of an interpersonal relationship, so that to
achieve, the subject must face some other person's expectations, or
alternatively must face the rivalry of another competitor, usually a
sibling, peer or parent. Anxiety about achievement in childhood is
primarily anxiety acquired in such interpersonal situations. This
leaves children with an interest in winning, particularly if there is the
possibility of doing so in some way that will reduce their fear of failure
and provide appropriate *matching* for their limited talents. Their
curiosity about achievement models has this origin.

1-b. Persons who are made curious about achievement by their conflict over it readily become involved in achievement as represented in expressive models.

Desiring to beat opponents but frightened to lose, the child is motivated to explore and to be curious about opportunities to deal with his conflict in a more manageable fashion. He is attracted to a variety of culturally provided expressive models. Some of these may be vicarious as in folktales, comics, and television, and may suggest that the small participant can win (Jack and the Giant Killer, Mighty Mouse), or that the central figure may have powers to overcome insuperable odds (Superman). Or the expressive models may be of the participant variety like physical skill games in which the consequences of winning and losing are drastically reduced. Noticeably, in the earliest forms of physical skill and strategy games such as tagging and hide-and-seek, both winning and losing are episodic and their intensity is decreased by the instability of the sides. There is, in addition, no final explicit outcome so that there is a lack of clarity about which players have actually won or lost. This reduction in the objective clarity of winning and losing, however, permits rather than prevents subjective estimates of success to assume relatively egocentric proportions. Thus Piaget has shown that very young children all imagine they have won in the games that they play.[9] And Maccoby has demonstrated that six-year-olds anticipate success with their peers in a way far exceeding the limits of possibility.[8] With the passing of chronological age there is a developmental change in the models in which children can find a statement for their problems of winning and losing. The diffuse skill models of the earlier years give way to games in which the requirements for winning are more rigorous and the penalties for losing more obvious (marbles, football).[14] Children of different maturity levels, therefore, can find a matching for the maturity of their achievement conflicts somewhere in each of the many series to be found in the cultural model array of tales and games, etc.

The second part of the present theory is that once the child becomes *involved* in games a further series of circumstances occur to which the broad term *enculturation* has been given. At the present time in the development of this theory, the term *enculturation* is being used to apply to two distinct processes, the first of which can be called *social learning* and the second *personality adjustment*. Both seem necessary to explain the players' continued involvement and the cultural significance of expressive models.

> 2-a. In the case of children, and to a lesser extent adults, participation in achievement games contributes to physical, intellectual, and social learning, each of which in due course may contribute to the participant's ability to survive in the full scale success systems of the larger culture.

It has been assumed traditionally that various physical, intellectual and, particularly moral, characteristics have been learned as a result of participation in games, more especially team games. Whether or not these traditional assumptions are well-founded, it is contended here that in achievement games a capacity is learned to master the contingencies of winning and losing in interpersonal competition, and that the development of this capacity is fostered by the game-contained demands. There is some, if partial, evidence for this latter claim.[6] The argument is, that because games reduce the scale on which the competition occurs, then winning and losing as complex interpersonal events become more readily assimilable by the child. Even loss is more acceptable when it is known that victory may occur in a second episode. The dangers and threats associated with both winning and losing are thus much reduced, while the gratification in winning is not. Furthermore, losers are defended by the play convention that the game is only for *fun* anyway. Privately, at least, a victor may think what he likes about winning. The view that expressive models make social and behavioral complexities more assimilable (both cognitively and emotionally) to the participants is a part of a more general argument of the present investigators that expressive models exist for the very reason that they can convey to participants information which cannot be assimilated more simply nor without overwhelming anxiety in large-scale cultural participation.

In sum, the first reason for player's involvement in any particular model is that the model has scaled down the dimensions of his conflict to a point where it is intellectually and emotionally comprehensible. In turn, the player's involvement in the clarity and safety of the model's presentation, facilitates learning.

> 2-b. Expressive models contribute to a player's adjustment to the cultural pressures which have given rise to his conflict (child

training pressures for children, current success pressures for adults), because they are exercises in mastery.

By scaling down the conflict dimensions the games give their participants the confidence that winning and losing as complex interpersonal processes and anxiety inducing ones can be mastered. It is in this sense that the game is a mechanism of personality adjustment. It is legitimate to call this an enculturative function, however, because the adjustment involved means that the underlying process of achievement training adopted by the parents has greater assurance of success, and that the pressures put upon children to achieve and be concerned about achievement will not lead to overwhelming despair and inferiority. Likewise with adults, contemporary pressures towards success may be similarly reduced to assimilable proportions. If this theoretical position be correct, then the various achievement models which have survived in our culture do so because they continue to have this culturally adaptive significance. It has, for example, always been something of a puzzle to explain the persistence of some of the most elementary of expressive models such as tagging.[16] We now consider that it is their function to preserve within the player the confidence that some of the incompatible pressures which afflict him are manageable and that he may continue to survive successfully in the cultural system that engenders his conflicts. This increased confidence in himself would be a second reason for the player's involvement in the expressive models.

An alternative conceptualization of this *adjustment* process would be to say that the game *involves* the player because it *resolves his conflict*. The difficulty with this formulation in the present case, however, is that the player's original conflict is not resolved. It continues and it must continue if the child training system or the adult cultural system is to be preserved, and to be successful. Perhaps a tension-reduction conceptual paradigm is not the most appropriate one. A level of aspiration paradigm might be more appropriate. The fantasied success and reduced loss would, in these terms, not change the large scale world directly, but by increasing the confidence of the players in analogous competitive processes, may elevate their general level of aspiration with respect to these same processes in the large-scale world. In this case the *fun* of the game derives from an exercise in competence rather than an exercise in tension assuagement. There is some supportive if not definitive evidence for this view in the earlier work of these investigators showing that those who prefer games of particular types (physical skill, or strategy) seem to be successful in the same ways (power or strategy) with their peers.[15]

Much of the preceding discussion necessarily deals with child training, but this paper is concerned with adults. In the various researches on achievement training in this culture there is suggestion of both reward and anxiety in the training of child achievers, though the various investigations are by no means consistent on this point.[3] What is neglected in most research on achievement training is the investigation of the achievement motivation of the parents. Since adults themselves are the mediators of the general pressures at work in the larger community, we might expect that the parents who induce high achievement training conflict in children will also be in similar conflict about achievement in adult concerns. The *conflict-enculturation* theory implies that the child training relationship to expressive models is but a part of a larger system which has in its total nature been adaptive in culture. Thus we would speculate that the adults most concerned to induce achievement in their children would themselves have high achievement aspirations in terms of the various status indices by which persons in this culture *score* their achievement—roles, houses, annual income, possessions, and the likes. The fact that high status adults will continue to play games of physical skill is supportive of this latter interpretation. The enculturative function, for the adults as compared with the children, however, is presumed to be dominantly adjustive. The game enables these adults to continue to be achievement motivated without succumbing to the pressures that this motivation entails. The game playing ensures periodic innoculations of manageable success and manageable failure, reassuring the participant that he is indeed one who can tolerate such pressures in his own psychic economy. To be sure, some game-related physical skills are learned even by adults, but it is doubtful that much important and progressive social learning takes place through games after biological and cultural maturity has been attained.

These statements do not preclude the possibility that even in adulthood, changes in life circumstances may induce achievement conflicts which will in turn lead to game playing.

In sum, the conflict-enculturation hypothesis says that child training induces conflict which leads to curiosity about representations (as in expressive models) of the dimensions of this conflict. Involvement in models follows because their microcosmic representation reduces the conflict's complexities to cognitive and emotional comprehensibility and because of the successes a player may gain while in the model. This involvement in turn has enculturative value because the participant can learn about the cognitive and emotional aspects of winning in a model in a way that he cannot do outside of it, and because his successes give him increased confidence that he can manage the achievement pressures in full-scale cultural participation. The models thus have the general cultural function that they contribute to the learning and adjustment of persons who must maintain a high level of achievement motivation if the general cultural norms are to be sustained.

This paper has presented the results of a subsystem replication among American adults which when conjoined with the earlier cross-cultural study and subsystem replication among Ohio school children supports a *conflict-enculturation* hypothesis of game involvement. Certainly, this hypothesis will require further study before it is proved, but the results thus far obtained are encouraging. At the very least, this study represents the first large-scale empirical substantiation of the view that psychological factors are of major importance in game preferences.

SUMMARY

In previous cross-cultural research, relationships were established between child training variables, game playing, and general cultural variables. Using three national surveys with adults the following hypotheses derived from the cross-cultural study were confirmed within this culture:

(1) Because games of strategy are associated cross-culturally with severe primary socialization, psychological discipline, high obedience training, and complex cultures, they will be preferred in this culture by the persons who have had greater experience of such a child training pattern, that is by the higher status groups as compared with the lower and by women as compared with men.

(2) Because games of chance are associated cross-culturally with

high routine-responsibility training, punishment for the display of initiative, and a belief in the benevolence of the gods, they will be preferred in this culture by members of the lower status groups as compared with the higher and by women as compared with men.

(3) Because games of physical skill are associated cross-culturally with high achievement training, they will be preferred in this culture by the upper as compared with the lower status groups and by men as compared with women.

The results were conceptualized in terms of a *conflict-enculturation* theory of games.

REFERENCES

1. CAILLOIS, R. Man, Play and Games. Glencoe, Free Press, 1961.
2. CLARKE, A. C.: Leisure and occupational prestige. *Amer Social Rev, 21*: 301-307, 1956.
3. CRANDALL, V. J.: Achievement. In H. W. Stevenson (Ed.): *National Society for the Study of Education: Yearbook.* pp.416-459, 1963.
4. DENNY, R., and MEYERSOHN, M. L.: A preliminary bibliography on leisure. *Amer J Sociol, 62*:602-615, 1957.
5. GRAZIA, S. DE.: Of Time, Work and Leisure. New York, Twentieth Century Fund, 1962.
6. GUMP, P. V., and SUTTON-SMITH, B.: The "it" role in children's games. *The Group. 17*:3-8, 1955.
7. KALTENBACH, J. E., and McCLELLAND, D. C.: Achievement and social status in three small communities. In D. C. McClelland *et al.* (Eds.), *Talent and Society.* New York, Van Nostrand, 1958.
8. MACCOBY, M.: The game attitude. Ph.D. thesis, Lab. of Soc. Relations, Harvard U, 1960.
9. PIAGET, J.: The moral judgment of the child. Glencoe, Free Press, 1948.
10. ROBERTS, J. M.; ARTH, J., and BUSH, R. R.: Games in culture. *Amer Anthrop, 61*:597-605, 1959.
11. ROBERTS, J. M., and SUTTON-SMITH, B.: Child training and game involvement. *Ethnology, 1*:166-185, 1962.
12. ROBERTS, J. M.; SUTTON-SMITH, B., and KENDON, A.: Strategy in games and folktales. *J Soc Psychol,* in press.
13. SUTTON-SMITH, B.: A formal analysis of game meaning. *Western Folklore. 18*:13-24, 1959.
14. SUTTON-SMITH B.: The games of New Zealand children. Berkeley, U Calif, 1959.
15. SUTTON-SMITH, B., and ROBERTS, J. M.: Rubrics of competitive behavior. *J Genet Psychol,* in press.
16. SUTTON-SMITH, B., and ROSENBERG, B. G.: Sixty years of historical change

in the game preferences of American children. *J Amer Folklore. 74*: 17-46, 1961.

17. VEROFF, J.; ATKINSON, J. W.; FELD, S. C., and GURIN, G.: The use of thematic apperception to assess motivation in a nation-wide interview study. *Psychol Monog, 74* (Whole No. 499): 1-32, 1960.

18. WHITE, C. R.: Social class differences in the use of leisure. *Amer J Sociol, 61*:145-150, 1955.

19. WHITING, J. W. M., and CHILD, I. L.: *Child Training and Personality.* New Haven, Yale, 1953.

PART TWELVE
COGENT COMMENTARIES

Chapter 36

ON THE THRESHOLD*

BRYANT J. CRATTY

IN THE NOT TOO DISTANT past, arriving at the truth was a relatively simple matter. One had only to listen to and obey the voice of authority. Adhering to the pronouncements of the clergy and obeying the commands of the reigning monarch took much of the hazard out of making individual judgments.

Today the world is more complex. Rational men test their beliefs by reference to the scientific method of problem solving. This newer avenue to the truth results in greater accuracy. Observations are confirmed or disproved through analyses of measurable evidence, employing techniques which others can understand and may replicate.

But this approach to the truth has also produced special problems. Examples are the debates in the medical literature concerning the influence of smoking upon lung cancer, the use of oral contraceptives, and the value of certain drugs in the treatment of psychotic disturbances. Similar disagreements are currently aired in educational journals. These controversies are brought about by the failure to agree upon two fundamental questions: (1) the type of evidence which is considered to be scientifically valid, and (2) upon the way in which research findings should be interpreted.

But controversy is healthy. Arguments refine the issues. Questions hone the edges of reason and should eventually lead men to an even greater capacity to understand their environment and themselves.

Physical educators have not been immune to controversy. In the 1930's it was decried that we were the salvation of America's edu-

* B. J. Cratty: On the threshold. *Quest,* Monograph VIII, 1967, 7-14. This paper was presented as the Merck, Sharpe, and Dohm Lecture sponsored by the Texas Institute of Child Psychiatry, Baylor University Medical Center, in December, 1965. Reproduced here with the Permission of the author and the *Quest* Board.

cational system. Overacting to the preachments of Dewey and Kilpatrick, certain of our leaders asserted that we were working with the whole individual through physical activities, and in this manner contributed directly to his social adjustment. We had become psychiatrists on the ball field!

However, objective evidence supporting this philosophical stand was tenuous to say the least. For example, one investigation indicated that sports participation aided social adjustment because college girls in physical education classes were able to name more of their classmates at the end of the semester than at the beginning. Participation in physical activity had been the cause advanced for increased sociality, although no causal relationship had been proved. The hyperactive physical social *lion* was revered . . . the happy productive introvert was abhorred despite some evidence that social hyperactivity may be reflective of neurotic behavior. The playfield does provide a dynamic workshop for social interaction, but so does the bridge game.

Other research indicated that boys scoring higher on personal adjustment scales had stronger grip strength scores. The implication? Of course, strengthen the grip and improve personal adjustment!! [13] It was assumed that because A was related to B, it must cause B. However, the logician would cry *post hoc, ergo propter hoc,* while the statistician would mutter that correlation is not causation.[18]

In 1956 Sputnik circled the world . . . shifts in educational goals occurred from emphasis upon producing an adjusted child to the development of curricula designed to fashion the productive child. Scientific mindedness replaced *well-roundedness* . . . math-science scholarships usurped athletic grants-in-aid as status symbols. Child rearing literature began to contain articles concerned with "Achievement Needs," "Reading at Two" and the role of the home in improving the child's learning capabilities.

Physical educators have not been slow to react. Spurred on by the theoretical pronouncements of a psychologist in the Mid-West, a school seating engineer in Florida, and a doctor of education in Philadelphia . . . it was discovered that motor activities contributed to an even wider variety of human capabilities than was dreamed about in the 1930's.[16, 14, 10, 3] Crawling improved hearing, speaking, thinking, seeing, perceiving, abstract thinking, and cognating. Walking a balance board aided reading by heightening laterality. *Physiological Optics, Neurological Organization,* and *Laterality-Directionality* supplemented bland educational terms. Rousseau's *recapitulation theory* appeared in a new suit.[17] The trampoline was raised in status from the prop of a carnival clown to the indispensable diagnostic tool of the clinical neurologist. The nervous system was reduced to four simple components that everyone could understand. Instead of handing their teacher an apple upon entering school each morning, children began the day by creeping around her desk.

But the presence of new theories have bred healthy controversy . . . and I believe raised several questions which demand answers. (1) Does one merely have the obligation to outline techniques for perceptual-motor training without providing a scientifically sound theory underlying these techniques? Is it important to know *why* you are doing something which *seems* to improve learning in the classroom? (2) What is the status of knowledge about the human nervous system, about learning, about motor activity, and about the interaction between classroom learning and movement activities? (3) What kinds of perceptual-motor training programs may enhance learning and which activities seem superfluous?

Elucidation of these questions is important because it seems to me that the type of parent and school district which quickly adopts new and controversial practices, i.e. crawling ten minutes a day . . . will be the same individuals and groups who, when subsequently failing to find the expected gains in measures of classroom learning success, will also be the first to relegate perceptual-motor activities back to their former underfinanced, understaffed, and *sweaty* position they previously held. And this I believe would be extremely unfortunate.

Let us then examine for a few moments the scientific validity of the practices and most important the tenability of the theories espoused by Kephart, Delacato and Harmon. This evaluation will be followed by some recommendations for positive action.

Basic to the correct application of the scientific method to the study of behavioral change is the determination of the influence of one variable at a time upon the performance measure under consideration. For if lots of things happen to people in a program of perceptual-motor training, is it not important to determine which of these really help, which are of no assistance, and which ones perhaps work against the expected objectives? Thus of paramount importance is to enumerate some of the variables which perhaps could influence relationships between A (crawling) and B (a reading improvement score). For example if we ask or require that a child crawl for thirty minutes (assuming that we do not ask him to do anything else) there are at least six accompanying factors which could change scores recorded on succeeding tasks. (1) The attention span might be lengthened, because the child has engaged in an activity longer than he usually attends to anything. (2) Personal rapport has been established between an instructor and his charge. An adult has been attentive to the child for a period of time. (3) Vigorous motor activity reduces biochemical indices of stress in the blood. Muscular tension decreases following exercise. The child becomes more relaxed. (4) Vigorous movements of the legs promote a heightened awareness of their location. They become stronger and begin to move more effectively in other tasks. (5) A *success syndrome* has been established; the child has perhaps accomplished something; while perhaps in the past he has performed poorly at nearly everything. (6) Most important, however, arising from these programs are positive and clear-cut formulas for improvement which undoubtedly aid in reducing parent-child tensions which are usually present, particularly when the child has a mild or severe perceptual-motor difficulty. The child perceives the parent acting positively, as opposed to rejecting or overprotecting him. A constructive course of action is apparently being taken to help improve his problem of which he is many times acutely aware.

Of equal importance is the examination of the theoretical underpinnings of some of these movement programs. The Philadelphian theory is widely published and discussed.[3] It is easy to understand because it is simple. Ontogeny parallels phylogeny . . . train the central nervous system rather than educate peripheral functions . . . neurologically *organize* the child by recapitulating his total development through practice of the gross movements which characterize various developmental stages. Five major deficiencies can be identified in this theoretical construct.

(1) The functioning of the nervous system is not as simple as it is assumed to be by the theory. Voluntary motor patterns are the product

of dynamic interactions of innumerable areas of the brain, some initiating, others suppressing, and others timing the actions.

Crawling, for example, is the product of a neuromotor *program* initiated in the cerebrum, involving both the associative and motor areas. The reticular system is involved via the general tension level accompanying the movement while the cerebellum may contribute to the smoothness of the act via involvement in certain of its timing components. The locomotor reflex, mediated at the spinal level, under-lies the gross characteristics of the cross-extension pattern evidenced in a normal crawling pattern.

Confirmation of this principle of dynamic interaction has been so thoroughly established in experimental neurology that it has been codi-fied as Hughling-Jackson's principle, i.e. motor output is a finite resultant of the interactions of several portions of the nervous system. Experimental evidence supporting this theory is obtained when a por-tion of the central nervous system is ablated, and then an attempt is made to assess the exact role of the structure damaged by observing motor output. The exact relationship between function and damage is rarely discernible as it is usually difficult to determine whether the ablated structure was a controlling mechanism, an inhibiting or a facilitating structure influencing the action pattern under consideration.

(2) There is a scarcity of data supporting the assumption that motor activity of the large postural and limb muscles affects the visual or the associative centers of the brain. While irradiation occurs be-tween neurons closely aligned, to hypothesize that a given set of nerve pathways somehow drastically changes other nerve pathways structurally or functionally which pass through a proximal portion of the central nervous system has little supportive evidence.

(3) The observational data which are advanced in support of these theoretical suppositions has been gained by clinicians watching the gross behavior of children, and then explaining their observations by hypothesizing neurological underpinnings. Physical educators and psychologists have engaged in this type of speculative neurology for years. It should be recognized for what it is, no matter where it occurs, or who utters it.

(4) This theory is based to a large degree upon the importance of establishing laterality and thus to improve complex symbolic behavior

and abstract reasoning. Some of the supportive evidence cited relates to the finding that the Australopithecine usually swung his bone club in his right hand when bashing out the brains of unfortunate baboons whom he encountered.[2] This four feet six inch, ninety-pound ape-man while possessing a round, human-like pelvis which enabled him to engage in erect locomotion could only boast of a cranial capacity which was less than one-third that of most modern men (600 cc as compared to 1500-2200 cc). Taken together these findings suggest that laterality has been with us for over 2,000,000 years. Thus Delacato postulates that a modern brain that has more than tripled in size has only to be *trained* by engaging in gross unilateral motor behavior that was characteristic of a subhuman living in South Africa about 2,000,000 years ago!

(5) Literature in child development provides a fifth source of information which is in conflict with Delacato's theories. Innumerable findings point to the superficiality of Delacato's observations with regard to the motor-mental development of children. Delacato suggests that the infant is *bound by his reflexes* when first born, although Preyer and others have found that the fetus evidences crude voluntary movements before birth. Delacato suggests that basic locomotor patterns proceed before the establishment of laterality, while Gierseke and others observe evidences of unilateral behavior based upon hand choice as early as seventeen weeks of age, well before the child has begun to creep. Gesell and the majority of child development experts state that children develop in a series of spirals, moving ahead in several types of behavior at a time, sometimes retrogressing and later *filling in* developmental skills rather than in the smooth, orderly sequence hypothesized by Delacato. Delacato seems unique in his observations concerning the characteristics of children's sleep patterns. All parents are aware of the multitude of positions that children fall into during a night's sleep. To suggest that a child who does not usually assume the tonic neck position may be headed for later problems is questionable. A child sleeping on his face *must* turn his head to one side to breathe, and due to the structural characteristics of the shoulder and hip region he *must* place his body in a position simulating a tonic neck position.

Others have advanced more palatable theoretical formulations which do not necessitate the assumption that the central nervous system is being trained by motor activities. Harmon and Kephart's theories are more peripheral in nature. They suggest that perceptual-motor training enhances classroom learning by adjusting and balancing postural tensions and by heightening the child's perceptions of his body, particularly left-right discrimination.[10, 11, 14] It is believed that these assumptions are supported by more valid evidence and are probably accepted by a reasonably large percent of the professional workers in education, psychotherapy, psychiatry, and psychology. The child development literature for the past thirty years supports the importance of sensory-motor experience in the early learning of children, while the importance of the body as the frame of reference from which perceptual judgments involving vision are formed has also been documented with some frequency in the experimental literature.[8, 9, 21]

However, these theories also lack sufficient concrete experimental evidence indicating *which* of the varied techniques suggested are actually affecting various perceptual attributes. Harmon, for example, published data which indicated that learning in the experimental classrooms in Winter Haven, Florida showed only slight improvement over that evidenced in the *control* classrooms.[11]

But what evidence *is* available which will shed some light upon the nature of motor activity and its possible relationship to classroom learning? The neurological journals, child development monographs, and experiments from the psychological laboratories for the past seventy-five years have fortunately contributed findings which do relate to these problem areas. So let us enumerate some of these and then from them attempt to derive a purposeful course of action which is suggested by this evidence.

Finding

The motor attributes of children are highly specific and tend to become more so with age and experience. For example, there are at least three kinds of balances, four kinds of strengths, several kinds of attributes involving agility and power. Manual dexterity may be factored into at least five components.[4, 5, 6, 7] A child may have a strong grip and a weak mid-section; or perhaps be able to balance well while standing still on one foot, but he quickly falls off when attempting to traverse a narrow balance beam.

Implication for Action. To properly evaluate and to improve the perceptual-motor ability of children one should engage in a number of tasks involving balance, agility, hand-eye coordination, manual dexterity, strength, and flexibility, depending upon the deficiencies assessed.

Finding

Perceptual judgments and motor functioning are at times impossible to separate. For example, catching a ball involves the visual tracking of a moving object in three-dimensional space, perceptually anticipating its pathway while moving the body to intersect it, and then placing the hands in proper catching position.

Implication for Action. Perception probably is being trained while engaging in many movement experiences. Handwriting, ball throwing, and visually tracking the words across a written page from left to right are not purely perceptual or motor acts but should be termed perceptual-motor tasks.

Finding

Muscular tension facilitates direct forceful acts, while inhibiting complex coordinations.

Implication for Action. To improve the perceptual-motor performance of a child, place him in a situation where social-emotional *tone* does not contribute to muscular tension if you expect him to learn complex skills.

Finding

Complex tasks many times can be learned by children with severe perceptual-motor problems if the skills are reduced to simple components and the child is reinforced, i.e. given reassurance from the instructor, etc. when even slight improvement is evidenced.[12]

Implication for Action. When working with children with mild to severe problems, reduce the tasks to basic components, and when these are mastered proceed to build up more complex response patterns upon these beginnings.

Finding

The manner in which the child perceives his body, moves his body, and locates and uses his body parts influences learning during early childhood.[21]

Implication for Action. Work with basic perceptual tasks prior to proceeding to more complex ones (i.e. reading). Find out if the child can locate his body relative to an object (i.e. stand in front of that box, put your left side toward the line/engage in tumbling tasks, trampolining, and other similar activities which will serve to heighten awareness of the large surfaces of the body. Require verbal feedback from the child as he identifies his hands, wrists, knees, etc., and engages in unilateral activities to heighten the ability to make different left-right judgments about his body. By constructing a solid *body platform*, a base is provided from which accurate and more complex judgments may then be made.

Finding

Often more important than the performance level in a task is how the individual *feels* about his level of achievement. Success is measured not in absolutes but in comparison with real or hypothesized norms.[1] If the individual perceives himself continually failing, an overlay of emotional-muscular tension results which further impedes learning.

Implication for Action. To heighten an individual's self-concept provide a situation in which he experiences success, even though slight. Success is related to the values of the individual performing. Thus, a boy between the ages of five to fifteen, whose peers highly regard prowess in sports can be expected to base a large portion of his self-concept upon his success or failure in physical activities. Thus, to heighten a youngster's self-concept part of his educational program should be devoted to improving socially valued physical skills. There is evidence that a *failure syndrome* on the playground will begin to generalize to the classroom . . . and that success in sports may also transfer to other behavior.

CONCLUSIONS

As you have been able to observe, I agree with some of the practices and theories which have been recently advanced while questioning others. We should, I believe, be critical but open-minded. Professional people visiting Philadelphia usually come away impressed; improve-

404 Contemporary Readings In Sport Psychology

ment does seem to take place in the concomitant behavior of children subjected to programs of motor training. But we should not overact. While some of these theories are difficult to defend with reference to available experimental evidence, perhaps some components of the practices arising from them do indeed influence the nervous system in ways not fully understood at the present time.

Those of us in universities with research budgets and the time to carry out well-controlled studies need to persist in our efforts to sub- stantiate or negate some of the theoretical assumptions advanced and the practices arising from them. And hopefully through these means, new and important dimensions will be reached in our service to children.

The movements people engage in are important. They comprise that component of overall behavior which others can see and react to. To a large degree the self-concept is based upon what a person can do with his body. And yet movement is not the key from which all the mental, emotional, and social facets of personality must neces- sarily stem.[1] Perceptual-motor malfunctions of a mild or severe nature can be caused by lesions in the nervous system, by biochemical im- balances, and/or can be attributed to deep-seated emotional problems. There is little evidence that any of these causative agents can be in- fluenced by crawling on the floor.

The key to helping a child with learning problems is to first attempt to understand the child. Improvement in behavior of people cannot be gained by inserting them into a formula. We should synthesize available knowledge, not ignore it. The answer to complexity is not a retreat to simplicity.

REFERENCES

1. CRATTY, BRYANT J.: *Movement Behavior and Motor Learning.* Philadel- phia, Lea and Febiger, 1964.

2. DARWIN, C.: *Adventures with the Missing Link.* New York, Harper, 1959.

3. DELACATO, CARL H.: *The Diagnosis and Treatment of Speech and Reading Problems.* Springfield, Thomas, 1964.

4. FLEISCHMAN, E. A.: The dimensions of physical fitness—the nation-wide normative and developmental study of basic tests. Technical Report No. 4, The Office of Naval Research, Department of Industrial Administra- tion and Department of Psychology, Yale, New Haven, August 1962.

5. FLEISCHMAN, E. A., and ELLISON, GAYLOR D.: A factor analysis of fine manipulative tests. *J Applied Psych, 46*:96-105, 1962.

6. FLEISCHMAN, E. A.; KREMER, ELMAR J., and SHOUP, GUY W.: The dimensions of physical fitness—A factor analysis of strength tests. Technical Report No. 2, The Office of Naval Research, Department of Industrial Administration and Department of Psychology, Yale, New Haven, August 1961.

7. FLEISCHMAN, E. A.: Factorial analysis of complex psychomotor performance and related skills, *J Applied Psych, 40*:2, 1956.

8. FROSTIG, MARIANNE, and HORNE, DAVID: *The Frostig Program for the Development of Visual Perception: Teacher's Guide.* Chicago, Follett, 1964.

9. GESELL, ARNOLD: *Vision.* New York, Hoeber, 1949.

10. HARMON, DARELL BOYD: *Notes on a Dynamic Theory of Vision,* vol. 1, Published by the Author, 1958.

11. HARMON, DARELL BOYD: *Winter Haven Study of Perceptual Learning.* Winter Haven Lions Research Foundation, Inc., Winter Haven Lions Club, Winter Haven, 1962.

12. HIRSCH, WILLIAM: *Motor Skill Transfer by Trainable Mentally Retarded and Normal Children.* Doctoral Dissertation, U of Calif, 1965.

13. JONES, HAROLD E.: Physical ability as a factor in social adjustment in adolescence. *J Ed Res, 40*:287-301, 1946.

14. KEPHART, NEWELL C.: *The Slow Learner in the Classroom.* Columbus, Merrill Books, 1960.

15. PIAGET, JEAN: *The Construction of Reality in the Child.* New York, Basic Books, 1954.

16. RADLER, D. H., and KEPHART, NEWELL C.: *Success Through Play.* New York, Harper, 1963.

17. ROUSSEAU, J. J.: *Emile* or *Education.* Translated by B. Foxley. London, J. M. Dent and Sons, 1911.

18. SLATER-HAMMEL, A. T.: Problem of evidence in research. Speech given to the International Federation of Sports Psychology. Rome, April 1965.

19. STOLTZ, H. R., and STOLTZ, L. M.: Adolescent problems related to somatic variations. In: *Adolescence,* 43rd Yearbook N.S.S.E. Part I. Chicago, U of Chicago, 1944.

20. WAPNER, SEYMOUR, and WERNER, HEINZ: *Perceptual Development, An Investigation Within the Framework of Sensory-Tonic Field Theory.* Clark U., 1957.

Chapter 37

INFLUENCE OF THE HAWTHORNE EFFECT UPON PHYSICAL EDUCATION RESEARCH*

Dale L. Hanson

INTRODUCTION

THE CONCEPT of the so-called *Hawthorne effect* emerged from research that was conducted at the Western Electric Company's Hawthorne plant in Chicago during the late twenties and early thirties of this century. Interest centered on discovering working conditions most conducive to the increased productivity of employees doing factory assembly work. The physiological variable of fatigue was not at issue here having been satisfactorily studied in earlier research. Focus was on the broader phenomenon of motivation and the effect of boredom or monotony on production.

Six girls working in a special observation room, called the *relay assembly,* were subjected to various experimental conditions. In an attempt to create a *natural situation* they were urged to work at a comfortable pace and under no circumstances to try to make a race out of the task. Variables were introduced which were presumed to affect production. It was found that it did not matter whether the variables were present or absent, the productivity of the six girls continued to rise over the two-year period of the experiment. This finding supported an earlier study of the effects of changing room illumination. Output rose during increased illumination, as might be expected. Contrary to prediction, it remained high even when illumination became so low it approximated bright moonlight. In both the illumination and relay assembly room experiments, it was found that workers produced beyond the management's expectations.[3, 4]

---

* D. L. Hanson: Influence of the Hawthorne effect upon physical education research. *Res Quart Amer Ass Health Phys Educ, 38*:1967, 723-724, 1967. Reproduced here with the permission of the author and the American Association for Health, Physical Education, and Recreation.

It was hypothesized that the special attention and treatment afforded these workers resulted in the development of an informal social organization with its own morale and common purpose. The existence of these new social forces served to enhance the favorable reaction of the individual operators to the experimental situation and to create new drives to increased output.[5] They became *insiders* as against *outsiders* and their increased motivation resulted in greater productivity.

One wonders if the *Hawthorne effect* appears in physical education research where experimental groups are set aside for special treatment, especially when the research task demands optimal motivation as would be the case for endurance study. Such curiosity prompted the reporting of the following studies:

Investigation I—Turner[7] divided thirty male college students of low motor fitness into two groups. The subjects of one group were given instruction on an individual basis with minimal opportunity allowed for group interaction. Subjects in the second group were instructed on a group basis exclusively, with maximal opportunity given for group interaction. The instruction and training exercises were identical; only the approaches differed. Within group improvement on a 600-yard run was significant at the .01 level for both groups; $t = 3.97$ and $t = 4.09$ for individual-centered and group-centered approaches, respectively. Improvement in the 600-yard run for the group-centered class was significantly greater at the .05 level than for the individual-centered class ($t = 2.14$).

Investigation II—Bruess[1] met with a group of fifteen male college students three times each week for six weeks following the administration of a muscular endurance test. The students were given a placebo each meeting period and engaged in discussion about its effect on their physical vitality. They were told that the placebo might increase their indurance. No training was provided and the subjects were restricted in physical activity throughout the experimental period. After 6 weeks, the group was retested for muscular endurance using a 23-pound load in the performance of forearm curls at a rate of 120 curls per minute. The mean improvement for the group was 18.86 curls; significant at the .01 level, with $t = 8.30$.

Investigation III—Hanson and Walker[2] tested twenty-four male college freshmen subjects for bench-stepping endurance on an 18-inch bench at forty steps per minute. A metal rod was horizontally extended above the subjects' heads which was touched each step-up to ensure a full leg extension. On the basis of random placement, two groups were formed. One group, the experimental group, met in street clothing three times weekly with the author to receive a fructose placebo and to discuss its apparent effect on their endurance. Group interaction was encouraged. Further attention was not given the control group. Four weeks later, both groups were retested for bench-stepping endurance in the before-mentioned manner. A one-tailed t-test was applied to the data as the author was interested in determining if significant increases in endurance resulted from the treatment.[6] The gains of the experimental group were significantly greater at the .05 level than the gains of the control group ($t = 1.75$).

DISCUSSION

The results of these three studies parallel the illumination and relay assembly room findings of the Hawthorne research. In one instance, the group-centered approach to endurance training provided significantly greater increases than did an individual-centered approach, even though training programs were similar. The use of special attention and placebos resulted in significant gains in forearm curl endurance with a similar approach resulting in significantly greater gains for an experimental group in bench-stepping endurance. It appears that it is possible to develop an *in-group* with increased motivation to perform endurance tasks.

The purpose of this study was to alert the reader to the Hawthorne effect, and to suggest possible implications to physical education research. It can be argued that the implications are minimal because our physical tasks are not at all similar to the piece work of industry, our testing time is minimal compared to the extensive time involved in determining industrial output, and our group interaction opportunities are more limited. Certainly these differences, as well as others, are important. The fact remains, however, that the Hawthorne effect can contribute to the improvement of physical performance. For this reason, it should prove fruitful for the researcher to consider its possible effect when designing experiments and interpreting findings.

REFERENCES

1. BRUESS, CLINT EDWARD: *The effects of training with two different programs of resistance loads upon muscuar endurance.* Unpublished master's thesis, U of Maryland, 1965.
2. HANSON, DALE, and WALKER, ROSS: Testing for the Hawthorne effect in a bench-stepping endurance event. Unpublished research, 1965.
3. HOMANS, GEORGE C.: *The Human Group.* New York, Harcourt, 1950.
4. OLMSTED, MICHAEL S.: *The Small Group.* New York, Random, 1959.
5. ROETHLISBERGER, FRITZ JULES, and DICKSON, WILLIAM JOHN: *Management and the Worker.* Cambridge, Harvard, 1939.
6. SLATER-HAMMEL, A. T.: The one-tailed test in physical education research. *Res Quart Amer Ass Health Phys Educ, 29*:117-19, 1958.
7. TURNER, EDWARD T.: *A comparative study of the effects of individualized and group instruction on motor fitness of low motor fitness college males.* Unpublished master's thesis, U of Maryland, 1965.

Chapter 38

HYPNOSIS AND MUSCULAR PERFORMANCE*

Warren R. Johnson**

In this paper I shall (1) review the experimental literature on hypnosis in relation to gross muscular performance, (2) illustrate some ways in which hypnosis has been useful to athletes, (3) suggest some uses of hypnosis as an experimental tool, and (4) endeavor to answer several questions concerning the use of hypnosis in sports competition.

Although in popular opinion hypnosis bestows superhuman powers and although some subjects do, indeed, display marked increments in performance under certain hypnotic conditions, the fact remains that the controlled studies conducted to date do not present clear-cut or consistent evidence of heightened performance in the hypnotic or posthypnotic states. Reviews by Hull [7] (1933), Gorton [5] (1949) and Crasilneck and Hall [2] (1959) dealing with the physiology of hypnosis include brief discussions concerning muscular performance. The conclusions reached by these reviewers were necessarily based upon experiments which involved small muscle and usually mild work, and few subjects. In those studies criteria of depth of trance were usually not clearly specified; the exact suggestions given were usually not reported; and it is often not possible to determine just what role hypnosis actually played in the experiments. A single short review concerned with hypnosis as it might relate to performance in sports is available (1960). [1]

Studies which have included measures of large muscle work, rigorous controls and reasonably large numbers of subjects have produced

* W. R. Johnson: Hypnosis and muscular performance. *J Sports Med and Physical Fitness, 1*: 1961, 71-79. Reproduced here with the permission of the author and publisher.

** Appreciation is expressed to Milton Erickson, M.D., of Phoenix, Arizona, for his critical reading of this paper.

evidence decidedly favorable to the hypnotic state. Roush, whose study is unique with respect to its large number of subjects—twenty— and very severe criteria of trance depth, reported statistically significant advantages to the hypnotic state in all her tests—grip strength, elbow flexion strength and a hanging by hands test of endurance.[17] Similarly, Hottinger found that the performance of his six subjects improved significantly in the hypnotic state in tests of back and leg strength and appreciably in the Sargent jump. However, their grip strength did not improve.[6] In a third study involving seven students, Ikai and Steinhaus reported results highly favorable to performance following hypnosis,[18] but hypnotic controls were not specified in detail.

On the other hand, Orne found that if sufficiently well-motivated, all of his nine subjects were able to hold a kilogram weight at arm's length longer in the nonhypnotic state even though his hypnotic suggestions were calculated to elicit maximum performance.[16] (Incidentally, Orne's paper, "The Nature of Hypnosis: Artifact and Essence" should be studied by anyone seriously interested in the range of methodological problems and pressing questions confronting research workers in hypnosis.) Our own studies of strength, endurance, and power in the nonhypnotic, hypnotic and posthypnotic states have also resulted in generally negative findings; however, there were indications that endurance performance (supine press of a 47 pound barbell to exhaustion) improved when hypnosis was introduced. Our only consistently positive findings have occurred when negative suggestions were given. That is, we have always been successful when we have given suggestions designed to make performance worse than usual.

Our experimental studies of the effects of hypnotic suggestions upon physical performance may be summarized as follows.

In our first experiment entitled "The Effects of Post-Hypnotic Suggestions on All-Out Effort of Short Duration," [12] the particular suggestions did not improve the performance of the subjects in an all-out dash of 100 revolutions on the bicycle ergometer set for 26.8 pounds resistance, (average time about 40 seconds). It is interesting to note, however, that these subjects invariably reported feeling better after the ride when the posthypnotic suggestions were given even though they had no recollection at nonhypnotic levels that suggestions had been given to them at all. Interestingly, this is apparently the only reported experimental study of hypnosis which has included severe respiratory and circulatory as well as gross muscle responses.

In a second study,[11] stereotyped hypnotic and posthypnotic suggestions designed to contain both cognitive and affective elements and presented at both deep and light trance levels as well as in the nonhypnotic state did not result in statistically significant improvements in the performance of twelve subjects. The physical tests were grip strength, Sargent jump and supine press to exhaustion of a forty-seven-pound barbell. However, although the group performance was not significantly different in the various conditions of the study, the performance of one subject in the supine press test was quite remarkable and his scores had to be excluded from the statistical analysis.

This subject was a professional football player and habitual weight trainer weighing about 235 pounds and having a mesomorphic body type of perhaps 5-7-1 by the Sheldon system. Like the rest of the subjects he had practiced the supine press in advance of the study so as to plateau his scores and to insure against muscular soreness during the study. In his first testing session, the suggestions were given but hypnosis was not utilized; his score was about as usual, 130. Hypnosis was then introduced and in the next three testings his scores were 180 (when he was stopped by the investigator), 230 and 333 respectively. In contrast, the next strongest athlete began the study at fifty-seven presses and reached a maximum of seventy-five.

To determine whether this individual was dependent upon hypnosis to perform in this way, he was later retested without hypnosis and was stopped by the investigator at 350 presses. Prior to this testing he spoke of having an entirely new idea of his potentialities and was absolutely certain that he could surpass his old record. It is noted that he recovered quickly after each exercise bout and reported a complete freedom from muscle soreness.

Some months later it was possible to employ the technique of age regression to ascertain possible reasons for the sudden tapping of performance resources. (In hypnotic age regression the subject does not *remember* in the ordinary sense, but presumably relives events of his past. Penfield has elicited what appears to be similar behavior by means of electrical stimulation of the temporal lobes.) When led to relive and verbalize his first trance state test this subject gave a distinct impression of having accepted the suggestions as vivid reality and apparently his performance, became literally, a matter of life and death to him. In the age regression to that first performance in hypnosis he confirmed what he had said after his posthypnotic performance. That is, he would give up in complete fatigue and then watch in amazement as his arms continued to raise the weight, seemingly by themselves.

A common explanation of heightened performance in the hypnotic state is that suggestibility is increased, inhibitions are removed and there may be selective anesthesia for pain and fatigue. However, this case led to the speculation that Gellhorn's explanation of exceptional muscular performance under conditions of emotional excitement might also have application to exceptional performance in the hypnotic state. That is, it may be "due not only to the action of the adrenal medullary secretions on the striated muscles but also to the intensification of discharges from the motor cortex resulting from impulses which reach the motor cortex from the hypothalamus." [4]

In a third experiment, when different types of hypnotic and posthypnotic suggestions were compared as to their effectiveness in altering performance in a test of endurance—the supine press to exhaustion of a forty-seven-pound barbell—it was found that although moderate *pep talk* type suggestions seemed to get better results with most subjects than more quietly reasoned suggestions or suggestions intended to take effect posthypnotically in response to a signal while the subjects exercised, this advantage was not at statistically significant levels. However, posthypnotic suggestions designed to deteriorate performance were invariably successful. This was true in spite of the fact that the subjects had no posthypnotic recall that such suggestions had been given to them, and they were completely mystified that their most desperate efforts failed to bring their performance up to customary levels.

So much for our very modest list of experimental studies. I will now briefly describe two case studies which illustrate quite different ways in which hypnosis may be used to affect gross motor performance. I would like to emphasize that although a number of subjects are not involved, I attach great importance to case studies which may reveal potentialities of the human nervous system.

In the first of these which was published with the title, "Body Movement Awareness in the Non-Hypnotic and Hypnotic States," [9] exceptional ability to verbalize complex bodily movement in the hypnotic state was demonstrated. A very successful baseball player requested assistance in getting out of a protracted batting slump. Before being hypnotized, he was asked to describe in detail just what had gone wrong with his batting; but he was unable to do this in spite of much effort to describe and demonstrate physically the several movements. Subsequently in the deep trance state and with instructions to verbalize spontaneously at a signal, the subject—to his own complete surprise—was able to make a meticulous analysis of his movements while batting and to pinpoint a number of errors of foot work, pelvic rotation, grip on the bat, timing of swing and use of his eyes. Moreover, when given a choice as to whether to recall this analysis posthypnotically or to have it more gradually *come to him* as he played, he elected the latter more gradual and less self-conscious choice.

This man's batting—which this investigator has at no time observed —immediately improved and he finished the season with a 400 average. Of psychological interest is the fact that when he returned to report on his season he attributed the entire analysis to the investigator and was quite sure that he remembered receiving direct and specific suggestions to correct his movements. To repeat, however, he alone was responsible for his corrective analysis. One must wonder at the extent to which vague or uncertain bodily states might be verbalized under hypnotic conditions such as these.

The second case study was published under the title "Hypnotic Analysis of a Case of Aggression Blockage in Baseball Pitching." [8] A professional baseball pitcher requested hypnotic suggestions which would make him more aggressive when he played because he could perform at his best only when he was unreasonably angry. Since psychiatric evaluation of this man did not contraindicate approaching the problem at hypnotic levels, he was trained to enter a deep trance and, in due course, to experience age regression.

When regressed to childhood he revealed that he had severely injured his younger brother and that the experience was especially painful to him bcause he had escaped punishment. This event seemed to provide the model of the cycle of rage, attack, guilt reaction and aggression avoidance which was later to manifest in the sport situation. That is, the rage which accompanied successful pitching was followed by a severe but unconscious guilt reaction from which the subject protected himself in subsequent games by *easy going* and *lackadaisical* play until, finally, his hostile feelings would build up and spill over in another highly successful rage.

This subject was soon able to realize that aggressive behavior need not be antisocial or unsportsmanlike and need not be followed by feelings of guilt. He was then able to pitch consistently well throughout the season with no further recurrence of the rage-guilt reaction cycle.

Before turning to the question and answer portion of my paper, I would like to describe a use of hypnosis as an experimental tool which I believe has a place in, for example, certain fatigue and nutrition studies. The phenomenon of posthypnotic amnesia makes possible the obliteration from conscious recall of what occurs in the trance state. In a recently published study of warm-up,[13] when the subjects were tested on the bicycle ergometer, it was always posthypnotically such that they were unaware they had warmed up or not; and, indeed, they remained in ignorance, at nonhypnotic levels at least, as to the nature of the study. Similarly, in food deprivation studies it would be possible to keep subjects in ignorance of whether or not they had eaten or how much or what; and it would be possible to give suggestions which would increase or reduce feelings of hunger regardless of whether or not food were eaten.

It is presumed—and I stress this emphatically—that any such research would be under strict medical supervision.

Let us turn now to several questions which my students have helped me to identify as being of special interest.

(1) **Question.** How might the discrepancies in the published reports concerning the effects of hypnosis on muscular performance be explained?

Answer. There are a number of possibilities. The most obvious are those related to experimental controls. For example, how about the trance depth? It is perhaps significant that Roush imposed the most rigid criteria of deep trance hypnosis that I am aware of in a study—and her findings were uniformly favorable to the hypnotic state. (In this regard it is important to realize that there are many degrees of trance depth ranging from the very light—in which the subject is well aware of his surroundings—to the very deep stuporous condition of the profound trance.) How about the suggestions given and their mode of presentation? The most dramatic improvement in performance that we have observed was in response to stereotyped suggestions, calmly stated and designed to persuade the subjects to do their best; but I am under the impression that efforts to *whip up* subjects with even very moderate *pep talk* type suggestions such as we used are more likely to be effective with most subjects. How about the possibility that a subject is faking hypnosis? Orne has shown that experienced hypnotists can be fooled by subjects who know relatively little about hypnosis.[16] How about the physical fitness level of the subjects? Although this consideration has not been tested experimentally and no study that I am aware of mentions the physical fitness level of the subjects, my experience has led me to suspect that hypnotic suggestions are more likely to improve the strength performance of nonathletes than of athletes; and conversely, that hypnotic suggestions are more likely to improve the endurance performance of athletes than nonathletes. If these observations are correct, it is probably because by training, athletes already know how to require something approaching maximum contraction from their striated muscles; and in regard to endurance, the athletes can stay with a task long enough to become bored and/or uncomfortable with it and are likely to be helped by suggestions which minimize discomfort and divert attention from the unpleasant side effects of the task. At any rate, nearly all of the subjects in our studies have been athletes and I gather that most of those involved in the other published studies have been nonathletes.

(2) **Question.** To what extent is hypnosis used by athletes today?

Answer. One can only speculate. Some psychologists, psychiatrists, and professional hypnotists have told me that over the years they have, on occasion, helped athletes in various ways. The recent publicity given to hypnosis, coupled with the popular impression that hypnosis bestows something like magical powers, has doubtless led many athletes to seek out this kind of assistance. Of course a few such instances have been publicized but most have not.

(3) **Question.** Has hypnosis actually helped athletes to perform better?

Answer. Yes, in a variety of ways some of which have nothing to do with increasing strength or endurance. And, of course, it has also failed to do so. There is no question in my mind that the baseball players referred to earlier in this paper were helped by their respective analyses at hypnotic levels. Many other examples of what appear to be improved performance due to hypnosis could be given; but I will mention only a few.

A renowned medical hypnotist told me recently of his having done such things as increase the aggressiveness and confidence of some athletes, improve the steadiness of marksmen and the performance of a shot-putter. An Australian psychiatrist and former champion swimmer has described to me the work with hypnosis of a physiologist-swimming coach in Australia; and he was quite confident that this man had helped his swimmers gain the self-assurance and self-discipline needed for high level performance in competition. This psychiatrist, by the way, was unequivocal in his belief that the Australian coach had used hypnosis quite legitimately, for it had merely helped the athletes achieve something like their full potential. Gale, a medical hypnotist, has described uses of hypnosis in sports along lines of relaxing athletes and helping them learn skills.[3] Other hypnotists have reported having helped athletes adjust more adequately to the rigors of training, sleep better, gain weight and so on. As far as I know no one has claimed to have elevated a mediocre talent to champion level performance by hypnosis.

When an athlete performs well after having received hypnotic suggestions it is always possible to raise the question: Might he not have done just as well on that occasion if hypnosis had not been employed? This question is unanswerable. Sports like track and swimming would provide an excellent testing ground for studying the entire question experimentally; but sports in which one is working directly against an opponent—sports like wrestling, boxing and football—would be useless in this regard because they lack controllable conditions.

(4) **Question.** Is it actually possible to increase the aggressiveness of athletes by hypnosis; and if so is it safe to do so?

Answer. Two men who deserve to be called authorities on hypnosis, one a psychiatrist and the other a psychologist, have told me of having done so successfully. Both were quite confident that no harm was done to the athletes psychologically. Indeed, the medical hypnotist explained that the only ill effect that he had observed in such cases was that the athletes were subsequently somewhat more difficult to hypnotize.

Now these men were professionally qualified to make judgments regarding the basic mental health of their subjects and the advisability of using hypnosis in this way. But generally speaking I am under the impression that students of mental health would recommend extreme caution when considering the matter of manipulating aggressiveness, for this is certainly one of man's fundamental conflicts and is often a major consideration in the behavior disorders. I personally have never been willing to use hypnosis in this way without psychiatric participation. However, I have asked quite a few subjects in deep trance states how suggestions designed to make them more aggressive in sports would make them feel. All were happy with the idea and wanted suggestions which would encourage them to be more aggressive in a sportsmanlike way. On the other hand, all but one felt threatened by the idea of receiving suggestions which might encourage unsportsmanlike aggressiveness; and typically they would begin to emerge spontaneously from the trance unless reassured that no such suggestions were intended. I have encountered only one athlete who did not care whether suggestions given to him would make him more aggressive in antisocial as well as social ways. The meaner the better was his motto. At any rate, it seems noteworthy that suggestions designed to heighten sportsmanlike aggressiveness were invariably acceptable and desired.

This question of the effects of hypnotic suggestions upon aggressive behavior can be studied experimentally with built-in safeguards to protect the welfare of the subjects.

(5) **Question.** When changes in behavior are brought about by means of hypnosis, do these changes last or are they transitory?

Answer. When hypnosis is used in therapy, its effects are sometimes lasting and sometimes not; and I suspect that the same is true of its use in relation to physical performance. If a change is for the better and is rewarding to the subject, then one might expect the behavior to be self-perpetuating. The professional football player referred to earlier who performed so remarkably in the endurance test when given hypnotic suggestions told of acquiring a new concept of his capabilities when he saw what he could do. Rightly or wrongly, he felt too that this new self concept was related to his subsequent achieving of first string all-star standing.

Be that as it may, experienced people with whom I have talked about this matter are inclined to think of hypnotic effects lasting for appreciable periods, especially if the suggestions are reinforced occasionally. Still, there are many cases in which nonreinforced, hypnotically induced changes have lasted for years.

(6) **Question.** Assuming that improvement in some muscular performance is accomplished by hypnosis, could not some other technique such as a pep talk, greater discipline or a drug have done just as well?

Answer. This is another unanswerable question; but it is like asking: Although penicillin stopped this infection, might not some other treatment have worked just as well? Penicillin is no less valuable because other means may also get results.

(7) **Question.** Does improving performance by hypnosis bring about dependency on it?

Answer. This has not been my experience nor that of other experienced persons with whom I have talked concerning the reactions of normal people. However, many people feel exceptionally good and relaxed after having been *hypnotized* and enjoy repeating the experience because it is gratifying to them.

(8) **Question.** Is it safe to hypnotize athletes?

Answer. The present state of uncertainty on this question is suggested by the fact that a recent article in a medical publication argued both that (1) hypnosis is dangerous because it may make athletes go beyond their limits and damage themselves and (2) hypnosis is useless because all it can do is help athletes attain their potential.[14]

My feeling is that it is not possible to give a yes or no answer to this question without knowing the circumstances in specific cases. One would have to know *how* hypnosis was used. None of the several psychiatrists—including the one who worked with me—who know of my previously mentioned work with the baseball players seemed to see anything hazardous in those hypnotic analyses; and neither young man seems to have suffered from the experience. Quite the contrary. These appear to be examples of cases in which hypnosis was definitely instrumental in improving performance in competition. Moreover, the sports-minded psychologists and psychiatrists with whom I have discussed this matter have all felt that the cases which they have participated in or observed were not hazardous to the athletes.

On the other hand, it is exceedingly important to emphasize that there may be very serious dangers associated with hypnosis even though the subjects are *known* to be in good mental health. For this reason I believe that it would be extremely unfortunate if coaches generally were to feel free to begin hypnotizing their athletes in the hope of improving their performance. Nothing that I have said in this paper should be interpreted to mean that I would encourage such a development. Following are some of my reasons for feeling this way.

Although there is far from universal agreement as to the nature or effects of hypnosis, I suspect that most experienced hypnotists would agree that generally speaking it is easier to make people sick than it is to make them well. That is, a healthy person can be made to feel very bad in a variety of ways by means of hypnotic suggestions, but one cannot be at all sure in advance that hypnotic suggestions will cure any given ill person. Moreover, it may be recalled that in a controlled experiment, our suggestions designed to damage physical performance were always successful—which was certainly not the case with our suggestions intended to improve performance. Considerations like these have led me to conclude that people tend to respond better to suggestions that will have a negative effect on them than to those intended to have a positive effect. I have wondered whether this situation might be due to our traditional methods of child rearing in which the young are led (or programmed) to believe that they have been or are chronically on the verge of being *bad,* in danger or sick.

At any rate, if one is to claim that hypnosis can increase muscular performance, improve self-confidence, reduce nervousness, and so on, he must also take into account the other side of the coin which warns that hypnosis can be used with greater probability of success to make such things worse.

Monroe, who has written on the possible dangers of hypnosis in medicine, has said: "It seems to the author axiomatic that any medicine or medical procedure that can be good for the patient might also be bad. Anyone who has observed the hypnotic trance is aware of the intense suggestibility and increased cooperation of the subject. . . . such increased cooperation might under certain circumstances be exploited by the unethical." [15] I would add to this the thought that this increased cooperation might also be exploited by the well-intentioned but ignorant, insensitive or careless. Thus, to cite one of many possible examples of the misuse of hypnosis, a woman physician recently told me that she attempted, by direct hypnotic suggestions, to *dispose of* a patient's nightmares—and of course profoundly upset the patient. Similar problems could and undoubtedly would arise in sports if coaches were to feel free to begin using hypnosis without intensive training and clear understanding as to its appropriate and inappropriate uses.

Another very important factor bearing upon whether or not hypnosis is safe is the hypnotist himself. What kind of personality should he have? The enormously respected behavior scientist Hilgard, who is now conducting intensive research on hypnosis at Stanford, commented in a personal communication: "Any investigation that intrudes as much as hypnosis does into the life of an individual must be conducted by mature and sensitive people. Under these circumstances I see no danger in it." Obviously, these qualities—which of course are not guaranteed by academic or professional degrees—must be coupled with suitable training in hypnotic technique and study of personality functioning.

CONCLUSIONS

The basic purpose of this paper is to encourage a variety of research projects which will shed light upon the nature and potentialities of hypnosis with reference to physical performance.

It is popularly believed that to *hypnotize* an athlete is to attempt to supercharge him by direct suggestions in something of the manner of a stimulating drug. This paper is intended to point out that direct suggestions designed to improve muscular strength and/or endurance cannot be counted upon to be effective—although under certain conditions they may be; and it is intended to emphasize that hypnotic or posthypnotic suggestions designed to reduce physical performance are much more likely to be effective. A further intent of this paper is to illustrate a number of uses of hypnosis in relation to physical performance and research which have nothing whatever to do with stimulating individuals to greater effort. These uses may have to do with investigating certain neuromuscular and psychological problems which may profoundly affect and perhaps limit physical performance, or they may have to do with controlling the psychological variable in certain types of experiments.

Finally, although this paper is intended to expand the general understanding of hypnosis and its applications in the study of human performance, it is not intended to encourage its use by individuals lacking training not only in hypnotic technique but in psychodynamics as well.

REFERENCES

1. COFER, CHARLES N., and JOHNSON, WARREN R.: Personality Dynamics in Relation to Exercise and Sports. Chapter in Science and Medicine of Exercise and Sports. Johnson, Warren R. (Ed.), N.Y., Harper, 1960.
2. CRASILNECK, HAROLD B., and JAMES A. HALL: *Physiological Changes Associated with Hypnosis: A Review of the Literature since 1948. J Clin and Exper Hypnosis, 7*:9-50, January 1959.
3. GALE, CONDAR K.: Quoted in *Hypnosis May Help Athletes Learn Skills.* Scope Weekly, Upjohn, March 9, 1960.
4. GELLHORN, ERNST: Physiology of the Supraspinal Mechanisms. *Science and Medicine of Exercise and Sports,* Warren R. Johnson (Ed.) N. Y., Harper, 1960.
5. GORTON, BERNARD E.: The physiology of hypnosis. *Psych Quart. 23* (Part I) : 457-485, July, 1949.
6. HOTTINGER, WILLIAM L.: *The Effect of Waking and Hypnotic Suggestions on Strength.* Master's Thesis, Urbana, U of Ill, 1958.
7. HULL, CLARK L.: *Hypnosis and Suggestibility.* N. Y., D. Appleton-Century, 1933.
8. JOHNSON, WARREN R.: Hypnotic analysis of a case of aggression blockage in baseball pitching. *Amer J of Clin Hypnosis.* October, 1961.
9. JOHNSON, WARREN R.: Body movement awareness in the non-hypnotic and hypnotic states. *Res Quart Amer Ass Health Phys Educ, 32*: May, 1961.

10. JOHNSON, WARREN R., and KRAMER, GEORGE F.: Effects of different types of hypnotic suggestions upon physical performance. *Res Quart Amer Ass Health Phys Educ, 31*:469-473, October, 1960.

11. JOHNSON, WARREN R., and KRAMER, GEORGE F.: Effects of stereotyped non-hypnotic, hypnotic and post-hypnotic suggestions upon strength, power and endurance, *32*:522-29. *Res Quart Amer Ass Health Phys Educ,* 1961.

12. JOHNSON, WARREN R.; MASSEY, B. H., and KRAMER, G. F.: Effects of post-hypnotic suggestions on all-out effort of short duration. *Res Quart Amer Ass Health Phys Educ, 31*:142-146, May 1960.

13. MASSEY, BENJAMIN H.; JOHNSON, W. R.,and KRAMER, G. F.: Effect of warm-up exercise upon muscular performance using hypnosis to control the psychological variable. *Res Quart Amer Ass Health Phys Educ, 32*: March 1961.

14. M.D.'s Frown on Hypnosis of Athletes. *AMA News,* July 11, 1960.

15. MONROE, RUSSELL R.: A Psychiatrist looks at medical hypnosis. *J. of the Louisiana State Medical Society. 112*:148-154, April 1960.

16. ORNE, MARTIN T.: The nature of hypnosis: Artifact and essence. *J of Abnormal and Soc Psychol, 58*:277-299, May 1959.

17. ROUSH, ELSIE S.: Strength and endurance in the waking and hypnotic states. *J of App Physiol, 3*:404-410, January 1951.

18. STEINHAUS, ARTHUR, and IKAI, MICHIO: Some factors modifying the expression of human strength. *J of App Physiol. 16*:157-163, January 1961.

19. THOMAS, STEPHEN E.: Hypnosis in athletics. *Hypnosis. 1*:11-14, March, 1955.

Chapter 39

SOCIOLOGICAL CONSIDERATIONS*

GERALD S. KENYON

INTRODUCTION

THE SCOPE is broad, the time is short. Upon considering the many ramifications of sport, exercise, and dance when viewed as social phenomena, I am compelled to be selective. Therefore, I have chosen to confine my remarks to the significance and implication of what we know about a particular social process, namely, *socialization.* Socialization is selected because it is my belief that when physical educators talk about sociological benefits they are referring to the objective of social development—a goal achieved through socialization.[†]

Albeit briefly, I will thus endeavor to examine fact and fancy inherent in the argument that physical education serves as a medium for socialization. My presentation is structured around three questions. First, what is socialization and, more particularly, how does it occur? Second, what is the state of our present knowledge concerning the extent to which experiences associated with physical education programs contribute to socialization? Third, to what extent can we expect physical education programs to facilitate socialization?

---

* G. S. Kenyon: Sociological Considerations. *J Hlth Phys Educ and Rec, 38:* 1968, 31-33. Reproduced here with the permission of the author and the American Association for Health, Physical Education, and Recreation.

† I have chosen the term *considerations* rather than *benefits* as in one sense it is somewhat of a misnomer to talk about sociological *benefits* just as it is to talk about chemical, bacteriological, astronomical, or geological benefits. Sociology as a social science tells us not what social reality *should* be like but rather what it *is* like. Thus, while there are many ways sociologists (including sociologists of education and sociologists of sport) might contribute to an *understanding* of the role of physical activity in society, we can't expect them to *justify* it. It remains the responsibility of the professional person, in this case the physical educator, to take the best available information concerning human behavior and use it to enhance the attainment of educational goals.

LEARNING ONE'S "PART"

First, by socialization I am referring to the *process* by which "persons acquire the knowledge, skills, and dispositions that make them more or less able members of their society." [4] In the sociologist's view,* each of us, as a member of various social groups, is called upon on different occasions to play one or more roles. Thus, the process of learning one's *part* is synonymous with socialization.

Learning to play a particular role occurs through the influence of *socializing agents,* of which there is a wide variety, including parents, other members of the family, teachers, peers, or any other community leader or close associate. Socializing agents function within various social systems (such as the family, the school, the community, or the nation), each of which is characterized by its own set of norms and values. Such values and norms are manifested in the behavior of social models,[†] both actual and symbolic, to which the learner is exposed. Through imitation and identification, he is socialized into a variety of roles.

The learning of social roles begins in early childhood and continues throughout the adult years. During the course of a lifetime persons learn and relearn to play many relatively *specific* roles. Some are *ascribed*, such as *teenager, daughter, father* or *mother-in-law* and some are *achieved*, such as *club president, teacher, doctor,* or *athlete*. Each of these roles, whether they be ascribed or achieved, are more or less circumscribed and defined. On the other hand, there are some rather *diffuse* roles that are more general in scope and tend to cut across the more definitive, such as *democratic citizen* or the person with *outstanding moral character*. Whether we refer to specific or diffuse roles, the socialized individual has acquired behaviors, behavioral dispositions, and certain normative information associated with a wide variety of each.

Obviously, physical education programs lend themselves to providing some of the necessary conditions for socialization, namely, the

---

* Obviously, social anthropologists, psychologists, and psychiatrists have also been very interested in socialization. As might be expected, however, each discipline takes a somewhat different approach.

† For a well-developed discussion of the functioning of social models and their imitation, see Albert Bandura and Richard H. Walters, *Social Learning and Personality Development* New York, Holt, 1963.

existence of agents, models, and social interaction. Nevertheless, a closer examination is needed before we can know the nature and degree of the socialization that actually occurs. On the one hand, one might expect children to be socialized into several different and, for the most part, specific roles, including the *participant,* the *spectator,* the *official,* and even the *nonparticipant.* On the other hand, the writings of physical educators over the years seem to have been referring to the acquisition of more diffuse roles, such as the *responsible individual* or the *adjusted personality.* Indeed, it is usually this aspect of socialization to which physical educators address themselves and to which they have directed their research.

However, when we ask the question, "What evidence is there to suggest that experiences provided through physical education programs facilitate socialization into either specific or diffuse roles?" the simplest and perhaps most honest answer is, "Very little." This is not to suggest that evidence abounds supporting the negative view. The truth is that despite the availability of both theory and empirical findings concerning the process of socialization in general and the contribution of the school system in particular, few investigators have undertaken studies to determine the unique contributions of the physical education curriculum. And, in fairness, this is not surprising in view of the difficulties to be expected in conducting the meaningful research in this area.

THE TRAITS OF SUCCESSFUL PARTICIPATION

Much of what we find in the literature is the result of efforts to determine the traits peculiar to those who successfully participate in physical activity and sport. In brief, research suggests the following, using the language of the investigator: that physical prowess, at least for males, tends to be associated with popularity and social prestige,[13] being esteemed by one's classmates,[3, 7, 22] unique character and personality traits,[2, 5, 14, 15, 19, 20, 27] personal and social adjustment,[1, 6, 8, 21, 24,25] leadership skills,[26] and social status.[9, 18, 28, 29] It should be pointed out that differences between the participant and nonparticipant are not always observed.[17]

It is sometimes argued from the results of such studies that certain traits reflect the characteristics of persons competent to play many specific and diffuse roles. However, to assert that such attributes were acquired through physical education programs is probably unjustified, since to do so may be to risk confusing cause with association. Another and equally plausible explanation of the observed associations, is that high levels of performance require, in addition to certain physical attributes, social and psychological characteristics already inherent in the successful performer. The observation that perhaps "being a champion was a matter of psychological necessity" may be significant here.[12]

What then can we expect from physical education as a medium for socialization? If socialization is taken to mean being able to function comfortably and effectively in a particular class of groups, such as athletic teams or dance groups, and thus be called upon to play certain specific roles, the associated behavior styles and dispositions would likely be acquired if members of the group met and interacted with considerable frequency and over some period of time.* Insofar as it is possible to create these conditions in a physical education instructional program, boys or girls would, in all likelihood, acquire the values and ways of the team and consequently would be able to function effectively with groups of that type. On the other hand, if socialization is taken to mean acquisition of traits reflecting more diffuse roles, such as the *democratic citizen* or *adjusted personality*, success may not be easily forthcoming. The more diffuse the role the greater the likelihood of being exposed to models (such as peers and those presented by the mass media) that may display characteristics quite unlike those models used by the teacher, including himself. That is, if the teacher attempt to inculate values that differ from those held by individuals and groups visible to the pupil, his influence as a socializing agent may be negligible when we consider both the small amount of time most school children are involved in a physical education program and the number and potency of competing role models. The strength of these counterforces is illustrated by the fact

---

* In view of today's social condition it might be interesting to study the attributes associated with roles played by those in training for high levels of performance in sport. What kinds of roles are being learned? As we foster participation in contemporary sport do we train persons to play the role of the *Olympic athlete,* or the *black athlete?* If so, is this accomplished at the expense of achieving competence in other roles?

that although active participation in physical activity is not a part of the life style of the majority of Americans this apparently is *not* the result of harboring negative attitudes toward exercise and sport. On the contrary, most people seem to accept the values of a wide variety of sports and games.[10, 16] No matter how sympathic a person may be for exercise, his life style is such that apparently he plays a variety of rewarding roles in which being physically active does not provide a significant *pay off*. Thus, the physical educator should not be considered a failure if his or her students play roles quite distinct from those reflecting the goals of the program.

The situation surrounding a varsity sports team, as opposed to the instructional program, may be quite different. Here, the athle'e spends much of his time in a restricted and more integrated social environment. However, as Schafer[23] has pointed out, sport itself— the games and the practices—may have little effect. While the player is a member of the team he is also a member of a subculture and consequently cannot escape exposure to the norms modeled by its members.

Although I have only scratched the surface of what is known and theorized concerning one aspect of a most complex phenomenon, with regard to the function of physical education programs in the process of socialization, the state of the art seems to be as follows.

1. When we think and talk about physical education as a medium for socialization, we must distinguish between the learning of particular roles associated with involvement in sport and physical activity and the learning of more diffuse roles cutting across several specific ones.

2. At present there is little evidence to support the proposition that instructional programs in physical education are particularly effective for socialization into diffuse roles.

    (a) Only a limited number of socializing agents, models, and fertile situations can be made available in the time given for physical education in most school systems.

    (b) It is unlikely that many teachers have delineated the socialization outcomes they desire, an essential prerequisite to purposeful socialization. Moreover, even if the teacher as the socializing agent is able to specify clearly the goals he seeks, he still faces the problem of selecting the most efficacious means, which is no *mean feat.*[11]

(c) Never before have school children been involved in so many social situations and exposed to so many social stimuli. It is only when a diffuse role is characterized in much the same way by several of the child's *significant others,* such as his parents, his peers, his television and sports heroes, and his teachers, that we can expect him to play such a role effectively.

3. If planned for and deliberate attempts are made there is no reason to doubt the proposition that instructional programs in physical education could contribute to socializing children into a variety of specific roles, such as the player, the substitute, the referee, the team captain, or perhaps the intelligent spectator.

4. Considering the frequency and intensity of the social interaction—sometimes lasting for a period of several years—which has become a part of today's interscholastic and intercollegiate athletic programs, it is likely that the athlete becomes socialized into a number of roles, both specific and diffuse.

5. Although it is conceivable that we could do a better job in planning our physical education curriculum to maximize socialization outcomes, to be really effective will depend upon the results of much more research, with respect to the socialization process in general and as it is fostered in school situations. While we have reached the point whereby we know how to go about lowering the resting heart rate, we have a long way to go before we can successfully alter a complex constellation of behaviors and behavioral dispositions.

REFERENCES

1. BIDDULPH, L. G.: Athletic adjustment and the personal and social adjustment of high school boys. *Res Quart Amer Ass Health Phys Educ, 25:* 1-7, 1954.
2. BOOTH, E. G.: Personality traits of athletes as measured by the MMPI. *Res Quart Amer Ass Health Phys Educ, 29:*127-38, 1958.
3. BRACE, D. K.: Sociometric evidence of the relationship between social status and athletic ability among junior high school boys in *Professional contributions, No. 3.* Washington, D.C., American Academy of Physical Education, 1954.
4. BRIM, O. G., and WHEELER, S.: *Socialization After Childhood.* New York, Wiley, 1966.

5. CAVANAUGH, J. O.: The relation of recreation to personality adjustment. *J Soc Psychol, 15*:63-74, 1942.
6. COLEMAN, J. C.; KEOGH, J. F., and MANSFIELD, J.: Motor performance and social adjustments among boys experiencing serious learning difficulties. *Res Quart Amer Ass Health Phys Educ, 34*:516-17, 1963.
7. COWELL, C. C.: Validating an index of social adjustment for high school use. *Res Quart Amer Ass Health Phys Educ, 29*:431-38, 1958.
8. COWELL, C. C., and ISMAIL, A. H.: Relationship between selected social and physical factors. *Res Quart Amer Ass Health Phys Educ, 33*:40-43, 1962.
9. FLOWTOW, E. A.: Charting social relationships of school children. *Elementary School J, 46*:498-504, 1946.
10. HEATH, E. H.: *A Semantic Differential Study of Attitudes Relating to Recreation as Applied to a Bicultural Setting.* Unpublished doctoral dissertation. U of Ill, 1966.
11. INKELES, A.: Society, social structure, and child socialization, in J. A. Clausen (Ed), *Socialization and Society.* Boston, Little, 1968.
12. JOHNSON, W. R.; HUTTON, D. C., and JOHNSON, G. B., JR.: Personality traits of some champion athletes as measured by two projective tests: Rorschach and H-T-P. *Res Quart Amer Ass Health Phys Educ, 25*:484-85, 1954.
13. JONES, H. E.: Physical ability as a factor in social adjustment in adolescence. *J Educ Res, 40*:287-301, 1946.
14. LaPLACE, J. P.: Personality and its relationship to success in professional baseball. *Res Quart Amer Ass Health Phys Educ, 25*:313-19, 1954.
15. KANE, J. A.: *Personality and Physical Ability.* Proceedings of the International Congress of Sport Sciences, Tokyo, 1964.
16. KENYON, G. S.: Values held for physical activity by selected urban secondary school students in Canada, Australia, England, and the United States. Report of U.S. Office of Education Project, Contract OE6-10-179. Madison, U of Wis, 1968.
17. KROLL, W., and CARLSON, B. R.: Discriminant function and hierarchial grouping analysis of karate participants' personality profiles. *Res Quart Amer Ass Health Phys Educ, 38*:405-11, 1967.
18. McGRAW, L. W., and TOLBERT, J. W.: Sociometric status and athletic ability of junior high school boys. *Res Quart, 24*:72-78, 1953.
19. MERRIMAN, J. B.: Relationship of personality traits to motor ability. *Res Quart Amer Ass Health Phys Educ, 31*:163-73, 1960.
20. OGILVIE, B. C.: The personality of the male athlete. *Academy Papers* (American Academy of Physical Education), *1*:42-52, March 1968.
21. RARICK, G. L., and McKEE, R.: A study of twenty third-grade children exhibiting extreme levels of achievement on tests of motor proficiency. *Res Quart Amer Ass Health Phys Educ, 20*:142-52, 1949.

22. SCANDRETTE, D. C.: Classroom choice status related to scores on components of the California Test of Personality. *J Educ Res, 47*:291-96. 1953.

23. SCHAFER, W.: Athletic success and social mobility. Paper read at Symposium on the Sociology of Sport, AAHPER National Convention, St. Louis, Missouri, 1968.

24. SMART, R., and SMART, MOLLIE: Kraus-Weber scores and personality adjustment of nursery school children. *Res Quart Amer Ass Health Phys Educ, 34*:199-205, 1963.

25. SPERLING, A. P.: Relationship between personality adjustment and achievement in physical education activities. *Res Quart Amer Ass Health Phys Educ, 13*:351-63, 1942.

26. STOGDILL, R. M.: Personal factors associated with leadership: A survey of the literature. *J Psychol, 25*:35-71, 1948.

27. THUNE, J. B.: Personality of weight-lifters. *Res Quart Amer Ass Health Phys Educ, 20*:296-306, 1949.

28. TUDDENHAM, R. D.: Studies in reputation: Three correlates of popularity among elementary school children. *J Educ Psychol, 42*:257-76, 1951.

29. TRYON, CAROLINE M.: *Evaluation of adolescent personality by adolescents.* SRCD Monograph 4 (no. 23). Washington, D.C., Society for Research in Child Development, 1939.

Chapter 40

STRESS ADAPTATION THROUGH EXERCISE*

ERNEST D. MICHAEL, JR.

INTRODUCTION

REGULAR EXERCISE PROGRAMS have been found to improve muscular strength, motor skills, and circulation.[4, 5, 8, 9, 13, 14] Increases in strength and motor skills improve the efficiency of movement and help prevent fatigue caused by physical exertion. The increase in muscular tone also aids the venous return of the blood which in turn augments the circulation. The improvement in circulation is reflected in the slowing down of the pulse rate during training, in the faster return to normal of the pulse rate after exercise and in the improved blood pressure responses following a training program.

Along with the general improvement in fitness, a sense of well-being or a feeling of good health usually results from exercise. The feeling is subjective and the report is not accepted by many as reliable data. This euphoria may well be emotional in nature and, therefore, result in part from an adjustment of the autonomic nervous system. If this is true, then exercise may prove to be important in man's adjustment to stress.

REVIEW OF THE LITERATURE

Selye[20] in his report of stress advanced the theory that man is faced with two types of stress, specific and nonspecific. If a nonspecific stress is encountered repeatedly there is an alarm reaction following this pattern:

(1) Shock—depression of the nervous system.

* E. D. Michael, Jr.: Stress adaptation through exercise. *Res Quart Amer Ass Health Phys Educ,* 28:1957, 50-54. Reproduced here with the permission of the author and the American Association for Health, Physical Education, and Recreation.

(2) Counter shock—enlarged adrenal cortex, increased activity of nervous system.

(3) Exhaustion—develops when further resistance cannot be maintained.

If the alarm reaction is repeated, either general adaptation or breakdown takes place. The general adaptation syndrome of Selye concerns the adrenal cortex and a *learning* process of defense against future exposures of the same stress.

Since Selye, other studies have provided evidence concerning similar adjustments of the body to the external changes in the environment. Engel [6] reports the use of increased steroids as evidence of adrenal secretion during stress. It was suggested that the presence of excess adrenal hormone sensitizes the organism to respond metabolically to stimuli of lower impact while absence of the anterior pituitary or adrenal cortex causes inadequate response to stress.

Further evidence of the relationship between emotional states and the endocrine system was provided by Kramar [12] who reported the increase and then the decrease of capillary resistance as a result of stress. He attributes the rise of resistance to increased pituitary—adrenocortical activity while the decrease, or capillary crisis, results from the adrenal cortex.

There is general agreement that the adrenal glands are very important with respect to stress. [19] Opinion differs, however, concerning the sympathetic and parasympathetic systems in regard to specific stresses. Arnold [1] and Ax [2] discuss the different viewpoints with respect to anger and fear. Arnold feels that fear is sympathetic and anger is both sympathetic and parasympathetic and that anger, though both sympathetic and parasympathetic is more parasympathetic. Both agree with the presence of a dominant sympathetic (epinephrine) reaction to fear and a combination reaction to anger. Arnold [1] suggests that fear corresponds to the stress of cold (balance restored during parasympathetic overactivity) and anger corresponds to the stress of heat (balance restored during sympathetic overactivity).

Regardless of which theory is preferred, it is agreed that stress affects the autonomic nervous system with the sympathetic and parasympathetic reactions adjusting until balance is restored. If there were some means of improving the autonomic system, more efficient reactions to stress would result. The shock phase should be minimal, and the counter shock mechanism should adjust rapidly. The result would reduce the chance for exhaustion because of minimum counter-balance activity.

PHYSICAL ACTIVITY AND THE AUTONOMIC NERVOUS SYSTEM

The effects of physical activity on the adrenal and the autonomic nervous system have been shown indirectly in recent studies by Richter[17] and Hoagland.[10]

Richter[17] reported that the wild rat had large adrenals compared with the domestic rat and that surgical trauma along with ACTH has little influence upon the ascorbic acid content, indicating maximum stimulation. When the adrenals were removed, the wild rat died more easily than the domestic, as if the active animal was more dependent on the adrenals. Hoagland[10] used the seventeen ketosteroids as a measure of adrenal response and pointed out that the higher skilled and less fatigued men have less adrenal activity. The production of the seventeen ketosteroids declined with age and also with fatigue during the afternoon. It seems that the more active and less fatigued men have better adrenal function.

Van Liere[23] in 1954 was one of the first to report a direct relationship between physical training and the autonomic nervous system. He found that exercised rats had increased propulsive motility of the small intestine compared to nonexercised rats. The possible explanation was a dominance of the parasympathetic system. This dominance of the parasympathetic system is also reflected in the lower pulse rates of the trained men.[4, 5, 8, 14]

Bartlett's study also showed a direct relationship between physical training and emotional stress. He pointed out that daily exercise produces a degree of inhibition to restraint hypothermia. Adaptation to exercise stress appears to protect against the emotional stress produced by restraint, and manifested through the body temperature drop when exposed to cold. Michael[13] also reported the response to cold to be more pronounced with highly trained athletes than with normal young men. Apparently, an exercise program causes an increased adrenal sensitivity, for, as Engel[6] points out, the presence of excessive adrenal hormones seems to sensitize the organism to respond to lower stimuli. In studies on athletes, Michael[13] and Johnson[11] reported heightened emotional responses of these men before athletic functions. The more *keyed* the group, the better playing ability.

Since repeated physical activity seems to sensitize and increase the size of the adrenal glands, it is possible that this results in a more efficient reaction to stress. The increased sensitivity would result in a shortened time-lapse between shock and counter shock, while the increased size of the adrenals suggests a greater reserve of the counter shock steroids. Thus, following a stress a *conditioned* person might expect an improved adjustment to the shock.

EXERCISE AND ADAPTATION TO STRESS

If Selye's theories of stress are tenable, then the stress of repeated exercise should cause either a breakdown or adaptation. Exercise, by affecting the adrenal glands, affects the mechanism by which the body combats stress and therefore should be considered as a possible means of helping to strengthen the adaptation process. Williams[25] and Steinberg[21] both showed that emotionally unstable groups have heightened levels of physiological activity and, as Steinberg reported, inferior physical fitness. Taylor[22] pointed out that forced bed rest has been found to reduce the body to a dangerous state similar to starvation. It is possible then that exercise provides a means of strengthening the adaptive mechanism of the body. Exercise might well be a means of increasing the survival potential in a tense, emotional age.

Persky,[16] in discussing stress, points out the difference between physical activity and psychological (emotional) stress. He reports that blood eosinophil and glutathione levels are affected only by psychological stress. Thus, exercise can affect the adaptive mechanism without itself increasing the reaction caused by emotions. The advantage of exercise lies in the fact that it stimulates the defense mechanism, not that it is similar to other stresses.

The implications of using exercise as a means of adapting to stress raises many questions that cannot be answered at this time. How much exercise and what are the best kinds of exercise might be asked. An investigation of these questions should result in a series of interesting studies.

CONCLUSIONS

The evidence reported here supports the theory that repeated exercise *conditions* the stress adaptation mechanism. The studies point out that the adrenocortical activity along with the autonomic nervous system are involved in adjusting to stress. This ability to adjust is helped with exercise if we assume that the more sensitive response to stress reduces the time necessary to elicit a response and therefore lessens the duration of the adjusting phase. The evidence indicates that adaptation to exercise produces a degree of protection against emotional stress. The increased adrenal activity resulting from repeated exercise seems to cause an increased reserve of steroids available to counter a stress. A lack of activity was reported to reduce the ability to withstand stress, as if the reaction to a shock is a *learned* process.

The questions raised by this theory are numerous and challenging. If we accept the theory, the possibility exists that exercise, being a stress, might aid adaptation and at the same time bring about a breakdown. As Selye points out, the dangers of a therapeutic agent might be in the resulting syndrome of adaptation.

REFERENCES

1. ARNOLD, MAGDA B.: Physiological differentiation of emotional states. *Psychol Rev, 52*:34-48, 1945.
2. AX, ALBERT F.: The physiological differentiation between fear and anger in humans. *Psychosom Med, 15*:433-442, 1953.
3. BARTLETT, ROSCOE G., JR.: Stress adaptation and inhibition of restraint induced (emotional) hypothermis. *J App Physiol, 8*:661-663, 1956.
4. COGSWELL, ROBERT, *et al.*: Some observations of the effects of training on pulse rate, blood pressure, and endurance in humans, using the step test, treadmill, and electrodynamic brake bicycle ergometer. *Amer J of Physiol, 146*:422-430, 1946.
5. CURETON, T. K.: Physical fitness improvement of a middle-aged man, with brief reviews of related studies. *Res Quart Amer Ass Health Phys Educ, 23*:149-160, 1952.
6. ENGLE, FRANK L.: General concepts of adrenocortical function in relation to the response to stress. *Psychosom Med, 15*:565-573, 1953.
7. HEBB, D. D.: Emotion in man and animal. *Psychol Rev, 53*:88-106, 1946.
8. HENRY, F. M.: Influence of athletic training on the resting cardiovascular system. *Res Quart Amer Ass Health Phys Educ, 25*:28-41, 1954.
9. ———, and BERG, W. E.: Physiological and performance changes in athletic conditioning. *J Appl Physiol, 3*:103-111, 1950.

10. HOAGLAND, HUDSON, *et al.*: Adrenal stress response in normal men. *J Appl Physiol, 8*:149-154, 1955.
11. JOHNSON, W. R., and J. HARMON: Emotional reaction of college athletes. *Res Quart Amer Ass Health Phys Educ, 23*:391-397, 1952.
12. KRAMAR, JENO.: Stress and capillary resistance. *Amer J Physiol, 175*:69-74, 1953.
13. MICHAEL, E. D.: Unpublished data. U of Calif, Santa Barbara College, Goleta, 1956.
14. ———, and T. K. CURETON: Effects of physical training on the cardiac output at ground level and at 15,000 feet simulated altitude. *Res Quart Amer Ass Health Phys Educ, 24*:446-452, 1953.
15. MITCHEM, JOHN C., and W. W. TUTTLE: Influence of exercise, emotional stress, and age on static neuromuscular tremor magnitude. *Res Quart Amer Ass Health Phys Educ, 25*:65-74, 1954.
16. PERSKY, H.: Response to life stress: Evaluation of some biochemical indices. *J Appl Physiol, 6*:369-374, 1953.
17. RICHTER, C. P., and D. E. WOOD: Hypophysectomy and domestication in the Norway rat. *Fed Proc, 12*:116, 1953.
18. ROGOFF, J. M.: A critique on the theory of the emergency function of the adrenal glands: Implications for psychology. *J Genet Psychol, 32*:249-268, 1945.
19. SAYERS, GEORGE: The adrenal cortex and homeostasis. *Physiol Rev, 30*,241-320, 1950.
20. SELYE, HANS: *Stress.* Montreal, *Acta,* 1950.
21. STEINBERG, D. L., and M. P. WITTMAN: Etiologic factors in the adjustment of men in the Armed Forces. *War Medicine, 4*:129-139, 1943.
22. TAYLOR, H. L., *et al.*: Performance capacity in acute starvation with hard work. *J Appl Physiol, 6*:624-633 (Report on Bed Rest). *J Appl Physiol, 2*:223, 1949.
23. VAN LIERE, E. J., *et al.*: Physical training and propulsive motility of small intestine. *J Appl Physiol, 7*:186-187, 1954.
24. WEISS, A. KURT: Adaptation of rats to cold air and effects on tissue O_2 consumption. *Amer J Physiol, 177*:201-206, 1954.
25. WILLIAMS, MEYER: Psychophysiological responsiveness to psychological stress in early chronic schizophrenic reactions. *Psychosom Med, 15*:456-462, 1953.

Chapter 41

FITNESS BEYOND MUSCLE*

ARTHUR H STEINHAUS

WITHIN OUR RECENT MEMORY, fitness has become a popular word. Many equate it with physical strength and stamina. Some speak of fitness exercises and think of calisthenics or isometrics. The Japanese Sports Medicine group composed entirely of physicians calls itself Society for Physical Fitness. The President's Youth Fitness Committee of Eisenhower has given way to the President's Physical Fitness Committee of the Democratic Administrations. Many people when puzzled or in a critical mood ask, "Fitness for what?"

It was Charles Darwin who about a century ago gave content and scientific status to the concept of fitness. To biologists generally, as to Darwin, fitness means survival. Contrary to common thinking, emphasis is primarily on species, not on individual survival. Thus the ultimate test of human fitness is whether it is adequate to perpetuate the human race. This means more than *brute animal* survival. It means survival of our race on a plane that is genuinely human; and this demands mental and spiritual as well as physical fitness.

As a species we are still beset with civil wars. Any war between members of a species is civil war; and that means self destruction—destruction of the irreplaceable germ plasma that Nature has uniquely accorded our branch of the animal kingdom.

As a species we must yet learn to combat the ills that beset mankind as a whole. Of these, disease and famine, malnutrition and overweight, and physical, mental, and moral decadence associated with plenty, should be mentioned. Unless we succeed on all these fronts, the human race will follow into oblivion the many other species that in past eons have been found unfit in the struggle for survival.

It is not comforting to admit that Nature's great experiment with the

* A. H Steinhaus: Fitness beyond muscle. *The Physical Educator*, 23:1966, 103-107. Reproduced here with the permission of the author and publisher.

teachable brain has yet to prove itself fit to survive, and it is no foregone conclusion that it will. Can the discoveries of man's brain be exploited for his survival before they destroy him—by explosion or by decadence? You and I must measure success in terms of our contributions to the positive side of this race against time.

Knowing me as a physiologist you might well expect a talk on the physiology of strength, speed, endurance, and flexibility; or at least an opinion on the significance of the T wave of the E.C.G.; but this occasion calls forth another mood in me. I would rather exercise the freedom you have afforded me to discuss some less scientifically based, but more important aspects of human fitness. I would like to discuss the foundations of mental, emotional, and spiritual fitness.

Modern day knowledge concerning the unity of man makes it impossible to separate physical fitness from any other aspect of fitness. Man is a totality that in health always acts as an indivisible unit. Divisions are only artificial matters of convenience, if not of ignorance. For the highest human accomplishments man must be strong in totality.

President Eisenhower, on June 19, 1956 put it this way: "National policies will be no more than words if our people are not healthy in body, as well as of mind, putting dynamism and leadership into the carrying out of these major decisions. Our young people must be physically as well as mentally and spiritually prepared for American citizenship."

Plato (in Phaedrus) likens the whole man unto a charioteer driving two horses. One horse, as you recall, is of lowly origin, driven by powerful and basic instincts. The second horse is of nobler nature, and being possessed of powers of thought and reason, seeks the higher ways of life. The charioteer must control both the baser and nobler steeds and with wisdom, use their respective capabilties in the pursuit of man's efforts to discover the light and truth which is the way of the gods.

You and I can identify in man's brain the two horses and the charioteer of Plato's whole man.

The spinal cord, brain stem, and limbic system including the primitive cortex and associated hypothalamic structures that connect with the endocrine glands, together represent the lowly horse. The cortex of parietal, temporal, and occipital lobes may well compare with

Plato's nobler steed. This leaves the prefrontal lobes, found only in modern man, as the charioteer. It is the prefrontal lobes to which have been ascribed the functions of wisdom or conscience in contrast to knowledge and ordinary intelligence that are functions of the remaining cortex.

To illustrate how modern science has come to recognize this total unity I need only to remind you of a few recent findings.

Today we have reason to consider the muscular system as man's most important sense organ. Without muscle sense we could not talk, walk, breathe, or feed ourselves. We would have no real conception of weight or the third dimension. We probably would not be able to think. We know that complete relaxation of body musculature stops our thought processes and thus rests what is generally called the mind.[14]

Professor Penfield's[9] stimulation of the cortex in conscious patients has produced indisputable evidence that the sights, sounds, and associated emotions of early childhood experiences, remain as traces in the brain which when stimulated electrically are completely relived again and again. Hypnosis with its demonstration of complete recall of the past, provides further evidence that all of our experiences continue to live in the brain to form what psychologists call the apperceptive mass, and, no doubt, determine our behavior in yet unknown ways.

Today we know there are nerve centers that turn on hunger and others that turn it off, surgical operations on nerve centers that can make a monkey eat a dead mouse, centers to put us to sleep and others to wake us up, centers that turn on sex and others that turn it off.[8]

In 1952 the late Professor Bykov reported to the Montreal International Physiological Congress that conditional reflexes evoked by signals of the second order can be made to overrule unconditioned reflexes. Thus he told us how the skin can be made to react as it normally does to warm water ($42°$ C) even though the water is hot ($62°$ C), if after a period of conditioning to warm, the subject is told the water is warm when it is really hot.

This is only one illustration of how words (signals of the second order, Pavlov) can cause changes in the circulation. Many other illustrations are emerging to show that stored memories may rule the body's chemistry and *body* does what *mind* thinks, if it is contrary to reality or not. Because of the great significance of this fact for fitness and survival may I illustrate it a bit more.

Gutman and Jakoubek of Prague[4] recently reported that there are increases in blood sugar and liver glycogen (adaptations) as needed for running, as soon as a dog is placed on the treadmill where habitually he was caused to run.

Petren of Stockholm[10] some twenty years ago reported that the liver glycogen in guinea pigs regularly increased at that hour of the day when the pigs were accustomed to run.

We know that baby lambs and goats if subjected, in the absence of mother, to stress conditions, very early in life, for just forty minutes a day, three times in a week, are likely to die in four weeks. (Liddell p. 215 in Ref. 2.) Survivors exhibit neurotic behavior even two years later.[7] If the mother is present they easily withstand the same stress. We know that monkeys subjected to experimentally induced stress conditions show cardiac disorders and get stomach and duodenal ulcers, sometimes resulting in death.[1]

Today there is evidence that the increase in heart rate and other circulatory adjustments in exercise are activated from centers in the cortex and diencephalon[12] thus explaining the rapidity of these adjustments in the trained athlete whose nervous system has learned to make them. This was well-illustrated in experiments reported by the Russian physiologist, Letunov to the International Congress of Sports Sciences in Tokyo in 1964. He found that the heart of the trained athlete reached its maximum rate in five to eight seconds after he started to run, whereas it took the untrained runner's heart from thirty to forty seconds to reach maximum. In fact the very first beat after starting was already within 75 percent of maximum, in the athlete.

The full meaning of other important mind-body findings to man's fitness can at this time be only surmised. May I venture a few guesses which I trust you will not consider to be entirely irresponsible ones.

1. *Every person possesses more strength and endurance than he is capable of demonstrating normally.* We have reason to believe that the psychologic limit which in some persons is far below the physiologic

limit is due to inhibitions implanted by parents, by peers, or by self—perhaps in early childhood.[5] This has important implications for child rearing.

2. *Self-confidence is important for winning in sports and for effectiveness in daily life.* No doubt the earliest experiences with physical activities in the home have much to do with this. A child that is permitted to enjoy success in activities that have an element of risk in them will gain self-assurance which an overprotected child that is forbidden to try dangerous activities, will never attain.

3. *The success-related feelings of self-worth, self-respect, and self-acceptance so essential to a high level of fitness take form early in life,* at a time when big muscle activity is virtually the only way the child has of expressing itself. The direction taken in this early beginning may well determine the direction for life. Equally if not more important is the fact that one can have no real confidence or respect for others if he does not have confidence and respect for himself. Positive attitudes toward self and others are basic to a social structure that places worth on the individual, as in a true democracy. The earliest feelings of confidence in self no doubt come to the child from success in the performance of large muscle activities.

4. *Fitness on the human level demands a social structure in which the rights of each individual are recognized by every other individual.* Where is there a better place for such lessons to be learned than in the play life of children. Here each child can demand its rights and in turn must concede such rights to all others. A child who infringes on the rights of his playmates is quickly controlled by all members of the group. People who in their childhood have enjoyed such play life are more likely to possess this sense of sportsmanship and therefore are easier to live with in a human sense.

5. *The effectiveness of man's physical and mental performances are most closely intertwined.* This interdependence is becoming more evident with each new discovery. From studies in neuromuscular relaxation we find that completely relaxing one's muscles, particularly those of the eyes, face, and voice, not only induces sleep but also in the waking state quiets the mind, lowers blood pressure, improves gastrointestinal function, minimizes body aches and pains, and generally counteracts the destructive inroads of stress on the entire organism.[13]

From the pioneer work of Kephart at Purdue[6] and Delacato in Philadelphia[3] we are amazed that children's difficulties with reading and writing often disappear most dramatically when they learn to control their bodies with precision, in space. But why should we be surprised? Is it not the same nervous system that moves the body through space and the hand and eye across the page!

6. In his most provocative book *The Word as a Physiologic and Therapeutic Factor*, K. I. Platonov[11] presents hundreds of illustrations *of the power of words, spoken or thought, as signals of the second order to augment or depress the function of internal organs as well as influence the normal and abnormal processes of thought, action, and emotion.* With many illustrations he shows the power of the physician's words to create hope or despair in his patient's mind and thereby changes in his body chemistry. Paralleling *iatrogenic* or physician induced neurosis he illustrates also *Didactogenic* or teacher induced neuroses. Quoting Danilo Samoilovich who as a physician observed the 18th Century plagues he says "hope raises the spirits of the patients, rendered weak by fear, and the internal symptoms cease to be serious and numerous from the very onset of the disease." And from Ivan Pavlov he quotes "there is no sense in life when the aim is lost—even the instinct of life and its worth-whileness decline." One is reminded of reports of our own soldiers who were taken as prisoners of war in Korea. Those who entertained strong hopes and faith that they would survive to a better day, often did. Those who stared hopelessly before them did not.[15] What else is this but fitness induced by the spirit of man!

7. *Closely related to hope* but in ways that are not easy to describe and even more difficult to prove, yet very frequently illustrated in the lives of individuals, families, and nations, *is the fact that a sound, wholesome, and fully accepted philosophy of life contributes to human strength and fitness.* Analysis brings truth but also sometimes paralysis. Synthesis brings strength and the will to action. You and I are victims of a scientific age in which we lay great emphasis on scientific analysis to discover the truth. But too often this leaves us with a multitude of disjointed facts which like the pieces of a jig-saw puzzle merely bewilder the mind. The resulting confusion breeds uncertainty and weakness. We must put the pieces together so as to see the whole

picture. We must take time to synthesize the facts into larger wholes. We must fit together a thousand and one facts into a comprehensive philosophy of life that explains to us the world in which we live, in a way that is satisfying to us.

This the mind of man needs. This gives it strength. Such strength can be seen in the lives of individuals, of families, and of nations that have accepted a philosophy of life and steadfastly believe it. Hitler's Germany had such a philosophy that made it strong and so have the followers of Marxism. Now let me hasten to say that for the strength of the individual or group it is not necessary that the philosophy be true, as long as it is fully accepted. *But for the good of the world it makes an endless difference!* It is also not difficult to see that a person whose mind is filled with conflicting ideologies and con-flicting senses of values will have great difficulty in gaining that internal unity which gives strength and internal serenity. Inner conflicts create stresses which in turn undermine organic fitness.

8. Finally, I would suggest that every human being, to remain truly fit on the human level, must work for a cause outside himself. He must work for something that is bigger than himself. It is not enough to be good or efficient. Every person needs to be good or efficient *for something.* For the young child that something may be the self; but very soon it will be something beyond the self.

Early in this century my boyhood hero, Theodore Roosevelt, a distant cousin of F. D. R. put it this way,

> The things that will destroy America are *prosperity-at-any-price,* peace-at-any-price, safety first instead of duty first, the love of soft living, and the get-rich-quick theory of life.

Here in the words of our *Rough Rider* President we have an admonition which I believe warns us even more sternly today. It points to a danger that besets every nation blessed with prosperity and the many good things that come with a high standard of living.

Most recently in the words of one who has taken much too early in life we hear again the same truth. "Ask not what your country can do for you; ask rather what you can do for your country."

That nation is strong whose people sacrifice for the national cause. How else can we explain the victory of little Israel over Egypt, or, when I was a boy, the victory of little Japan over Russia.

When at war we readily rise to a common cause. In peace we become self-centered and therefore weaker. The peoples of younger nations such as the Soviets and the Red Chinese feel such a cause. Unfortunately it is often not good for all mankind and thus brings strife between members of the human species. In 1932 I asked a question of a young student at the newsstand in my Moscow hotel, of which I am still ashamed. He somehow saw through the intent of my question when I asked him what he had had for breakfast. His answer came quickly. "I had black tea and black bread; but I am glad to do this for a greater tomorrow." A nation is most fortunate whose citizens are willing to sacrifice for a better tomorrow.

Many efforts for cause seem illy-directed and hardly constructive as witness some student demonstrations and mob scenes. Nevertheless, these fill needs in the lives of people and disclose the power that could under wiser leadership, be hitched to more significant causes.

A youth may find his cause in playing football for his high school or university, in swimming for his country in the Olympics, or in the Peace Corps. A man or woman may find it in service as a teacher, a physician, or a volunteer worker in civic and other philanthropic measures. In the last analysis the most truly worthy causes are ones that serve to advance all mankind.

That species will be found fit whose members place species goals above individual good. It remains the ultimate test of nature's experiment with brain, whether or not the human race can unite in a cause that advances the entire human species in the face of its common enemies such as famine, flood, poverty, ignorance, insects, disease, self-indulgence, and other forces that would destroy it from within or without.

In a democracy, as this is understood in the free world, such concern for the common good cannot be legislated—or forced on people from above. It cannot be extracted under fear of banishment to Siberia. It must, instead, be freely given by each individual. This makes it a spiritual force. For ". . . he that loseth his life for my sake shall find it" is as true today as it was when first spoken nearly two thousand years ago.

To make human beings truly fit is no easy task. It is one that demands the best thought and dedication of all who guide the development of youth in their home life, in their sports life, in their school life, and, in fact, wherever any person has opportunity to help another. It is not easy but it is the ultimate test of human fitness—physical, mental, and spiritual. It is *one,* total fitness that is in truth indivisible, and will determine our ability to survive, in the Darwinian sense, on the human plane.

When some months ago I spoke to Japanese physicians, the pagoda came to me a fitting symbol for ideas such as these. It may serve, also, to summarize my thoughts here.

Even as every pagoda needs a strong foundation to carry its beautiful structure, so every person must be possessed of physical fitness to support the burdens that life will place on him. But as we look upward we find that every pagoda culminates in a point that is directed to the heavens. It is as though the entire structure is for the purpose of permitting this upward thrust, that transforms a mere wooden structure into a pagoda.

So also man's entire being must support an upward thrust which in giving purpose to his life, transforms man the animal, into man the human being, and makes of him in the words of Plato, a whole man fit to know the ways of the gods.

Truly human fitness is a many splendored thing. It has been called fitness of body, of mind, and of spirit. It is fitness beyond muscle!

REFERENCES

1. BRADY, J. V.: Ulcers in Executive Monkeys, *Sci Amer,* October, 1958.
2. BRAZIER, M. A. B. (Ed.): First Conference on the *Central Nervous System and Behavior.* New York, Josiah Macy Jr. Foundation, 1959.
3. DELACATO, C. H.: *The Diagnosis and Treatment of Speech and Reading Problems,* Springfield, Thomas, 1963.
4. GUTMAN, E. and JAKOUBEK, B.: Preparatory reactions to muscular work. *Physiol Bohemsol, 10,* 275-82, 1961.
5. IKAI, M., and STEINHAUS, A. H: Some factors modifying the expression of human strength. *J Appl Physiol, 16,* 157-63, 1961.
6. KEPHART, N. C.: *The Slow Learner in the Classroom,* Columbus, Merrill, C. E., 1960.
7. LIDDELL, H. S.: Conditioning and Emotions. *Sci Amer,* January, 1954.
8. MacLEAN, P. D.: The limbic system with respect to two basic life principles, trans. Second Conference on the *Central Nervous System and Behavior.* Brazier, M. A. B. (Ed.): New York, Josiah Macy Jr. Foundation, pp. 31-118, 1959.

9. PENFIELD, W.: *The Excitable Cortex*, Springfield, Thomas, 1958.

10. PETREN, TURE: Die 24 Stunden Rhythmik des Leberglykogens bei Cavia Cambay nebst Studien uber Einwirkung des "Chronischer" Muskelarbeit Auf Diese Rhytmik. *Morphol Jahrbuch, 83,* 256-67, 1939.

11. PLATONOV, K. I.: *The Word as a Physiologic and Therapeutic Factor,* Moscow, Foreign Languages Publishing House, 1959, p. 262.

12. RUSHMER, R. F.: Effects of nerve stimulation and hormones on the heart; the role of the heart in general circulatory regulation, *Handbook of Physiol,* (Sec. 2) vol. 1, pp. 345-47.

13. STEINHAUS, A. H: Facts and theories of neuromuscular relaxation, *Quest,* Mon. III, 3-14, December, 1964.

14. STEINHAUS, A. H: Your muscles see more than your eyes, Address before General Session, Southern District A.A.H.P.E.R., February 27, 1966 (In press).

15. WOLFF, H. G.: What Hope Does for Man, reprinted from *Science and Humanity* in *Saturday Review* by State Com. on T. B. and P. H., and New York State Heart Assembly, Inc., 105 E. 22nd St., N. Y.

16. WRIGHT, J. (Translator): *Phaedrus* in #456 of Everymans Library, New York, Dutton, 1910.

INDEX

A

Ability, 53, 57, 188
  leadership and, 359
  personality and, 359
  range of, 100
  See also Skill
Academic achievement, 220. *See also*
  Learning
Accidental factors, 53
Accuracy
  concentric circle, 26, 27, 29 (T),
    30 (T), 31
  horizontal deviation, 26, 27, 29
    (T), 30 (T), 31
  information feedback and, 25, 26,
    31, 32, 33
  practice and, 31-32
  -speed relation, 32, 33
  in throwing, 23-35
  vertical deviation, 26, 27, 29 (T),
    30 (T), 31
Achievement, 403, 442
  status and, 375
  traits of, 426-429
Achievement training, 374, 375, 377,
  381, 382, 383-389
Activation, 55
Activity, *See* Physical activity
Adaptation, 432-437
Adrenals, 6, 433, 434-435, 436
Aesthetics, 88 (T), 90 (T), 91 (T),
  92 (T), 93 (T)
Age
  juggling and, 207-212
  learning time and, 210 (T)
  movement time and, 69, 70 (T), 71
  personality change with, 309-310,
    311, 313-314, 317
  physical skill and, 207
  response time and, 69
  responsiveness and, 18-19

satiation and, 14-15, 18, 20
skill movement separation and, 62 *n*.
target throwing and, 211
Age regression, 412-413, 414
Aggression, 115-116, 291, 292, 298
  in boxers, 284-290
  competition and, 284, 288
  direction of, 285, 286, 287, 288, 295
  hypnosis and, 414-415, 417, 418
  prematch vs. postmatch, 295, 296
  sports and, 284-285
  type of, 285, 287, 288
  in wrestlers, 284-290
Agility, 194
  two-handed, 154, 192, 197
Alarm reaction, 432-433
Alcoholism, 131, 132, 134, 135 (T),
  137
Alertness, 63
American Institute of Public Opinion,
  376, 378 (T)
Anaerobic metabolism, 161, 170
Anger, 433
Angular rotation, 235, 237 (T), 238
  (T), 239 (T), 241
Animal experimentation
  exercise and emotionality in rats,
    5-9
  play and exploration in
    chimpanzees, 10-20
Anxiety, 143, 318, 319-320
  achievement and, 384, 387, 388
  drive and, 143
  about masculinity, 273
  prematch vs. postmatch, 295
  stress in learning and, 144, 146 (T),
    147 (T), 148 (T), 149-150
  task complexity and, 143
Apparatus
  augmentation and reduction, 260
  ball, 65, 66
  bicycle ergometer, 163

Prowess. *See* Power
Pseudogeneral ability, 184-185
Psychiatric patients, depression in,
130-139
Psychiatric service
athletes vs. nonathletes use of,
111-117
dropout rate and, 113-114
presenting problem for, 113, 114-
115
referral sources for, 112-113, 114
Psychoanalysis, 271-272, 273, 280
Psychogalvanic studies, 333-342
Psychogalvanometer, 335
Psychosexual factor, 334, 336, 337,
338, 339
Puberty, 5-9
Pulse rate, 343
Purdue Motor Fitness Test, 357, 358
Pursuit tracking task, 37 *n.*, 40, 41

R

Rats, prepuberty exercise and
emotionality in, 5-9
Reaction, 62, 63
Reaction key, 65, 66
Reaction latency, 68
increased, 60-73
movement complexity and, 63
Reaction time, 60, 133, 258, 262 (T)
age and, 69
complexity and, 64, 67-79, 68 (T),
72
disjunctive, 60
movement and, 68
-movement time intercorrelation,
70-71
practice and, 65
sex and, 69
small muscle, 133
theory of, 60-63
Reaction-time apparatus, 259
Readiness, 61, 62, 63
Reading retardation, 222
Recapituation theory, 397
Recording technique, 13
Recreation, 374

polls, 123, 376-377, 378 (T), 379
(T), 380 (T)
See also Leisure
Reflex, 60, 61
Rejection, 275, 276
Relaxation, 442
Reliability
of attitude scales, 85, 88, 90 (T)
of individual differences in learning
research, 180 (T), 183
Reliability analysis, 96-101
Reliability coefficients
in performance research, 369
in projective testing research, 279
(T), 280
Reliability estimate, 99
correlation coefficient as, 100-101
Reliability theory, in criterion score
selection, 95-105
Reliability undetermined, 81
Research decision, 95-106
Resistance increase, 244
Response strength, 143
Response time. *See* Reaction time
Response time chronoscope, 65
Responsibility training, 374, 375, 377,
381
Responsiveness, 12, 13, 14, 15, 16,
17-18, 19, 20
Restraint, 434
stress and, 6
Retesting, 77. *See also* Test-retest
Rhythm, 189, 190, 192
Role playing, 425, 426, 427 *n.*, 428,
429
Roper-Fortune Survey, 376-377, 380
(T)
Rosenzweig Picture-Frustration Study,
285, 286, 287, 288, 289
Rudder control test, 154

S

Sargent jump, 411, 412
Satiation, 12, 14-16, 19, 20
Scale stability, 92 (T), 93 (T)
Schizophrenics
employment of, 119, 120